THE 1001 REWARDS & RECOGNITION FIELDBOOK

BOB NELSON ★ DEAN SPITZER

WORKMAN PUBLISHING · NEW YORK

Library of Congress Cataloging-in-Publication Data
Nelson, Bob, 1956–
The 1001 rewards & recognition fieldbook : the complete guide / by Bob Nelson and Dean Spitzer.
383 p. cm.
ISBN 0-7611-2139-0 (alk. paper)
1. Incentives in industry. 2. Employee motivation. I. Title: One thousand and one rewards and recognition fieldbook. II. Spitzer, Dean R. III. Title.
HF5549.5.I5 N457 2002
658.3′142—dc21
2002029605

Interior design by Sophia Stavropoulos
Cover and interior illustrations by Burton Morris

All company logos used in "Bob & Dean's Recognition Honor Roll" are property of the companies referenced and used with their permission.

"CEO Santa" and "A Modern-Day Guardian Angel" are used with permission of *Corporate Meetings & Incentives* magazine.

Workman books are available at special discount when purchased in bulk for special premiums and sales promotions as well as for fund-raising or educational use. Special editions or book excerpts also can be created to specification. For details, contact the Special Sales Director at the address below.

Workman Publishing Company, Inc.
708 Broadway
New York, NY 10003-9555

Manufactured in the United States of America
First printing: March 2003
10 9 8 7 6 5 4 3 2 1 0

In memory of Sally Kovalchick,
1938–2000

Editor,
1001 Ways to Reward Employees

Contents

PART I
RECOGNITION FUNDAMENTALS

PART II
GETTING STARTED WITH RECOGNITION

PART III
ORGANIZATIONAL RECOGNITION

PART IV
ISSUES AND CHALLENGES IN RECOGNITION

PART VII
SELECTED ARTICLES

Recognition Technique Reminder Cards

Quick Reference Cards

Recognition ASAP[3]

Getting Started with Recognition

Recognition Cycle

Recognition Planning

Team Recognition

Virtual Team Recognition

Recognition Evaluation

Recognition Troubleshooting

Acknowledgments

"Appreciation is a wonderful thing: it makes what is excellent in others belong to us as well."

—Voltaire,
writer

The authors would like to acknowledge the contributions of the following people, without whom this book would not have been possible:

Dr. Aubrey Daniels, pioneer in the science of positive reinforcement; Dr. Ken Blanchard, mentor and role model; and Dr. Peter F. Drucker, father of modern management, for their wisdom and inspiration, and their contributions to the disciplines of motivation and management.

Drs. Don Griesinger, Harvey Wichman, and David Drew of the Peter F. Drucker School of Management at Claremont Graduate University, who served on Bob's Ph.D. advisory committee for his doctoral dissertation on the use of nonmonetary recognition; Dr. Joseph Maciariello and Dr. Don Griesinger for helping to inspire and encourage Bob to pursue his interest in employee recognition and motivation.

Peter Economy, longtime friend, confidant, and business writer extraordinaire, for suggesting that the authors collaborate on a book about recognition and rewards, and for his extensive help in researching, interviewing, and drafting many of the cases found in the manuscript, and for reviewing and editing the manuscript.

The fine staff at Workman Publishing Co., including Peter Workman, Bruce Harris, Susan Bolotin, Jenny Mandel, Kim Cox, our editor Richard Rosen, and the rest of the team that helped bring this resource to fruition: Paul Gamarello, Lisa Hollander, Sophia Stravropoulos, Anne Cherry, Kelli Bagley, Megan Nicolay, and Katherine Adzima, among many others.

Rebecca Taff, managing editor of *Bob Nelson's Rewarding Employees* newsletter, who helped to compile much of the marginalia used in this book; and Daryl Magziack, administrative coordinator for Nelson Motivation Inc., for his assistance in typing and compilation of various portions of the manuscript.

Bob would also like to thank his spouse, Jennifer, and children, Daniel and Michelle, for their ongoing patience, love, and support.

Dean would like to thank his wife, Cynthia, and son, David, who give him all the rewards and recognition he will ever need.

Foreword

When Bob Nelson and Dean Spitzer approached me about writing the foreword to their new book, *The 1001 Rewards & Recognition Fieldbook,* I was honored. I've known them both for many years and appreciate their work. Bob's *1001 Ways to Reward Employees,* now in its thirty-ninth printing, with close to 1.5 million copies in print, indicates that the topic has tremendous appeal to business audiences and that he has written about it in a way that has practical value. I am sure that all who read it get ideas about how to use recognition more effectively.

I know of Bob's passion for the topic of recognition and for helping others see its potential. He is known for generating a host of new ideas that can be applied immediately. He provides an easy method for the busiest managers to work recognition into their daily behavior. Although Bob has spread the word about the power of recognition through his many lectures and seminars, he finds time to be a student and researcher. He recently completed a three-year doctoral study on the subject, and shares his findings in this fieldbook. His efforts to anchor what he writes about in scientifically derived principles of human learning marks a key difference between this book and many others written on this topic.

Bob and Dean have created a substantive treatment of reward and recognition in the workplace. *The 1001 Rewards & Recognition Fieldbook* goes well beyond anecdotes, suggestions, and quotes to show readers why and how recognition works to achieve desired results. In this comprehensive resource, they present evidence—from research, surveys, and actual practice—that recognition and nonmonetary rewards, properly applied, are great motivators.

Bob and Dean show you how you can act spontaneously in implementing recognition and reward programs, while keeping a long-term strategic focus and moving toward creating a true recognition culture where you work. *The 1001 Rewards & Recognition Fieldbook* walks you through a detailed organizational recognition plan to sustain long-term initiative at multiple levels across the organization. Their plan allows managers the freshness and flexibility to build a culture of positive reinforcement that gets people excited! And their plan allows the employee to be active in defining and applying recognition and reward for others as well as themselves. This kind of approach creates the right conditions for personal accountability and commitment at all levels.

Bob and Dean make the case that recognition matters, perhaps more now than ever before, in our relationships and in our organizations. They show that recognition is doable, regardless of your constraints or limited resources, and that recognition is for everybody, and everybody needs to play a part in making it happen.

The authors have poured their extensive experience into this book, and from each page you will learn a little more about what I consider to be "the greatest management principle in the world." Thank you, Bob and Dean.

—Dr. Aubrey Daniels
Chairman, Aubrey Daniels International;
author, *Bringing Out the Best in People, Other People's Habits,* and *Performance Management: Improving Quality and Productivity Through Positive Reinforcement*

Preface

We wrote this book to advance the practice of recognition—to make it a more viable part of as many relationships, groups, and organizations as possible. Although this book primarily focuses on the value of recognition in the world of business, we'd like to think it also serves as a manifesto of sorts.

Heaven knows we could all use more recognition and appreciation in our lives! More than ever, we live under the stress of trying to achieve more, achieve it faster, and with fewer resources. As a result, our relationships are strained, and our sense of connection and purpose gets misplaced. Whether or not we succeed in slowing down, at the very least we should try to incorporate more recognition—giving it and getting it—into our lives so that we can enjoy the ride and appreciate those we're with along the way.

But recognition is more than a salve for the negative effects of an increasingly stressful world around us; it is also a lubricant for the achievement we aspire to in the first place. Recognition is the greatest motivator for performance of all types. When you get serious about performance, you *have* to get serious about recognition. And for that reason we hope that this book is read by every team leader, supervisor, manager, or executive who is trying to get things done through others and inspire employees to new levels of creativity, productivity, and performance.

Obviously, recognition is easier to give when times are good, but it is during difficult times that people most need it. Maintaining an environment in which recognition is encouraged and can flourish is one of the hallmarks of great organizations that are truly committed to its people.

Challenging times provide an opportunity to discover the real value of recognition—not recognition based on money or other tangible rewards, but recognition that derives from valuing what others have done. It benefits the giver, the receiver, and—in business—the bottom line. True recognition has the greatest value, yet costs little or nothing!

This book can help you initiate low-cost recognition in a systematic way, ensuring that you can build a culture of recognition in

your company that will survive and thrive in good times and bad. It will show you how to be a catalyst for change and how to help recognition flourish in your organization and also become a greater part of your life outside of work.

Recognition is crucial for effective human relations of all types. If enough people catch the wave, the practice of recognition will enhance not just the effectiveness of our organizations but the effectiveness of our families and communities, and even society at large.

—Bob Nelson, Ph.D.
   San Diego, California

—Dean Spitzer, Ph.D.
   Mulberry, Florida

INTRODUCTION

Motivation—
the Fire Within

"You get the best effort from others not by lighting a fire beneath them, but by building a fire within them."
—Bob Nelson

Why do people do what they do? This question has fascinated and bewildered mankind since the dawn of time. At the most basic level, unmet needs drive people's actions: If we're hungry, we eat; if we're thirsty, we drink; if we're tired, we sleep. But once our most basic physical needs are met, our attention turns to higher-level needs, such as a desire to belong, or to achieve something meaningful in life. Most of us spend almost one-third of our adult lives at work, so it should be no surprise that we often look to the work-place—and to our coworkers—to help us satisfy many of these needs.

Motivation is the internal human energy that propels people to satisfy their unmet needs. While we all have the same *basic* needs, our priorities are in a state of constant flux. Moreover, everyone has his or her own set of

"Brains, like hearts, go where they are appreciated."

—**Robert Mcnamara,**
former U.S. Secretary of Defense

additional *personal* needs. One person is most motivated to spend more time with his family, another to obtain a pay increase; another craves more responsibility and does whatever it takes to get it.

By its very nature, motivation is *intrinsic*—you can't motivate others, you can only provide an environment that is more conducive to their self-motivation. True, you can force others to do what you want at times, but such motivation is apt to be short-lived, lasting just as long as the direct force or threat exists. Once the coercion stops, so does the person's motivation—and the desired behavior. In fact, the traditional emphasis on coercion has given rise to misconceptions about motivation. One such misconception is exemplified by the old joke: If you tell someone to do something and be rewarded, that's called *incentive*; if you tell someone to do something or be fired, that's called *motivation.*

In recent years the use of coercion, fear, and threats have become increasingly ineffective motivational tools, due in part to larger social changes—greater affluence, the emergence of "knowledge workers," and the proliferation of job choices—that have made the use of force much less acceptable in the workplace and society. Employees now have more decision-making power about where they choose to work, and more control over how they choose to spend their energy while at work.

A controlling style of management simply cannot get the best results from today's workers. Employees are increasingly expected to use their own best judgment—to make decisions on their own—and not to do just what they are told to do. Moreover, today's employees want to be given even more authority, and greater autonomy in using that authority. They want to be trusted and respected to do the work they are hired to do, so they can do that work to the best of their abilities. The role of managers has shifted from an authoritative "command-and-control," "my-way-or-the-highway" style—the predominant style of management since the Industrial Revolution—to a role in which effective managers act more like coaches, colleagues, counselors, and even cheerleaders for their employees.

It is possible to create an environment in which each and every individual in your organization can be motivated. In fact, creating such an environment is perhaps the most important and challenging role of managing today. The key element in shaping a motivat-

"If human beings are perceived as potentials rather than problems, as possessing strengths instead of weaknesses, as unlimited rather than dull and unresponsive, then they thrive and grow to their capabilities."

—**Robert Conklin,**
teacher, author, and speaker

ing work environment is the management of consequences, particularly *positive* consequences.

Every employee wants to be magnificent. Every employee starts a new job excited about doing his or her best. Yet, for many employees, the initial excitement of the job quickly wears off, and motivation dissipates. We believe this outcome is the direct result of how managers treat their employees on a daily basis. Show us an unmotivated employee, and we'll show you a manager who has failed to help that employee achieve his or her full potential on the job.

It's up to managers to establish a supportive environment in which people can perform at their best. Managers need to create a new partnership with employees to help reach the goals of the organization, as well as the employee's personal goals. The effective use of recognition and reward is the primary means for creating a supportive work environment in which employees can be—and are—highly motivated, helping to assure the success of your organization.

YOU GET WHAT YOU REWARD

It seems that not a month goes by without the emergence of some new management fad "guaranteed" to increase employee performance, improve morale, and cure whatever ails your organization. Truth be told, most of these methods are soon discarded by those who employ them—to the chagrin of the employees who feel like Ping-Pong balls, bounced from one new management approach to the next.

There are, however, certain basic truths in management that you can always rely on. One is, "You get what you reward"—sometimes referred to as the Greatest Management Principle in the World. We know from extensive research that human behavior is shaped by its consequences, and that one of the most powerful ways to enhance employee performance is by providing positive consequences for that performance. If you notice, recognize, and reward a specific behavior—for instance, excellent customer service—that behavior will tend to be repeated.

Given that positive reinforcement is one of the most validated principles in management and psychology, it is surprising how few managers use it on a regular basis. It's common sense, but far from common practice. Yet it *needs* to become common practice if your organization is to thrive, let alone survive.

NO-COST IDEA 1

The Gold Star Award

Markeeta Graban, associate director of the Department of Psychiatry at the University of Michigan Health System, reports: "It's really true that anything can be a significant form of recognition. Over three years ago I drew a star on a piece of scrap paper, colored it, and gave it to someone for helping me out that day. They in turn gave it to someone who gave it to someone else. It took on special significance with each use. Now we have it on a magnetic backing and pass it on to someone who has helped or is having a rough day. People love it!"

DEALING WITH CORPORATE CULTURE

Q We are a small owner-managed real estate services company—appraisers, tax agents, administrative support. Our company culture, starting at the top, is very businesslike, with closed-door, production-driven, non-participative management styles. I'm trying to develop an employee recognition program that would fit our culture and not be too loose.

—**Bea Lytle**, anonymous company and location

A First, realize that almost anything can serve as a form of recognition (time off, gifts, activities, or giving additional work if done in the right context). So eliminate any preconceived notions of what to do. You will be best served not to decide what to do in a vacuum. Ask your employees what they would be excited about doing. Try to use their ideas, not yours, and if you're stuck for ideas, pass around a copy of *1001 Ways to Reward Employees* to get people thinking, and have them flag what appeals to them.

Everyone likes to be recognized and appreciated. But how many managers consider "appreciating others" part of their job description? Indeed, how many managers are expected by their organizations to recognize their employees when they do good work? Very few, we would venture.

At a time in which employees are being asked to do more than ever before, to make suggestions for continuous improvement, to handle complex problems quickly, and to act independently in the best interests of the company, the resources and support for rewarding them are at an all-time low. Budgets are tight; salaries are frozen. Layoffs are rampant; promotional opportunities are on the decline. More than ever, employees need to be told by their managers that their efforts are appreciated, and that they play an important role in their organizations.

In today's business environment, however, managers tend to be too busy and too removed from their employees to notice when they have done exceptional work, or to thank them for it. Working at the computer frequently replaces personal interaction between manager and employee. Futurist John Naisbitt predicted this would happen over two decades ago in his book *Megatrends*.[1] He stated that the more highly technical our work environments, the greater the employee's need for human contact. He called this emerging need "high-tech/high-touch." And this change has happened at a time when people are looking for greater meaning in all aspects of their lives.

The widespread lack of rewards and recognition programs at the time they are most needed is particularly inexcusable, because what motivates people the most takes very little time and money to implement. It doesn't take a fat bonus check, a trip to the Bahamas, or a lavish annual awards banquet to get the best out of people. It just takes a little time, thoughtfulness, and energy—consistently applied—to make a difference to employees.

Rewards and recognition are tools that can be used by every manager and leader in any organization to help realize enormous business benefits. This book will show you how.

THE BENEFITS OF RECOGNITION

Improved morale. One of the more immediate effects of increased recognition is improved morale. When employees are recognized for doing good work, they feel special, and consequently happier and more satisfied with their employers.

Enhanced productivity. Employees who feel good about their jobs tend to perform at a higher level; the performance itself becomes a further motivator for wanting to continue to do a good job.

Increased competitiveness. When companies recognize and reward performance that is aligned with the organization's key objectives, the organization becomes more successful, competitive, and efficient in reaching its goals.

Higher revenue and profit. Any organization that wants to make money and be profitable will find that recognizing progress in those areas will encourage employees to work harder to make money, and realize greater profits for the company.

Decreased stress. There's a fine line between stress and excitement. Recognition helps to make work more fun and exciting, increasing the likelihood that employees will "rise to the challenge" when needed, rather than feel out of control and swamped by their work.

Decreased absenteeism. When employees are thanked and valued for the work they do, they begin to look forward to the time they spend on the job. Absenteeism declines.

Decreased turnover. A study by the Gallup Organization—based on interviews with two million workers at seven hundred companies—revealed that the number one factor affecting the length of an employee's tenure at a company is the quality of that employee's relationship with his or her immediate supervisor.[2] More recognition equals better relationships, equals decreased turnover and increased tenure.

Lower related costs. When employees are happy to come to work and are excited about doing their best work, the need for—and costs of—interviewing, hiring, and training new employees declines drastically.

Morale

Productivity

Competitiveness

Revenue & Profit

Stress

Absenteeism

Turnover

Related Costs

NO-COST IDEA

The Spark Plug Award

Beverly Cronin, book manager for Hastings Books, Music, and Entertainment in Rio Rancho, New Mexico, recalls receiving a "Spark Plug" award in the mid-sixties from a department store manager in Akron, Ohio, who said, "This is for you, because you add a spark to our workplace." The award was a spark plug painted gold and hung on a ribbon. She still keeps the award in her jewelry box to commemorate the first time she was recognized on the job and felt she made a difference.

HOW TO USE THIS BOOK

We set out to create the most comprehensive and most fully integrated book on the topic of employee recognition and rewards. Although there are many good books available to supplement this one (including those by the authors!), we wanted this book to stand alone as both a resource and an application guide to help you get the best results from your reward and recognition efforts. This book is not intended just to be read, but is meant to be used "in the field," where it can have the greatest impact.

We also wanted this book to be helpful to you whether you are a manager, a team leader, a human resources professional, an executive, or a regular employee—regardless of your level of experience with rewards and recognition, or the nature of the existing recognition programs in your organization.

Here's what you can expect to find in the book's seven sections:

PART I: Recognition Fundamentals. An overview of what we know about motivation and recognition.

PART II: Getting Started with Recognition. Initial approaches for using recognition.

PART III: Organizational Recognition. An overview and review of the primary steps in effectively designing, planning, implementing, and managing organizational recognition programs.

PART IV: Issues and Challenges in Recognition. Some of the most common and challenging problems that arise when applying recognition in an organization.

PART V: Recognition Tools. A variety of assessment and measurement tools, planning worksheets and checklists, and "best practices" to serve as your models for recognition.

PART VI: Recognition Resources. Additional information and ideas, and the authors' personal "honor roll" of companies that excel at employee recognition.

PART VII: Selected Articles. Some of the authors' most popular and useful articles elaborating on points not covered in the book.

In addition, you will find in the margins of this book not only thought-provoking quotes, but the following features:

NO-COST RECOGNITION IDEAS 101 new real-world examples of no-cost recognition ideas that the authors have collected.

Q&A Questions about rewards and recognition from people across the country and abroad, with answers by the authors.

WRECKOGNITIONS Real-life examples of common and not-so-common mistakes that can wreck the effectiveness of recognition.

Signposts Markers directing you to recognition tools and resources.

At the end of the book are quick-reference cards that can be removed and used to cue your own *real-time* reward and recognition activities.

TERMS AND DEFINITIONS

Motivation: The internal human energy available to inspire a person to act.

Motivator: Anything that increases motivational energy.

Demotivator: Anything that reduces motivational energy and/or triggers negative behaviors.

Recognition: A positive consequence provided to a person for a behavior or result. Recognition can take the form of acknowledgment, approval, or the expression of gratitude. It means appreciating someone for something he or she has done for you, your group, or your organization. Recognition can be given while an employee is striving to achieve a certain goal or behavior, or once he has completed it.

Reward: An item or experience with monetary value (but not necessarily money) that is provided for desired behavior or performance, often with accompanying recognition. Harvard Business School professor and management consultant Rosabeth Moss Kanter defines a reward as "something special—a special gain for special achievements, a treat for doing something above-and-beyond."

Incentive: Recognition or reward that is promised in advance for

DEFINITION, PLEASE

Q What is the difference between recognition and reward?

—**Mary Ann Short**,
Ohio State University,
Columbus, OH

A I usually think of re-cognition as more of an activity (a social or interpersonal activity), while a reward is more of a thing (money, merchandise, travel). You reinforce progress toward desired performance or behavior through recognition, and you reward after those results are achieved.

an anticipated achievement based on meeting certain criteria. Incentives create anticipation and excitement and thus can result in stronger, clearer motivation.

BUILDING A RECOGNITION CULTURE

Once you've applied the principles and ideas discussed in this book, you will be well on your way to shaping a more motivating workplace. If you keep at it, you will soon have employees who are dedicated to your (and their) success, and a work environment in which people are excited about their jobs, enjoy their coworkers, and want to do the best work possible each and every day. Not only will this give your organization a competitive advantage, it will also make you proud to be a leader.

Your job, however, will not be done. To sustain the results you obtain, you will need to align desired behaviors and performance with your company's systems of hiring, orientation, and training, and with the use of traditional incentives such as raises and promotions. When this happens, you will have truly created a culture of recognition. You will have created the kind of work environment we all dream of—an environment that puts people first, and rewards and recognizes their contributions to their customers, coworkers, and organizations. We wrote this book to help you create that vision.

"The capacities of the average human being for creativity, for growth, for collaboration, for productivity (in the full sense of the term) are far greater than we have yet recognized."

—Douglas MacGregor, management theorist

PART I
RECOGNITION FUNDAMENTALS

CHAPTER I

The Rewards and Recognition Revolution

"There are two things people want more than sex and money: recognition and praise."

—**Mary Kay Ash,** founder, Mary Kay

There's a revolution going on in today's work-places. Workers want respect, and they want it now. They want to be trusted to do a good job; they want autonomy to decide how best to do it; and they want support, even if they make a mistake. Most important, they want to be appreciated when they do a good job.

These considerations are more important to today's employees than they were to employees in previous eras. Providing workers with respect and autonomy can make a world of differ-ence in keeping them, and in getting the best efforts out of them.

A SHIFT IN LOYALTY

Q I've been teaching for eleven years and am beginning to see issues related to what I believe is the contemporary lack of employee loyalty, versus the old '50s and '60s mentality of always looking up to the employer. What's your viewpoint?

—**Jeff Sumner,**
Yorktown, VA

A **Employee loyalty has shifted dramatically. I'm convinced that employees today are no longer loyal to organizations as much as they are loyal to people, especially to managers who treat them with trust, respect, and consideration, and who systematically seek to act in their best interests.**

RECOGNITION TODAY

Everyone likes to be recognized for doing a good job; smart managers and business owners have known this for years, and have successfully used it to motivate employees and enhance their performance. But now, more than ever, the use of recognition is a critical ingredient in the success of an organization. Here are five major business trends that have influenced the importance of recognition in today's work environment.

1. The decline of traditional incentives. Over the last decade, traditional incentives such as money and promotion have lost their power to shape employee behavior. According to an article in *Compensation and Benefits Review,*

- 81 percent of workers claim they do not receive any reward for increases in productivity;

- 60 percent of managers report that their compensation will not increase if their performance improves; and

- only 3 percent of base salary separates average from outstanding employees.[1]

Clearly, the traditional system of rewards in business is in crisis if it fails to differentiate and encourage high performance on such a widespread basis. Just as clearly, employee loyalty is negatively affected by the failure of managers to make the proper connection between pay and performance. According to a recent survey by human capital consulting firm Aon Consulting, only 48 percent of surveyed workers would recommend their organization as one of the best places to work, and 58 percent would leave to work for another employer, even if offered only a slight increase in pay.[2]

Part of the problem stems from a past overdependence on financial rewards and the exclusion of other potential reinforcers. In the words of management guru Peter Drucker, "Economic incentives are becoming rights rather than rewards. Merit raises are always introduced as rewards for exceptional performance. In no time at all, they become a right. To deny a merit raise or to grant only a small one becomes punishment. The increasing demand for material rewards is rapidly destroying their usefulness as incentives and managerial tools."[3]

And it gets worse. Cash and other material rewards have in some cases actually been found to have a *demotivating* effect on employees. As Cecil Hill, corporate manager of improvement programs at Hughes Aircraft Company in Los Angeles, explains,

> *I found certain aspects of the cash awards approach would be counterproductive at Hughes Aircraft. For example, cash awards would reduce teamwork as employees concentrated primarily on individual cash gains. We also found that United Airlines had dropped its longtime cash awards system because of litigation problems. Other companies pointed out a negative boomerang effect whenever ideas were turned down, while many firms reported an ongoing problem with timely response, and others noted disagreements on determining dollar amounts and conflicts regarding what constitutes "a part of normal job performance."*
>
> *We have also found instances where "pay" for certain types of intellectual performance tends to denigrate the performance and remove it from the intellectual achievement category, which elicits pride and satisfaction, reducing it to a more mundane "pay-for-performance" concept. In short, cash awards seemed to have an overall demotivating effect.[4]*

In addition, organizations today are less able to offer their high achievers promotions or similar incentives. Because of increasing competition in the global marketplace, most organizations have been forced into extensive internal changes manifested by downsizing, cost-cutting, and the flattening and elimination of numerous levels of hierarchy. These changes have greatly reduced the number of positions available for employee promotions. In a recent survey reported in *The Washington Post,* 43 percent of respondents from seven hundred organizations indicate that they will be able to offer fewer opportunities for advancement in years to come.[5] As management consultant Rosabeth Moss Kanter observes, "In this time of corporate hierarchy-shrinking and organizational layer-removal, companies cannot afford the old-fashioned system in which promotion was the primary means of recognizing performance. Greater accessibility to rewards—at all levels—is a necessity when employees stay in place longer; and recognition is an important part of this."[6]

"Human beings need to be recognized and rewarded for special efforts. You don't even have to give them much. What they want is tangible proof that you really care about the job they do. The reward is really just a symbol of that."

—**Tom Cash,**
senior vice president,
American Express

"To create a competitive edge in today's business world, organizations are trying to do more with fewer employees, so it's imperative that employees are rewarded for using problem-solving and decision-making skills. No activity is more important to an organization."

—David W. Smith,
president,
Action Management Associates

2. The rise of nontraditional incentives. In the meantime, non-monetary incentives have actually come to rank higher in importance for most employees than traditional organizational rewards such as cash and promotions. In multiple studies conducted first in the 1940s[7] and more recently in the mid-1990s,[8] employees have consistently ranked feeling fully appreciated for work done and feeling "in" on things as being more important to them than more traditional incentives such as good wages or job security. In a more recent survey of workers conducted by the Society of Incentive Travel Executives Foundation, 63 percent of the respondents ranked even a pat on the back as a meaningful incentive. In another study, 68 percent of respondents said it was important to believe that others appreciated their work, and 67 percent said that most people need appreciation for their work.[9]

To illustrate the power of positive reinforcement, Daniel Boyle, vice president and treasurer of Cascades Diamond, in Thorndike, Massachusetts (formerly Diamond Fiber Products), describes the impact that the award of a "100 Club" nylon and cotton jacket had on one employee:

> *You might think this is a trivial thing, but it means a lot to the people who earn a jacket. A teller at a local bank told me once that a woman came in and proudly modeled her baby blue 100 Club jacket for bank customers and employees. She said, "My employer gave me this for doing a good job. It's the first time in the eighteen years I've been there they've recognized the things I do every day." During those years she had earned hundreds of thousands of dollars in wages, which had paid for cars, a home mortgage, food, other essentials, vacations, college educations. In her mind, she had provided a service for her earnings. The money wasn't recognition for her work, but the 100 Club jacket was.[10]*

Think of the impact recognition could have had on this employee if it had been used on a daily basis, instead of only once in her eighteen years of service to Cascades Diamond!

This shift in desired incentives is further demonstrated by Beverly Kaye and Sharon Jordan-Evans's recent study of the reasons employees stay with a particular company.[11]

TOP 10	REASONS TO STAY
I	Career growth, learning, and development
2	Exciting work and challenge
3	Meaningful work; making a difference and a contribution
4	Great people
5	Being part of a team
6	Good boss
7	Recognition for work well done
8	Autonomy, sense of control over one's work
9	Flexible work hours and dress code
I0	Fair pay and benefits

Note that the traditional incentives of fair pay and benefits are last on the list. Pay and benefits are a foundation upon which managers need to build, but they are not the main reason that employees are loyal to their organizations—far from it. A survey of executives by Robert Half International, a staffing company, further confirms the importance of recognition in employee retention. That survey found that the number-one reason employees leave organizations today is "limited recognition and praise" for the work they do, which was ranked higher than all other responses, including inadequate compensation, limited authority, and personality conflicts.[12]

3. The increased use of variable compensation. There is an emerging trend in employee compensation toward variable compensation systems in which base salaries are fixed and merit increases are paid only on a bonus basis, in accordance with specific performance targets. While variable compensation makes a lot of sense for the organizations that employ it—tying pay and performance tightly together—employees can become demotivated

NO-COST IDEA 4

Special Delivery

At Armstrong Machine Works in Three Rivers, Michigan, paychecks are delivered personally to about three hundred workers by the general manager or the controller each week in order to give everyone a chance to be heard. At least once a week, each employee has the opportunity to ask questions, make suggestions, and receive feedback from management.

See page 371 for article, "The Care of the Undownsized."

when targets are not met and bonuses are not forthcoming. This effect becomes even more pronounced when the targets are outside the control of the employees who are expected to meet them.

Such systems place pressure on organizations to find ways other than traditional pay to reinforce desired behavior. Informal rewards can help accommodate this need for new reinforcers, and they are perfectly compatible with variable compensation systems.

4. The increased need for empowered employees. Increasingly, employees are expected to be self-directed and self-empowered. If they work in a different location (or on a different shift) from their managers, have flexible work hours, or telecommute, employees are expected to act independently and in the best interests of the organization with less direct management supervision than in the past. As Joseph Maciariello and Calvin Kirby observe in their book *Management Control Systems,* "the challenge for managers is to build adaptability into the controls of an organization, thus providing workers with more flexibility and freedom to innovate, while managers still direct their activities toward the common purpose of the organization."[13] Recognition and rewards are tools of empowerment that can be used by managers and workers alike to reinforce desired behavior and improve performance in their work environments.

5. More change and uncertainty. Businesses of all types and sizes are experiencing change at a much faster rate than they have in the past. The nature of effective rewards and recognition is changing quickly as well. As management professor Henry Mintzberg observes, "in today's dynamic, changing work environments, management must use more flexible, less formalized coordinating mechanisms."[14] The result is a reduction in the reliance on formal management controls.

Informal, flexible systems work better during times of uncertainty—whether the need is to stabilize operations or to more quickly and better meet organizational demands during times of crisis. As Maciariello and Kirby explain, "The association between the informal and formal changes with the degree of uncertainty. As stability and predictability increase, the use of formal systems increase. In times of major change, the informal system should be the dominant management system. The formal system, that is, the policies and procedures that applied to the past products and customers, may actually be looked upon by management as a potential barrier."[15]

The use of informal rewards provides just the right combination of relevance, immediacy, and individual value. Considering that a reported 33 percent of managers would rather work in another organization where they could receive better recognition,[16] this issue is critical to motivation and performance in today's fast-moving organizations, and to an organization's ability to thrive—let alone survive—in the future.

Although employees put high value on recognition and appreciation, the impact goes far beyond workforce contentment. Recognition can also increase a company's revenues while decreasing its costs—a potent combination in any business. The consistent use of recognition not only results in a higher level of productivity and performance from employees, it also makes it easier to attract new employees as the organization develops a reputation as an "employer of choice."

In addition, employees who are treated well inevitably treat their customers better. Chances are, you'll never get employees to treat customers better than they are being treated themselves. As J. W. Marriott, chairman and CEO of Marriott International, puts it, "We know that if we treat our employees correctly, they'll treat the customers right. And if the customers are treated right, they'll come back."

THE RECOGNITION AND PERFORMANCE LINK

Recognition and performance are closely linked. A fundamental reason for the use of recognition is that it has a measurably positive impact on the job performance of employees. When you get serious about enhancing performance, you have to get serious about recognition! Bob Nelson's doctoral study (discussed in more depth in Chapter 3)[17] found evidence to support the link between the use of recognition and enhanced performance in at least three different ways.

First, most of the managers in Bob's study agreed with the notion that the use of recognition leads to enhanced performance in many ways (the percentage of managers who agreed with the following statements is indicated in parentheses):

SELL THE IMPACT

Q What can you do when the owners of a company just don't believe in rewarding their employees?

—**Anonymous**

A Somehow you've got to get on management's radar screen. The point is that rewarding employees isn't a good idea just because it makes employees feel better, but also because it makes good business sense, too. Happy employees are more productive, they provide better customer service, and they are less apt to leave a company for other opportunities. Share the research and sell the bottom-line impact that recognition can have on the organization.

- Recognizing employees helps me better motivate them (90 percent).

- Providing nonmonetary recognition to my employees when they do good work helps increase their performance (84 percent).

- Recognizing employees provides them with practical feedback (84 percent).

- Recognizing my employees for good work makes it easier to get the work done (80 percent).

- Recognizing employees helps them be more productive (77 percent).

- Providing nonmonetary recognition helps me achieve my personal goals (69 percent).

- Providing nonmonetary recognition helps me achieve my job goals (60 percent).

Second, 73 percent of managers in the study reported that they received the results they expected immediately or soon after they used recognition, and 99 percent said they felt that they would eventually obtain the desired results.

Third, of the employees who reported to the managers in this study, 77 percent said that it was either "very important" or "extremely important" to be recognized by their managers when they do good work. Employees expected recognition to occur immediately (20 percent), soon thereafter (53 percent), or sometime later (18 percent).

It's true: Recognition really does motivate employees and enhance performance!

THE ECONOMICS AND BOTTOM-LINE IMPACT OF RECOGNITION

Effective recognition programs, even at the individual and team levels, require a substantial investment of time and money. Let's consider, for example, an organization in which one hundred supervisors are spending, as a realistic average, two hours and

$25 a week each on recognition. If the fully burdened cost (hourly wage plus the cost of benefits) of each supervisor is $50 an hour, the time that the supervisors devote to their recognition efforts alone costs the company approximately $650,000 per year.

And that's just the beginning. Say that ten teams (with ten employees on each team) are spending one hour per person (at a fully burdened rate of $25 per hour) and $30 a week per team on recognition-related activities. That works out to an additional $140,000 per year in real cost to the company. The grand total of this very simple approach to individual and team recognition is close to $800,000! And this is before we even think about adding in the costs of an organizational recognition program.

If you were the CEO of this company, wouldn't you want to know what benefits the organization was getting for this significant investment of company resources?

A smart CEO, of course, would have no problem with the $800,000 expenditure, provided he or she were confident that the program was an investment that would produce in excess of the cost. Unfortunately, recognition done poorly can easily turn a huge investment into a huge expense with low return and major morale consequences for the organization. However, as we will demonstrate throughout this book, when recognition is executed properly, the benefits can far exceed the time and money put into it.

Numerous studies support the important role that employee recognition plays in achieving a company's financial and performance goals. Some companies have specifically tracked the financial payback of their recognition efforts; here are some of the results:

- Pegasus Personal Fitness Centers asked employees to make a list of the rewards they would like to receive (up to a value of $25) when they achieved performance goals. The company reports that this practice helped double sales in a six-year period.

- Oil giant Amoco offered employees a variety of gifts and contests. One plant saved $18.8 million in two years from such efforts.

- Amtech threw "Victory Parties" for its employees and credits the technique with helping to obtain a phenomenal 890 percent growth in revenue over a five-year period.

NO-COST 5 IDEA

Fishy Stuff

The New England Aquarium allows employees to recognize coworkers with a "thank-you cod" (a card shaped like a cod fish)—a play on New England accents. "Half of the card goes to the employee and the other half into a quarterly lottery for gift certificates for paid time off, the company store, and local restaurants," reports Linda Hower, learning technologist for Gilbane University in Providence, Rhode Island.

➔ **See pages 287-308**
for "Recognition Best Practices."

RECOGNITION MAGIC AT DISNEY CORPORATION

How does Disney do it? Year after year, Walt Disney World Company excels in service excellence. To learn about the more than two hundred recognition programs at Disney, we interviewed Dee Hansford, former manager.

Q: Walt Disney once said, "You can dream, create, design, and build the most wonderful place in the world . . . but it requires people to make the dream a reality." How do you focus on people today to keep Walt's dream alive?

A: *We are constantly looking for new ways to recognize people, both informally and formally. Informal things are happening all of the time. An example of a new formal recognition program we just introduced is the Partners in Excellence program.*

Q: What is the Partners in Excellence program?

A: *Partners in Excellence was created by a cross-divisional, multilevel team of Cast Members. It implements a formal recognition program that upholds the company's performance excellence initiatives. It provides one global recognition program for guest satisfaction, cast excellence, and operational/financial excellence.*

Q: How did you come up with this program?

A: *We sought input from other great companies and used them as a benchmark. However, you find that you can look at what other companies do, but if* your program doesn't support your philosophy your people are not going to respond. To be well rounded, employees need skills reinforcing Disney's "performance excellence" initiatives. That is, we need to be great with fellow Cast Members, we need to be great with guests, and we need to understand the impact we have on our business every day. Those principles helped form Partners in Excellence.

Q: How do employees win, and who does the evaluation?

A: *You can be nominated by anyone, whether they belong to your work team or not. So the nomination can and should reach across business units. A Cast Member is evaluated by establishing local criteria for excellence. The criteria cover three foundations that we consider crucial:*

1. *Cast excellence.* How good a team player are you? Do you know your role in the team? Are you always ready to help your fellow Cast Members?
2. *Guest satisfaction.* Is the guest you serve a paying guest or a fellow Cast Member?
3. *Operational and financial excellence.* Do you always look for ways to streamline a process? Can we save labor hours or labor dollars? Can we do this more efficiently?

Q: Are there different levels in the program?

A: Yes. There are several levels. There is the first-time recipient, who receives a 10k gold pin, a statue, and a celebration hosted by our top leadership. The statue is a reproduction of the statue in front of the Magic Kingdom. The pin also has those symbols on it.

At the second level, partners who are selected a second time meet additional criteria and are expected to set higher levels for themselves.

One of the things we ask our current partners to do is to be involved in helping set local criteria for those areas where we do not have any. We ask them to develop their fellow Cast Members as potential Partners in Excellence candidates. If they meet both the first- and second-level criteria, then they are eligible to receive a second award. They receive a diamond in the pin, their statue is upgraded with an engraved plaque, and they receive a two-night resort stay at the property. They also attend an annual local celebration hosted by our executives.

Q: How many people receive awards?

A: The program is open to all Cast Members part-time and full-time through the manager level. It affects upwards of 35,000 people. Last year we did not set a limit, and we celebrated 1,307 Cast Members. This year we will try to recognize 1 to 3 percent of our top performers.

"You can dream, create, design, and build the most wonderful place in the world, but people make the dream a reality."

Q: What has been the reaction from the Cast Members to these programs?

A: We have seen and heard feedback from our leaders that the Partners program has improved teamwork and attendance, and that communication between management and nonsalaried Cast Members has improved.

Q: Are employees happy with these programs and do they motivate them to work harder?

A: Yes, they are very pleased. When we started Partners in Excellence, we were retiring some existing programs. The feedback we received was that employees wanted to be recognized for outstanding performance and behaviors. First, they wanted to be recognized for guest satisfaction. Second, they wanted to be recognized for longevity. Our Cast Members have experienced a great sense of pride when receiving the recognition. They realize that it is the highest honor our company can bestow, and they take it very much to heart.

Q: What advice would you give to other companies looking to start a similar program?

A: Be sure you create a program that supports your company's culture and business objectives. Solicit input from employees and leaders, because they are going to be the owners. Be very, very aware of the diversity of your population.

TOO BUSY

Q A few years ago, after a survey indicated that employees felt unrecognized by their managers, I put together some recognition items such as thank-you cards and offered training to all employees in how to use them. Unfortunately, the managers and supervisors didn't attend because they were "too busy." They also seldom used the items available to recognize their employees. How can I get managers involved in this process?

—**Alice Rumph,**
Gambro Renal Products,
Lakewood, CO

A **First, congratulations on the initiative you've shown. I've found that making recognition happen is iterative, so try to build on and expand from your successes. Discuss with the managers the increasing problem of attracting and retaining employees, and the hidden costs, the loss of productivity and competitiveness. Show what your competition is doing. Relate the issue to the bottom line. You can't force managers to recognize their employees, but you can make a persuasive case for why they should want to do so. Remember too that having too little time is usually just an excuse.**

- American Express used a "Great Performers" poster campaign to help increase net income by 500 percent in eleven years, with a return on investment of 28 percent.

- American Airlines' AAchievers points-for-merchandise rewards program awarded employees points for making suggestions about how the company could save money, fix a problem, and so on. These suggestions resulted in cost savings that allowed the company to purchase a new airplane.

- Boardroom's "I-Power" program recognized and rewarded every employee for submitting two suggestions per week, resulting in a fivefold increase in the company's revenues in just a few years.

Despite the wealth of evidence supporting the effectiveness and financial benefit of employee rewards and recognition, we have found that managers must make a "leap of faith" to believe that recognition is worth doing. No single study or example of company success will convince the person who doesn't want to believe in recognition. Individually, managers and executives in the organization have to be convinced not only that recognition is the right thing to do, but also that it will work.

CHANGES IN THE USE OF EMPLOYEE RECOGNITION AND REWARDS

In the past decade, recognition has gained credibility as an effective performance management tool, and the use of employee recognition and rewards has undergone significant changes:

- **From one size fits all to multiple programs and activities.** During more stable times, companies could have a few traditional recognition programs, such as a years-of-service or employee-of-the-month program, and be able to keep employees relatively motivated. That's not enough to satisfy most employees today.

- **From centrally oriented programs to leader-oriented programs.** Recognition programs of the past could be centrally created and managed by the human resource department; today the task of motivating employees in a leader's sphere of influence must fall to each leader.

- **From formal programs to informal behaviors and activities.** Although formal recognition is still important to employees, informal, spontaneous recognition—specifically tied to those things that most matter on a day-to-day basis— is even more so.

- **From few choices to many options that constantly change.** Greater choice equals greater alignment and freshness, since what is motivating to one employee may have no meaning to another. The best incentive programs today allow greater choice among available options, including merchandise choices, as well as development opportunities, family-shared activities, special considerations, team activities, and spontaneous celebrations.

- **From infrequent use to greater frequency and flexibility.** The days of expecting a great performance review to motivate an employee for the next twelve months are over. Recognition must be used on an ongoing basis with employees who have earned and deserve it. This in turn means that greater creativity and flexibility are required to generate new recognition ideas to be used, and that they must be used more often.

- **From cultures of entitlement to cultures of performance.** Organizations, especially larger and older ones, are moving away from a mindset of "taking care of people" toward "helping employees help themselves" to learn, grow, perform, and produce in ways that benefit the employees and the organization.

- **From selective use for top performers to use for everyone.** Incentives such as travel and merchandise used to be reserved primarily for the organization's top sales employees. Now, not only are incentives used throughout the organization, but all employees are encouraged to recognize each other and their managers.

Every business has its share of problems, which can include poor product quality, low morale, poor customer service, and low productivity, to name just a few. In some cases, such problems might require millions of dollars to fix. Recognition, however, offers a low-cost strategy with a big-impact effect on morale, performance, recruiting, and retention. Recognition works, and when managers recognize their employees' efforts, employees will respond by giving their best efforts.

"People will forget what you said. People will forget what you did. But people will never forget how you made them feel."

—Anonymous

THE TAKE-AWAY

- Now more than ever, the use of recognition is a critical ingredient in the success of any organization.

- There is a strong link between recognition and performance, with a positive effect on the bottom line.

- More than ever before, leaders are responsible for motivating employees in their immediate sphere of influence.

- Positive reinforcement really does work, and anyone can benefit from its use by learning to reward and recognize effectively.

CHAPTER 2

The Salary Fallacy and the Seven Facets of Recognition

"Compensation is a right; recognition is a gift."

—**Rosabeth Moss Kanter,** management consultant

Ask any manager what his or her employees want from their jobs, and you'll probably get a list of items heavy on financial incentives such as increased pay, bonuses, promotions, and so forth. Ask any employee what he or she really wants from his or her job, and you'll likely get a very different answer.

Yes, salary is important, but even more important are the intangibles of trust and respect, the chance to learn new skills and be involved in decision making, and being thanked for doing good work.

RECOGNITION FALLACIES

In a series of studies originally conducted by Lawrence Lindahl in the late 1940s[1] (and subsequently repeated with similar findings by Kenneth Kovach in the 1980s and Bob Nelson in the 1990s), what managers believed that their employees most wanted

OVERCOMING EXCLUSIVITY

Q Don't staff members who are not recognized become frustrated?

—**Gary Flaxman**,
City of Long Beach, CA

A Yes, this can be the case, but the problem can be alleviated. When staff members are frustrated about not being recognized, it's often a clear indication that there's not enough recognition and it's too infrequent. If the criteria are clear, people can self-select to be recognized through better performance. If they are doing the desired behaviors, but no one is noticing, allow people to nominate themselves or come up with another means of giving the behavior visibility. Expand the types of recognition; don't put all your focus on a single program.

from their jobs was in sharp contrast to what the employees themselves reported as being most desirable.

	Employee Ranking	Manager Ranking
Full appreciation for work done	1	8
Feeling "in" on things	2	10
Sympathetic help on personal problems	3	9
Job security	4	2
Good wages	5	1
Interesting work	6	5
Promotion/growth opportunities	7	3
Personal loyalty to workers	8	6
Good working conditions	9	4
Tactful disciplining	10	7

While managers thought the traditional motivators of good wages, job security, and promotion/growth opportunities (each of which has a financial cost) were what employees most desired, the employees most highly valued full appreciation for work done, feeling "in" on things, and sympathetic help on personal problems—all items, ironically, that have no direct financial cost.

In a 1991 study, Professor Gerald Graham, of Wichita State University, asked fifteen hundred workers to rank the importance and frequency of use of sixty-five motivators in the workplace. All five of the top employee-ranked items were nonmonetary forms of recognition. Of these five top-ranked items, three required little or no financial resources and very little time to implement successfully. The top-ranked item, "Manager personally congratulates employees who do a good job," had the highest-ranked impact, although almost 58 percent of respondents said their managers seldom if ever provided such thanks. The second-highest-ranked employee motivator, "Manager writes personal notes for good performance," was reported as being seldom if ever provided by their managers by 76 percent of respondents.[2] The following table indicates the motivational importance and frequency of use of the top employee-ranked motivators in Graham's study.

TOP 5 — GRAHAM'S MOTIVATORS

Rank	Motivating Behavior	Frequency of Use[a] (%)
1	Manager personally congratulates employees who do a good job	42
2	Manager writes personal notes for good performance	24
3	Organization uses performance as the major basis for promotion	22
4	Manager publicly recognizes employee for good performance	19
5	Manager holds morale-building meetings to celebrate successes	8

[a]Percentage of respondents who say their manager or organization typically uses these techniques.

Dr. Graham found two common characteristics among the top five motivating practices in his study. The practices most motivating to employees are ones that are:

❶ Manager-initiated rather than organization-initiated.

❷ Contingent on performance, not just on being present.

Dr. Graham found that the type of reward most preferred by employees was personalized, "spur-of-the-moment recognition from their direct supervisors."

In his conclusion, he writes, "It appears that the techniques that have the greatest motivational impact are practiced the least even though they are easier and less expensive to use."

Other studies reinforce Graham's findings. "National Study of the Changing Workforce," by the Families and Work Institute in New York, reveals the importance of nonmonetary factors on employees' choice of their current employer.[3]

Of reasons considered to have been "very important" by respondents, the top ten reasons cited required no direct financial cost, with "open communication" ranked as the most important reason by 65 percent of respondents; "position salary" was ranked sixteenth.

NO-COST 6 IDEA

Welcome Cards

Joan Padgett of the learning resources center of Veterans' Medical Center in Dayton, Ohio, reports, "I recently decided to take the time to give a welcome card to a new employee and wrote a personal note, saying: 'At the end of some days you'll feel elated; after some you'll feel completely drained; but may you always leave your office knowing you contributed to our organization.' The employee was thrilled and said she would keep the card always. Her emotional response convinced me of the value of giving cards to thank, congratulate, welcome, and celebrate employees."

❶	Open communication	**65%**
❷	Effect on personal/family life	**60%**
❸	Nature of work	**59%**
❹	Management quality	**59%**
❺	Supervisor	**58%**
❻	Gain new skills.	**55%**
❼	Control over work content	**55%**
❽	Job security	**54%**
❾	Coworker quality	**53%**
❿	Stimulating work	**50%**
⓰	Position salary	**35%**

Most of the items in this survey are factors related to what is often called the "softer" side of management, the *people* dimension of work. This study found that "open communication" is most important to people at work. Everybody wants to know what's going on—especially as it affects them and their jobs. Simply telling them what's going on, and providing them with the information they need to most effectively do their jobs, is a motivator.

And in a 2002 survey conducted by Bob Nelson, the top ten recognition factors for employees were:

TOP 10   NELSON'S RECOGNITION FACTORS

1	Support and involvement	6	Manager availability and time
2	Personal praise	7	Written praise
3	Autonomy and authority	8	Electronic praise
4	Flexible working hours	9	Public praise
5	Learning and development	10	Cash or cash substitutes

Survey after survey consistently indicates this simple truth: when it comes to recognizing employees, the simple, intangible considerations are the most important to their motivation.

THE MONEY MOTIVATION MYTH

Most people don't come to work just for money. We're not saying money isn't important; clearly it is. We all need money to pay our bills and live in the manner to which we are accustomed. We're also not saying money has no motivational value; clearly it does, and the strength of that motivation will vary over one's career. If you are about to buy a new home, have some unexpected medical bills, or have children in college, you're going to be more keenly aware of your monetary needs, and much more motivated by cash.

But for most of us, most of the time, once we are able to comfortably keep up with our monthly bills, our self-esteem quickly and inevitably turns to other factors that have much greater significance: feeling we are making a contribution, having a manager that tells us when we do a good job, having the respect of our peers and colleagues, being involved and informed about what is going on in the company, and doing meaningful, interesting work.

The point is, the money employees are paid is *compensation*. Compensation is a function of your company's compensation philosophy and policies, its market, and geographic considerations. Recognition is not compensation; it's what you offer employees above and beyond compensation to get the best effort from them.

According to management theorist Frederick Herzberg, a fair salary is considered a "hygiene" factor; something everyone needs in order to do the job they are hired to do. Hygiene factors include other basic needs such as adequate workspace, sufficient lighting, a comfortable environment, and more. These factors enable you to do your job—but aren't enough to encourage you to do your *best* job. Getting people to do their best job is the function of what Herzberg calls "motivators." Motivators include praise and recognition, challenging work, and growth and development opportunities. In essence, there is a huge difference between just getting people to come in to work and getting them to do their best work.[4]

A QUEST FOR CASH

Q What does it mean when employees consistently ask for money as a reward? This is exemplified by informal surveys, employees choosing cash instead of merchandise for service recognition, and unsolicited comments about requesting money in place of parties, luncheons, etc.

—**online forum participant**

A Money is a definite motivator, so it comes as no surprise that employees would ask for it. However, if that is all they ever ask for, you might have a different situation going on. I've seen some organizations in which money has become the only motivator; that is, money was always used as thanks or included as a choice for recognition, to the point where employees viewed it as the only acceptable form of recognition the company had to offer.

Recognition is different from money and needs to be used regardless of what cash bonuses you give employees.

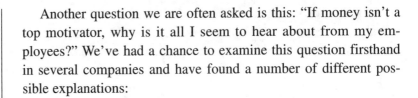

Another question we are often asked is this: "If money isn't a top motivator, why is it all I seem to hear about from my employees?" We've had a chance to examine this question firsthand in several companies and have found a number of different possible explanations:

❶ In some organizations where people are doing jobs they don't enjoy, while working for managers who never show their appreciation, employees conclude: "If this is what it's like to work here, at least they had better pay me well." In the absence of recognition, money becomes a form of psychological reparation for enduring a miserable job.

❷ In other organizations, we have found managers who use *only* money to thank people—for example, they award bonuses for completing projects, on-the-spot cash for desired behavior, or an extra percentage in the employees' annual salary increase. Without intending to, these managers implicitly send the message to employees that cash is the only medium of gratitude. They *train* employees to expect cash as the only true form of thanks.

Unfortunately, many people equate the amount of money they earn with their perceived worth to the organization. You need to be careful that you do not respond just to those individuals who constantly ask for more money. Why? Because you want to reinforce *results,* not requests. This is a critical point: You will never get the best effort from employees merely by paying them more. Employees who only want more money will never be satisfied with what they are paid, and their expectations will rise with each salary increase.

But since money is a basic need, don't you sometimes have to pay employees well first, *before* the other factors we've discussed, to begin motivating them? This question came up at a conference keynote presentation one of the authors was giving, and he was delighted to have a member of the audience stand up and say, "Not necessarily! I found that by using positive reinforcement I was able to increase the performance level of my employees, which led to increased sales revenues, which ultimately made it possible to pay people better." In other words, nonmonetary incentives were the catalysts for improving employee productivity—enabling *everyone* to gain financially in the process.

Another way to look at the relation between money and motivation is that most of us cannot influence what employees earn, but there are a lot of things we can do to influence their excitement and motivation on a daily basis. Treating employees well is of paramount importance if you want them to come to work energized and committed, and to bring their best thinking and initiative with them. Management's daily interactions with employees can do one of two things: promote trust and respect between managers and employees or erode it. Not much of a choice, when you think about it.

The focus of management used to be on "renting" employee behavior; in some work environments staff was even referred to as "hired hands." Today it's not good enough to simply rent the behavior you want from employees—you've got to find a way to tap into their hearts and minds, and to elicit their best effort. You have to make employees feel valued so that they *want* to do their best work on a daily basis, and to consistently act in the best interests of the organization.

If you truly want your company to be competitive in today's fast-moving global marketplace, you need to obtain extraordinary results from ordinary people. You can get such results from your employees by focusing on how you treat them. For the best results, pay employees fairly, but treat them superbly.

THE SEVEN ASPECTS OF EFFECTIVE RECOGNITION

The act of recognizing an employee has to take into account seven different considerations in order to be effective, genuine, and fully appreciated:

1. Contingency. The best forms of recognition are contingent. Contingency relates to how closely recognition is tied to desired behavior or performance. Contingent recognition is given only when an employee exhibits some sort of desired behavior or performance—for example, when an employee handles a difficult customer request or completes a project on time. Noncontingent

---

NO-COST IDEA 7

Reach Out

Store managers at the St. Ann branch of Famous-Barr department stores, based in St. Louis, Missouri, go to each employee at the end of the day to see what went well for them that day, rather than wait for a weekly or monthly report. Those positive items are worked into the next morning's store rally. "It's been a very effective way to reinforce good news on a timely basis and charge employees up to do their best every single day," says Dan Eppler, merchandise sales manager for the company.

"Treat others the way you'd like to be treated."
—**The Golden Rule**

"Treat others the way they'd like to be treated."
—**The Platinum Rule**

NO-COST IDEA

John's Day

When John Gur-den made his monthly sales target of $125,000 in automated voice processing system sales, David Woo, CEO of Automatic Answer in San Juan Capistrano, California, asked him what he would like as a reward. His response: Designate a John Day.

Soon, John Day banners were plastered throughout the offices, and receptionists answered the phone, "It is a good morning at Automatic Answer, where we are celebrating John Day." Woo also let Gruden use his office for the entire day. Finally, at a lunch in his honor, Gruden was presented with a special John Day photo album.

recognition is generalized; for example, given when an organization holds a company picnic for all employees, or celebrates an employee's birthday.

2. Timing. Recognition is most meaningful when it is given soon after the desired behavior or performance. Recognition loses meaning (or can even become alienating to the recipient) when it is not timely, which means that saving up individual recognition for an annual performance appraisal or rewards banquet can be counterproductive.

3. Frequency. Positive reinforcement is most effective in shaping desired behavior or performance when it is frequent, at least until the behavior becomes established. Frequency should always be considered when designing rewards and recognition programs. When organizations initially conduct recognition it tends to be on a formal, yet infrequent, basis around specific *events,* such as a celebration of a record sales quarter. When a company expands its recognition efforts, it often establishes more frequently awarded recognition *programs,* such as years of service, employee-of-the-month or safety award programs. If a company goes further in instilling recognition in the organization, it typically becomes a daily part of management *practices,* such as the use of personal one-on-one praising, frequent thank-you notes, and public praise.

4. Formality. The formality of an award affects its impact on an employee. A formal reward is one that stems from a planned and agreed-upon program of incentives. Examples of formal rewards include employee-of-the-month programs, years-of-service awards, and attendance awards. An informal reward is more spontaneous and flexible, often stemming from the relationship between the parties involved. Examples of informal rewards include a personal word of thanks for a job well done, or recognition in a staff meeting for excellent customer service.

5. Recognition setting and context. Recognition can be given to an employee privately, or in front of some or all of the company's personnel. While everyone likes a spontaneous personal word of thanks, formal praise tends to be more highly valued by recipients—although shy individuals (perhaps 20 percent of the population) usually prefer private and less formal displays of gratitude. Make sure you take into account your employee's personal nature. Recognition can be presented impersonally—for instance, by mail—or it can be very personal, even anecdotal and emotional. But most employees prefer recognition that is presented with a personal touch, no matter what size the audience.

6. Significance of the provider. We know that, in general, manager-initiated recognition is highly valued by employees. But who should provide the recognition? The individual with the most status or the one with a special relationship to the recipient? As a rule of thumb, personal recognition is most meaningful from those we know well or work closely with: public recognition tends to mean more when provided by someone of higher status. When a choice of providers is possible, ask the employee who he or she would most prefer to be recognized by.

7. Value to the recipient. Recognition is more meaningful when the form it takes is valued highly by the recipient. One individual may value rewards that relate to his or her job, such as a specialized work tool, a software upgrade, or an educational opportunity, while another individual may value rewards that relate to his or her personal and family life and can be shared with others. Such rewards might include dinner out with a significant other, a weekend getaway, a barbecue set, or tickets to a sporting event. Customize rewards and recognition for the recipient. Consider whether the recipient would most value tangible recognition, intangible recognition, or both. Tangible recognition might be a trophy or plaque, while intangible or symbolic recognition includes ceremonies, public announcements, time off, or the gift of more responsibility or more space in which to work. Research suggests that managers today need to consider a range of options for getting results from their employees that only a few years ago might have been considered too fuzzy, abstract, and ill defined to be taken seriously.

"You never know when a moment and a few sincere words can have an impact on a life."

—**Zig Ziglar,**
speaker and author

LUV IS IN THE AIR
AT SOUTHWEST AIRLINES

The employees are dressed in shorts, polo shirts, and athletic shoes. They are telling jokes and generally having a great time on the job. Sound like a group of camp counselors? Try again. These are the employees of Southwest Airlines. At Southwest Airlines, where the corporate culture emphasizes fun and playfulness, the strong sense of camaraderie and high spirits is evident as soon as you arrive at the ticket counter. These ticket agents and flight attendants are enjoying themselves, and their enthusiasm rubs off on the customers.

While many aspects of the airline's business cannot be taken lightly, what the employees of Southwest don't do is take themselves too seriously. For this, Southwest employees and customers can thank Herb Kelleher, the longtime CEO, and now chairman of Southwest Airlines. Kelleher has always believed that "a company is stronger if it is bound by love, rather than by fear." While many businesses have sterilized their workplace environments with restrictions and uniformity, Southwest has based its culture around a deep respect and accountability that comes from freedom, and, because of this, the company has become one of the most successful and admired in the world.

The mission at Southwest Airlines is simple: "At Southwest Airlines, employees are our first customer." Think about it: If your employees aren't happy, how can they put on a happy face and deliver good customer service? If you treat your employees right, they'll treat your customers right. And if your customers are treated right, they'll keep coming back, which makes shareholders very happy.

PARTICIPATION, NOT CONTROL

When employees know they are appreciated, and are given the opportunity to be themselves, enhanced employee loyalty, commitment, and initiative naturally follow. "I've never had control and I never wanted it," says Kelleher. "If you create an environment where people truly participate, you don't need control. They know what needs to be done and they do it."

Just how committed are Southwest employees? Immediately following the terrorist attacks of September 11, 2001, employees generated a grassroots response to help their employer. They announced plans to help the airline save money by working some hours without pay. The program was named Pledge to LUV. (LUV is the company's stock symbol—representing its home at Dallas Love Field, and also its emphasis on customer and employee relationships.) During November and December 2001, employees donated a portion of their pay (between one and thirty-two hours) back to the company. "It's completely voluntary, completely generated and inspired by employee suggestions," Ginger Hardage, vice president of communication at Southwest Airlines, told *HR News*.

Here are some unique ways Southwest cultivates this level of employee loyalty:

When employee Ed Stewart turned down a better-paying offer to stay with Southwest, Kelleher walked into his office and kissed him.

■ In 1996—when for the fifth year in a row Southwest had the best record among major airlines for on-time performance, baggage handling, and the fewest per-customer complaints—Southwest dedicated an airplane to all of its twenty-five thousand employees and put the names of all the employees on the outside of the overhead bins.

■ Southwest sends cards to all of its current 34,000 employees on their birthdays, on the anniversaries of their employment with the company, and on major holidays.

■ The company runs contests for the fun of it, such as a Halloween costume contest, a Thanksgiving poem contest, and an annual chili cook-off.

LUV STORY

One story sums up perhaps better than any other the employee-focused attitude at Southwest Airlines. When employee Ed Stewart turned down a better-paying offer to stay with Southwest, Kelleher walked into his office and kissed him.

At Southwest, you know that LUV's got something to do with it.

What impact does all this have on company performance? Southwest is profitable and expanding—in fact, it was one of the only airlines to add flights after September 11, 2001. Because so many people want to work for the airline, only 3 percent of applicants are hired, but because of its financial success the company is able to pay employees better and offer better benefits than the competition.

And all this has happened as the company has consistently grown in size, with more than 30,000 employees at present. Southwest stuck with the principles that made it successful and fought the tendency to become overly bureaucratic, relying more on its people than on policies and procedures that could easily have killed the company's spirit and competitive advantage.

THE TAKE-AWAY

- Studies show that what managers believe their employees most desire from their jobs often differs considerably from what employees actually want.

- Nonmonetary forms of recognition are generally more effective than monetary ones—including cash.

- Although simple forms of recognition such as verbal praise and written thank-you notes are proven to work, many employees report that they seldom receive them—an enormous opportunity lost for countless organizations.

- For employees, the most motivating incentives are manager-initiated rather than organization-initiated, and are contingent on performance, not just on showing up.

- Recognition is most meaningful when it is given soon after the desired behavior or performance occurs.

CHAPTER 3

Why Managers Use and Don't Use Recognition

"If success were determined by good intentions alone, everyone would be successful."

—Dean Spitzer

Employees expect to be recognized when they do good work. This is a truism supported by dozens of studies and surveys, and easily confirmed by asking almost any employee. Thanking employees for doing good work increases the likelihood that they will want to continue to work for your organization, and it serves as a catalyst for attracting talented new recruits.

For these reasons alone, you would think that the use of recognition would be standard operating procedure in today's organizations. It's not. In fact, the opposite is most often the case.

Bob Nelson recently conducted a three-year study as part of his doctoral work in conjunction with the Peter F. Drucker Graduate School of Management at Claremont Graduate University in Los Angeles, California.

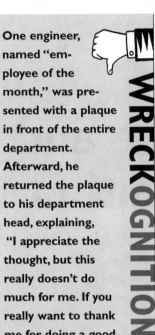

One engineer, named "employee of the month," was presented with a plaque in front of the entire department. Afterward, he returned the plaque to his department head, explaining, "I appreciate the thought, but this really doesn't do much for me. If you really want to thank me for doing a good job, give me some time off." In a similar example, one executive proudly arranged a golf outing as a team-building experience, oblivious to the fact that most employees did not golf, nor did they want to.

He sought to answer a simple question: Why is it that so few managers recognize employees when they do good work? One hundred and forty different variables were considered in the study, ranging from individual (such as awareness, skills, and demographics) to organizational (such as age, size, and culture). The results were illuminating, and often surprising.

A group of managers were drawn from thirty-four organizations, representing seven industries: health care, financial services, insurance, hospitality/restaurant/retail, information technology, manufacturing, and government. Within each organization, managers identified as frequent users of recognition were matched against infrequent users. A broad-based survey of all managers was then conducted, exploring their motivations for using recognition, which ranged from past experience with it to present reinforcement of recognition to future expectations from it. Open-ended questions were also used to collect each manager's perceptions of the primary factors that help or hinder use of recognition. The validity of the study was enhanced by an exceptional response rate of 69 percent.

WHY MANAGERS RECOGNIZE

Why do some managers embrace recognition while others shy away from using it?

Here were the top reasons reported in Bob's study:

1. Personal responsibility. Managers who frequently used recognition ("high-use managers") had internalized the importance of the behavior and made intentional plans to practice it on a daily basis. This variable was the most important in distinguishing high-use managers from low-use managers.

2. Skills and confidence. High-use managers had the interpersonal skills and confidence to use recognition, got better at using it, and continued to use it over time. Low-use managers lacked the skills and confidence to recognize employees.

3. Reinforcement for recognition use. High-use managers were reinforced for using recognition—first and foremost by employees who received the recognition, then by others as well.

4. Manager's age. Older managers (over fifty) were more likely to feel that it was not important to practice recognition. This was also true of managers who had worked many years in the same job or for the same organization. In fact, age was the only highly significant demographic factor that distinguished the group of high-use managers from the group of low-use managers; there were no significant differences in other demographic factors such as gender, ethnicity, nationality, and educational level between frequent users and infrequent users of recognition.

5. Role models. High-use managers were significantly more likely to have had parents who used recognition, although neither high-use nor low-use managers reported that their current managers recognized them very often. There's little that we can do about the upbringing of those with whom we work, but it is encouraging to know that high-use managers recognize their employees despite not receiving similar recognition from their own managers. This suggests that a culture of recognition can be built from the bottom up, and not just from the top down.

UNEXPECTED FINDINGS

What makes any research especially rewarding is obtaining results that differ from what the researcher expected—or was even looking for. Following are some of the unexpected findings identified in this study.

Limited time. High-use managers did not see time as a major constraint, but rather ranked it as a *positive* factor, in that recognizing an employee for doing good work takes so little time. Low-use managers, on the other hand, cited limited time as one of the main reasons why they didn't use recognition. It seems that a lack of time is not a true obstacle to giving recognition; it's merely an excuse for those managers who don't want to give it.

Recognition inequities. Most managers are concerned about the possibility of overlooking deserving employees when people are singled out for recognition. Evidence from this study indicates,

"Common sense is not always common practice."

—Stephen Covey,
management author

however, that concern over leaving someone out when using recognition is more an *excuse* for low-use managers and more a *consideration* for high-use managers. Low-use managers use it as an excuse not to recognize employees, whereas high-use managers take it into account as a consideration and are careful not to exclude anybody who deserves recognition.

Programs and tools. The practice of recognition was more greatly influenced by a manager's beliefs, experience, and training with the technique than by the quantity or quality of existing recognition programs and tools. Having organizational programs and tools in place can help facilitate recognition, but it is not a prerequisite for recognition. A manager who believes in recognition will make it happen regardless of the programs or tools available.

Budget and resources. Available budget and resources were also not prerequisites for the effective use of recognition. Although financial resources can greatly facilitate the practice of recognition in almost any organization, high-use managers find ways to recognize employees whether or not they have a budget or resources set aside for that purpose.

PATTERNS OF RECOGNITION USE

It's easy to see that there are positive and negative cycles that perpetuate high and low use of recognition behaviors among managers.

High-use managers tended to have a positive experience with the behavior, which made them more likely to use recognition. Their use of recognition was reinforced by the following (in order of most to least important): their employees, themselves, other colleagues, suppliers, and their own managers. Using recognition also helped them obtain the results they desired, which included increased performance and morale on the part of their employees. Based on this success, they were more likely to use the behavior again and again to the point that it became a daily part of their behavioral repertoire.

The Experience of High-Use Managers

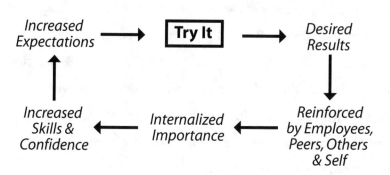

Increased Expectations → **Try It** → Desired Results

Reinforced by Employees, Peers, Others & Self

Internalized Importance

Increased Skills & Confidence

Low-use managers, on the other hand, did not have a positive experience with the use of recognition and thus had little or no chance of being reinforced for the behavior. No benefits were derived from the use of recognition, and any concerns or fears about the behavior became excuses for not doing it. The result: neither skills nor confidence were enhanced, and the behavior was avoided.

The Experience of Low-Use Managers

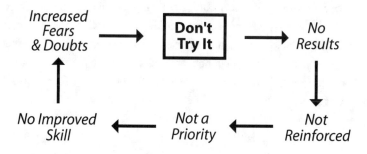

Increased Fears & Doubts → **Don't Try It** → No Results

Not Reinforced

Not a Priority

No Improved Skill

NO-COST IDEA 9

Dump a Dog

Susan Frankel tells of a fun program instituted by the company she worked for, a major insurance provider: employees could pass on to their manager the assignment they least wanted to handle. The program stemmed from a holiday contest, but its potential as a widespread reward for completion of a successful case or for overall outstanding work was quickly realized. Employees liked being able to pass on an undesirable assignment. It was both a motivator for higher performance and a fun way for management to show they really were there to help.

RECOGNIZING RECRUITING EFFORTS AT LANDS' END

Through its mainline Lands' End catalog, as well as other specialty catalogs, such as Lands' End Kids, Coming Home, Beyond Buttondowns, and First Person Singular, as well as its Web site and factory outlet stores, in 1998 the company had revenues of more than $1.2 billion, 13 percent more than the previous year. This ranks Lands' End as the country's largest direct-retail apparel merchant. It's also one of the best. According to a survey by the Great Place to Work Institute, Lands' End is among the top one hundred places to work in the United States.

24 HOURS A DAY, 7 DAYS A WEEK, 364 DAYS A YEAR

The company is closed one day a year—Christmas. However, while employees are never at a loss for something to do—on average, the company sells a men's dress shirt every ten seconds—things get particularly hectic during the holiday season, a three-month period during which the company does 40 percent of its business for the entire year. On its busiest days during the holiday season, more than 150,000 orders will go out the door.

All of this activity makes for employees who need a little extra. Management at Lands' End is very well aware of the need for an extensive system of rewards and recognition to keep employees happy and productive, for several reasons. For one, cows outnumber people in Iowa County, Wisconsin—where Lands' End's Dodgeville headquarters is located—with just under 23,000 people, and the unemployment rate is only 2 percent. For a company of 9,000 workers, processing more than 13 million orders a year, this makes for an extremely tight job market, and it's essential for the company to be able to hire and retain the best workers, especially during the holiday crunch.

Another reason is that the company's management team believes it's the right thing to do. Says former CEO Richard Anderson, "I think the first principle of the company, the foundation, is to treat all our people as we would like to be treated. This is not a company where people stand on titles or things like that. People talk to each other. People call me by my first name. The better they feel, the better their benefits, the better they're taken care of, the more we prosper. And we believe if our people feel good, their positive attitude comes out over the phone. It's kind of simple, but that's about the truth of it."

Here are some of the things that Lands' End does to reward and recognize its employees:

- Jackie Johnson-Caygill, the Dodgeville phone center manager, keeps employee morale high by conducting drawings for massages in the department's "cruise room," a closet plastered with posters of cruise ships in exotic locations, complete with the scent of coconut suntan lotion.

- Seasonal sales reps get to park in the parking lot closest to the office building during the holiday season, the lot normally used by permanent employees. Permanent employees are asked to park in a lot farther away from the building.

- To encourage temporary holiday season employees to commit to coming back to work the following year, Lands' End gives a variety of incentives, including a 40 percent discount on merchandise, a $500 tuition reimbursement, health insurance, and year-round access to the company's activity center. Regular employees receive a $35 bonus for every seasonal applicant they refer who is hired by the company.

- Regular employees receive a $500 bonus for referring new professional or hourly workers who are eventually hired into permanent positions. Says Pam Peterson, senior recruitment and development specialist, "The best candidates we have on board were recommended by our own employees."

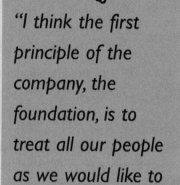

"I think the first principle of the company, the foundation, is to treat all our people as we would like to be treated."

- The company recently offered its employees $1,000 for every employee they helped recruit into the company's newly formed computer department.

- The company held a drawing for tickets to a Green Bay Packers football game, open to all employees who made successful referrals that season. Winners of this drawing were transported to the game by a bus hired especially by Lands' End for the event.

- The company is experimenting with allowing employees to work at home, taking orders from customers. Under this popular program, initially open only to the company's top-performing order takers, the company provides each employee with a computer, a modem, and dedicated phone lines.

- Chairman Gary Comer, founder of Lands' End, built an 80,000-square-foot activity center as a $9 million gift to his employees. During the design process, Comer asked his employees to submit their ideas about what facilities the center should include. The completed center includes a 25-meter swimming pool (high on employee wish lists), a glass-walled indoor track, an exercise equipment room, a whirlpool, a gymnasium, a photographic darkroom, outdoor tennis courts, and picnic areas.

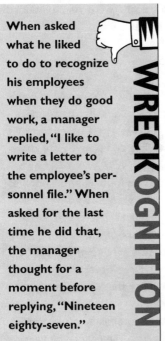

See page 347
for article,
"You Want ToMAYtoes,
I Want ToMAHtoes."

When asked what he liked to do to recognize his employees when they do good work, a manager replied, "I like to write a letter to the employee's personnel file." When asked for the last time he did that, the manager thought for a moment before replying, "Nineteen eighty-seven."

WRECKOGNITION

CONVERTING LOW-USE MANAGERS INTO HIGH-USE MANAGERS

Can a low-recognition-use manager ever become a high-recognition-use manager? And, if the answer to this question is yes, will the change last? How can you:

❶ Raise managers' awareness of recognition and its benefits?

❷ Help managers learn and use the relevant skills to recognize employees?

❸ Encourage managers to take the first step in recognizing others?

Managers need to personally experience the behavior and its potential and then systematically build upon its use and subsequent successes. The trick lies in finding a catalyst—an event or trigger mechanism that will help low-use managers personally experience recognition in a positive, meaningful way. For some managers, this happens when they are personally recognized by others for an accomplishment, skill, or achievement on the job. Other stimuli can include evidence of and research about the importance of recognition, watching an admired mentor or role model recognize someone, attending a presentation or training on the topic of recognition, or even reading an article that persuades the individual to act differently. Any of these practices can lend credibility to the behavior and start the person on a journey toward increased recognition usage. A seemingly small step can make a profound difference.

Likewise, simple techniques may also be effective—having the manager place a stack of thank-you cards his desk and getting his commitment to write a few notes to deserving employees at the end of each day, or encouraging the manager to leave positive voice-mail messages during the commute home, thanking employees for work they had done. Techniques such as these can go a long way toward making recognition simple and doable. Once someone is convinced of the value of recognition, further training, tools, resources, and encouragement help to make the identification of recognition opportunities and the practice of recognition routine.

By creating a cycle of behavior and response that leads to escalating use of recognition on the part of managers, it may be possible

RECOGNITION BEHAVIOR CYCLE

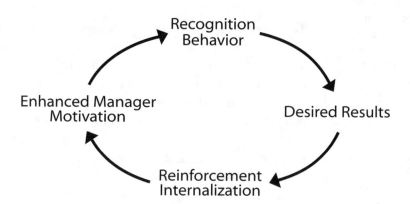

Recognition Behavior: By getting one low-use executive to list all direct reports on his "to do" list and acknowledge each employee weekly for some aspect of his or her work, that executive was able to see firsthand the benefits of the behavior.

Desired Results: By sharing the results of best practices from other organizations within the same industry, a human resources manager was able to convince her low-use management team to test a recognition program for a trial period.

Reinforcement/Internalization: By thanking a low-use department manager for introducing her to a key client when he visited the office, one employee made introductions a routine part of every client visit to the office.

Enhanced Manager Motivation: By bringing in an outside expert to address all managers at a quarterly meeting, one company was able to simultaneously raise awareness of the importance of recognition, and the expectation that it would be practiced by all managers.

to initiate a low-use manager at any point of the cycle and convert him or her to a high-use manager.

THE SIX EXCUSES

Organizations must confront the beliefs of low-use managers if they are going to make recognition a personal, practical, and positive experience. Misperceptions and constraints must be overcome, objections and obstacles removed, excuses con-

MASSAGING MANAGERS

Q I'm in the salon and spa business, and employee turnover is very high. Money has not been a major motivator for me, as I like to service customers and help them feel beautiful inside, and I've found that's how most of my employees feel. Could you help me find ways to coach owners and managers in how to do positive reinforcement? I know that employee retention would surely increase with bosses who knew how to give daily (even hourly) pats on the back and appreciation.

—**Alayne White,**
Alayne White Success Group,
Bristol, RI

A **First, lead by example by providing recognition and thanks to your owners and managers. Managers who receive recognition have an easier time passing it on to others. Second, get everyone involved in discussing and coming up with ideas of what types of recognition they'd most appreciate. Third, put tools in place that can facilitate recognition on a daily basis: praising cards or notes, pass-around trophies, gift certificates, bulletin boards, time in staff meetings, and so forth.**

fronted. Here are the six leading "excuses" for not using recognition, as reported by low-use managers themselves, and examples of how to deal with each excuse:

1. "I don't know how best to recognize my employees." Most low-use managers consider giving recognition a difficult task. They need to become aware of the importance of recognition, be trained in the skills of recognition, be provided with individual feedback, and be shown positive examples and techniques that they can actually *do,* no matter their time and resource constraints. To get buy-in, managers should discuss potential recognition strategies with their staff and seek feedback on their own recognition behaviors.

At BankBoston (now a part of Fleet Bank), managers give employees a blank index card on their first day of work and ask them to make a list of those things that motivate them. The manager ends up with an individualized motivation checklist for every employee.

2. "I don't feel that providing recognition is an important part of my job." Organizations need to set up the expectation that providing recognition is not an optional activity, but rather an integral part of the organization's strategy, specifically linked to achieving the company's goals. Furthermore, managers should be evaluated on their efforts at providing recognition in a frequent and meaningful way. Recognition should be made an important part of the planning of organizational, team, and individual goal setting, and not "management by announcement," where an initiative is announced once and then never again heard of again.

A vice president at AAA of southern California personally writes notes of thanks to individuals in field offices, demonstrating to all managers under him that if he can find time to acknowledge employees, they need to do so as well.

3. "I don't have the time to recognize my employees." As we've said, high-use managers actually rate time as a facilitator for conducting recognition because they've found that some of the best forms of recognition (personal or written praise, positive voice-mail or e-mail messages, public recognition, and so on) require

very little time to initiate and complete. Thus, the claim of low-use managers that they don't have enough time for recognition is often no more than an excuse for not doing it.

All managers and supervisors at Busch Gardens in Tampa, Florida, are provided with tokens inscribed "Thank you" to use as on-the-spot recognition for any employee caught demonstrating one of the organization's core values.

4. "I'm afraid I might leave somebody out." Another common concern of managers is the possibility that they will leave out someone who deserves recognition. Whereas low-use managers interpret this concern as an excuse for not recognizing employees at all, high-use managers convert it into a greater commitment to recognize *everyone* who deserves it. This might, for example, mean checking with a team leader to see if you have all the names of people who assisted with a successful project before commending the team in public. If at any time someone deserving is left out, simply apologize.

One of the authors recently attended an awards presentation at which the presenter personally checked to see that every recipient who was present was on the list and that no one who was absent would be called (those individuals were acknowledged later, in person).

5. "Employees don't value the recognition I have given in the past." Instead of being put off by what might not have worked in the past, low-use managers should make a fresh start and seek to find out what forms of recognition their employees would most value. Managers can talk with employees one-on-one or have a group discussion about potential rewards and incentives, or ask each person to bring two suggested motivators to the next staff meeting to share with the group. By involving employees in decisions that affect their own motivation, managers increase the employees' commitment and buy-in as well as the likelihood that what is done will be successful.

A manager at the Hyatt Corporation asked her employees at a staff meeting what ideas they had for increasing recognition. One of the employees suggested that the department rotate the responsibility for recognition throughout the group so that each week one

WRECKOGNITION

One corporation specifically invited top-performing employees to a headquarters meeting, telling them they would be publicly recognized at the meeting, only to run out of time at the end of the meeting so that numerous honorees were not mentioned at all.

REMEMBER: *If it's important, make sure recognition happens as planned, or start the meeting with recognition.*

NO-COST IDEA 10

Grab Someone's Potential

Shaheen Mufti, women's manager at Emporio Armani in Costa Mesa, California, shares the following "breakthrough" she had with an employee: "When faced with again disciplining an employee whose productivity, attendance, adherence to the dress code, and attitude were all out of line, I was so frustrated I blurted, 'I'm really disappointed in you! I *know* you can do this job, but you're just throwing all your potential away.' To my amazement, he decided to live up to my positive opinion of him; he became the top salesperson in the next accounting period."

person would be responsible for finding an individual or group achievement and then recognizing it in their own way. Creativity flourished, and recognition skyrocketed.

6. "My organization does not facilitate or support recognition efforts." Although recognition efforts can flourish even in the absence of formal organizational support, such support, if made available, can help managers maintain their commitment. Information, training, tools, funds, and programs that reinforce recognition activities should be made available on an ongoing basis—even if not all managers use these resources—to support recognition efforts and the organization's expectation that every manager take the responsibility for providing recognition seriously.

HOW TO APPLY THESE FINDINGS

The insights and lessons of this study can be applied to your workplace in many ways. Let's look at some that might affect you.

If you are a manager, you need to realize that giving recognition is well within your abilities. It depends far more on your internal sense of competence and your simple commitment to try it than on formal organizational efforts, programs, tools, and resources. Opportunities to recognize your employees and make recognition part of your behavioral repertoire are all around you on a daily basis, extending even to how you delegate assignments.

At American Express, all managers are taught a concept they call "link and label," in which every manager who provides a development opportunity to an employee is asked to explain why he thought of the employee for the recognition, what the employee can expect to learn from it, and how it will lead to other opportunities and responsibilities the employee values.

If you are a human resources professional, you can be a leading advocate of the importance and ongoing use of recognition in your organization. Consider asking managers to use and discuss recognition behaviors, activities, tools, and programs with those who report to them, and you establish a cross-functional recognition task force to deal with recognition recommendations and concerns of the organization. You might also want to consider ways to target low-recognition managers (many of whom are likely to be older, upper managers) for individualized attention.

At BankBoston (now Fleet Bank), a member of the recognition committee was given the task of calling on managers who did not use the organization's programs and explaining and updating those executives on the use and impact of the programs, often inviting them to discuss these issues with other managers who were more active users.

If you are an executive, realize that you set the tone for what everyone else in your organization feels is important. What you notice, they notice; what you model, they model. Look at what employees in your organization value and then support doing more of those things, leading the charge with your own actions.

A general manager at Xerox Corporation saves time at the end of each of his management team meetings for going around the room and having everyone share one thing they have done to recognize someone on their staff since the group was last together. Not only does this make the energy level of the group rise, but managers will take notes on one another's ideas—and plan to use those ideas themselves.

If you are a consultant who works with employee motivation, you should be able to assess and articulate remedies for improved employee recognition efforts. You should also be able to explain and defend such recommendations to both upper and middle management. And you should help managers and executives tie recognition to desired performance and to the strategic objectives of the organization.

Based on quantitative improvements in the employee recognition scores that were obtained from pre- and postassessments, one consultant was able to show significant progress toward the organization's goals of increasing recognition, decreasing turnover, and moving the organization closer to becoming an "employer of choice" in its industry.

"Ninety-five percent of American managers today say the right thing. Five percent actually do it."

—**James O'Toole,**
management professor

THE TAKE-AWAY

- Employees expect to be recognized when they do good work.

- The top reason given by high-use managers for why they frequently recognize employees is that they feel that it's their responsibility as managers to make recognition happen. They also have—and continue to develop—their skills and confidence in recognizing employees.

- The top reason given by low-use managers for why they seldom recognize employees is that they don't know how best to recognize their employees.

- Older managers (over fifty) are more likely than younger managers to feel that recognition is not an important behavior to practice.

- The excuses for not using recognition need to be addressed head-on.

PART II
GETTING STARTED WITH RECOGNITION

CHAPTER 4

The Context for Recognition

"The way positive reinforcement is carried out is more important than the amount."

—**B. F. Skinner,** behavioral psychologist

U nderstanding the organizational context—the environment in which you and your colleagues work—is crucial for the success of your recognition efforts. Contextual understanding is important for all types and levels of recognition, but, as recognition efforts become more sophisticated and ambitious, this understanding becomes even more essential for the ultimate success of your recognition efforts. In this chapter, we will show you how you can make the context of recognition work *for* you—not *against* you.

ACTIVITIES AND THEIR CONTEXT

E verything exists in a context. Context can greatly affect—sometimes totally shape—the way we experience an activity or event. To take an obvious example,

"The only way to motivate an employee is to give him challenging work for which he can assume responsibility."

—Frederick Herzberg,
management theorist

a graphic joke will elicit more laughs among close friends in a restaurant than the same joke told at a funeral. As quality expert Peter Scholtes says, "Everything is part of a larger system. For leaders to understand what is going on, they must understand the larger system of which any effort is part and with which it interacts."[1]

In the workplace context, judgments about competence and performance are usually seen as more threatening than they would be, say, on the tennis court or golf course. Measurement in sports is accepted as scorekeeping, but measurement at work is more heavily loaded with issues of fundamental self-worth and self-esteem.

THE CONTEXT OF GOLF AND THE CONTEXT OF WORK

Our favorite example of how context affects perception of an activity is from the game of golf. When you play golf, you spend half a day of your leisure time walking long distances just to hit a tiny ball into—or, more likely, in the general vicinity of—a little hole.

To those who haven't tried it, it doesn't sound very exciting. But it's the context surrounding the basic activity of hitting a little white ball with a long metal stick that makes the game so addictive. Contextual factors such as variety (different clubs, strokes, and terrain), competition, scorekeeping, challenge, social interaction, exercise, and so on make the game of golf anything but boring to those who are playing it.

Just as there is far more to the game of golf than simply hitting a ball, there is far more to a job than just the work activities performed. Every employee is immersed in a sea of contextual factors. These factors, more than the work itself, determine how motivating or demotivating the environment is—and they have a measurable impact on employee performance.

Imagine for a moment that the experience of golf was designed as many work situations are. Your job is to drive the ball off the twelfth tee, all day long, over and over again. Your boss tells you exactly how, when, and where you are supposed to hit the ball, every single shot, all day long, every week, year in and year out, and then rates your performance. How enjoyable would golf be under these circumstances?

As Ralph Stayer, CEO of Johnsonville Foods, says, "I had come to realize that I didn't directly control the performance of the people at Johnsonville, and, as a manager, I didn't really manage people. . . . *But I did manage the context.*"[2] As we'll soon see, managing the context of recognition is *everything*.

THE CONTEXT OF RECOGNITION

Organizations include a large number of factors that we might collectively define as the *culture* of the organization. Peter Scholtes has defined this culture as "what makes the experience of working at one company different from doing the same work at another company offering similar products and services."[3] When most employees talk about their company, chances are they are really talking about their company's *culture*. Their feelings about the culture can have a major impact on how they experience recognition—and how they respond to it.

What exactly is an organization's culture? It includes things such as these:

- Common behaviors
- Visible symbols
- Core values
- Ethical standards
- Shared assumptions
- Patterns of interaction with coworkers and supervisors

- The physical workplace
- Policies
- Rules
- Training
- Rewards
- Operating standards

Energy giant Southern Company of Atlanta, Georgia, describes its culture in the following way:

Southern Style is our definition of an attitude and culture that defines who we are and where we are going. Our values showcase teamwork and emphasize mutual respect and shared learning. We are committed to a work environment where we put the customer first *and demonstrate* ethical behavior *in all we do.* Teamwork *attracts and develops talent; Southern Company fosters open communication and we listen!* Superior performance expectations allow you to take responsibility for your success.

> "What makes employees come to work is a sense of pride, recognition, and achievement. Workers committed to their jobs and recognized for their work will work whatever hours it takes to get the job done."
>
> —**Thomas Kelley,**
> chairman of the board,
> Society for Human Resource
> Development

NO-COST IDEA

11

Wash & Watch

Managers sponsored a car wash for employees at Parrott Creek Child and Family Services in Marylhurst, Oregon. Says Kelley Gutman, who originated the idea, "Employees sat in the shade and drank iced tea while the managers washed their cars. It's a small thing, but employees seemed to feel appreciated and everyone had a great time!"

We encourage champions of change and always try to act with speed and decisiveness.[4]

Susquehanna International Group, a global trading and technology company headquartered in Philadelphia, Pennsylvania, has boiled its unique culture down into several paragraphs, which read in part:

Susquehanna maintains a highly distinctive small firm culture despite our tremendous growth. The dress is casual and the work environment is friendly and familial. At Susquehanna, it is clear that all employees share the common goal of achieving the organization's objectives. At Susquehanna, advancement is based on how well people contribute to the overall organization—employees are limited only by their own drive, creativity, and skill. Furthermore, we have a flat corporate structure, absent of hierarchies. Our unique environment allows employees to excel without being bogged down by red tape, job descriptions, or other "corporate" constraints. This unrestrained atmosphere has attracted some of the smartest, most competitive, and most creative people to our doors.[5]

But an organization's culture is largely invisible. The practices and behaviors in a company reflect the culture, which in turn reflects its core values. This is depicted in the figure below.

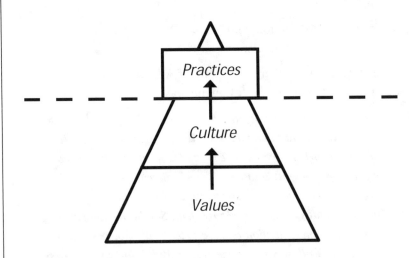

An organization's practices include those in areas such as:

- The management style of its leaders
- Patterns of interpersonal interaction
- Hiring preferences
- Orientation and training methods
- Rewards and punishments

Probably more than any other practice, recognition reflects the underlying culture of an organization. One can get a fairly good sense of an organization's values by observing what is recognized, how frequently, and in what ways. For example, organizations that are more performance-oriented tend to recognize achievements. Weyerhaeuser Company recognizes twenty-five or so high-achieving employees every year with its President's Award; winners are recognized at a company-wide event hosted by top management, where they receive a cash bonus and a personalized award to remember the occasion.[6] On the other hand, organizations that are more tradition-focused tend to recognize things that have little or nothing to do with performance, such as years of service. At rental car company Budget Group of Daytona Beach, Florida, president Mark Sortir hosts a monthly celebration, featuring a big cake, to recognize headquarters employees who are having an anniversary with the company.[7]

Needless to say, organizations that are energetic and creative tend to have more celebrations than companies that are staid and traditional. At Priceline.com, headquartered in Norwalk, Connecticut, anonymous employee volunteers improve morale with offbeat events and activities, such as a carnival, complete with dunking tank for company executives and a Velcro wall, a remote-control car derby, and a golf tournament with putting greens and water hazards—all built on the company grounds.[8]

The culture and underlying values of an organization also can have quite a profound effect on its receptivity to recognition activities. Organizations that are more creative, collaborative, communicative, people-oriented, flexible, and learning-oriented are likely to be more fertile grounds for trying out new approaches to individual, team, and organizational recognition. In contrast, organizations that are more individualistic, task-oriented, traditional,

"When someone does something well, applaud! You will make two people happy."

—**Samuel Goldwyn,**
movie producer

PARTY!

Q Do you have any fun ideas for activities or prizes for a holiday party?

—**Amy Peacock,**
Nextel, Norcross, GA

A **Get people involved! Each department can present a skit or give an award to another person or department that has been helpful to them in the past year. A Hallmark store manager made up certificates of achievement, such as Most Willing to Help a Team Member, Most Positive Attitude, then read each award aloud and let his group guess who the designated recipient was. This is a fun way to thank employees for important attributes they've displayed throughout the year.**

"A well-timed memento, presented in the right context with sincere words of thanks, becomes a reward that keeps giving recognition each and every time the employee sees or uses the gift."

—**Bob Nelson**

autocratic, and unionized present a real challenge to practicing widespread and innovative recognition.

To find out where your company stands in terms of its organizational cultural environment, there is a host of recognition assessments in the "Recognition Tools" section of this book. These assessment instruments will help you measure how conducive your organization is to recognition. Later in this chapter, we will discuss the implications of this kind of assessment.

FIGURE AND GROUND

The context of recognition can be understood by considering two powerful scientific concepts: *figure and ground* and *signal/noise ratio*.

The phrase *figure and ground* refers to the way humans perceive things; specifically, the contrast between a figure (an object in the foreground) and the ground (the background). The nature of the background affects how we see the figure.

Examples abound in ordinary life. While driving 70 miles per hour on an expressway, you are usually unaware of the speed, especially if the other cars are driving at similar speeds. Against a "ground" of speeding cars, the velocity of the "figure"—the car you occupy—is disguised. You may even be shocked when you glance at the speedometer. To take another common instance, whatever your height you probably have a different feeling about yourself depending on whether you're talking to someone taller or shorter than yourself. In business, this phenomenon operates constantly. Consider the situation of an employee who is delighted with his $1,000 bonus—until, that is, he finds out that his colleague received a $2,500 bonus. An employee's delight can turn to resentment with quite amazing speed.

How can we use what we know about context, and about figure and ground, to improve recognition in our organizations? In *SuperMotivation*, Dean discusses the power of *motivators* and the negative impact of demotivators (see lists on pages 51 and 52).

On the next page is a list of motivators that will enhance and facilitate any recognition efforts. These often hidden conditions in the *background* of the work environment have enormous potential for transforming (positively) the way employees feel about their jobs. The more of these motivators are present in the context, or "ground," of work, the more likely that the "figures," the employees, will be motivated to perform well and to get and give recognition.

PRIME MOTIVATORS

Action:
Being actively engaged in productive work

Fun:
A work environment that includes enjoyable activities—not just drudgery

Variety:
Opportunities to perform new and different tasks

Input:
Feeling that one's opinions matter

Stake-sharing:
Feeling ownership in the organization—financially or psychologically, or both

Choice:
Being empowered to make discretionary decisions

Responsibility:
A role in decision making, such as being responsible for a whole task, rather than just doing piecework

Leadership opportunities:
A chance to manage a team, meeting, or event

Social interaction:
The freedom to communicate with other employees at work without being reprimanded for loitering

Teamwork:
Being a member of a productive team

Using strengths:
Being encouraged to do the things that one does well

Learning:
Enhancing one's capabilities

Error tolerance:
Being allowed to fail, without punishment, and being helped to learn from the experience

Measurement:
Being encouraged to keep one's own score, rather than being micromanaged by a supervisor

Goals:
Being encouraged to set one's own goals, rather than having them imposed by others

Improvement:
Being in an environment that enables people to become a little better every day

Challenge:
Being given appropriately difficult tasks that cause one to stretch, without feeling anxious

Encouragement:
Being in an environment in which others believe in people

Appreciation:
Receiving acknowledgment of contributions

Significance:
Feeling part of a "mission that matters"

On the flip side of organizational context are *demotivators,* or negative factors in the work environment. When demotivators outweigh motivators in the "ground" of work, the "figures," the employees, will be too demoralized to strive for recognition.

COMMON DEMOTIVATORS

Organizational politics:
An environment in which the competition for power, influence, resources, and promotions is based on subjective or hidden criteria

Unclear expectations:
Unclear, confusing, and/or contradictory goals, objectives, and standards

Unnecessary rules:
Rules are necessary, but too many of them are demotivating.

Poorly designed work:
Poorly engineered work gets in the way of satisfying internal and external customers and frustrates employees.

Unproductive meetings:
Employees often leave meetings exhausted, battered, and bored.

Lack of follow-up:
Most employees could write a book about the "latest and greatest programs" that died on the vine.

Constant change:
Change is necessary, but is detrimental if it seems arbitrary and capricious.

Internal competition:
The healthiest organizations compete against their competition, not against themselves.

Dishonesty:
Employees hate being lied to.

Hypocrisy:
How can you trust leaders who say one thing and do another?

Withholding information:
Lying by omission

Unfairness:
When organizations are full of policies and practices perceived as inequitable

Discouraging responses:
Negative and instantaneous responses to employees' ideas and suggestions, such as "It won't work," "You can't do that here," or "That's not feasible"

Criticism:
Work environments that make employees feel that they are "guilty until proven innocent"

Capability underutilization:
When people feel that the skills and capabilities they were hired for aren't being used

Tolerating poor performance:
When one poor performer can cause everyone to look (and feel) bad

Being taken for granted:
When employees quietly do a good job, and are systematically ignored

Management invisibility:
It is amazing how many employees wouldn't even recognize the division vice president, much less the CEO.

Overcontrol:
Most employees are willing to be empowered, but few managers are willing to give them enough authority to be empowered.

Take-aways:
Reversing a benefit or policy so as to create another passing fad—here today and gone tomorrow

Being forced to do poor-quality work:
Work rules that don't allow quality-conscious employees to take pride in the work they do

No motivational program can ever be successfully implemented in the face of the demotivators listed here. No matter how powerful the new motivational initiatives might be, existing demotivators will eventually cancel them out. Remember: The bad taste that demotivators leave with employees remains long after the good taste of rewards and recognition is gone.

SIGNAL/NOISE RATIO

The other powerful scientific concept that has profound implications for the effective use of recognition is borrowed from the field of communication—*signal/noise ratio*. This principle describes the relative strength of a message—the "signal"—versus the noise that gets in the way. The "signal" is the message that you want to convey to a receiver; "noise" is everything extraneous that interferes. For example, when talking on a cellular telephone, static (noise) can detract from your message (the signal). The signal/noise ratio is a measure of how strong the signal is compared to the background noise.

The signal/noise ratio doesn't relate just to communication. It can be used to understand why so much of what we do doesn't have the expected effect. Organizations are full of noise. This doesn't necessarily mean a high decibel level. It means that there are extraneous factors that can (and do) get in the way of the primary message—in this case, recognition. Organizational factors such as business conditions, organizational changes, and a constant bombardment of information can distract from existing recognition efforts the same way that background noise can get in the way of a conversation.

If an organization is being downsized, this is very likely to have a negative impact on the recognition programs. The same is true of an organization in the throes of a major reengineering project, or of a large company whose forced-distribution performance appraisal process is widely viewed as punishing by top performers who miss the cut for the top performance rating.

Situations such as these can make any nonfinancial recognition initiatives suspect, and undermine their effectiveness. The noise of the downsizing program, the reengineering project, or the appraisal system can undermine the signal of the organization's well-intentioned recognition efforts.

WRECKOGNITION

A bookstore employee in Orlando, Florida, left her job in New York after her unappreciative boss of twenty years announced some major changes by saying, "If you don't like it, you can just quit!" She stood up and said, "Okay, I quit!" This same manager, who had never complimented her work in twenty years of employment, called his ex-employee a few weeks later at her new job in Florida to ask her to come back to work for him, with an increased salary and more benefits. She declined.

CYNIC CURE

Q How do you deal with an employee who distrusts management?

—online forum participant

A It's likely that his or her past managers have failed to uphold promises or commitments, perhaps on more than one occasion. First, build a bridge of trust between the employee and yourself. This evolves as a function of your daily interactions with employees. If you keep your promises, and if you are fair in your dealings with your employees, you can establish trust with even the most negative worker. Second, reward the behavior you want to see more of. Focus on your employee's performance and then reinforce any positive individual or team behavior that he or she exhibits. A simple word of thanks or a written note about an employee's accomplishments can be very effective. Be patient. It's probably taken your employee a long time to get to a level of distrust. It will probably take a long time to rebuild a new foundation.

The bottom line is this: A negative context can seriously undermine recognition efforts unless one spots the challenges and adapts very quickly to the conditions. In fact, it is just such sensitivity to the context of recognition that differentiates the novice from the virtuoso recognition provider.

AVOIDING MOTIVATIONAL SABOTAGE

Don't let your recognition efforts be sabotaged by factors that, although beyond your control, can be anticipated and rectified. If your organization scores low in receptivity to recognition efforts, there are things you can do to improve the situation. For example, you can stick with recognition procedures that are already in place within the organization, but do them more frequently. In addition, you can avoid recognition that is too visible across the organization, and therefore has lost meaning, and instead stick to recognizing your own work group or team. In such an environment, it is better to be an *evolutionary* change agent than a *revolutionary* one.

Other considerations include:

Business or operational climate. The business or operational climate of an organization can significantly affect its receptivity to recognition, and the type of recognition that is appropriate. Is the organization going through financial difficulties? Has there been severe cost-cutting? Has there been a merger, acquisition, or downsizing? Is any business-process reengineering occurring? Is there a major structural or technological change in progress? All these factors can hamper the reception of recognition in your organization.

Changes in department or business unit. The same is true, naturally, about changes in a department or business unit. Has there been significant turnover? Has there been a change in management? Have particularly aggressive work standards been imposed? Virtually any major change in the context of work can affect recognition, create a negative context, and increase *noise* in the organization's motivational systems. Understanding the context, however, provides a great opportunity to do something positive about it.

Other motivational efforts. Another important contextual consideration is whether other motivational efforts are going on in the organization at the same time. While other programs can enhance the climate for recognition, too many can cause motivational clutter. Too much of a good thing can cause employees to take your recognition efforts for granted. As a business manager in a large organization once said to one of the authors: "I think I've overdosed on praise!"

Potent monetary or high-value rewards. Remember, potent monetary or high-value rewards can negatively affect the use of smaller rewards and nonmonetary recognition. For example, a high-stakes sales contest with high-cost incentives (vacations, automobiles, and similarly expensive awards) can overshadow informal recognition.

Demographics. Don't forget to consider some of the demographic variables that can affect recognition—such as average age, experience level, ethnicity and education.

Workforce trends. Mobility, reduced loyalty, low unemployment, salary levels, and cost of living in the area can also have a significant impact on your reward and recognition efforts, so be sure to consider them while designing recognition programs in your own organization.

The good news is that none of these contextual factors needs to be a recognition-killer. One of the most valuable tools at your disposal in adapting to the context of recognition is timing. Timing is crucial to the success of any intervention. Sometimes there are just too many changes occurring in an organization to begin any more— even a recognition initiative. A key question to ask is: Is this the right time to do this? Would it make sense to delay it for a while?

Understanding the context of recognition can also help you to become more sensitive to the factors that can make or break your recognition efforts. For example, how should you handle recognition during a downsizing, when employees are feeling threatened and realize that they could be next? What kind of message do you send by recognizing someone who then gets laid off shortly there-

---

NO-COST IDEA 12

Say It Electronically

Katherine A. Kawamoto, director of Americas Sales Contracts in Irmo, South Carolina, shares the following tip: "There are many electronic greeting card services. They all have a great selection and are really a pick-me-up for our employees when they are having a bad day or are far away on business. You can plan to send anniversary and/or birthday cards up to a year in advance. It just takes filling out a form electronically, and the services send reminders out via e-mail when the date approaches."

DELIVERING WORLD-CLASS REWARDS AND RECOGNITION AT FEDEX

The FedEx Corporation, headquartered in Memphis, Tennessee, is loved both by its employees (FedEx has more than once made *Fortune* magazine's list of the 100 Best Companies to Work for in America) and by its customers (FedEx ranked eighth on *Fortune*'s Most Admired Companies in America list, and seventh on the magazine's Most Admired Companies in the World list). The company's 213,000 employees earned the company more than $19 billion in revenues in 2001.

A slowing economy, combined with the aftereffects of the 9/11 terrorist attacks, caused many airlines—of which FedEx Express is one of the nation's largest—to enact massive lay-offs. Bucking the trend and the pressure, FedEx Express tightened its belt rather than lay off any employees. They've also continued their recognition programs in the face of these cutbacks, which has encouraged employees to work all the harder to help the company meet its goals.

FORMAL RECOGNITION

FedEx Express (the largest of the FedEx Corporation's family of companies) has an extensive program of rewards and recognition, including these formal awards:

1. Bravo Zulu. The term *Bravo Zulu* comes from military terminology and means "well done." Any employee who makes an outstanding effort, or who has a great accomplishment to celebrate, is eligible to receive a "BZ." Every manager is authorized to give this award, and employees can also recommend their coworkers for it.

Historically, a financial award (cash bonuses under $100, theater tickets, dinner gift certificates, and the like) accompanied the award, but because of the recent cost-saving initiatives, people are on the lookout for low- or no-cost creative ways to give Bravo Zulus. For example, management has found that a well-written, personalized Bravo Zulu letter presented in front of a person's work group is often just as meaningful as getting cash.

2. Five Star Award. This is an annual performance award given to employees who have attained the ultimate level of achievement during the past year. The recipients, specially selected by senior management, also receive a reward of cash or stock options.

3. Golden Falcon. This award is given to employees who have been the object of complimentary customer reports to the company, have demonstrated exceptional performance achievement, or performed unselfish acts that enhance customer service. An example would be the courier with a misaddressed package who goes the extra mile to deliver it in a timely manner.

4. Humanitarian Award. This is given to employees who promote human welfare, particularly in life-threatening situations. One employee received it for rescuing a man from a burning car in an expressway accident.

INFORMAL RECOGNITION

FedEx Express takes great pride in its formal recognition programs, and it also strongly supports the efforts of managers and employees who participate in informal recognition. Here are just a few examples of how managers recognize employees informally:

- One manager gives chocolate as a reward for well-packed units. She found a certain chocolate bar that just happens to look like the back of a unit load device (ULD). When she sees a really well loaded ULD, she takes a quick photo

One manager gives chocolate as a reward for well-packed units. Another manager (who can carry a tune!) sings to the employees as they are sorting packages.

of it. In the next group meeting, she passes around the photos of the well-loaded ULD, and rewards those who packed them with the chocolates.

- Every morning, one manager (who can carry a tune!) sings to the employees as they are sorting packages.

- At another station, the work team chipped in and bought a boom box. Each employee gets to be "DJ for a Day." Employees get a chance to tease one another about their taste in music, and they get to know each other better too.

- Workers selected as employee of the month receive a copy of the notice placed on the company's wall of fame, and another copy is FedExed to their home. When they arrive home from work that day, they have good news to share with their family.

The FedEx Express approach to business is based on the values of people, service, and profit—if you take care of the people, they in turn will deliver the service that customers love, which in turn will drive the profits right back into the people. Applying this philosophy has made FedEx truly a company to be admired, and the best in the business.

A partner of a major consulting firm thought he'd be nice and stock a bowl with candy in the common area in the office. When no one touched it, he figured he needed to buy better sweets, so he dumped the hard candy and filled the bowl with chocolates. After a few weeks, during which no one touched the chocolates, he finally asked why no one appreciated his thoughtfulness— only to be told that virtually everyone in the office was dieting.

after? It may appear that being recognized is the kiss of death! One of the keys to successful recognition in such a climate is to create a sense of bonding among the survivors. This is not the time for singling individuals out. It could be a great time for thanking the team for sticking together and getting the work done under suboptimal conditions.

CONTEXT ASSESSMENT TOOLS

There are many ways to assess the organizational context and its implications for recognition. Among the assessment methods that can be used are personal observation, individual interviews, focus groups, and surveys. Let's look at some of the pros and cons of each.

Personal observation. On the surface, it would seem that the easiest way to assess the organizational context is by personal observation. Just being in an organization gives us plenty of clues as to what is appropriate or inappropriate. But personal observations are often unreliable because of the inevitable biases we all have, and because observations will very likely differ from person to person. One way to overcome personal bias in personal observation is to use a standardized list of things to look for, which helps you to be consistent.

- Is communication positive and constructive?

- Do employees listen to and respect one another?

- Do employees seem to enjoy their work?

Personal interviews. Interviewing employees is another way to take the pulse of your organization. In one-on-one interviews, these questions can be open-ended ("What do you think about . . .?), closed-ended ("Is this the case or not?"), or they can use a rating scale ("How strongly do you agree or disagree with the following?"). However, interviews are time consuming and don't promote much interactive discussion.

Focus groups. When interviews are done in small groups, they are referred to as focus groups, which have the advantage of generating many opinions in a relatively short period of time. They also allow for an active interchange of ideas among participants, and therefore tend to result in richer information. Ask questions such as:

- "What is the motivational climate in this organization?"

- "Do you feel that you are being fairly recognized for your efforts and accomplishments?"

- "What are some of the things you like *most* about working here?"

- "What are some of the things you like *least* about working here?"

These kinds of questions give you a quick snapshot of the motivational climate, and also identify some issues that need to be resolved—and that can often be resolved quite easily.

Surveys. Another way of assessing organizational climate is through the use of a survey. Many organizations do annual surveys on employee perceptions. Administering your own informal surveys can be very useful, allowing you to better understand the motivational climate in the organization and in your work unit. You might consider using one of the organizational assessment tools provided in the Recognition Tools section, such as the "Recognition Practices Inventories" or the "Recognition Context Assessment." These provide you with a way of directly assessing the health of your organization's recognition climate and help you determine the organization's readiness for more ambitious recognition efforts. Furthermore, answers to the individual questions will help you determine whether there are any areas in which you need to enhance the "recognition readiness" of your organization. This is particularly important if you are considering putting a major recognition program or initiative into place.

In this chapter, we have merely scratched the surface of understanding the context of recognition. We hope we have presented some thoughts, tools, and suggestions that will be useful as you proceed with your recognition efforts—whether individual, team, or organizational. As we've said, context can provide an opportunity and a threat—an opportunity for the prepared, and a threat for the unprepared.

Do all you can to be prepared!

NO-COST IDEA

13

Strength Barrage

When he worked as a manager for the City of San Diego Housing Commission, Peter Economy shares how, at the end of a weeklong management training workshop, all participants would write down one positive thing on an index card for every other person in the training session. Each individual would then receive their index cards and read what everyone else had to say about them.

THE TAKE-AWAY

- An organization's culture—what makes it different from similar companies—has a major impact on how employees experience recognition, and how they respond to it.

- Motivators—background environmental conditions that positively energize people in an organization—must outweigh demotivators for any recognition program to be successful.

- Noise in an organization—business conditions, organizational changes, information overload, and the like—can interfere with the messages you are trying to send employees, undermining the messages' effectiveness.

- The use of high-value monetary rewards can overwhelm the use of informal recognition and nonmonetary rewards.

- Organizational context can be assessed through personal observation, individual interviews, focus groups, and surveys.

CHAPTER 5

The Recognition Cycle

"He who does not learn from history is doomed to repeat it."

—**George Santayana,** philosopher

The best leaders know the power of positive reinforcement; that is, catching other people in the act of doing something right, and letting them know how much it's appreciated. They know that a positive consequence—a word of thanks, being taken out to lunch, a special award you have devised for them—greatly increases the chances that the desired behavior will be repeated and even enhanced. They know that the greatest management principle in the world is "You get what you reward."

THE RECOGNITION LEARNING PROCESS

But how does a person learn recognition skills? Recognition is much more than a single skill; it is a collection of closely related knowledge, attitudes, and skills. The right knowl-

Fun at Microsoft

One of the great honors at Microsoft is to have your office sodded: While you are away all the furniture is removed from your office and a wall-to-wall layer of sod is laid down. This got to be such a popular prank at the company that a memo was distributed, saying, "Whoever wants to sod someone's office, call this number and we'll do it." Legitimizing the prank, however, made it less fun and the sodding soon stopped, to be replaced by other high jinx, such as filling offices with Styrofoam peanuts or popcorn. In one memorable case, a manager returned from a business trip to find his office door removed and the space Sheetrocked over and painted to perfectly match the corridor wall.

edge and attitudes enable the right skills. These skills should then produce the right behavior, and the right behavior should produce the desired results. This sequence is depicted in the following diagram:

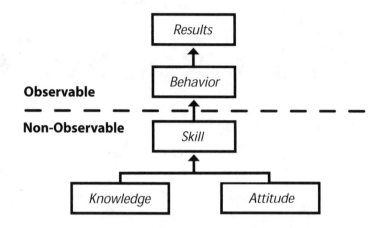

Only the behavior and results are directly observable (above the dotted line), but building a basic foundation of knowledge, attitudes, and skills is essential for the behaviors and results to manifest themselves.

All learning involves risk—risk of failure, risk of feeling stupid, risk of wasting time. The progression of learning any new skill typically occurs in the following stages:

Unconscious incompetence. This is the beginning stage, before you start learning a skill. You are incompetent, but you don't realize it because you don't even know how much you don't know. As for recognition, you aren't doing it—it isn't even on your radar screen.

Conscious incompetence. As you learn a skill, you soon become aware of your own incompetence in it. You lack not only proficiency but also confidence. Whether you're learning how to give recognition or ride a bicycle, the challenge of learning can appear overwhelming early on. Persist, however, and you will gradually acquire the skill and move to the next stage.

Conscious competence. At this stage, you are able to demonstrate the skill, but doing so requires a lot of conscious effort. As you practice the skill, however, you become more competent, and your proficiency and confidence build. Although giving recognition requires significant effort, as you continue to practice and receive feedback the skill improves and the effort required decreases.

Unconscious competence. After sufficient successful experience in using the skill, it becomes a self-reinforcing habit that can be demonstrated effortlessly without your even thinking about it. You are now unconsciously competent.

> "No one lives long enough to learn everything they need to learn starting from scratch. To be successful, we absolutely, positively have to find people who have already paid the price to learn the things that we need to learn to achieve our goals."
>
> —**Brian Tracy,**
> author

The Learning Ladder

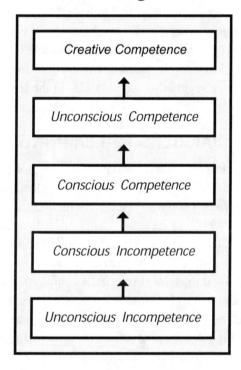

Creative Competence

↑

Unconscious Competence

↑

Conscious Competence

↑

Conscious Incompetence

↑

Unconscious Incompetence

Anyone can become competent, but individuals do not necessarily become competent at the same rate. Some people learn more quickly than others. It is the speed of learning—not the capacity for learning—that differs among people.

Unfortunately, it is all too easy to give up early in the learning process; the inevitable discomfort of the conscious incompetence period often leads to resignation. Many people simply quit at that point and stop using the skill. But others persist, overcoming the initial discomfort, practicing the skill, refining it, and gradually achieving higher and higher levels of competence and confidence.

Stand Up and Holler

When Norwest Banks hosted a sales and service conference in Orlando, Florida, last year, all the executives lined up on the sidewalk and applauded employees as they disembarked from the buses and entered the resort. "It really made everyone feel very special," reported Victoria Gomez, a vice president of Norwest from Columbia, Maryland.

When we feel competent, we are more likely to be creative. Experts are people who not only are highly competent, but who can go beyond the basics to seek new and different ways of demonstrating the skill. Experts are more than unconsciously competent; they are *creatively competent*. That is why we add a fifth stage to the learning ladder: *creative competence*. If we use the example of riding a bicycle, some people stop at unconscious competence, and are satisfied to ride their bike effortlessly. Others continue on, to enhance their skill further; some learn tricks or enter competitions. This is the difference between competence and expertise. While everyone has the capacity to achieve a high level of competence, not everyone becomes an expert.

The bottom line is that we believe it is possible for any manager or employee to develop competence in recognition, though only after successfully negotiating the obstacles in the learning process.

BARRIERS TO LEARNING

Although learning is a natural process, it is not necessarily an easy one. The degree of difficulty differs from person to person. So some people have a greater inclination to give recognition than others, and have an easier time learning to do so. Obviously, we tend to be attracted to learning more about things we already do well and, conversely, we tend to avoid trying to learn more about things that thwart us. As children, we were forced to learn; as adults, we choose to learn . . . or choose not to.

The major psychological barrier to new learning is fear of the unknown, which leads most of us to remain in our "comfort zones"—the same old behaviors that have worked for us in the past. When we are doing "just fine" with our existing repertoire of skills, why should we bother adding a new one to it? Why should we take the chance of feeling consciously incompetent when there is no pain in unconscious incompetence?

The decision to learn a new skill comes with risk—the risk of looking and feeling incompetent. Philip Crosby, the quality guru and author of the classic book *Quality Is Free,* put his finger on the exact nature of this problem when he said,

There is a theory of human behavior that says that people subconsciously retard their own intellectual growth. They come to

rely on clichés and habits. Once they reach the age of their own personal comfort with the world, they stop learning and their mind runs on idle for the rest of their days. They may progress organizationally, they may be ambitious and eager, and they may even work night and day. But they learn no more.[1]

We must be aware of our comfort zones and venture outside them in order to learn and improve. Newton's First Law of Motion (also referred to as the Law of Inertia) states that "an object in motion will remain in motion, and an object at rest will remain at rest until acted upon by an outside force." When applied to the development of recognition behaviors, this means that your tendency to resist change (inertia) will win out unless you're pushed to make a change. People will continue *not* giving recognition if that is their habit, or they will continue giving the same forms of recognition over and over again, until there is some impetus to change.

Fear of making mistakes and of looking bad causes many of us to shy away from learning new things. We often fail to realize that making mistakes is actually the raw material for learning. Learning almost always results from some degree of trial and error—and some kinds of learning are more of a trial than others. For most people, beyond-the-basics recognition requires venturing into situations beyond their current levels of ability. This "stretching," however, will ultimately increase effectiveness.

THE PDRI CYCLE
(PLAN, DO, REVIEW, IMPROVE)

As people move up the learning ladder to higher and higher levels of competence in recognition, the learning path is not usually a straight one. Probably the best way to think about learning is in terms of a PDRI cycle.[2] PDRI stands for:

- **P**lan to take some action or perform some activity.
- **D**o the action or activity.
- **R**eview and assess how well the action or activity worked.
- **I**mprove and refine the action or activity to make it even better when it is used next.

Let's apply this to the process of learning recognition behavior.

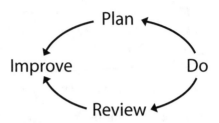

Silly Things Can Mean a Lot

Charles, a government contractor based in Pensacola, Florida, tells us, "I'm the maintenance manager supervising sixty-four jet mechanics for a company that contracts out to the U.S. Navy's flight school. These rough-and-tough men love it when I tape a pinwheel or a balloon to a plane they're working on, signifying that the jet engine has passed every test with flying colors."

Plan. This is the decision to use some form of recognition. This need not be the creation of an elaborate plan with a documented action model. A plan can simply be the desire or intention to take a particular action. You might just ask yourself, "How can I make a motivational impact on my employee or work group?" Obviously, the more complex the activity, the more important a formal plan will be, as you will see when we discuss organizational recognition. Furthermore, the greater your commitment to action, the more likely it is that you will implement your plan.

Until a skill or behavior is habitual, some planning is necessary. Although about 80 percent of our behaviors are habitual and require little or no thought, all new behaviors—or existing behaviors in new situations—require at least some amount of advance thought, planning, and commitment.

Do. Doing turns intention into action. Many people have good intentions but never follow through on them. If intentions were sufficient, *everybody* would be successful. The best performers understand the difference between intending to do something and actually doing it; they are action-oriented. They know that without action everything is just theory. And they know that although their actions at first might be incompetent, it is important to get the learning-by-doing process started. As Nike says, "Just do it!"

Review. Once you have engaged in a recognition activity, review it to see what effects it had. Feedback is a critical step in the learning process. The review reveals answers to such questions as: How well was the recognition received by the recipient? How did it make her feel? Was the objective of the recognition met? Were there any unintended positive or negative consequences?

This review can be elaborate or very simple. Sometimes you will do this review yourself, based on direct observation, and sometimes someone else will coach you through it.

After conducting a review, you can do one of three things: (1) stop giving recognition (fortunately, most people will not choose this option); (2) give it in exactly the same way next time, or (3) decide to improve the way you give recognition.

If you felt *really* successful, you can decide to repeat the recognition exactly as it was done the last time, but success is not the friend of improvement. In fact, we usually learn more from behaviors that fall short of the mark. Success gives us an opportunity for positive reinforcement; failure gives us yet another opportunity to succeed.

Improve. Most people who repeat activities do so because they want to do better the next time. This is the step at which you implement the information you received during your review, using it to improve your own performance. The more you engage in an activity, review, and improve it, the better you will become at that behavior.

It's easy to see the greater value of the PDRI cycle, compared with the linear learning model, which lacks the added benefits of repeated practice and feedback. Using the PDRI model and the wealth of recognition knowledge contained in this book (and in Bob's *1001 Ways* books), you *will* get better and better at giving recognition. As you use recognition more often, you'll become more competent and confident in doing so, and this will encourage you do it more frequently. The PDRI cycle will increase your effectiveness until recognition-giving becomes an ingrained habit.

Routines are good, but they do have a downside. They can seem mechanical—and *nobody* wants to be recognized by a machine. The president of a large manufacturing company walks through his plant once a month to say "hello" to his staff, which makes him feel like he's a great manager. But if you ask his people, they see this behavior as little more than a joke. Says one front-line worker, "Each month, Mr. Johnson asks me how my family is. And each month, I tell him, 'I'm still not married, sir.'"

In another company, upper management appears to be more interested in impressing their management peers than in thanking employees. In their management team meetings, company managers will talk about the great job one of their employees is doing, but the comments rarely get back to the employee who is acknowledged.

A FACILITY FOR RECOGNITION

Q We have two facilities with the same managers over both. In one facility the employees are caring and willing to help; in the other it is the opposite. How can we change the atmosphere in the second facility?

—online forum participant

A Learn from what has worked, and is working, in the first facility. Start sharing information and practices between the two facilities. What exactly does the one facility have going for it that the other doesn't? Are there key people who help perpetuate the attitude and practice of recognition? If so, what, specifically, do they do, and can those in the other facility replicate that? Perhaps start a recognition task force made up of members of both facilities so they can share experiences.

SINCERITY COUNTS

Q What tips can you suggest to overcome early resistance to new motivational techniques—for example, if workers question the motives of management?

—from the Canadian International Development Agency, Hull, Quebec, Canada

A Tell people what you are up to. After all, the best management is what you do *with* people, not to them. For example, say something like "I'm going to be trying to give more feedback when I see good work in our department. I know I haven't done a lot of this in the past, and I'm not really comfortable with it, so let me know how I did if I give you such feedback." If you come at it sincerely, with the best interests of your employees at heart, people will not feel manipulated.

It's very easy to fall into a pattern. When you lose the spontaneity, freshness, and sincerity of being thankful for an employee's good work, recognition becomes mechanical, and will likely be perceived by employees as manipulative. This is why it is vital to take the PDRI cycle to the next level.

BREAKTHROUGH IMPROVEMENT: GETTING TO THE NEXT LEVEL

It is important—for both you and your employees—that recognition behaviors do not stop developing when they become rote. When recognition becomes routine and boring, it loses its power to motivate, and inevitably diminishes in frequency.

Once you feel comfortable with your mastery of basic recognition giving, it is time to develop new skills, which means moving out of your *new* comfort zone. This can involve expanding possibilities through discovering new types and varieties of recognition, leveraging uses of recognition to get maximum impact, connecting and aligning different types of recognition, and, of course, linking it to desired performance.

Giving recognition can be very motivating for both the giver and the recipient. As you master the PDRI cycle, you should be willing to seek new recognition challenges. Fortunately, the PDRI cycle provides for this progression.

PDRI cycles should not just continue going around and around ad infinitum. This would simply get the same skill more habitually ingrained. Habits can actually become addictive, because it feels so good to be in our comfort zones—what Philip Crosby is talking about when he says that "people subconsciously retard their own intellectual growth." Ironically, the more we repeat the same PDRI cycle, the less likely we are to move on to other behaviors and grow. One of the most important self-development skills is to know when to move on to new learning.

Once you have mastered your first PDRI cycle, you will want to innovate and become even more effective. You will want to attempt something that is beyond your current self-perceived level of ability.

But a breakthrough improvement for *you* doesn't have to mean a quantum leap for all of humanity! Breakthroughs are relative; a breakthrough for one person might be an incremental step for another. When you become ready for the next recognition breakthrough, make the decision to move forward. This will take your recognition behavior to the next level. The following diagram shows what this process looks like:

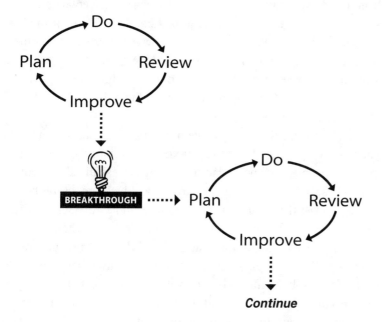

"Continuous learning drives everyone to find a better way, every day. It's not an expense, it's an investment in continuous renewal."

—**Jack Welch,**
former CEO,
General Electric

A breakthrough need not involve a long drawn-out process. A breakthrough improvement decision can result from the realization that "I am not satisfied with giving the same old recognition. . . . I want to go to the next level," and an *aha* about what to do next.

For example, one IBM manager decided that she was not satisfied with just saying "thank you" to her team for a job well done. She decided to try something different. She ordered coffee mugs for the team with her personal thank-you written on the mugs, even though it required a considerable effort to get approval, track down a vendor, and come up with the right words. Then there was the matter of how the mugs would be presented—especially since it was a virtual team, with members spread out all over the United States.

Moreover, this manager used the opportunity to involve other managers who might have been less willing to strive for a recognition breakthrough on their own. She gave them the opportunity to participate, so that their employees could also be recognized. You too can help others achieve recognition breakthroughs.

NO-COST IDEA 17

Bragging Sessions

At Petro Canada, a large energy company, management hosts "bragging sessions" to allow employees to share progress they were making against goals with upper management. The meetings have a fun and celebratory feel and generate high energy to continue efforts.

See page 269 ◄
for "Recognition
Training Designs."

The key point is that *she did it:* she had a breakthrough improvement in the way she gave recognition. And the $2 coffee mugs were highly motivating to the team.

Interestingly, the idea for this recognition breakthrough came from one of her employees, and the manager's acceptance of that suggestion was very reinforcing to that employee. One of the best ways to achieve breakthroughs in any area is to borrow from others what has worked for them. One of the biggest mistakes we make is thinking that we need to invent our own breakthroughs. We don't—there are plenty of great ideas out there that will work well for your situation and circumstances.

Don't be afraid to ask for advice from trusted colleagues, and even your own employees. No doubt, in your organization or elsewhere, there are people you know who have been successful using recognition. These recognition models are invaluable sources of breakthrough ideas. If you are unable to find examples firsthand, "steal" from articles, books, or any other resource you can get hold of.

Another method for facilitating breakthrough recognition is rehearsal. Try role-playing the new recognition behavior with friends or family members before using it in the workplace. Or you can visualize the situation and its impact mentally. Some form of rehearsal will very likely give you the confidence to move forward and achieve a recognition breakthrough.

One of the best ways to achieve recognition breakthroughs is recognition training. A training environment allows for discussion, dealing with obstacles, and learning from others.

Another good path to recognition breakthrough is recognition coaching. Find someone you respect who uses effective recognition behaviors and ask him or her to coach you. If you are fortunate enough to know someone who is more expert than you are, enlist that person to be your recognition coach. Actually, it can be mutual—you can coach each other.

Breakthrough improvement rarely occurs when we are overstretched or overstressed. As busy as most managers are today, it's important to take time for your own needs. Relaxing and giving yourself a chance to regenerate is essential to staying fresh and effective, whatever your position is. It is also essential for breakthrough improvement. Get off the treadmill and consider how you can improve the morale and performance of your work group using recognition.

Jack Canfield, coauthor of *Chicken Soup for the Soul,* advises,

Increase the amount of time you get away from the office so you can increase the high-level thinking required to come up with big ideas. When I come back to work from a long vacation, I immediately see the results. I'm more productive and creative. While on vacation, I'll also get incredible ideas that wouldn't happen at home because I'm too busy putting out fires.[3]

What works best to relax and recharge your batteries varies widely from person to person, so it is important to be aware of what you find most satisfying and rejuvenating.

Another great way to increase breakthrough improvement is to participate in a support group. Jack Canfield further explains that he gets energy injections by spending time with others. He belongs to a Master Mind group, a term coined by legendary motivational guru Napoleon Hill, author of *Think and Grow Rich,*[4] who suggests that people form support groups to motivate and inspire each other. Canfield explains, "We all get locked into our own myopic viewpoints and very rarely get to see other, broader points of view. Regular meetings with successful people from different professions help open our thinking to new, bigger possibilities."[5] If you can't find a recognition support group or idea exchange, why not start your own?

RECOGNIZING THE RECOGNIZER

One of the reasons recognition isn't used as widely as it should be is that the recognizers don't get recognized themselves. How often do employees take time to recognize their managers for recognizing them? And how often are managers recognized by one another?

Never forget that the recognizer also needs recognition; otherwise you end up taking that person for granted. If you are managing people who give frequent and effective recognition, make sure you recognize their efforts.

Creating a "culture of recognition" demands that this cascading recognition be formalized, but until that happens, it is up to individual managers to do the right thing and recognize the recognizers.

If you are not currently getting recognized for recognition, you might want to try some form of self-recognition. When you have reached a milestone in recognizing others, reward yourself!

"Knowledge is not information—it's transformation."

—**Osho,**
author

IN RECOGNITION WE TRUST AT THE OFFICE OF PERSONNEL MANAGEMENT

As director of performance management for the U.S. Office of Personnel Management, Doris Hausser guides and inspires all federal government agencies, which employ 1.8 million people, to develop creative recognition programs that will work for them. We interviewed her to learn her secrets of success for working with—and motivating—the most diverse workforce in the world.

"The challenge that the Office of Personnel Management faces," says Hausser, "is to encourage people to be innovative and creative, yet keep them from doing something that the law does not allow them to do." This challenge is made all the greater by constant public scrutiny, having to use public funds, and the requirement to adhere to rigid legislative constraints. In addition, says Hausser, "The organizations in government are so diverse, we have everything from astronauts to cowboys, so the award has to be something the employee will value."

Until 1993, the Office of Personnel Management was very controlling with federal agencies—they told them exactly what they were allowed and not allowed to do when it came to employee recognition and rewards. But tight control over government recognition programs did not work because there is no one-size-fits-all recognition program that works for everyone. So the government got rid of their strict regulations and developed more lenient guidelines for the agencies. With the removal of regulations, OPM has had to change their perception with the agencies from that of *police officers* to *recognition and reward consultants.*

Hausser realized just how difficult this change was going to be when she attended a meeting where the Department of Energy was brainstorming innovative and nontraditional ways to reward employees. "I walked into the meeting in the middle of a discussion. People stopped talking when I walked in. After I was introduced to the group, the woman who had been speaking did not want to continue. She said she was describing a new team reward program and she did not want to describe it in front of the Office of Personnel Management. She was hesitant because traditionally OPM emphasized individual recognition, not group recognition. I promised her I would keep quiet unless I heard something that was illegal. She then proceeded to describe how the lives of the individuals who fix power lines depend on employees working as a team. She proposed having team goals and team rewards. After hearing the proposal, I got up and applauded and said that I wanted to go on record as saying it was a wonderful plan! The experience was a good lesson for me."

So the OPM now bends over backward not to be directive. They give the agencies guidelines that preach the principles of recognition. The OPM has also learned that the agencies have to design their own programs to be successful. They encourage agencies to exchange ideas and they bring in outsiders to train agencies on the principles of recognition. When asked for help, OPM assists an agency in designing its own program by asking questions such as the following:

What is the nature of the work? "Do employees interact with the public? If so, then you probably want to reward good customer service. For people who interact with a computer all day, you can have the computer monitor performance in keystrokes, but you need to set up performance goals for individuals and publicly reward their achievements."

What is the setting of the work? "Let's say you have a government employee sitting at the top of a ranger station. What is good performance for that person and who is going to know about it?"

What do you want to reward? You need to reward behavior that you want to see happen again. "One agency has started the Giraffe Award to recognize people who stick their necks out, where you are really awarding risk taking, and that's the whole idea. The award is symbolic of the nature of the contribution that the employer wants to see."

"One agency has started the 'Giraffe Award' to recognize people who stick their necks out, where you are really awarding risk taking."

What kind of people do you have? "Some employees, like scientists, would rather die than be publicly appreciated."

Where are the boundaries of the culture? Complex organizations can include very different employees and functions. "You might have general consuls on one floor, a room full of people working on computers on another, and a research team on a third floor. You need to define the boundaries and tailor the recognition program to each culture."

Hausser and her office also help agencies balance legal issues with incentive issues. "We sometimes get calls from agencies that want to use some sort of lottery as an incentive program. The law does not allow for this type of award program because there is the element of chance to receiving the award. So we try to help the agency find something that would be more effective. We ask them questions to understand what they were trying to achieve, and we try to find out why the lottery was so intriguing to them. Usually they like the lottery because they can purchase one thing of value, but they can have a group participate in the program. So what it boils down to is that the agency has a limited budget and a whole team of people they want to recognize. We then suggest that instead of getting a great big expensive crystal vase with a logo, they give everyone a button with "Great Job!" printed on it. It doesn't need to be a crystal vase to be valuable. People need to understand that the power of recognition is as important as the crystal vase."

THE TAKE-AWAY

- Anyone can learn to become proficient at recognizing employees.

- Learning is a process of improvement that can be expressed as a PDRI cycle: Plan, Do, Review, and Improve.

- As PDRI cycles are mastered, further learning requires breakthrough improvements.

- Take time to recognize the recognizers—your managers and colleagues—and yourself.

CHAPTER 6

Getting Started with Individual Recognition

"I can live for two months on a good compliment."

—**Mark Twain,** author

The most powerful type of recognition occurs at the individual level, one-on-one. A leader can attain some of the greatest levels of motivation with today's employees through the effective use of one-on-one praise and recognition. Every leader needs to take personal responsibility to see that they recognize their employees, and they need to keep at it on a daily basis.

QUICK TIPS FOR GETTING STARTED

What's the best way to get started using recognition with individuals? Here are some guidelines that we've found valuable:

Start in your immediate sphere of influence. Motivation is very personal. To be successful with recognition, you need to operate on a very immediate, one-on-one level. A great thing about recognition is that you don't need anyone's permission to start using it.

SLACKERS—OR NOT?

Q I work for the City of Golden, Colorado, as the supervisor of youth programs. The nature of the jobs I hire for tends to attract nineteen- to twenty-four-year-olds. This age group seems so busy with their lives that I have a hard time motivating them to push themselves to give their all, especially working with young kids. Do you have any suggestions?

—**Matt Hess,**
Golden, CO

A **Find out what excites them and then try to see how you can do more of that. In my experience, younger workers are often motivated by their social context, so you might create opportunities for them to interact more with their peers more, both on and off the job. Younger workers also are often very resourceful and thrive on challenging assignments and variety in their jobs.**

Do *one* thing differently. The best goals are ones that are attainable and reasonable, so it is best to start small—perhaps by doing just one thing differently. After you achieve some success and momentum, you can expand your efforts. It is far better to focus on one thing and do it consistently than to try to do a dozen things that never go beyond an initial announcement. For example, start each staff meeting with good news and praise for individuals who deserve it, perhaps reading thank-you letters from satisfied customers or from other employees in your organization. It's estimated that over 90 percent of our daily behavior is routine; don't underestimate the power of selective daily focus.

Ask employees what motivates them. Start with employees' preferences for recognition—have them jot down ways they like to be thanked or complete a simple recognition survey of things they find motivating. Motivational preferences differ from person to person, and over time. Spend time with employees to find out what types of work activities most interest them, the skills they'd like to learn or develop in their jobs, and the direction they want their career to take. Learn about their personal hobbies and family situation. All of this information is fodder for motivation, and the more you know about your employees, the better you will be able to motivate them. Help them reach their goals, and your employees will want to help the organization succeed in return.

Focus on what you can do, not on what you can't do. In almost every work environment, there are constraints that can keep you from implementing recognition activities. Large companies may seem impersonal and bureaucratic, while smaller companies or nonprofits may not have many resources to devote to recognition. Public organizations must be careful how they use public funds for recognition activities, older companies may be slow to change from ineffective paternalistic incentives, and many organizations are unionized, which restricts some recognition practices. But don't dwell on what you can't do; focus on the hundreds of things you *can* do. Anyone can write a simple thank-you note expressing heartfelt appreciation for a job well done. It only takes a moment, and it doesn't cost a dime.

Don't expect perfection. Far too many managers abandon their initial efforts when they don't meet their expectations. There is no perfect way of doing recognition, and any new behavior or change will be awkward at first. Instead, try out some small things, learn from what works, then seek to improve. Ask others in your work group to provide feedback and ideas as you try your new behaviors. Have fun in the process and you will seldom go wrong.

Now let's build on some of these initial strategies in a more systematic way by examining how best to plan individual recognition.

"Many know how to flatter; few understand how to give praise."

—Greek proverb

PLANNING INDIVIDUAL RECOGNITION

The best way to get any new behavior started is to plan for it to happen. Individual recognition is no exception. Planning doesn't need to be elaborate or even formal. A plan can be as simple as deciding to tell someone who has done a good job that you appreciate it.

To be most successful, your plan should take into account the stages before and after the recognition:

BEFORE YOU RECOGNIZE

When planning individual recognition, a good (and simple) approach is to use the *who, what, where, when, and how* format. This planning format doesn't even need to be written down, but systematically thinking it through will help you do a better job of recognition—especially when you are just getting started with it.

➤ **See page 258** for the "Individual Recognition Planning Worksheet."

- **What** do I want to recognize? The best recognition is contingent; that is, in response to a specific behavior or performance.

- **Who** do I want to recognize? Identify the person or people most responsible for the desired behavior or performance.

- **When** should the recognition be done? The best recognition takes place soon after the desired behavior or performance.

- **Where** should the recognition be done? The best recognition is personal; that is, delivered directly to the individual being acknowledged—ideally, in person.

- **How** should the recognition be done? The best recognition is done in a way that enhances its motivational value to the recipient. Who performs the recognition? Is it done in public or private? Asking yourself these questions will help make sure that the recognition activity has the greatest impact.

GUIDELINES FOR EFFECTIVE PRAISE

One of the best ways to start appreciating others is with simple praise. Praise is priceless, yet it costs nothing. Although giving effective praise may seem like common sense, a lot of people have never learned how to do it. We suggest an acronym—ASAP[3]—to remember the essential elements of a good compliment: As Soon, As Sincerely, As Specifically, As Personally, As Positively, and As Proactively as possible.

As Soon. Timing is critical. To be most effective, the thank-you should come soon after the achievement or desired activity has occurred. If you wait too long to thank a person, the gesture will lose its significance. Your employee will assume that other things were more important to you than taking a few minutes with him or her.

As Sincerely. Words alone can seem hollow if you are not sincere. Your praise should be based on a true appreciation of and excitement about the other person's successes; otherwise your thanks may come across as a manipulative tactic—for instance, a ploy used only when you want an employee to work late. As the saying goes, "People don't care how much you know, until they know how much you care."

As Specifically. Avoid generalities in favor of details of the achievement. Compliments that are too broad tend to seem insincere. Specifics give credibility to your praise. Say *what* the employee did and *why* her effort was of value. For instance: "Thanks for staying late to finish those calculations I needed. It was critical for my meeting this morning."

As Personally. Here it is in a nutshell: The most effective forms of recognition are the most personal ones. This shows that recognition is important enough for you to put aside everything else you have to do and focus on the other person. Since we all have limited time, the things you do yourself indicate that they have a high value to you. Recognition by way of a quick e-mail or voice-mail message is certainly appreciated, but praise in person means much more, when you can do it.

As Positively. When you say something like "You did a great job on this report, but there were quite a few typos," the "but" erases all that came before. Save the corrective feedback for the next similar assignment. Separate even constructive criticism from your acts of praise.

As Proactively. Praise progress toward desired goals. Don't wait for perfect performance; praise improvements and behavior that are approximately right. You will get the results you want faster.

In summary, the essence of a good praising communicates:

- I saw what you did. (Make sure others know what you see.)

- I appreciate it. (Place value on the behavior or achievement.)

- Here's why it's important. (Always provide a context.)

- Here's how it makes me feel. (Give it an emotional charge.)

The act of delivering simple, direct praise for a job well done is extremely easy to do, yet so few people do it. Make the extra effort to appreciate employees, and they'll reciprocate in a thousand ways.

SIMPLE GESTURES COUNT THE MOST

Recognition does not have to be anything fancy; in fact, the simpler and more direct the better. The more we work with recognition and rewards, the more we are intrigued by the simple and sincere ways employees appreciate each other with a minimum of cost, paperwork, and administration. One of our favorite examples of how literally *anything* can be viewed as recognition comes from Hewlett-Packard. An engineer burst into his manager's office in Palo Alto, California, to announce he'd just found the solution to a problem the group had been struggling with for many weeks. His manager groped around his desk for some item to acknowledge the accomplishment, and ended up handing the employee a banana from his lunch and saying, "Well done.

"Most of us would rather be ruined by praise than saved by criticism."

—**Norman Vincent Peale,**
pastor and author

NO-COST IDEA 18

Thanks a Million

Chris Ortiz, in systems and applications at NASA's Johnson Space Center in Houston, Texas, offers, "After reading *1001 Ways to Reward Employees*, I created an award for all my team members who helped me. I call it my Thanks a Million award. It contains a thank-you note taped to ten $100 Grand candy bars. Recipients break them up and pass them on to others who have helped them."

Congratulations!" The employee was initially puzzled, but over time the Golden Banana became one of the most prestigious honors bestowed on inventive Hewlett-Packard employees.

Another simple yet effective approach is to put notes on business cards. John Plunkett, director of employment and training for Cobb Electric Membership Corporation in Marietta, Georgia, says, "People love to collect others' business cards. Simply carry a supply of your cards with you and as you 'catch people doing something right,' immediately write, 'Thanks,' 'Good job,' 'Keep it up,' and what they specifically did in two or three words. Put the person's name on the card, sign it, and give it to the employee." One hospital in Chicago even uses these praising cards as a recruiting device: "Thanks so much for your service today. If you ever consider leaving your job here, we'd be glad to consider hiring you for our firm. Please give me a call."

At Tektronix, in Beaverton, Oregon, the company instituted a simple way for managers and employees alike to focus on recognizing others for doing something right. Simple memo pads were printed with a cartoon and the heading "You Done Good Award," which could be given to anybody in the company from anybody else in the company. On it, individuals state what was done, who did it, and when, and then give the memo to the person. By providing this vehicle for employees to thank one another, praise happens much more often. The idea has caught on and is now part of life at Tektronix.

ARAMARK, headquartered in Philadelphia, Pennsylvania, proclaims days in honor of high-performing employees. The honorees enjoy all sorts of frills, such as personalized computer banners and a free lunch.

MAKE RECOGNITION PART OF YOUR JOB

Have a reminder system. Hyler Bracey, CEO of the Atlanta Consulting Group, keeps five marbles in his pocket and transfers one to another pocket each time he praises someone. His goal is to transfer all five marbles from one pocket to the other each day. The technique has helped Bracey make praise a habit and a routine part of his workday.

Write notes at the end of the day. If your days fly by before you ever get a chance to recognize anyone, take a few minutes before you go home to jot some personal notes to individuals who made a difference that day. Get some personalized note cards made up and keep a stack of them next to your telephone on your desk as a constant reminder of this powerful tool. Many managers may find it difficult to recognize during a busy time, but possible once things slow down at the end of the day. Use that time to scrawl a few notes to the individuals who made a difference that day.

Harness the power of technology. When you get a positive e-mail, pass it on to others, or print it out to read at your next staff meeting. When you send a positive e-mail, copy the recipient's manager. Instead of just using voice mail to assign tasks to employees, try leaving messages of praise. You can do it from your cell phone as you commute home after work.

Single out individuals in group meetings. A group setting provides numerous opportunities to acknowledge individuals—reading a positive letter of thanks that an employee has received from a client, allowing time for anyone to publicly thank anyone else in the group, or hosting a "praise barrage," during which everyone focuses on what one member of the team is doing well.

Vary your routine. Take different routes to your office so you can mingle with all of your employees. Enter your facility at different entrances from time to time to get a chance to greet others and ask them about their work. Learn the names of your employees and take breaks with groups of them. If you are pressed for time, ask him or her to reschedule a meeting with an employee so as to be able to give him or her your undivided attention.

Be accessible. If you have an "open-door" policy, make sure you are actually around for employees to use it. Be accessible when your employees need you to be, not just when it is convenient for you. As Roy Moody of Roy Moody and Associates in Phoenix, Arizona, says, "The greatest motivational act one person can do for another is to listen."

Following is our top-ten list of motivators for today's employees.

SMALL IS BEAUTIFUL

Q Many suggestions you make seem like they'd be best in large companies. We have two full-time and three part-time employees, as well as a couple of family members. I think that a reward should not only shore up the confidence of the recipient, but also encourage others to do a better job. In a small place, this could seem like favoritism.

—Jon Leer,
Leer Technical Communications,
Bedford, NH

A Given the flexibility and greater degree of interaction and visibility of management in a small company, you can offer more than a large company does—special assignments, lunch with the boss, fun certificates, celebrations of milestones, training and growth opportunities, and so forth. Have a session in which everyone lists two or three things that motivate them. Although you can give rewards to increase morale, whenever possible, you should link the rewards to some kind of performance so as to keep it as objective as possible. The result will be increased performance and improved employee morale and satisfaction.

TOP 10	WAYS TO MOTIVATE EMPLOYEES		
1	Personally thank employees for doing a good job—one-on-one, in writing, or both. Do it quickly, often, and sincerely.	7	Recognize, reward, and promote people based on their performance, and deal with low and marginal performers so that they improve or leave.
2	Take as much time to meet with and listen to employees as they need or want.	8	Provide employees with a sense of ownership in their work and in their work environment; let them decide how best to do their work.
3	Provide specific feedback about performance of the person, the department, and the organization. Catch people doing something right!		
4	Strive to create a work environment that is open, trusting, and fun. Encourage new ideas and initiatives.	9	Create a partnership with each employee. Give people a chance to grow and learn new skills; show them that you can and will help them meet their goals within the context of meeting the organization's goals.
5	Provide information on the company's prospects, upcoming products, and strategies for competing in the marketplace, and how the individual fits into the overall plan.		
6	Involve employees in decisions, especially those decisions that directly affect them.	10	Celebrate the successes of the company, of the department, and of the individuals in it. Take time for team- and morale-building meetings and activities.

Make people a part of your "to do" list. Add the names of those individuals who report to you to your weekly "to do" list and check them off when you "catch them doing something right."

As relatively simple and easy as these activities and techniques may seem, they can have a significant impact on the morale, productivity, and performance of your employees. Try one or more of these techniques and stick with those that work for you.

MAKING TIME FOR EMPLOYEE RECOGNITION

Lack of time is probably the biggest obstacle to leaders providing more recognition in the workplace. Managers are often too busy focusing on what's *urgent* to focus on what's *important*—namely, the people they manage.

The situation is made worse by the false perception of many managers that they are already providing employees with plenty of

"Every single person you meet has a sign around his or her neck that says, 'Make me feel important.'"

—**Mary Kay Ash,**
founder,
Mary Kay

praise and recognition. According to Aubrey Daniels, chairman of Aubrey Daniels International of Atlanta, Georgia, and a leading authority on the topic of performance management, "Those managers who feel they use positive reinforcement the most, in my experience, often do it the least."

Managers may have learned that they need to positively reinforce their employees, and feel they are doing so, but often they are actually doing very little on a daily basis to catch their employees doing something right. Worse, the reinforcement they are providing is often far from positive—the feedback is nonspecific or insincere; the praise is random, overlooking employees who have contributed equally to a given success; or the facts about the acknowledged behavior or performance are wrong.

How can managers start recognizing their employees more? As reported earlier, a "lack of time" is just an excuse and needs to be addressed. Like any behavioral change, you have to find a way to make it a natural part of your daily routine.

Even managers who *are* busy can find time to make recognition a part of their daily behavior. If they cannot bring themselves to praise employees personally, they can focus on other recognition activities they are willing and able to do. For example, a manager can approve a department celebration, even if he or she doesn't personally attend the party.

TECHNIQUES FOR MAINTAINING COMMITMENT

What keeps people from acting on their best intentions to recognize employees more frequently? Usually, you can raise managers' levels of awareness about the importance of recognizing employees, and you can have them practice their interpersonal skills so they can increase their ability and comfort level, but you can't force them to keep up the desired behavior once they get back on the job. We're convinced that the ratio of success increases when we help people develop an individualized strategy and support plan to stay committed.

Following are several tactics we've seen work in a variety of different organizations. Try them, adapt them, and combine them as you see fit for your circumstances.

"Good words are worth much and cost little."

—**Dag Hammarskjöld,**
former secretary-general
of the United Nations

NO-COST IDEA

The Praising Board

From Connie Maxwell of West Des Moines Community Schools: "I post notes from other departments that have something positive to say about any of us; this way, people who work with me are more inclined to write one to someone else, so there's a mutual sharing of thanks. It's become a point of pride to have a note that one wrote posted."

VIKING FREIGHT: A VERY REWARDING PLACE TO BE

Viking Freight (now FedEx Viking West), a $419 million wholly owned subsidiary of Federal Express based in San Jose, California, is a shipping company with a vast network of sixty-six service centers in eleven western states. Viking has long attracted attention for its rewards and recognition programs, unprecedented in its industry. The company has a number of entries in Bob Nelson's book *1001 Ways to Reward Employees,* and others have picked up on the company's unique, employee-centered culture.

Here is a brief look at some of the company's many different awards and programs:

Moment of truth award. This employee-nominated award is given to workers who generate additional revenue for the company, most often by referring new customers. Awards of a plaque and $100 are given out to recipients on a quarterly basis.

EZTDBW award. This employee-nominated award—named after the company's slogan, "Easy to Do Business With"—is given quarterly to workers who go out of their way to help their coworkers. Honorees receive a certificate and a logoed item such as a flashlight, pen and pencil set, or clock.

Safety award. This self-nominated award, also given quarterly—is based on ratings earned for a variety of safety-related factors.

Employee appreciation week. During this week in August, Viking shows appreciation for its em-ployees in a variety of ways. Breakfast and lunch are served to employees, and the company throws a big midweek barbecue lunch at all of its locations.

Holiday celebration. During the holiday season, all employees are treated to a cele-bration centered around a barbecue or catered dinner.

Holiday turkey. During the holiday season, every employee gets a personal greeting card signed by his or her manager, along with a gift certificate for a turkey.

BLT ("Breakfast, Lunch, and Talk"). Once a quarter, Viking corporate officers pull together a group of five or six new employees for a breakfast or lunch full of questions and answers, and informal conversation.

Officer visits. Viking's officers regularly drop in on employee meetings and bring food for the meeting's attendees.

All-star award. These on-the-spot-awards (up to $100) and an accompanying certificate can be given out at any time and for any reason with the approval of a director or higher.

Extra mile award. This award of $500 and an accompanying certificate—given with the approval of a director or higher—recognizes employees who do something really special.

Viking Performance Earnings Plan (VPEP). When company profit exceeds 5 percent, all employees share in the additional profit above that mark. The company has paid out more than $9 million in incentive pay in a single year.

Employee of the month. Each month, every Viking service center selects an employee to receive this award.

Lifesaver award. At one service center, employees give one another rolls of Lifesavers when they get an extra hand in solving a problem.

Quarterly service center competitions. Each quarter, service centers vie for cash awards based on ratings on a variety of business factors. Cash awards—which range from $650 for a small service center to $6,000 for a large service center—are shared by all employees in the center.

> *Company drivers are eligible to participate in the Viking-sponsored truck-driving championships, and show off their driving skills in a variety of events, such as maneuvering a tractor trailer through a barrel course.*

Jeans days. Administrative employees who contribute to charity (making a $3 contribution from their paychecks, matched by Viking) are allowed to wear jeans to work on a designated day.

Gold and more gold. An incentive award given to salespeople who achieve certain revenue goals.

Truck-driving championships. Company drivers are eligible to participate in the Viking-sponsored truck-driving championships, and show off their driving skills in a variety of events, such as maneuvering a tractor trailer through a barrel course. Winners are then sponsored (with all expenses paid) by the company in statewide and national competitions against other truck drivers.

Many of the awards center around food. Why this focus on the stomach? Because, according to Viking's vice president of human resources, Tom Suchevits, "We've found that it's important to 'break bread' with our people. It's part of the family feeling that we want to convey. Our product is service, and our employees are our best ambassadors."

Says Suchevits, "We hope that our employees feel positive about their jobs and about the company, so that when they deal with the customer, they give them their positive feelings. These positive feelings come back to the company many-fold."

NO-COST IDEA

Keeping in Touch

At the Department of Mental Health and Mental Retardation in Austin, Texas, Claudia Smith reports, "We assign a mentor to each new employee who comes on board so the people feel connected right away. The mentor is available for any type of day-to-day questions. At the end of sixty days, there's a follow-up with the mentor, employee, and manager to see how everything's going. It's really made a difference in our retention rate and in how fast people feel 'on board.'"

Link the activity to your day planner. For many people, the key to changing their routine is to make the new behavior part of their current planning and organizing system. As we've said earlier, we've been successful at getting analytical, task-oriented managers to start praising employees more by getting them to think of their people as "things to do." We have these managers put on their weekly "to do" list the name of each person who reports to them, and cross each person off the list once they have given praise based on that person's performance. For some managers, such a specific technique helps them to understand praise as a finite action rather than an intangible activity, and the task becomes much easier to complete. The manager can also write reminders in his or her calendar for future dates, such as employees' birthdays or the anniversaries of their hire dates—or, better yet, when performance milestones are achieved.

Elicit the help of others. Managers are likely to have significantly better results when they involve others and discuss what they are trying to do. They could have people work with a partner for recognition activities; this could be a colleague they met in a training session or someone from a different area of the company with whom they want to keep in touch. Have them exchange action plans with specific times for follow-up and discussion of progress. In this "buddy system," the partner acts as a designated monitor, counselor, and enforcer all in one—essentially, a soul mate to encourage and act on the new behaviors.

Alternatively, at the next staff meeting, a manager can say, "I'm going to be trying some new tactics and would appreciate your feedback on it. Specifically, I'm going to be acknowledging people when I see them doing a good job. I'm trying to do this in a timely, specific way. Let me know how it feels to you and give me feedback as to how I can do it better."

Hold one-on-one meetings. One systematic approach for making more time for your employees is to start holding one-on-one meetings. The idea is to set a minimum acceptable standard for "face time" with each employee. At the Ken Blanchard Companies, in San Diego, California, such meetings take fifteen to thirty minutes at least once every two weeks. Since that time is the employees' to

THE POWER OF I'S: NO-COST ON-THE-JOB RECOGNITION THAT WORKS

Praise and simple gestures of sincere thanks are important to employees today, but there are many other things that can be incorporated into the job itself to acknowledge an individual and make him or her feel special, such as:

- **Interesting and important work.** At least part of every job must be of high interest to an employee. As the management theorist Frederick Herzberg said, "If you want someone to do a good job, give them a good job to do." Yes, some jobs may be inherently boring, but you can give anyone in any job some variety or at least one task or project that's stimulating. Send him to meetings in your place, or assign her to a suggestion committee, or to some other special group, that meets once a week. The time away from the regular job is likely to be more than made up with increased productivity, creativity, and fresh insight and ideas.

- **Information/communication/feedback.** With the presumption of lifetime employment largely a thing of the past, more than ever employees want to know how they are doing in their jobs, and how well the company is doing. Start telling them how the company makes money and spends it. Make sure there are ample channels of communication to encourage employees to ask questions, and get and share information. At least some of the communication channels should directly involve management in non-intimidating circumstances. Soon you'll have employees taking initiative to suggest ideas that can improve processes and save the organization money and time.

- **Involvement in decisions/ownership.** Involving employees, especially in decisions that affect them, is both respectful to them and practical for the organization. People closest to the problem or to customers typically have the best insight into how a situation can be improved. They know what works and what doesn't, but are rarely asked for their opinion. As you involve others, you increase their commitment and the ease of implementing new ideas or change.

- **Independence/autonomy/flexibility.** Most employees—especially experienced, top-performing ones—value being given room to do their job as they best see fit. All employees also appreciate having flexibility in their jobs. When you make your decision and communicate your intentions to provide these things to employees based on their performance, you increase the likelihood that they will perform as desired, and bring additional initiative, ideas, and energy to the job as well.

- **Increased visibility/opportunity/responsibility.** Everyone appreciates a manager who gives credit where it is due. Chances to share the successes of employees with others are almost limitless. In addition, most employee development happens on the job; give employees new opportunities to perform, learn, and grow as a form of recognition and thanks.

use as they desire, the meetings frequently start with the manager asking, "What's on your agenda?" (They even have one-on-one forms to help the employee prepare for these meetings.) One employee might want feedback on a project she recently completed, another may want to get advice on how he can improve a working relationship with another employee (they may try to figure it out through role-playing), and another person might want to discuss career options and skills she would like to learn on the job.

Schedule time for recognition. You can also provide structures or systems in your work environment that will encourage praise. As mentioned earlier, some managers save time at the end of every staff meeting to ask if anyone has any praise they'd like to share. Typically, people do. Other companies have scheduled "bragging sessions" with upper management in which they update (and celebrate) the progress of major projects.

THE TAKE-AWAY

- The best way to get individual recognition behavior started in an organization is to make plans for it to happen.

- When planning individual recognition, consider, "Who, what, where, when, and how?"

- Effective recognition is ASAP[3]: As Soon, As Sincerely, As Specifically, As Personally, As Positively, and As Proactively as possible.

- Simple gestures count the most to employees.

- A top motivator for many of today's employees is being personally thanked for doing a good job, either in person or in writing—or both.

CHAPTER 7

Getting Started with Team Recognition

"When things succeed the superior leader takes no credit. And because he takes no credit, credit never leaves him."

—**Lao-Tzu,** philosopher

"It's amazing what can be accomplished when no one cares who gets the credit."

—Sign in Boston College locker room

Few issues in business today are as challenging and critical as knowing how best to recognize teams—whether they're quality-improvement teams, cross-functional, self-directed, or even remote and virtual teams. Recognizing teams can feel complicated, but in many ways it's just an extension of what we know about recognizing individuals—with some adaptations.

WHAT WE CAN LEARN FROM INDIVIDUAL RECOGNITION

Recognition works with individuals when it is immediate, sincere, specific, and based on performance. It works best when it is personal and comes from an employee's imme-

NO-COST IDEA

Sharing a High Note

Norman Groh, a customer service manager of Xerox Corporation in Irving, Texas, ends management staff meetings on a high note by asking that all managers share one thing they have done to thank their employees since they last met. Besides generating a surge of energy and an exchange of practical ideas, he also captures those thanks and places them in the employee newsletter for broader visibility.

diate manager or from other highly regarded people in the workplace.

The same principles hold true for teams. Some of the best forms of team recognition are personal, whether it's a manager thanking his group members for their involvement, suggestions, and initiative, or sending a letter to all team members thanking them for their contributions. A manager can also take personal interest in a special project team's work by attending its first meeting. Managers can conduct informal retreats for team members during which they can set goals, stimulate communication, or focus on problems. They might order in special food as a way to celebrate a team's progress, thus expressing appreciation and encouraging the team's continued energy. And at the end of the project, managers can send the team on an outing.

A manager at the Gap, based in San Francisco, California, wanted to thank everyone for working madly to meet a big deadline. She handed out gift certificates from a spa. Says Carol Whittaker, another Gap manager, "It was a much appreciated treat to help employees calm down and relax after a tough time."

Simple ideas can go a long way toward developing team spirit and positive group morale. Creating symbols of a team's work or effort (T-shirts or coffee cups with a special motto or project logo), or including photos of work teams in different company publications—as is commonly done at Advanced Micro Devices in Sunnyvale, California—can help reinforce effective behavior.

Another idea is to create a lasting memento of a significant group accomplishment. For example, executives at JASCO Tools in Rochester, New York, made a formal presentation to employees who helped produce the components that won a quality award. They put the award on permanent display on the shop floor.

Ideas such as these are limited only by the creativity of the people in an organization. Gestures of recognition do not have to be elaborate. To ensure that recognition is carried out personally and in a timely fashion, think small. Simple ideas are easier to implement, they are no less appreciated than complex ideas, and they work.

Recognition can take the form of simply empowering employees: involve the team in the goal-setting, brainstorming, or problem-solving process; place a priority on open communication by encouraging and making time for questions; or grant the group sufficient authority to achieve their objectives.

What drives team members to take on responsibility at GDX Automotive's new plant in Shelbyville, Indiana, is having the autonomy to determine exactly how to do their jobs. According to Gary J. Goberville, vice president of human resources, teams have the authority to pick a coworker as their team leader. He explains, "If you want a motivated workforce taking on the responsibility for good-quality products delivered on time, you have to give them the fullest authority to work out the best way to do it."

All eighty employees at Techmetals, a small metal-plating company in Dayton, Ohio, are involved in plant layout, scheduling, and delivery. And self-directed teams at Motorola's cellular equipment manufacturing plant in Arlington Heights, Illinois, not only decide on their own training programs and schedule their own work, but are also involved in the hiring and firing of coworkers.

WHAT MAKES RECOGNIZING TEAMS DIFFERENT?

The task of recognizing teams differs in many respects from individual recognition, and this presents a dilemma. In recognizing a team en masse, a manager runs the risk of alienating the team members who contributed most to the team's work, while reinforcing the slack behavior of team members who contributed little or nothing to the team's efforts.

"Jelly bean motivation"—giving equal recognition for unequal performance—is detrimental to the sustained performance of the group. Your best performers will feel unappreciated and either quit the group (or the entire organization) or cut back their efforts—reducing their productivity to match the team's norm.

It is a rare occasion in which all members of a team contribute equally to the group's work—each participant brings a different degree of skill, knowledge, experience, and enthusiasm to the work at hand. One way to resolve this conflict is to make sure the team leader knows how to recognize individual members of the group when their performance warrants it, and does so. Then, as the group develops into a team, each member can assume this leadership role of recognizing others (among other roles) as warranted.

By the time the group becomes a high-performing team, all members should be skilled at recognizing and praising one another, and your job will be that much easier.

Another solution is to find ways to recognize both individual and team contributions simultaneously. When a project is finished, the team can be publicly praised as a group for its work, and additional individual praise can be given to top performers.

You can create a team challenge or contest in which a team competes against its own goals or against another group. When the team is successful, let its members decide how to celebrate: bowling, playing laser tag, visiting a state fair, or having a "popcorn lunch" (going to a lunchtime movie), a pizza party, potluck dinner, or catered lunch.

Of course, although money is not necessarily a strong motivator by itself, it can be used effectively as a facet of team recognition. In the team program at Cal Snap and Tab, in the City of Industry, California, everyone can win, but one team wins big. "We're using a combination spoilage/attendance program," says marketing manager Richard S. Calhoun. "We put $40,000 into a special fund, and every time a mistake was made we deducted its costs from the $40,000. We ended up giving out about $7,000." The next year the employees were divided into four teams, with a prize kitty of $1\frac{1}{4}$ percent of shipments. One fourth of a percent was credited to each team, and spoilage by any team member was deducted from it. At the end of the program, each team got to keep its $\frac{1}{4}$ percent kitty, and the team with the lowest spoilage also got the leftover one fourth.

At Boston's Beth Israel Deaconess Medical Center, the PREPARE/21 program has increased employee involvement, teamwork, and creativity. Under PREPARE/21—which stands for Participation, Responsibility, Education, Productivity, Accountability, Recognition, and Excellence for the 21st Century—employees are encouraged to organize teams to study ways to cut costs and improve the organization. However, Beth Israel Deaconess goes a step further by allowing employees to share in the monetary savings that accrue as a result of team suggestions. In the first year of the program, participating employees split $1 million—half of the $2 million that Beth Israel Deaconess saved as a result of employee suggestions.

PLANNING TEAM RECOGNITION

Because there are more factors to consider, planning team recognition can be a little more involved than planning individual recognition. The key is simply to get started; don't make team recognition more complicated than it needs to be. It's for this reason we suggest you use the same simple "Who, What, Where, When, and How" planning format we suggested for individual recognition when planning team recognition.

Who should be recognized? Involve the individuals you are trying to motivate. Discuss the topic of recognition with the team and ask, "Does anyone think we need to do more recognition in our

"You can hire people to work for you, but you must win their hearts to have them work with you."

—**Anthony Jay,**
management theorist

10 WAYS TO PRAISE AND RECOGNIZE TEAMS

1	Have a manager pop in at a special project team's first meeting to express appreciation for the members' involvement.
2	Open the floor for team members to praise anyone at the beginning or end of a meeting.
3	When a group member presents an idea or suggestion, encourage other team members to thank the person for his or her contribution.
4	Create symbols of a team's work, such as T-shirts or coffee cups with a team or company motto or logo printed on them.
5	Hold a "praise barrage," where team members write down and share things they like about another member of the team.
6	Assign one member of the team the job of creating and presenting an award for another member of the team.
7	Alternate the responsibility for team recognition among different team members each week or at each meeting.
8	Host a refreshments gathering, a potluck, or a special breakfast or lunch to celebrate interim or final results.
9	Ask an upper manager to attend a "bragging session" with the team, during which the group shares its achievements, and team members are thanked for their specific contributions.
10	Write letters to every team member at the conclusion of a project thanking them for their contribution, and include a copy in their personnel file.

NO-COST IDEA

Popcorn Lunch

Jennifer Wallick, a computer software manager working for Four Pi Systems, a subsidiary of Hewlett-Packard in San Diego, California, would reward her work group after finishing a demanding project by taking them to see a movie over lunch hour. As she explains, "It meant a slightly longer lunch hour, but it was a great break and a lot of fun!"

See page 259
for the "Team Recognition Planning Worksheet."

team?" We have never heard of any employee saying, "I get too much recognition where I work." Focus the discussion on ongoing recognition efforts, not just on a onetime celebration or activity. Take the initial interest you receive in having more recognition and ask, "Who is willing to help get a recognition program or activities going?" Volunteers who see a need and have an interest in the topic drive some of the best recognition programs and activities.

What should be recognized? Team recognition should reward desired behavior done either by the whole team or by outstanding individuals within it. Activities can range from thanking individuals who completed team assignments to celebrating an important team milestone or achievement.

Where should the recognition be done? Recognition can be done wherever members of the team interact: at team meetings, between meetings, or in planned, off-site celebrations for team accomplishments. Teams can also be recognized for their achievements within larger groups, such as at an organization-wide awards banquet or at an annual "all-hands" employee meeting.

When should the recognition be done? As with individual recognition, team recognition should follow soon after the desired behavior or performance. Recognition can be done instantly, as in the case of a helpful suggestion made within a team meeting, or it can be planned to coincide with the completion of a significant contribution by the entire team.

How should the recognition be done? Ideally, team recognition should match group values. Ask team members to give you feedback on the effectiveness of your personal style of praising. Your openness in seeking their feedback will make it easier for them to try new behaviors as well. Here are a few other examples for you to try: Start your staff meetings by reading a letter of thanks or praise from a customer, or set aside some time at the end of your meetings to ask if anyone has any praise to share. Create a "Successful Projects" scrapbook, with photos of different teams and their accomplishments, or a "Team Spirit" wall for photos of past and present teams in the organization and what each has achieved or is trying to accomplish.

DEVELOPING A LOW-COST TEAM RECOGNITION PROGRAM

What if you feel you can't afford to set up a team recognition program? Fortunately, the best forms of team recognition cost little or no money. For example, the Ken Blanchard Companies in San Diego, California, created an Eagle Award to recognize team members "caught delivering exceptional customer service." Any employee can nominate any other employee for the award. Typical examples of recognized behavior include staying late to ship materials, helping a customer locate a lost order, resolving a billing problem, or rearranging schedules to deliver a last-minute customer request.

The employee's name is submitted with a brief description of the activity that is considered worthy of recognition. A committee reviews the recommendations, primarily to screen out actions considered a normal part of someone's job. The Eagle Committee then surprises the winners with a visit, and takes a picture of the person holding an Eagle Award. The photo is displayed on a lobby bulletin board along with a brief description of the recipient's special efforts. The winner gets to keep the trophy on his or her desk until it is needed for a new recipient—typically a week or so. At the end of the year, an "Eagle of the Year" winner is selected from a list of multiple award winners. That person is presented with an engraved clock at the company's annual celebration program.

Let's look at other guidelines for creating an effective, low-cost group recognition program.

Focus on areas that have the most impact. You'll make the most progress if you focus on only a few goals at a time. Select one or two objectives that would make the biggest difference in your group's success. At Blanchard, management focuses on improving customer service, which would create a significant positive impact on sales and generate repeat business for the company.

Involve your target employee group. After helping the team establish goals, have the team develop the criteria and mechanics for the recognition program. By involving the group, team members will feel a sense of ownership and be vested in the program's

DEALING WITH SHIFTS

Q I own a reprographics company with twenty employees who work very hard and are dedicated. Most of the functions are performed by several people at a time. I stress teamwork more than anything else. I have several ways to reward teams, but due to having three shifts, I can't present awards in front of everyone, which I know you strongly recommend.

—**Susan Holland,**
Mirror Image, Inc.,
Houston, TX

A Public recognition is generally powerful, but is by no means the only way to recognize your team. Turn the problem over to your shift employees and see what they would value most, and how they'd like to have everyone know about their accomplishments. Maybe photos of the high performers receiving their awards can be posted on a bulletin board, or a project scrapbook can be made. Do whatever seems to raise the most enthusiasm with the employees you are trying to motivate.

Improved Appearance

Shannon Kearns, RN, in quality management at Jackson Health System in Miami, Florida, writes, "We wanted to improve the appearance of our security guards so we started giving those who were dressed appropriately in full uniform their choice of work schedule as an incentive. We were surprised to find that peer pressure is making the biggest difference. At the beginning of each shift, the shift commander has everyone who is in their correct uniform stand up, and the staff call each other on any slipups."

success. Remember, the best management is what you do *with* people, not what you do *to* them. Make employees partners in their own success. At Blanchard, the group of employees that was pulled together to create the program to improve customer service came up with the specific criteria of the Eagle Award.

Announce the program with fanfare. A recognition program should be fun and exciting, starting with how the program is announced. If you are going to use merchandise incentives, show pictures or have samples of the goods available for members of your team to look at and touch. The Eagle Award program was announced and explained at a group meeting, and nomination forms (and refreshments) were distributed to all who attended.

Publicly track progress. If you don't measure it, you can't manage it! If you do measure it—and do so publicly—you will increase the chances that members of your team will pay attention to the behavior you want. In addition to being featured on the highly visible bulletin board of Eagle Award recipients, all Eagle Award honorees are listed in the company newsletter, along with a description of how they had demonstrated exceptional customer service.

Have lots of winners. Since some of the best forms of recognition—personal, written, or public praise—are free, why not do as much of it as possible? The Eagle Award had no top limit: Any number of people could be honored, and, subsequently, additional "traveling trophies" were added to the mix so that recipients could keep them on their desks for a longer period of time.

Allow flexibility of rewards. What motivates one person may not motivate another, so allow individuals some flexibility in their choice of rewards whenever possible. You could allow them to choose their recognition activities, assignments, or merchandise. All Eagle Award recipients, for example, were given a choice of a car wash coupon, a restaurant discount coupon, or a zoo pass.

Renew the program as needed. Even the best recognition program eventually runs its course, often within just a few months.

Build on the success of the program, learn from your mistakes, and try something new to keep things fresh. Although it was implemented inexpensively, the Eagle Award was highly successful and customer service became one of the group's top attributes. After some 60 percent of employees had received the award, the criteria of the program were modified to include measures of *internal* service so that even more employees could participate.

Link informal and formal rewards. Get the best of both informal and formal rewards by combining their use. For example, recipients of an informal recognition program that encourages employees to use "praising forms" can be tracked and given a formal award that permanently signifies the event. A team merged informal and formal award programs when it revised the Eagle Award program, presenting recipients with stickers each time they received the award. Employees placed the stickers on a card that, when completely filled, could be redeemed for a wall plaque (a formal award), which would be presented at a company meeting with much fanfare. At the end of the year, all recipients of a wall plaque were invited with their spouse or significant other to have dinner with the president and founder of the company.

Find ways to perpetuate new behaviors. To sustain new levels of performance, organizational systems—hiring, orienting, communication, training, career development, merit pay, and promotion

SILLY SOUNDING

Q A lot of recognition ideas seem silly to my staff of younger employees at the store. How should I deal with that?

—**Katherine,**
online conference participant

A Although it's true that no single idea will appeal to everyone, it is also true that everyone wants to feel valued, and you need only discover what does it for them. Ask them what they'd prefer to do and try to use their ideas. It might be increased flexibility, or autonomy, or an invitation to join a professional association or to go on a team outing. There's no limit to the possibilities! Also, remember not to let a few cynics undermine what the others in your store would appreciate.

TEAM RECOGNITION TIPS

- Acknowledge a good comment, contribution, action item, or follow-through.

- Recognize small in-process accomplishments that contribute to an end result.

- Reward punctuality and the honoring of commitments.

- Make a special effort to encourage and thank shy employees for their contributions.

- Praise someone for bringing up a not-so-popular opinion or idea.

- Recognize and praise positive group dynamics, such as not interrupting one another.

practices—may need to be tweaked to reinforce the desired behavior. The Eagle Award became a starting point for making customer service a core value for the entire organization and an established part of the company's culture—far beyond its humble beginnings in the sales department.

MANAGING REMOTE AND VIRTUAL TEAMS

According to a U.S. Labor Department report, about one in ten employees has an alternative work arrangement. Managing employees who are not physically located near you is a particular challenge. Managers must be more systematic and proactive in looking for opportunities to recognize their employees when those instances are less obvious.

Tom Coffey, a manager at Oscar Mayer in Madison, Wisconsin, is in charge of five different geographical sites in North America, each of which has a technical expert who works on team development for site-specific managers. Coffey's challenge is that he wants his employees to spend more time helping one another, even though they work in different locations. With some thought, and application of the ideas that follow, he was successful in achieving this goal, and helped his dispersed employees bond together.

BUILD A FOUNDATION OF TRUST

The starting point in almost any strong working relationship—virtual or not—is trust. Without daily face-to-face contact between manager and employee, trust is more vulnerable to breakdown. Virtual and remote employees, in particular, must know that their managers trust them to carry out everyday work functions, to do their basic job with little or no supervision, and to perform to the established standards.

MAKE TIME FOR PEOPLE

Despite the advances in virtual offices and remote locations, there's no substitute for "face time" when it comes to building trusting relationships. Managing is a people job, so, naturally, you need to make time for people.

If your employees are in the office infrequently, meeting with them when they *are* around has to be a higher priority. This could mean establishing a set time each week for meeting with virtual employees, meeting during "core hours" when everyone is present, or coordinating schedules so that you are in the office at the same time as your employees. One executive we know schedules office hours at his company's plants so that anyone can sign up for a meeting. Employees sign up using a deli-style "Now serving #47" electronic billboard on the plant floor.

How time together is spent makes a difference as well. Talk about issues of real importance to employees. Ben Edwards, CEO of the stock brokerage A. G. Edwards and Sons in St. Louis, Missouri, conducts a nationwide audio conference call with *all* employees on the last Friday of each month. The meetings begin with a brief state-of-the-company talk; then Edwards opens the phone lines for a real-time question-and-answer session.

MAINTAINING A SENSE OF TEAMWORK

When employees are not in the same place, organizations must still create and sustain a strong sense of camaraderie, commitment, and collaboration. Managers can take a proactive role in fostering a sense of teamwork by establishing regular times for telephone calls, e-mails, teleconferences, videoconferences, and computer chats. Electronic message boards can be used for on-going communication about progress in critical aspects of the team's work. Communicating in these ways gives virtual employees the opportunity to exchange ideas with team members, talk about the problems they may be having, discuss ways to improve, evaluate the team's progress, share ideas, get feedback, brainstorm, and discuss strategies. Everyone needs a forum in which to share problems and acknowledge successes.

This last point is critical. For team recognition to be effective, you must acknowledge success. If you don't focus on positive results along the way, you won't continue getting them.

On page 102 are some ideas for recognizing teams even if they do not physically meet together.

REMOTE WORKERS

Q I work for a privately held software company based in Chicago with about three hundred employees. We have a severe case of bad attitude, lack of motivation, and extremely high turnover. The majority of our workforce is made up of consultants who work remotely and are on the road with clients about 75 percent of the time. The remote workforce cannot participate in our headquarters' motivational events, such as going to baseball games, happy hours, and lunch-and-learns. We've tried gift certificates to Borders or for American Express purchases, but we just don't have a way to set up a program. Do you have any suggestions?

—**Laura Jones,**
Cyborg,
Chicago, IL

A **You need to do at least as much for your employees in the field as you do for the headquarters staff. Don't let distance be an excuse for inadequate recognition. Consider an enhanced use of e-mail and voice-mail praise, as well as recognition activities and programs just for field staff.**

RECOGNITION SHINES IN THE CITY OF SEATTLE

The City of Seattle has dedicated itself to rewarding and recognizing the efforts of the people who help to make the city a great place to live and work. It begins with a commitment to excellence, and it is put into action through the support of management and the participation of employees from all levels and departments within the organization.

A city of Seattle's prominence doesn't just happen. It takes the dedicated and concerted effort of the public, the city's corporate citizens, and its elected officials and government. Indeed, as in most American cities, local government employees touch almost everyone at one time or another— whether they're in parking enforcement, fire and police, utilities such as water and power, street repair, parks and recreation, or any number of other programs. With this in mind, Seattle created an employee recognition strategy to recognize and celebrate employees as the city government's greatest resource.

Seattle Works!, the heart of the city's recognition plan, is a citywide program that encourages employees to nominate coworkers in any one of seven different categories for recognition— Outstanding Public Service, Inspiration, Community Ambassadorship, Innovation, Employee Involvement, Environmentalism, and Heroism— with the winners being honored at a traditional annual awards presentation.

Nominations, submitted on preprinted forms or via the city's intranet, are reviewed by a committee of nine employees representing eight different city departments. However, while the primary duty of the committee is to select the best candidates in each category, it also has the responsibility of making sure that every department and each of the city's ten thousand employees is identified and has a chance to be recognized. Says Theresa Chambers, program manager of Seattle Works!, "We make sure that recognition is spread around so that employees from departments who weren't recognized last year maybe have a better chance this year. We also look at the different job categories because we're trying to make sure that field employees, front-line employees, and teams get the recognition they deserve."

Winners in each of the seven award categories receive a cash award ($500 for individuals, up to $2,000 for teams) or two days of paid vacation, an award, and recognition at the annual awards ceremony. The city's budget for Seattle Works! is in the approximate range of $14,000 to $16,000, with more than half of the funds going to the individuals and teams selected for the annual awards.

Most of the city's thirty departments and offices have their own formal recognition

programs, in addition to the citywide program and more than half have annual or quarterly recognition programs that include formal ceremonies. Cash awards in these programs range from under $100 to more than $2,500 for each individual or work team. Outstanding employees are also eligible for paid leave or "off" shifts.

Formal programs are the tip of the recognition iceberg. Many of the city's departments give informal types of recognition, such as celebrations with light refreshments at the end of long-term projects, and plaques and mementos to recognize jobs well done. The city's Executive Services Department supports these efforts with a variety of materials and programs. For example, through its REV (Recognizing Employee Value) program, the department has prepared employee recognition toolkits, which are given out at employee recognition workshops, new-supervisor orientations, and new-employee orientations. The toolkits contain low- and no-cost ideas for recognizing employees, such as giving out a Seattle Works! thank-you note, creating an on-line "kudos" bulletin board, creating a "hall of fame" with photos of outstanding employees or teams and notes about recent successes, holding a staff appreciation day, and much more. Included in the toolkit is a mug that says, "We make Seattle work!," Kudos candy bars, and Seattle Works! buttons and stickers.

The department also uses recognition "road shows" to get employees out in the field "REVed" up. In this popular program, a department

A department employee dresses up as a "recognition sprite," and showers the recipient with "recognition dust."

employee dresses up as a "recognition sprite," and showers the recipient with "recognition dust." The celebration includes an impromptu party with cookies and soft drinks. At the end, the recipient is presented with a recognition toolkit with tools and ideas for recognizing others.

The Seattle Public Utilities, Drainage, and Wastewater Division has a program that's called "Thanks a million, here's a 20," which provides on-the-spot recognition in the form of a twenty-dollar bill for a job well done.

City Light has a newsletter with a column called "Pause for Applause," where employees are invited to submit thank-yous to coworkers via the newsletter. The Seattle Center purchased books of coupons from Starbucks to be passed out to deserving employees. One department has an award for "grace under fire," another has a mentor award, and yet another has a facilitator award. Each of these programs has helped to create an organizational environment that supports and fosters employee recognition.

Says Theresa Chambers, "I've seen it make a difference in our organization. Our efforts have created a ripple effect in the city, where employees are thinking about recognition as part of their jobs now. It's about introducing the concept that recognition is an action, not an item. One of the things I try to emphasize is that there are lots of ways to recognize an employee. The most important thing is that you do it. It's that immediate, spontaneous recognition that really makes a difference and makes people want to come to work every day and be motivated to do a good job." Kudos!

TIPS FOR RECOGNIZING VIRTUAL TEAMS

- Ask team members to keep the leader and other team members apprised of their accomplishments, since they can't be as readily seen.

- Keep a recognition log of remote team members so that they don't fall through the cracks—a particularly important consideration for "mixed" teams (ones with both traditional and virtual team members).

- Make sure that virtual team members are appropriately included in recognition programs (by passing around recognition item catalogs, and by ensuring that remote employees are kept fully in the loop).

- Provide some "treat" for virtual team members who can't join in face-to-face socials and celebrations.

- Keep a list of recognition items that are appropriate for a mobile workforce and can be mailed to the employee, such as greeting cards, gift vouchers, and discount coupons.

- Become more aware of the recognition capabilities of e-mail, such as sending virtual flowers or greeting cards, "mood stamps," or paste-on icons.

- Don't forget: Virtual teams require *more* recognition, not less.

- Involve executives in recognition activities by way of conference calls.

- Team identification items (such as logoed coffee mugs, T-shirts, jackets, and so forth) are more important for virtual team members because they help remind them of their team membership.

- Make a point of employing a variety of team recognition tactics when rewarding members of virtual teams.

INCREASE COMMUNICATION AS YOU INCREASE DISTANCE

A basic principle of electronics is that the farther the source, the weaker and more distorted the signal and the greater the need for amplification. Likewise, the greater the distance from one's manager, the greater the effort both parties have to make to keep in touch. This can be done through periodic updates or through more frequent scheduled meetings and visits.

CEO Hal Rosenbluth of Rosenbluth International, a chain of travel agencies headquartered in Philadelphia, Pennsylvania, is accessible to all his employees through a toll-free voice-mail box. Employees are encouraged to call in with suggestions, problems, or praise, and about seven employees do so every day. Fargo

Electronics, based in Eden Prairie, Minnesota, established a daily electronic newsletter to share sales and production figures, customer feedback, and profit-sharing updates with employees.

Also, be sure to go out of your way to provide the same types of communication, recognition, and rewards to virtual workers that you give to those employees who are located closer to you so that all employees can participate. Ask for questions in advance from all locations, and make sure that each employee in every location gets answers to the questions that arose.

USE TECHNOLOGY—DON'T LET IT USE YOU

Too often, managers use technology like voice-mail or e-mail as another method of assigning work to their employees. It may seem faster and more efficient to do so, but employees are denied a chance to ask questions about projects that are assigned when work is delegated in a one-way communication.

However, it is possible to use technology to *reinforce* the human element at work, and to increase the opportunity to provide meaningful recognition and appreciation to others. This won't happen by accident; it takes forethought and planning.

As more employees work off-site on either a full- or part-time basis, managers will need to incorporate the Internet and other technology into their reward and recognition programs.

Voice mail. How did we ever survive before voice mail? A recent study by Pitney Bowes shows that e-mail is now the primary message tool used by U.S. knowledge workers.[1] Still, most of us have had times when we felt we were slaves to the voice message system. Consider leaving positive voice-mail messages simply to thank others for something they have done well. Don't offer any criticism or assign additional work—simply leave a message of thanks. A great voice mail (from a client or customer, for example) can even be transcribed and distributed.

E-mail. When you praise someone via e-mail, copy that person's manager and others on their team. When you get a positive e-mail

---

NO-COST IDEA

24

Keep in Touch

Chris Higgins, senior vice president of project planning at Bank of America's Services Division in Virginia, says, "It is so important to give everyone credit. I always try to find out who is going above and beyond the call of duty. My team is usually spread out over the country, so I wander over the telephone wires or pop in unexpectedly on conference calls. I go out of my way to thank people for their work. It is not a huge effort; it mainly takes discipline, but has tremendous payoff."

NO-COST IDEA

25

Applauding Separately as One

Barbara Green, office manager for Buckingham, Doolittle and Burroughs in Canton, Ohio, shares this idea: "We sent an e-mail to our entire staff asking everyone to applaud the great efforts of our office services department at 4 P.M. at their desks. Members of that department work throughout the building and are rarely in one place at the same time, so this was a terrific way for each staff member to receive the benefit of the praising at exactly the same time and in the same way."

about someone's performance, pass it on to others or print it out and save the message to share in person, in an upcoming team meeting, or on a company bulletin board.

Cellular phones. Use the time away from your office to call and thank individuals you work with.

Pagers. Many pagers today allow you to leave a text message, which you can use to transmit a word of praise.

Screen savers. You can create a screen saver that reminds you to recognize people and their performance.

Virtual recognition. The Internet opens a wide range of opportunities for you to recognize others. You can send employees virtual flowers, greeting cards, or postcards, and use the Internet to order a book, gift, or other recognition item for deserving employees.

Company Intranet. Hughes Network Systems in San Diego, California, created what they call an "Applause" bulletin board on their company's intranet system that pops up when employees first log onto their computer. Anyone can post praise for anyone else in the organization, and most employees take a moment or two to read through the compliments. After a few days, the messages are deleted to make room for new praise. The company intranet is a fantastic place for sharing "best practices." One manager used to make over sixty visits a year to her company's various locations. "There were some fantastic ideas out there," she said, "and it was my job to share these stories and ideas within the company." Now she has created a special site on the company intranet for sharing "best practices." "We've saved thousands of dollars doing it this way," she reports, "and the managers love it!"

Certificate software. You can recognize people instantly and creatively by creating your own colorful recognition certificates. Several companies offer certificate-making software and hundreds of styles of papers, seals, presentation folders, embossers, and other items to make your certificates special.

TIPS FOR USING TECHNOLOGY TO RECOGNIZE OTHERS

- Use it, don't abuse it. Use technology sparingly and make it meaningful. Overusing technology to deliver praise and recognition will undermine the value of your messages and simply make it part of a person's daily noise.

- Get personal. When leaving praise messages, be as specific and sincere as you can. Avoid the simple "Good job." Embellish the praise with specifics.

- Do it now! The beauty of technology is that it allows you to act immediately. Recognition is most effective right after the desired behavior or performance. Seize the moment and follow through.

- Say it right the first time. We all love to dash off e-mails, but take a second look and make sure it says what you want it to say. We know of one employee who was more than a little perplexed when she received an e-mail that said, "Great job on that affair."

- Follow up face-to-face. To anchor recognition in memory, follow up any technological communication with face-to-face interaction. "Face time" is still the best way to convey heartfelt appreciation and sincerity.

PERSONALIZING VIRTUAL RECOGNITION

When creating a virtual recognition program, managers should start by identifying the baseline motivational needs of their employees. A corner office or a prime parking space does not have much significance in a virtual environment, but what about a faster or better computer, or a state-of-the-art cell phone or text pager? "Technology—actually the access to technology—can be a very effective reward in itself," says Roz Cleveland of Continental Mills in Seattle, Washington. "I've found that giving employees new computers is a very motivational act. Getting employees involved in the selection process and seeking their input is also an important motivator, as well as allowing them to actually purchase the items."

Alternatively, virtual team members might value learning and development opportunities, a bright houseplant to liven up their home office, or a reward that is linked to a hobby or personal interest, such as a gift certificate to a local restaurant or passes to a local movie theater.

"The ratio of 'We's' to 'I's' is the best indicator of the development of a team."

—**Lewis D. Eigen,**
executive vice president,
University Research

To find out what virtual employees want, ask them. Conduct a survey asking them what kinds of recognition would be meaning-ful to them, have a discussion with your work group about the topic, or ask your virtual employees to select recognition and cele-bration activities for the end of the project. Not only does this involve your employees in the process of planning their own recognition, but it also stimulates their desire to perform and gives them something concrete to look forward to when the project is successfully completed.

THE TAKE-AWAY

- Team recognition works when it is immediate, sincere, specific, based on performance, and comes from the employees' immediate manager or from other highly regarded people in the workplace.

- "Jelly Bean motivation"—giving equal recognition to all members of a team for unequal performance—is detrimental to the sustained performance of the team and should be avoided.

- Where possible, provide both individual and team recognition simultaneously.

- When planning team recognition, con-sider "Who, what, where, when, and how?"

- Managers can promote a sense of team-work among virtual team members by establishing regular times for group com-munication, including conference calls, videoconferences, and computer chats.

- Virtual rewards must be tailored to vir-tual employees who do not have or require the standard job accoutrements of their nonvirtual counterparts, such as corner offices and parking spaces.

CHAPTER 8

Getting Started with Organizational Recognition

"Men and women want to do a good job, a creative job, and if they are provided the proper environment, they will do so."

—Bill Hewlett, cofounder, Hewlett-Packard

Organizational recognition refers to formal recognition programs and activities that are organized and executed on a company-, facility-, or group-wide basis. This commonality aside, organizational recognition can be very diverse—as simple as recognizing an outstanding employee in the company newsletter or as complex as a multitiered process culminating in an award presentation by the company's CEO at a glitzy annual ceremony.

However it's practiced, an effective organizational recognition program can help create a culture of recognition that will perpetuate itself—outlasting individual employees and managers who may come and go.

ORGANIZATIONAL VERSUS INDIVIDUAL AND TEAM RECOGNITION

Organizational recognition is, to some extent, an elaboration of the same recognition principles we advocate for individual and team recognition, but it is also a unique phenomenon whose special challenges can neither be minimized nor ignored.

By their very nature, the effects of individual and team recognition tend to be limited, with rarely more than a momentary impact on the organization as a whole. Without an organizational system to maintain it, such recognition tends to be short-lived.

In contrast, organizational recognition, with its larger scope and greater complexity, has the capacity for much broader ongoing impact.

As the scope of a recognition program increases, the entire culture of the organization can be deeply and permanently affected. Of course, there's a price: with greater scope comes greater complexity, and greater potential for problems.

Organizational recognition requires a very different perspective— a broader, more strategic, more systemic perspective—than individual and team recognition. One has to be much more aware of the consequences of putting an organizational recognition program into place, and one has to keep a close eye on its impact on employees. The negative repercussions can be as extensive as the benefits, and it's essential to deal with unforeseen consequences as soon as they are discovered. But discovery itself can be difficult. In individual recognition, feedback is usually fairly immediate. With organizational recognition programs, if you make a mistake you might not even know about the problem until the consequences have become quite severe.

For example, one company implemented a nonmonetary employee recognition program at the same time that large executive bonuses were being announced. Employees were not happy with the financial disparity of the two programs, and understandably viewed the recognition program with cynicism and contempt. Unfortunately, because senior managers did not receive feedback for some time, they continued the programs—adding insult to injury in the eyes of most employees. This well-intentioned organizational recognition program became a major demotivator.

Whereas an individual award is typically viewed as the isolated action of an individual supervisor or peer, and a team award is

> *"Never believe that a few caring people can't change the world. For indeed, that's all we ever have."*
>
> **—Margaret Mead,**
> anthropologist and author

viewed as the isolated act of a manager or team leader, an organizational award is viewed as "policy" by members of the organization.

THE IMPACT OF ORGANIZATIONAL RECOGNITION

Organizational recognition is distinguished from individual and team recognition by three characteristics: extensiveness, visibility, and formality.

Extensiveness.　Organizational recognition affects a large number of people—directly or indirectly.

Visibility.　The message sent by the recognition is seen or heard throughout the organization. Once an award becomes highly visible, it tends to be viewed differently. This can be a blessing, because the award can operate as a positive model for a wide range of the company's employees; however, it can also be a curse, because any mistakes are greatly magnified. A supervisor who personally recognizes an undeserving employee will do minimal damage, but one who publicly recognizes a clearly undeserving employee as part of an organization-wide program can create enormous and long-term damage to the employees' morale and trust, to his own credibility, and to that of the organization.

Formality.　There is greater structure needed for organizational recognition; that often means less flexibility and more difficulty in initiating the program or changing it once it has begun. Structure is good because it can increase the consistency of recognition and the likelihood that recognition will occur at all. The downside is that design flaws are hard to fix. Organizational recognition that is changed or discontinued can become a major demotivator to employees as they become increasingly cynical about the sincerity of management.

WHY BOTHER WITH ORGANIZATIONAL RECOGNITION?

There are three primary reasons why organizations find it desirable to establish organization-wide recognition programs:

PRESCRIPTION: START SMALL

Q I recently took on the role of admitting supervisor at our hospital. The department has an 80 percent turnover rate! The problem had been diagnosed as stemming from stressful conditions and low pay, but I interviewed employees who say they get no recognition for their hard work and feel extremely unappreciated. I want to start a recognition program right away, but I feel a bit overwhelmed by the task, as senior management seems inaccessible and also afraid of change. Unfortunately, we've also just merged with another hospital, so everyone is nervous about job security and learning new systems. Do you have any suggestions?

—**Khristina Newell,**
Baptist/St. Vincent's Health System,
Jacksonville, FL

A **Yes! Start small and build. Small changes can have an immediate impact and give you momentum, and if you wait until you create the perfect program, it may never get implemented, and, as you've indicated, it's often the simple considerations—consistently applied—that help the organization become a more positive place to work.**

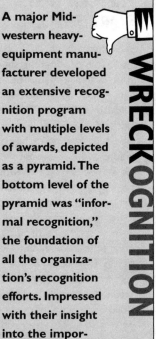

A major Midwestern heavy-equipment manufacturer developed an extensive recognition program with multiple levels of awards, depicted as a pyramid. The bottom level of the pyramid was "informal recognition," the foundation of all the organization's recognition efforts. Impressed with their insight into the importance of informal recognition, one of the authors asked what they did to manage that activity. "Nothing," came the response, "we don't know how."

Improving performance: To reinforce specific behaviors and results that management would like to see more frequently.

Modeling core values: To highlight company core values established by management.

Showing appreciation: To demonstrate management's gratitude for extra effort.

As you will see, these purposes are not mutually exclusive. Recognition can include a combination of any or all of these purposes. Now, let's look briefly at each.

IMPROVING PERFORMANCE

Every organization has plenty of opportunities for improvement in sales, quality control, productivity, safety, customer service, knowledge sharing, and employee retention, among other areas. Although recognition is frequently an important component in organizational performance-improvement programs, we believe that recognition should be an integral component of *every* organizational improvement effort.

Recognition geared at improving performance is goal-oriented. It is targeted at helping an organization achieve a desired outcome.

People do things largely for the positive consequences they anticipate. Recognition in the form of contingent promises (incentives) and after-the-fact recognition (positive reinforcers) for desired behaviors or results are a major motivator of both individual and group performance of all types. Our books *1001 Ways to Reward Employees* and *SuperMotivation* both showcase numerous examples of organizational recognition provided to reward employees for meeting or exceeding performance expectations.

In one of the most frequently cited applications of recognition to work performance, Emery Air Freight used positive reinforcement to dramatically reduce its costs of doing business. Emery was losing a lot of money because its containers were not fully loaded when shipped. Workers knew that they were supposed to ship fully loaded containers; the performance expectations had been communicated to them many times. However, while workers reported that their containers were fully loaded 90 percent of the time, a review

found that the containers were actually fully loaded only 45 percent of the time. Through the use of positive reinforcement and feedback on performance (primarily just praise from management!), the percentage of full containers increased from 45 percent to 95 percent, saving the company millions of dollars.

In a similar type of praise-for-performance program, Weyerhauser Paper Company increased the productivity of logging trucks from 60 percent to more than 90 percent.

MODELING CORE VALUES

Sometimes the purpose of organizational recognition is to provide models for other employees to emulate desirable core values of the organization. For example, when Lou Gerstner, former CEO of IBM Corporation, was at American Express, he instituted a highly visible Great Performers program, in which posters of outstanding employees were displayed along with posters of more famous American heroes. Modeling was also used successfully by Gerstner to promote IBM's services organization, IBM Global Services. In newspaper and magazine ads, high-achieving employees were pictured along with a description of their accomplishments. Although aimed primarily at customers, this advertising campaign also served the purpose of establishing role models within the organization.

Other examples are plentiful. Each month, Nordstrom department stores select a Customer Service All-Star who has demonstrated the greatest commitment to customer service. From looking at those selected for recognition, it is very clear to employees exactly what types of behaviors Nordstrom's management considers most important. Stew Leonard, of Stew Leonard's Dairy in Connecticut, is well known for his front-line leadership in his grocery stores, providing very visible employee-of-the-month recognition for those who modeled his "customer first" philosophy. Jack Stack, Chairman of Springfield Remanufacturing Corporation, has put so much emphasis on recognizing cost-consciousness among employees that they are reputed to know how much the toilet paper costs!

All managers and supervisors at Busch Gardens in Tampa, Florida, are provided with tokens they can use as an on-the-spot award to give to an employee they see doing something that reinforces the organization's core values (such as helping a coworker

NO-COST IDEA 26

Put it in Print

Bob Gaundi, human resources manager of Mental Health Systems in San Diego, California, says: "Certainly recognition from supervisors is important, but praise from one's fellow employees is of the highest order, so we allow employees to recognize coworkers through a monthly newsletter. We ask employees to write a short statement about laudable efforts they witness from fellow employees. All of the examples are published in a special section of our monthly newsletter. Employees always turn to this section first!"

Secret Agent Dad

Michael L. Horvath, director of environmental projects for FirstEnergy Corporation, reports, "An engineer on my staff spent an extended amount of time on the road doing environmental evaluations of companies. I sent a letter to his three school-age children explaining why their dad was gone so much lately and that he was doing special 'secret agent' work that was very important for our company. His wife called the next day to say how excited their kids were that Dad was a 'secret agent'!"

without waiting to be asked, being pleasant to a customer on a hot day, or cleaning up after himself). The recipient can redeem the token for an additional $10 in his or her next paycheck, though most employees keep the tokens as keepsakes.

Jack Welch, former CEO of General Electric, installed a special telephone in his office for the company's purchasing agents to call him directly and report price concessions they had won from vendors so he could thank them immediately. No matter what he was doing, he would answer the special telephone, and then scribble a personal congratulatory note to the agent. This became part of GE folklore and a powerful example for other executives to follow.

SHOWING APPRECIATION

Organizational recognition shouldn't be restricted to rewarding people for quantifiable results. Appreciation is recognition that is not based on the achievement of predetermined goals. For example, at Dow Corning Company, management hosts ice cream socials where managers make and serve sundaes as a way to thank employees for special accomplishments. Another company sends flowers to the spouses of employees who have to travel extensively. Many organizations host surprise celebrations when the staff meets major milestones, such as working to satisfy a difficult customer or hurrying to meet a rush-order deadline. Signs of appreciation can range from one company's distribution of chocolate cookies to another's celebration of a new product by having an ice cream party in its plant, complete with a mariachi band.

Thank-you events such as these energize employees to work hard and improve their performance. They also become ingrained in the company's culture and part of the organizational folklore.

STARTING POINTS FOR ORGANIZATIONAL RECOGNITION

There are three "starting points" for organizational recognition, representing where the impetus for a program originates:

At the top. Senior executives decide that the organization needs a recognition program.

In the middle. A unit within the organization designs a recognition program that is expanded to the rest of the organization.

At the bottom. An existing individual or team recognition initiative is expanded throughout the organization. (This is much less common than the other two models.)

Let's look briefly at each of these.

STARTING AT THE TOP

A significant amount of organizational recognition begins with a CEO's or other top executive's inspiration or with a program started by top management. This was the genesis of the program initiated by Martin Edelston, CEO of Boardroom, in Greenwich, Connecticut. After reading about suggestion programs used in Japan, he decided that his company needed a similar program. His initial effort to recognize employee suggestions for improvement had such a positive impact on employee creativity and morale that it was expanded into I-Power, a proprietary program Boardroom marketed to other companies. I-Power uses a lot of social recognition and some very small monetary rewards to generate a large number of employee suggestions. As one employee said, "I never realized that making suggestions could be so much fun."

Management can assign someone the responsibility to see that recognition programs are initiated. That person can help lead a recognition task force, for example, to develop some simple, low-cost programs, celebrations tied to organizational milestones, and an information feedback system to keep management informed of various individual, departmental, and organizational successes as they occur.

STARTING IN THE MIDDLE

In this scenario, a group within the organization, such as the manufacturing division, might sponsor a program to recognize the most productive, the most quality-conscious, or the safest employees. It is not unusual for the success of such program to get the attention of other divisions and of senior management. Nothing succeeds like success! These successful functional programs are often then expanded or replicated throughout the organization.

NO-COST IDEA
28

Joint Appreciation

Colin Service Systems in White Plains, New York, has recognized employees with awards such as Most Helpful Employee and Nicest Employee. Coworkers vote for the employees they think should win the titles, and executives make the presentations.

See page 289 for Boardroom's "Best Practice."

RECOGNITION THE CHEVRON WAY

The Chevron Corporation, based in San Francisco, California, is an international company that produces energy and chemical products and employs about 35,000 people worldwide. Chevron has developed a set of corporate recognition and award guidelines that each division uses to design its own specific recognition program. In addition, Chevron has developed a company-wide recognition program called the Chairman's Award, which rewards individuals or teams who've achieved extraordinary accomplishments, such as developing new technology, improving their work progress, or devising innovative solutions to complex problems.

Recognizing and rewarding employees is a very important part of Chevron's philosophies. Chevron Way is a set of principles, values, and strategies that was published to help guide employees in their day-to-day work. With this publication, each division has an increased interest in specifically linking recognition to business goals and compensation policies, and in coming up with new ways to make recognition meaningful.

For a long time, oil companies made a lot of money, but when the market crashed and they weren't doing well, Chevron's management started focusing on results. At first they concentrated on quality because they knew they needed to have good processes to achieve good results. This improved results for a number of years, but after a while the organization reached a threshold—they weren't getting any more efficient or getting better results. So the executive team looked at best practices of other companies, like Eastman Chemical. Eastman had been incorporating recognition programs in its organization and was seeing great business success.

Chevron tries to encourage and reinforce people's potential by rewarding the behaviors that they want to see again. The most effective reinforcement comes from what they call the "natural" or the "self sources." If you turn the key in your car and the car starts, that's a natural reinforcement that you are going to do again and again. But these natural reinforcers are not always present for the behaviors that organizations need to be successful. Even incentive programs can be limiting. Incentive programs are different from behavioral reward programs in that incentives are set up in advance so that employees get the incentive after attaining their goal. Take the example of an employee who is paid to talk to a certain number of customers per day. What tends to happen is that the employee will work only to the set goal. Instead, Chevron tries not to set limits—but rather to communicate to people where they fit, and encourage them to do what they can. And when they notice a behavior or a result that they want to see repeated, they recognize it and publicize it so that others will know. The real goal is to use recognition as a business tool—to reinforce and encourage behaviors that are good for the business.

All employees are eligible for the Chairman's Award. Last year they had an organization that saved the company millions of dollars—so they gave everyone in the organization the award because it was a team effort—everyone contributed and all were awarded equally.

In addition to the Chairman's Award, each division develops its own customized recognition programs. At the division level, recognition is highly valued and explicitly encouraged. Everyone is encouraged to integrate the principles and philosophies of the Chevron Way into their work. Chevron is in the process of training its managers on "reinforcement-based leadership." In this training program, managers learn about positive and negative reinforcers—when to use consequences to continue and extinguish behaviors. If a division needs explicit help in setting up their recognition program, they can always go to their group for help with designing and implementing the program. Once a division decides what it wants to do, they include the cost of the recognition program in their budget.

The real goal is to use recognition as a business tool—to reinforce and encourage behaviors that are good for the business.

The corporate recognition team helps the division work through the process step by step. First they are helped to clarify what their business goals are. Next they are assisted with determining what behaviors are needed to meet those goals. Finally, everyone works through the nuts and bolts of the best ways to reward and recognize the desired behaviors. The divisions are encouraged to have equitable programs with very clear, specific criteria for recognition, "volunteering to support a project"—not vague criteria like "above and beyond the call of duty."

All of Chevron's divisions have some type of recognition program, but they are all very different, and are customized to reward the specific behaviors that make a particular division successful. To list a few:

- In one division, everyone has signature authority to purchase recognition and reward items without formal approval, so individuals in the organization are empowered to reward as they see fit.

- In another organization, committees evaluate nominations for awards using scoring charts.

- Some groups use only instant awards—say, coupons worth $20 that anyone can give to anyone. One of Chevron's refineries uses decals that can be placed on an employee's hard hat.

Sometimes organizational recognition programs start with a spontaneous gesture on the part of an individual manager. Earlier we talked about Hewlett-Packard's Golden Banana award, which started as a spontaneous act on the part of a single manager and ultimately became a formal organizational award for top performers that expanded over time.

STARTING AT THE BOTTOM

Spontaneous tokens of recognition can evolve into major organizational awards. There are numerous examples in which team or department recognition gains visibility and sponsorship and is expanded to other areas in the organization. Janitors on a shift at the Renaissance Worlington Hotel in Ft. Worth, Texas, were asked to create an award for their job function and came up with the Golden Broom award, which evolved into a highly successful organization-wide program.

THE FOUR PHASES OF ORGANIZATIONAL RECOGNITION

There are four key phases of putting organizational recognition programs into practice. We will discuss each of the major phases in greater detail, but let's end this chapter with a quick overview of a process that, if properly executed, will have a profound and positive effect on an organization's employees and bottom line.

DESIGN

Everyone can appreciate the importance of the blueprint for a house. No matter how outstanding the subsequent construction work might be, the house will be no more functional than the blueprint design permitted. Likewise, no matter how well constructed a bridge or a road, if there are serious design flaws neither the bridge nor the road will be safe. While individual or team recognition is much more dependent on the initiative and skill of the recognition givers, organizational recognition is more dependent

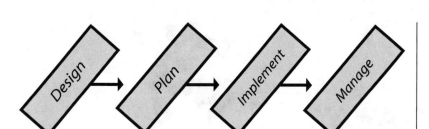

on the design of the program, which will be discussed in greater depth in Chapter 9.

PLAN

Once an organizational recognition program has been designed, an implementation plan needs to be developed. In Chapter 10, we present and discuss the six elements of organizational recognition planning that will help you leverage your program design into a successfully implemented program. A detailed example of an organizational recognition plan is also provided.

IMPLEMENT

Once an organizational recognition program is designed and the program plan developed, implementation can begin. As the saying goes, once you plan your work, you need to work your plan. That is implementation: working your plan. (See Chapter 11.)

MANAGE

An organizational recognition program must be managed after it is implemented. Implementation will launch organizational recognition programs, but that initial launch is not enough to sustain it for very long. As you will see in Chapter 12, organizational recognition programs have "life cycles." Understanding and managing these cycles are critical to the ultimate success of your organizational recognition programs. The one constant in organizations, as in life, is change. Organizational recognition must be kept dynamic and actively managed to address all the shifting circumstances, conditions, and problems that might occur.

SUPPORT STAFF

Q I am having the most difficult time putting together a recognition program for our support staff. The group consists of five administrative and ten sales support employees. They have various roles and responsibilities and are rarely recognized for all that they do. This creates an issue, as the support people ask why the sales staff is so successful. Any suggestions?

—**Lucy Morris,**
Nabisco, Tempe, AZ

A **Bring your support employees together and ask them how they'd like to be recognized. You can prime the discussion with some examples from other companies or even create a list of activities or items that the group members can rank or vote on. Also consider discussing recognition opportunities with the sales staff and what they might like to do to reward exceptional support. The sales reps who receive assistance and support are in a key position to notice and act on good work—and many of them will enjoy being able to "pay back" the dedication they receive from support staff.**

THE TAKE-AWAY

- Effective organizational recognition programs can help create a culture of recognition that will perpetuate itself—outlasting individual employees and managers who may come and go.

- Remember, organizational recognition requires a different perspective than individual and team recognition—a perspective that is broader, more strategic, and more systemic.

- There are three starting points for an organizational recognition initiative: at the top, in the middle, or at the bottom.

- There are four stages of effective organizational recognition: (1) design, (2) plan, (3) implement, and (4) manage.

PART III
ORGANIZATIONAL RECOGNITION

CHAPTER 9

Designing Successful Organizational Recognition

"The best recognition programs inspire people to new levels of performance, helping ordinary people attain extraordinary results in the workplace."

—Bob Nelson

O rganizational recognition programs, if properly designed, have the potential to radically and positively alter the entire climate and bottom-line outcomes of an organization. But organizational recognition should never be viewed as a substitute for individual or team recognition, nor is it just an enhanced version of individual and team recognition; it requires an entirely different approach.

ARTICULATING THE PROGRAM GOAL

T he starting point of organizational goal setting is always dissatisfaction with one or more aspects of the current state of the organization. However, these concerns are often rather vague at first. For instance:

R·E·S·P·E·C·T

Q We're in the process of identifying two or three organizational goals that everyone can rally around. One area that we believe has strategic importance and focuses on employees is respect. The notion of setting an organizational goal around respect for self, colleagues, students, and vendors has potential, but we don't know how to go about measuring changes.

—**Nancy Griffis,**
Regents College
Albany, NY

A **Respect and trust may not be as abstract as you think. If you look at** *Fortune*'s **100 Best Companies to Work for in America, there is a strong undercurrent of individual trust and respect in each one. The Gallup Organization, for example, has recently reported a strong correla-tion between employee satisfaction and positive responses to the state-ment "My manager has praised or recognized me within the past seven days." Try to determine what behavior members of your organization con-sider indicators of respect in their environment, and then periodically check for improvement.**

❶ The motivational climate is negative.

❷ Employee turnover is high.

❸ Training attendance is low.

❹ There are too many product defects.

❺ The accident rate is high.

❻ There are frequent customer service problems.

❼ Not enough recognition is being given.

In order to create meaningful goals, it is important to define problems by expressing them in measurable terms. Let's see what the above list might look like when the dissatisfaction is quantified:

❶ Motivational climate score is 4 out of 10 on the recent Motivational Climate Assessment survey.

❷ Turnover rate is 8 percent.

❸ Twenty-three percent of employees who sign up for training classes don't attend.

❹ Defect rate is 5 percent.

❺ There have been twelve lost-time accidents at the plant this year.

❻ Customer complaints have increased 18 percent compared with the previous year.

❼ Only 12 percent of employees report in the annual Employee Attitude Survey that they have received recognition from their supervisors.

Once you have defined your *current* situation precisely, you can precisely define your *desired* situation. The examples above can now be converted into goals:

SAMPLE GOALS

1 Motivational climate score of 8 out of 10 on the next "Motivational Climate Assessment" survey

2 Turnover rate of only 5 percent

3 At least 90 percent attendance

4 Defect rate of less than 1 percent

5 No more than five lost-time accidents at the plant next year

6 Zero customer complaints

7 At least 80 percent reporting that they have received recognition from their supervisors during the current performance period

> "You've got to give people a voice in their jobs. You've got to give them a piece of the action and a chance to excel. You've got to give them the freedom to have fun."
>
> —**Mike Cudahy**,
> president,
> Marquette Electronics

HOW TO WRITE GOALS

All performance starts with clear goals, and the key to effective goal writing—articulating goals that clearly communicate their intent—is specificity. "Fuzzy" goal writing produces employees who don't know what to do or what they are supposed to achieve.

The format of an effective goal is quite easy to master.

- First, make sure your goal is an *action statement.*
  (What will be achieved?)

- Make sure that the *target group* is understood.
  (Who will achieve it?)

- Specify the *time frame.*
  (When will it be achieved or for what period?)

Now let's rewrite each of these, using proper goal-writing syntax:

- Attain a motivational climate score of 8 out of 10 on the Motivational Climate Assessment survey to be administered to all company employees on May 1.

- Achieve a company-wide turnover rate of no more than 5 percent for the next fiscal year.

- Increase the retention rate of hourly employees who sign up for training classes to 90 percent or higher during the third quarter.

- Reduce the monthly average defect rate in production to less than 1 percent by July 31.

See page 260
for "Organizational
Recognition Goal-Setting
Worksheet."

- Reduce the number of lost-time accidents at the plant to five or fewer during the next fiscal year.

- Reduce customer complaints to zero for the month of April.

- Achieve a rate of at least 80 percent of employees reporting on the next Employee Attitude Survey that they have received recognition from their supervisor at least once during the current performance period.

ORGANIZATIONAL RECOGNITION DESIGN FACTORS

Once you've clearly expressed the goals of your organizational recognition program, it's time to design the program itself. As you consider the following list of factors, keep two things in mind: (1) not every factor must be in place every time for your organizational recognition program to be effective, although the more in place the better, and (2) factors will be effective only if properly applied.

FOCUS

Make what you want to recognize the bull's-eye of your recognition target. Aim for it, hit it, and you will get what you want—from more productive employees to a bigger bottom line.

In organizational recognition, focus is particularly vital because there may be many other factors competing for attention. It is vital that only the critical behavior is recognized—not one that merely mimics the desired result. For example, if your focus is on increased workplace safety, make sure you quantify the result you want in terms of decreasing actual accidents, or you might end up simply recognizing a decrease in *reported* accidents!

CLARITY

The conditions that will trigger recognition, and the criteria that will be used to make recognition decisions, must be clear to everyone in the organization before "the game" begins. In addition,

the person receiving the recognition must be able to easily see how it is directly related to his or her actions, and realize that they deserve it. This is called "creating a clear line of sight."

We have found it quite startling how frequently employees are confused about why they or others are being recognized, and how seldom they feel that the recognition in their organizations is given objectively. In fact, it is not at all uncommon for senior executives to choose their favorites for recognition, vetoing candidates who might actually be more deserving. But when employees come to believe (either correctly or incorrectly) that politics is influencing the program, it's the kiss of death for organizational recognition.

When objective criteria are not stated up front, it's easy for people to manipulate or misinterpret the system. Ill-defined recognition standards are an invitation for mistakes, misunderstandings, and confusion. It is vital to use unambiguous recognition criteria that are widely publicized and out in the open. How will you know when recognition is working in your organization? You'll know it when you hear employees say, "We certainly deserved that!"

READINESS

The organization must be ready to implement an organizational recognition program, and many companies fail to appreciate the challenge. Make no mistake about it: implementing an effective program isn't easy. It is usually better to begin implementing an organizational recognition program when there are no other major programs competing with it, and when the organizational recognition program is linked to some other key initiative, such as quality or safety improvement.

This is exactly what the Tennant Company, a manufacturing company based in Minneapolis, Minnesota, did. At Tennant, quality improvement had already emerged as the company's signature initiative, so it was natural for them to link their recognition initiative to the quality initiative. When Tennant's management team began developing a recognition program, there was no question that one of the company's chief goals would be to recognize superior contributors to quality improvement.

NO-COST IDEA

29

Take Suggestions Seriously

American Strap in Diamond City, Alaska, found that employees became more and more creative after their suggestion system was launched. Just finding that their suggestions were being taken seriously changed the workers' attitudes, and they became even more willing to find ways to help the company improve.

➡ **See page 302**
for the Tennant Company in "Recognition Best Practices."

> *"Every great and commanding movement in the annals of the world is the triumph of enthusiasm. Nothing great was ever achieved without it."*
>
> **—Ralph Waldo Emerson,**
> American writer

SPONSORSHIP

Any organizational recognition program, or, for that matter, any organizational change initiative, begins with strong sponsorship. Sponsorship means that an executive, or somebody with similar stature and credibility within the organization, actively supports and champions the program. Often management support comes from too low a level and is passive in nature.

Sponsorship means more than having an executive say, "Go ahead!" It means that an executive owns the program, and is willing to do whatever it takes to make it successful. Sponsorship is crucial not only to getting an organizational recognition program successfully launched, but also to making it sustainable long enough to have the desired impact. Bottom line: Upper management must sponsor the recognition initiative from the tip-off to the closing buzzer.

ALIGNMENT

It is crucial that recognition activities being done at different levels and in different areas of the organization are consistent and coordinated. If the most critical behaviors and results are not recognized uniformly at all levels (individual, team, and organizational), the organization goals will be compromised.

Some organizations allow supervisors and managers to recognize any positive behavior they approve of. At first glance, this might appear to be a good thing, but it can actually cause confusion and wasted resources. Recognition should be a strategic leadership tool, and it is most effective when used in a coordinated manner. To achieve maximum organizational impact, supervisors and managers should be directed to recognize the positive behaviors that are aligned with the desired goals, not just any positive behaviors that they might observe. Alignment is instrumental to achieving maximum return on recognition investment.

ENHANCEMENT

It is more efficient to enhance a successful existing recognition program than to start from scratch. There's no need to reinvent the wheel. Organizations that are serious about recognition ought to benchmark recognition that has already been successful within

See pages 287–310
for "Recognition
Best Practices."

the organization—and in other organizations. Maintaining a database of organizational recognition "best practices" increases the cost-effectiveness of subsequent programs. In addition, there are a tremendous number of excellent ideas for recognition programs that you can use as the platform for your own. Books like *1001 Ways to Reward Employees* and *SuperMotivation* can give you a strong foundation upon which to customize your program.

INTEGRATION

Recognition is often a part of a larger initiative. Consider, say, a safety-improvement program that is already charged with identifying the most critical safe and unsafe behaviors, setting up behavioral checklists, selecting safety observers, establishing the measurement system that will be used to monitor the behaviors, and figuring out the feedback process through which the measurements will be communicated to participants. The point? Recognition cannot merely be an add-on component, but must be integrated into an organization's other relevant programs. In fact, it's our firm belief that recognition should be an integral part of *all* organizational improvement programs.

SYSTEMIZATION

When you are giving one-on-one or small-group recognition, a "system" isn't usually necessary, but as the size and complexity of recognition increase, so does the need for a more reliable, orderly way of doing things.

Most individual and team recognition is fairly spontaneous, but no matter now successful individual and team recognition may have been, companies need to *formalize* the program when embarking on organizational recognition. The introduction of a systematized approach to recognition reduces the dependency on individual initiative and provides the consistency and quality control so crucial for highly visible recognition. While this does not mean the end of fun and spontaneous recognition, it acknowledges that such gestures must occur within a formal structure. In order to be successful, organizational recognition must occur when it is officially earned, not when a manager happens to see a positive

THE IMPORTANCE OF BEING SINCERE

Q I'd like to come up with some creative ways to inspire motivation, but my bosses point out Alfie Kohn's book *Why Rewards Don't Work.* Kohn claims that incentives result in only temporary compliance and can destroy morale. What do you say about this?

—**V. Pike,**
online forum participant

A Kohn's book is provocative, but I believe it's misguided. Not all rewards are short-term and manipulative. If you start with what is important to the individual you want to motivate, and help that person move toward his or her goals, you are also reinforcing his or her intrinsic long-term needs. Ethical managers with sincere intent need not be manipulative. [See the article "Punished by Rewards: A Rebuttal," on pages 375–77.]

CLEANING UP AT TENNANT COMPANY

Founded in 1870 by George Henry Tennant, the Tennant Company started out as a sawmill, quickly grew into the largest manufacturer of wood flooring in the upper Midwest, and is now one of the premier manufacturers of industrial and commercial floor maintenance equipment.

Tennant's mission is simple: to become the world's preeminent provider of nonresidential floor maintenance equipment, floor coatings, and related products. In 1999, sales were $429.4 million, up more than 10 percent from the year before, and net income had grown 22 percent, to $19 million. Tennant's strong and steady growth is no accident; the company built its business on a firm foundation of quality, support for employee initiative, and an innovative multidimensional program of employee rewards and recognition.

Back in the 1970s, many American companies struggled with a problem that threatened to put many of them out of business: poor quality. Somewhere along the way, American business had forgotten the importance of building a quality product. It took the phenomenal success of quality-obsessed Japanese manufacturers during the '70s and '80s to wake up their American counterparts.

For the Tennant Company, this realization didn't come about easily. By 1979, Tennant's Japanese customers were loudly complaining about numerous hydraulic oil leaks in Tennant's best machines. In reality, almost all of the company's machines were defective, but the Japanese, who expected a higher level of quality, were the only customers to complain.

The Tennant Company rose to the occasion, sparking a quality revolution that has been accompanied by an equally significant revolution in employee initiative and recognition. As a result, whenever a problem is found today, or whenever a system or process can be improved, employees are encouraged to take action.

WELDING A NEW SOLUTION

To take one notable example, a group of Tennant welders asked the company's engineers to design a new system for streamlining a welding operation that would allow the unit to reduce its stockpile of finished units and thereby reduce the cost of moving and storing them. But the projected cost of $100,000 was unacceptable to company management. The engineers returned with a new solution that would cost $25,000. Again, management rejected the expense. Rather than give up, however, the welders took action to solve the problem themselves. The solution? An overhead monorail system built of scrap iron purchased from a local junkyard. The cost? Less than $2,000 in materials, and about two days of effort from the welders. The system worked like a charm—saving the company more than $29,000 in its first year alone—and the welders became heroes for refusing to give up and for taking the initiative to create an affordable solution. Tennant's support of an environment that encourages employee initiative has unleashed a flood of great ideas from workers, particularly from the line employees who actually produce the company's products.

When Roger Hale initiated the quality revolution at Tennant in 1979, he invited quality guru Phil Crosby to play a major role in setting the company's course. Tennant adopted Crosby's groundbreaking book, *Quality Is Free,* including Crosby's fourteen-step quality-improvement process, as its guide. Step twelve—employee recognition—received special attention.

DIFFERENT STROKES

Tennant began by defining an objective: to recognize superior quality performers. The company then discovered a very important principle: different people respond to different kinds of rewards and recognition. So Tennant developed a three-dimensional program of rewards and recognition.

First is Tennant's formal awards program, in which honored employees (up to 2 percent of the workforce each year) receive a ten-carat gold and diamond ring, and a plaque at an annual banquet. The program has three rules governing the selection of award recipients:

1. The program is peer-driven. An employee can nominate anyone of higher, equal, or lesser rank (but not anyone to whom he or she reports directly).

2. Recognition recipients are selected by a committee of employees of different rank and from different departments of the company.

3. The company's established criteria for selecting recognition recipients are printed on the nomination forms.

Second, an additional "formal" award grew out of employee feedback for more frequent recognition. Winners of the Koala T. Bear (a take-off on the word *quality*) are surprised with a visit from a costumed bear and recognition committee. Each recipient receives a stuffed Koala T. Bear and a certificate of his or her achievements. There's a less stringent nomination process, and the awards are presented monthly.

The third dimension of the program is Tennant's informal rewards program, designed to recognize people who meet specific goals. It is flexible and can be tailored to meet the needs and preferences of individuals and groups. Informal recognition is immediate recognition given by managers and supervisors to those employes doing something right.

While any one of these dimensions might be considered a complete program in many organizations, Tennant firmly believes that all three have to be present to maximize employee motivation and performance. According to former human resources manager Rita Maehling, "We believe that the three-dimensional approach is key. Like a three-legged stool, each dimension plays a critical role. Take away one leg of the stool, and it falls."

Winners of the Koala T. Bear (a take-off on the word quality*) are surprised with a visit from a costumed bear and recognition committee.*

NO-COST IDEA

30

Customer Connection

Pioneer/Eclipse, a manufacturer in Sparta, North Carolina, takes customers to meet line workers who have had a part in developing their products. Workers love to tell customers about their ideas and listen to what's needed.

behavior or feels like playing Santa Claus by handing out a few gift certificates.

RESPONSIBILITY

Although having a sponsor confers legitimacy to a program, someone else needs to be responsible for running the program on a day-to-day basis. Program leadership or coordination responsibility should be vested in an overall organizational recognition coordinator (discussed in more detail in Chapter 11), or with separate coordinators for each program.

INVOLVEMENT

Too often, recognition programs are perceived as impersonal. Too many recognition programs appear to be run by distant management or a Wizard of Oz–like administrative system operating behind a curtain.

In our discussions of individual and team recognition, we emphasized the importance of gaining employee ownership through involvement, which can significantly increase the impact of organizational recognition, along with employee morale.

Involvement can take different forms, including involving employees in designing the program, selecting recognition recipients, administering the program, or physically giving recognition. We like the idea of an "advisory team" that includes representatives from key organizational units. Although not essential, an advisory team provides a vehicle for communicating wishes to the organization and can engender greater rank-and-file involvement.

ACCESSIBILITY

Recognition should be accessible to everyone, and everyone should have a chance to be a winner. This doesn't mean that recognition should be easy to attain or given to everyone, but it *does* mean that everyone should be a candidate for recognition and feel that it is an attainable goal.

We are often amazed by the number of recognition programs that pit one employee against another in a competition that only one can win. The ubiquitous employee-of-the-month programs are

a perfect example of this kind of recognition. In our experience, employee-of-the-month programs are not nearly as effective as their proponents believe; they limit the amount of recognition in the organization and make recognition stale, irrelevant, and unexciting to recipients.

The purpose of recognition should be to give as much of it as possible, as long as it is deserved. If your program is properly focused, the more recognition you give, the more highly motivated your employees will be to achieve the organization's goals. We strongly recommend that recognition be triggered by behaviors and outcomes that are within *every* employee's reach; otherwise the recognition will become demotivating, rather than motivating, to most employees.

VISIBILITY

One of the virtues of organizational recognition is its ability to influence a large number of people, directly and indirectly. In fact, the cost-effectiveness of organizational recognition programs depends on the ability to leverage the investment beyond what one could reach with individual or team recognition. As management consultants Garry Jacobs and Robert Macfarlane write, "If a list on the wall or a letter home can have that much impact, how much more powerful can be awards and celebration programs that generate widespread social recognition for high achievement?"[1]

One of the best ways to make organizational values visible is to make heroes out of employees who best personify them, as one company did by renting a football stadium and having its "sales heroes" enter the stadium to the rousing cheers of friends, family, and other employees. At Apple Computer, T-shirts were created with a core company value printed on each shirt, and they were given to employees who personified each core value.

Visibility is a primary benefit, but it can also be a major challenge. Remember, while individual or team recognition is typically viewed as an isolated action taken by peers or supervisors, employees tend to see organizational recognition as company policy.

KNOWLEDGE SHARING

Organizational recognition magnifies the potential for learning, as individuals share the techniques they have found most

➡ See page 269 for "Recognition Training Designs."

HOW MANY RECIPIENTS?

Q Is it more important to hold out for an exceptional nomination or to reward a lot of people?

—**Susan Schmitz,**
Department of Transportation

A **It's more important to establish clear, objective criteria and then to recognize all those who meet them. When there are not many nominations, it may be a red flag that the program is dead or dying. Recognition should be a celebration of success and excellence. If people are just going through the motions, focus on re-energizing or replacing the program. Do not recognize average or marginal nominations or you will lose credibility and the program will be viewed as a joke. People you honor should be role models for others in the organization.**

effective. Chances are, individual managers, supervisors, and teams have learned quite a lot from their recognition experiences. Identifying and sharing "best practices" and lessons learned is one of the hallmarks of a learning organization, and it has the added benefit of publicizing successful recognition programs.

Unfortunately, by failing to share knowledge, far too many organizations keep reinventing the wheel. Organizations need to have a method for capturing "best practices" and lessons learned. This can be done manually or by using a computer database. Collaborative software, such as Lotus Notes, is particularly valuable for encouraging on-line exchanges and capturing knowledge so that it can be shared.

SIGNIFICANCE

The meaningfulness of recognition to the employee is more important than its monetary value. Strive for high *recognition value,* not necessarily high *financial value.*

The key to the success of any reward or recognition is the message it sends. Recognition should say to the employee, "What you have done is important and we want to celebrate it with you." The most significant forms of recognition are typically those that are symbolic of the accomplishment. There is no magic formula, but the more creative and personalized it is, the better. We like what Bell Atlantic did: they named cellular telephone tower sites after top-performing employees.

PRESENTATION

The *way* recognition is delivered to recipients can be as important as the recognition itself. Too often, though, organizational recognition is treated as "factory recognition" or "mass-produced recognition." No matter how large the program, there should never be a feeling of impersonality.

To be effective in today's knowledge-based and highly technical workplace, it's more important than ever that recognition be "high-touch" as well as high-tech. That's why smart companies make the effort to recognize as personally as possible, rather than just have the recognition show up anonymously on the employee's desk or in his or her paycheck. Employees remember the presentation long after the prize is forgotten.

MEASUREMENT

The whole notion of measurement is often viewed negatively because it frequently implies negative consequences of evaluation and judging others. However, when used appropriately, measurement can motivate, and even excite—just as scorekeeping heightens fans' interest in a game. There are several reasons why measurement is important.

First, measurement makes things happen; what you measure is what you get. All of us tend to concentrate harder on things that measure our skills, whether it's an exam, a race, or an assessment of job productivity.

Second, without measurement we would have little way of knowing how well recognition is working. As the well-known saying goes, "Only those things that are measured can be managed." If the impact of recognition is not quantified, the organization's leadership may wrongly believe that recognition has no value to the organization, so when times get tough financially, recognition is often one of the first things to be cut back. And, when recognition is trimmed—or eliminated entirely—the resultant losses in employee morale and productivity can make a bad financial situation far worse. We take this up in further detail in Chapter 13.

MODIFIABILITY

Rarely do we get things perfect the first time, or even the second or third. In the real world, most improvements are repeated continuously until they become successes. Therefore, we recommend that you design your organizational recognition programs to be easily modified, or at least fine-tuned. This will allow you to make the changes or minor modifications that might turn a good program into a great one.

One of the best ways to do this is through piloting. Pilot projects allow you to try something out on a small scale and test alternative approaches in a low-risk situation, before rolling out the initiative across the entire organization.

WRECKOGNITION

Many organizations use competition—at the expense of collaboration—to energize employees, especially sales. One fast-food chain publicly ranked each of its fifty-two district managers every month, regardless of how long each person had been in the position, their previous experience, or the size of the district. Additional recognition, prizes, and trips were provided to the top 20 percent, whereas the bottom 20 percent were constantly in fear of losing their jobs. The situation became ugly, and led to unethical behavior, as district managers would fight to improve their position, often at the expense of their peers and public safety.

Take the Day Off

Jeff White, a Chick-Fil-A manager in the Renaissance Tower in Detroit, Michigan, rewards individual team members with a paid day off based on excellent performance. Other Chick-Fil-A managers will feature any student employee who makes the honor roll in a newspaper ad, and give them free restaurant coupons to share with their family and friends.

Don't try to accomplish too much too quickly. It is much better to focus the initial efforts on one part of the organization, concentrating the energy and resources you need to better overcome the inevitable organizational inertia.

It is obviously a good idea to pilot the program in an area where it is likely to succeed. Every organization has some areas that are more receptive to change than others—often reflecting the leadership within those areas. It's your job to figure out which those are, and to design your programs accordingly.

CLOSURE

Since recognition programs are frequently modified and sometimes terminated, it's important to know how to end a program without leaving employees feeling that you've taken something of value away from them. Too often, when a recognition program is discontinued the decision comes without warning and the demotivational effect on employees can nullify the program's gains. This problem can best be avoided if the effective dates of the program are communicated when the program is announced—we call this "time-bounding." You can always extend the length of the program, but you want to reserve the right to end the program if it has served its purpose or hasn't lived up to expectations from a business perspective. Putting a fixed time limit on recognition programs also forces you to continuously introduce new approaches, keeping your program fresh and your employees interested.

SUSTAINABILITY

Probably the greatest challenge of organizational recognition is sustaining it. Organizational recognition programs that are implemented and discontinued tend to lead to considerable employee cynicism about the programs, and to reinforce employees' perceptions that recognition is just another "program of the month," and not a genuine commitment. Employees get excited about recognition and then become disappointed as motivational programs come and go.

Without an overarching strategy for organizational recognition, no recognition effort can be sustained for long. As Dean has explained, "Management, especially upper management, is ultimately responsible for creating a working environment that is conducive to self-sustaining, organization-wide, high motivation."[2] The real power of organizational recognition to transform the motivational climate of organizations is rarely realized.

A CASE STUDY IN RECOGNITION PROGRAM DESIGN

Let's now look at a composite case that exemplifies the application of many good design factors. In the next chapter, we'll again use this case to illustrate successful planning in an organization recognition program.

A major department store chain had a customer loyalty problem. Senior management decided to define their goal for customer loyalty as a 20 percent increase in repeat sales by the end of the current fiscal year. To achieve this, they figured that they would have to reduce customer complaints by 50 percent and department manager attrition by 30 percent. They based these conclusions on research that revealed that unresolved customer complaints were the leading cause of the lack of repeat business. Further analysis indicated that most customer problems were never solved because sales associates reported only vague symptoms to management, instead of pinpointing specific customer concerns. The customer loyalty problem was further exacerbated by the instability caused by frequent turnover in department management. To their dismay, senior managers discovered that the same problems occurred over and over again in stores, and that most of these problems—if they had been identified, communicated, and acted upon by the department manager—could have been relatively easily, and permanently, resolved.

Once the effort had a clear focus, management could start designing a solution. The focus of the primary initiative was limited to modifying the behavior of sales associates, since department manager attrition was immediately remedied by bringing salaries and incentive compensation up to market standards.

Based on previous experiences with recognition, the senior leadership team was convinced that a well-designed organizational

THE MOTIVATION TAX

Q We will be rolling out a recognition system in the near future. Our accounting department just informed us that gifts valued over $25 are taxable. It seems that something so easy and beneficial has been turned into something difficult. What do other companies do to get around this issue?

—**Tiffany Keith,**
Dallas Semiconductor,
Dallas, TX

A **Some companies use play money that is given to someone and then turned into payroll and added to the paycheck, less taxes on anything over $25. Others pay for recognition activities from general funds. Of course, you can still do a lot with $25 per employee, you just have to be more creative!**

One of the authors once worked with a firm in Seattle, Washington, helping to evaluate their formal recognition programs. One of the firm's managers told him that only about *4 percent* of the organization's employees were eligible for any of the company's seven established recognition programs. Fortunately, the company had several informal recognition programs that worked well with a large percentage of its employees.

recognition program would solve the problem. There was complete commitment to solving this problem; the future of the department store chain depended on it. Sponsorship was at the CEO level. The

Building Customer Loyalty: The Plan

senior management team also had the support and resources of an external consultant who could help them build a robust program.

Once the effort was clearly focused and readiness assessed, the senior management team committed to a completely aligned organizational effort focused on the sales associates' difficulty in identifying and reporting behaviors. Everyone would be involved in the improvement effort, and every store would handle the situation in the same way. Some local customization would be permitted, but the overall program design was to be the same throughout the organization.

Senior management realized that the current challenge could not be solved through isolated activity. Managers were not going to correct this organization-wide problem by leaving things up to the individual senior executives to influence the store managers, or by relying on the initiative of the individual store. They realized that a systemized approach was essential for an effective and sustainable solution.

A multifaceted intervention was needed, composed of a number of integrated components: communication, tools, training, *and* recognition. The senior management team (with the assistance of the consultant) decided on the following integrated intervention:

- Communications that clearly, consistently, and appropriately conveyed the desired behaviors and results to sales associates and their managers, as well as the details of the improvement program

- Training to help sales associates recognize problems and use their new tools

- Measurement that identified when the right behaviors and results were occurring

- Recognition that would energize employees, reinforce the desired behaviors, and celebrate the achievement of results

The senior management team based their program on a model recognition program—which they identified in a benchmarking study, and which they felt matched their needs—and customized it to their specific situation. They decided to use a scorecard approach to recognition because they wanted to systematize the intervention and make it fun.

The recognition criteria were clearly defined and communicated: every time sales associates identified a customer problem and communicated it to the department manager, they would get their scorecard signed. When sales associates got five signatures, they would receive a $20 store gift certificate with the inscription "Thanks for helping us create loyal customers." When sales associates obtained twenty signatures, they would receive a "Loyalty Bear" teddy bear and they could choose a $50 dinner-for-two gift certificate from one of five local restaurants.

Department managers personally delivered all awards, and recipients evaluated their presentation efforts. For their part in the program, department managers would receive cash awards for solving the problems that were reported to them. A program coordinator was selected to handle the daily logistical aspects of the program.

Once senior management had communicated the program, distributed problem-recording tools, developed scorecards, and

NO-COST 32 IDEA

Say It with a Gorilla

Tandy Corporation in Ft. Worth, Texas, uses a three-and-a-half-foot stuffed gorilla to recognize initiative and innovation. The gorilla visits and stays with a person who had a useful idea until another idea comes along. The person who has the most ideas in a quarter receives another prize.

➡ **See page 369** for article, "Beware Tax Implications of Recognition Rewards."

See page 363 ◀

for article, "How to Design a High-Motivation Compensation System."

"You've got to give people a voice in their jobs. You've got to give them a piece of the action and a chance to excel. You've got to give them the freedom to have fun."

—**Mike Cudahy**,
president,
Marquette Electronics

trained employees and managers, the recognition program was launched. It didn't take long for the results to manifest themselves.

This program energized the sales associates like nothing ever had. Not only did customer loyalty increase dramatically within two months, but many other aspects of sales associate performance that weren't part of the program, like customer service behaviors, showed improvement. The increased pay, plus the cash awards for customer problem solving, reduced department manager attrition far below industry norms. The program goals were reached, and after three months, each store had a big celebration to mark the milestone. After the program ended, the benefits were sustained. Because the problem had been solved at its root cause, and because employees had learned a new set of behaviors, the customer loyalty benefits kept increasing.

This is a case of powerful intervention, well designed and imaginatively implemented. In it, you'll find that many of the organizational recognition program success factors were used, directly or indirectly.

THE TAKE-AWAY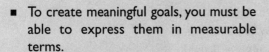

- To create meaningful goals, you must be able to express them in measurable terms.

- Effective goals have three essential parts: (1) an action statement, (2) an understandable target group, and (3) a definite time frame.

- There are many factors that will enhance the probability of success for your organizational recognition program, including: focus, clarity, sponsorship, alignment, integration, involvement, visibility, measurement, modifiability, and many more.

CHAPTER 10

Planning Successful Organizational Recognition

"Those who fail to plan, plan to fail."

—**George Hewell,** business writer

What's planning? Simple. Planning is an investment of time made in the present to improve performance in the future. Every hour spent in effective planning can save many hours—and much frustration—during execution. Although there are times when everyone is tempted to improvise (the urge to "wing it" is decidedly human), keep in mind the six P's of planning: Prior Planning Prevents Pitifully Poor Performance!

Planning is the way we transform intentions into reality. It's the bridge we build to cross the gap between our current state and our desired one. Planning is the

NO-COST IDEA

33

Shine a Light

At Sea World in San Diego, California, team leaders are given "spotlight cards" to hand to employees they catch in the act of doing something well. The team leaders write down what they saw and what they appreciated about it, and then have at least two other team leaders or supervisors sign each card before it is presented to the employee. A copy is also posted on the employee bulletin board.

next step—after articulating the goal and designing the program—in the process of realizing a successful recognition program.

Planning does not need to be a lengthy or tedious series of tasks. In fact, planning is essentially not a series of tasks at all; as Richard Sloma, a former corporate CEO and renowned expert on planning, puts it, "'Planning' is *not* a task or an event. Planning is first and foremost an attitude, a frame of mind. . . . [It means] cutting through all the B.S. and getting right to the heart of the matter."[1] Planning is actually *the thinking process* individuals and organizations use to prepare for more effective action. Written plans are the visible product of planning, but shouldn't be equated with it.

THE SIX ELEMENTS OF GOOD ORGANIZATIONAL RECOGNITION PROGRAM PLANNING

If planning is a "frame of mind," what are the considerations that should "frame" your thinking? We strongly feel that any effective organizational recognition program planning should consider the following six elements:

❶ **Action plan:** The heart of the plan—the steps needed to make your program design operational

❷ **Schedule:** The proposed time frame for implementing your plan of action

❸ **Program resource requirements:** The human and nonhuman resources required for successful program implementation

❹ **Budget:** The estimated cost of the program

❺ **Potential failure factors and preventive actions:** The factors that could, if not addressed, cause the program to fail or fall short of expectations, plus the preventive actions that should be taken to avoid or mitigate their possible impact

❻ **Measurement strategy:** The approach for determining how well the program is being implemented and how effective it was in meeting its goals

THE SIX PLANNING ELEMENTS IN PRACTICE

Let's return to the department store case study discussed at the end of the last chapter and see how management applied these six elements in their program to address their customer loyalty problem.

You might recall that management operationally defined its customer loyalty problem in terms of volume of repeat sales. The current level of repeat sales was $125,000,000. The desired level of repeat sales (the goal) was $175,000,000. The gap was $50,000,000, or 40 percent of the current level of repeat sales volume. It was determined that, in order to achieve the goal, customer complaints would have to be reduced by 60 percent and department manager attrition would have to be reduced by 30 percent.

ACTION PLAN

The best way to prepare an action plan is to identify the major categories of activities, and then identify the activities under each category.

Developing an action plan usually involves some degree of systematic brainstorming ("What do we need to do to make this program design implementable?"). It's also typically an iterative process—a process that normally involves going over the same material numerous times before the necessary activities can be identified.

It's also important to remember that action plans are rarely linear. Most action plans identify many activities that branch off from one another, resulting in some activities that must occur simultaneously. Here's a little diagram to help you visualize this:

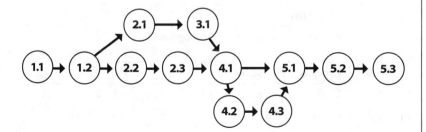

ROLL OUT THE RECOGNITION

Q What do you think about rolling out a formal recognition program in stages?

—**Carolyn Strumbly,**
Progressive Insurance,
Mayfield Village, OH

A I like it! It's much better to start small and build, based on your learning and experience, than to have the perfect program that you roll out five years from now—if then! And remember to use a mix of rewards—not just monetary ones.

LOW MORALE

Q I work for a developmental services agency that provides day and residential services for developmentally challenged people. We are looking for a way to reward staff who have been here for several years for doing a great job. They need to be pumped up to do what they do on a daily basis! Our agency is, of course, financially limited, and on the front lines of providing services to the public. Thanks for any help you can give.

—**Susan Bontaine,**
Ontario, Canada

A **Recognize performance when it happens, not after several years! It's easy to notice great performers in any work environment—more easily than steady, dependable workers. Yet recognizing the day-to-day, behind-the-scenes performers is important as well. Brainstorm some options with the group, and try the ideas that create the most energy. I'm convinced that the best things you can do are things that cost little or no money, but they need to be fun and fresh. Ask those individuals if there's anything they need to do their jobs better—then try to fulfill that need.**

Here's what the action plan for the department store chain looked like:

ACTION PLAN

Step #	Major Activity	Responsibility
1.0	**Executive Approvals and Budgeting**	
1.1	Present plan to executive committee	Design team
1.2	Make revisions (if necessary)	Design team
1.3	Finalize plan	Design team
1.4	Obtain budget approval	James Johnson
1.5	Obtain finance codes for requisitions	James Johnson
2.0	**Tool and Material Preparation**	
2.1	Schedule announcement events	Laurie Lewis
2.2	Design recognition items	Jill Macy
2.3	Order recognition items	John Jenkins
2.4	Prepare training plans	David Owens
2.5	Develop training	Training department
2.6	Design scorecards	Design team
2.7	Develop recognition presentation aids	Lisa Lambert
2.8	Develop problem-recording tools	David Owens
2.9	Prepare for kickoff meetings	Design team
2.10	Prepare kickoff meeting materials	David Owens
2.11	Prepare measurement tools	Bill Calvert
3.0	**Communications and Training**	
3.1	Run kickoff meetings	Senior management team
3.2	Train managers	David Owens
3.3	Train employees	David Owens
4.0	**Program Implementation**	
4.1	Implement scorecards and recognition	Senior management team
5.0	**Program Measurement**	
5.1	Collect interview/survey data	Bill Calvert
5.2	Monitor measurements	Bill Calvert
5.3	Take corrective action (if needed)	Bill Calvert

continued on next page ➤

Step #	Major Activity	Responsibility
6.0	**Program Modification** (based on program measurement feedback)	
6.1	Fine-tune program (as needed)	Design team
7.0	**Prepare for Program Success Celebration**	
7.1	Plan for celebration event	Jill Macy
7.2	Order items for celebration	John Jenkins
7.3	Implement celebration event	Senior management team
8.0	**Evaluation and Debriefing**	
8.1	Analyze measurement data	Bill Calvert
8.2	Debrief program participants	Bill Calvert
8.3	Document lessons learned and "best practices"	Bill Calvert
8.4	Input into database	Laurie Lewis
8.5	Close out program	Senior management team

Notice that the activity categories are identified by whole numbers (1.0, 2.0, 3.0, and so on) and that categories do not name responsible persons or teams because they are not activities. The activities are identified under the category headings, and are numbered sequentially (1.1, 1.2, 1.3, and so on). All activities must have a person responsible for the successful completion of that activity.

> *"Planning is damn scary if you do it right, because what you're really talking about is change. It's much easier to just say, 'Next year's going to be better' and leave it at that."*
>
> **—Graham Briggs,**
> vice president of finance,
> Charles River Data Systems

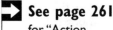 **See page 261**
for "Action Planning Worksheet."

There are two keys to effective action planning:

1 Will the identified activities result in a successful program?

2 Is there sufficient accountability to make sure that the activities are accomplished?

Once you are confident that the action plan is complete, the next step in the planning process is scheduling.

SCHEDULE

An action plan provides a basic outline of what needs to be done, but it doesn't usually explain *when*. This is the purpose of the

TRACKING CHANGE

Q Is it important to have a systematic data-collection process in place before implementing a rewards and recognition program?

—**Margaret Frederick,**
Florida Department of Education,
Tallahassee, FL

A If you want to demonstrate the improvements you've made—or plan to make—a process of measurement is essential. As a baseline, start with one type of performance your organization would like to see more of and set up a recognition activity around it. Report the best improvement (as determined by group vote) at each staff meeting. Then give an award of some kind, such as a pass-around trophy, an afternoon off, or a gift certificate. Expand from this simple approach.

See page 262 ◀
for "Schedule
Worksheet."

schedule, which provides another perspective on the program—especially in terms of time frame and dependencies.

Activities are rarely independent of each other. The most important scheduling consideration is when activities are going to be completed, since the start dates of some activities are often dependent on the completion dates of other activities. If a plan is to be successfully implemented, key milestones usually must be completed by a certain date, and there must be clear accountability for critical schedule dates.

The schedule should identify major milestones—not necessarily every task—and assign actual dates to them. Here is what a partial schedule for the department store's recognition program might look like:

SCHEDULE (PARTIAL)

Major Milestones	Critical Dates
Plan approved	February 20
Budget available	February 22
Tool and material preparation begins	February 23
Tool and material preparation review checkpoint	March 5
Tool and material preparation completed	March 20
Kickoff meetings begin	April 2
Kickoff meetings completed	April 5
Training begins	April 7
Training completed	April 14
Scorecards and recognition use begins	April 15
In-process measurement begins	April 15
Preparation for celebration begins	May 20
Preparation for celebration completed	June 5
Celebration event implemented	June 16
Program participant debrief begins	June 17
Lessons learned and "best practices" documented	June 22
Program knowledge entered into database	June 29

Notice that the milestones are specific dates. This provides the accountability that is so vital for successful accomplishment. Furthermore, if a key milestone is missed, other milestones—

	FEBRUARY	MARCH	APRIL	MAY	JUNE	JULY
Approvals obtained						
Budget available						
Tool and material preparation begins						
Tool and material review checkpoint						
Tools and materials completed						
Kickoff meetings begin						
Kickoff meetings completed						
Training begins						
Training completed						
Scorecards and recognition used						
Measurement						
Preparation for celebration begins						
Preparation for celebration completed						
Celebration event implemented						
Program particpant debrief begins						
Lessons learned and "best practices" documented						
Program knowledge entered into database						

which are dependent on that milestone date—might have to be changed.

Above is a supplemental diagram that illustrates not the schedule's actual deadlines, but the flow of activities over time.

PROGRAM RESOURCE REQUIREMENTS

The step element in organizational recognition program planning is to identify the resource requirements needed for success.

Almost every organizational recognition program will require at least some resources—people, tools, training, materials, recognition items. And almost all resources are time-critical. They must be designed, ordered, or otherwise acquired before they are needed. Slippage in meeting these resource acquisition dates can cause the entire program to be delayed.

The resource requirements can be identified from the action plan and the schedule. As explained in the previous chapter, there is often a trade-off between the ambitiousness of the program goals and the resources required. Furthermore, the more aggressive the program schedule, the more resources might need to be invested to achieve ambitious milestones.

HUMAN RESOURCES REQUIRED	
Personnel	**Program Role**
William Wilson, chief executive officer	Program executive sponsor
Robert Evans, vice president, retail operations	Senior management team member
Samuel Sharp, vice president, merchandising	Senior management team member
Norma Matthews, Vice President, Purchasing	Senior management team member
Lee Green, vice president, information systems	Senior management team member
James Johnson, financial analyst	Design team member
Laurie Lewis, administrative assistant	Design team member
Jill Macy, manager, graphics department	Design team member
John Jenkins, graphics associate	Design team member
David Owens, training manager	Design team member
Lisa Lambert, trainer	Design team member
Bill Calvert, information systems associate	Design team member
Mary Macdonald, external consultant	Program consultant

It is wise to separate "human resources" from "other resources," because they need to be handled quite differently. In the current example, the human resources allocation for the department store loyalty-improvement program is shown on page 146.

OTHER RESOURCES REQUIRED		
Resource	**Purchase or Develop**	**Date Required**
Sales associate scorecard	Develop	March 20
Problem report form	Develop	March 20
Store gift certificates	Develop	March 20
Restaurant gift certificates	Purchase	March 20
"Loyalty Bears"	Purchase	March 20
Kickoff meeting materials	Develop	March 20
Training materials—managers	Develop	March 20
Training materials—employees	Develop	March 20
Measurement tools	Develop	March 20
Celebration event recognition items	Develop	June 5
Celebration event refreshments	Purchase	June 5

The chart on this page lists the other resources required, including whether they need to be purchased or developed internally and the date each is required. Not all of these resources are costly, but all of them are critical to the program's success.

BUDGET

Next prepare the budget, an estimate of the amount of money needed to fund the various elements of the program. Without one, you won't get funding approval, and people won't think proactively or economically. The budget estimate should be as accurate as possible, but understand that it will always be an estimate.

Of course, budget estimates should be compared with actual expenditures, as they occur, to determine if the program is over budget, on budget, or—miracle of miracles—under budget. This

NO-COST IDEA

Names Are Magic

Whenever possible, allow employees to connect their names with their work. Home Depot posts workers' names on signs, such as "This aisle maintained by Jerry Olson."

Employees at Cooper Tires of Findlay, Ohio, are allowed to stamp their names on the inside of the tires they produce so they can be recognized for their contributions.

| PROGRAM BUDGET | | |
Items	Estimated Cost	Actual Cost
Sales associate scorecard	$500	$500
Problem-solving form	$240	$300
Store gift certificates	$3,500	$3,250
Restaurant gift certificates	$5,000	$5,000
"Loyalty Bears"	$3,400	$3,400
Kickoff meeting materials	$200	$600
Training materials—managers	$150	$200
Training materials—employees	$100	$150
Measurement tools	$120	$175
Celebration event recognition items	$1,200	$1,400
Celebration event refreshments	$850	$850
Consultant	$5,000	$4,000
Miscellaneous/contingency	$500	$200
TOTAL	**$20,760**	**$20,025**

See pages 263–65 for "Required Resources" and "Budget" worksheets.

will often enable you to take action on a performance issue before it is too late. In the current example, the estimated budget items are listed below. No internal personnel costs are included. As you can see, the actual cost came in just under budget, because some expenses, such as consulting fees, were reduced when other items exceeded the budget estimates. This is all part of good project management. Budgeting does not have to be a chore. As Bob Nelson and Peter Economy explain in *Managing for Dummies,* "Experienced *budgetmeisters* know that once you understand your costs of doing business—and where they come from—the budgeting process is actually quite simple."[2]

POTENTIAL FAILURE FACTORS AND PREVENTIVE ACTIONS

Most of us are familiar with Murphy's Law: "If anything can go wrong, it will." Here's a corollary: The most likely cause of problems in any program is the factor that was ignored, the key thing that was forgotten or overlooked.

The way to avoid ambushes is by closely examining the many "contextual" factors in your organization that can undermine or sabotage the best intentions—and then plan how to avoid them, or deal with them if you can't.

POTENTIAL FAILURE FACTORS AND PREVENTIVE ACTIONS

Factor	Probability	Preventive Actions
Lack of continued sponsorship	10%	No action needed
Plan not approved	10%	
Budget not funded	10%	
Failure to meet critical milestones	50%	Identify critical milestones and ensure that adequate plans are in place.
Resources not developed/ordered on time	30%	Allow adequate lead time for all resources; order as early as possible.
Key program personnel cannot perform roles	20%	Select backups for each role.
Customer problems too difficult to solve	40%	Focus on problems that can be solved; don't let difficult problems delay the program.
Sales associates do not respond as predicted to the recognition	30%	Make sure social recognition is in place. Pretest recognition in focus group.
Results take longer than expected to manifest themselves	40%	Manage appropriate expectations; make sure stakeholders are aware that program might take longer than expected.
Managers lose enthusiasm for program	40%	Keep department managers engaged in the program; senior managers must stay in constant contact with them.
Department manager attrition increases	20%	Senior managers should be ready to take over department manager responsibilities if needed during the program.

➤ See page 266
for "Potential Problem Worksheet."

WRECKOGNITION

One large pharmaceutical company gave watches to all its employees around the world to celebrate a company anniversary. While many employees appreciated the gift, others were less than thrilled. Says one employee, "I already have several watches. What I really would like is a software upgrade, but that's not in the budget. I wonder if I can hock this watch to purchase the software I need?" A Spanish affiliate of the firm wondered why Americans were so obsessed with time, and the Chinese affiliates were confused, because in their culture timepieces are exchanged only to grieve a death.

One company gave every employee a birthday card on their birthday along with two movie passes. What they didn't take into account was that some employees lived in other states, where the theater chain did not have locations. So what did the company do? It wrote a check to each out-of-state employee for a total of $1.12, the value of two bulk-purchase movie passes!

REMEMBER: *Think through the possible pitfalls of recognition.*

The chart on page 149 lays out the major potential failure factors and proposed preventive actions in the current example.

You will notice that probability estimates exist for each potential failure factor. Preventive actions are provided for all factors with probabilities greater or equal to 20 percent. The factors with probabilities of less than 20 percent were considered too remote to require preventive actions.

One of the best ways to mitigate potential failure factors—and particularly with a high-risk initiative—is to implement a pilot project. As we mentioned in previous chapters, a pilot project is a small-scale implementation that can serve to identify problems with the program before full-scale implementation.

Pilot projects are particularly useful in large, ambitious programs—they are usually unnecessary in smaller ones. Another consideration that must be weighed in the decision-making process is that pilots can add to costs and extend the time frame for full implementation. Of course, these costs are often offset by a significantly increased probability of success in a full implementation.

There are times when a program—despite all the good intentions of those who designed and implemented it—fails to produce the intended results. Although there's always terrific resistance even to contemplating it, it's possible that the program should be terminated prematurely. In Chapter 15, we discuss the importance of anticipating program termination and also planning for program revitalization.

HOW TO MEASURE THE EFFECTIVENESS OF REWARDS AND RECOGNITION

Measurement is such an important—yet often overlooked—part of program planning that it deserves some special consideration. We will return to the department store example to discuss how its measurement strategy was developed.

As more attention is placed on recognition activities and programs, there is an increased need to measure their effectiveness. Too often we regard measurement as something to be done *after* we've completed the work, but, in fact, measuring appropriately at different stages is one of the keys to getting greater benefits from rewards and recognition.

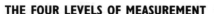
THE FOUR LEVELS OF MEASUREMENT

In 1959, Donald Kirkpatrick introduced a four-level model of measuring training, and it still serves as the industry gold standard. By applying this model to rewards and recognition, we (and you) have a viable means of determining the value of recognition programs and activities.

- **LEVEL 1-Reaction.** This level of measurement describes employees' reactions to, or satisfaction with, the rewards or recognition activities and programs. Level 1 includes such questions as: How are employees responding to your recognition efforts? Are your employees excited about your company's recognition programs? Do they consider the recognition valuable? Are the recognition materials and tools easy to use? What is employees' favorite part of the recognition programs or activities? Have they shared any suggestions for improving recognition? Remember, surveying or interviewing employees can help determine the effect of rewards and recognition on attitudes and perceptions.

- **LEVEL 2-Learning.** This level of measurement pertains to the skills that exist relative to recognition, and the learning that occurs as a by-product of reward and recognition activities. As we have explained throughout this book, recognition is not necessarily something we are born with; it is a set of skills and attitudes that must be learned. Level 2 includes such questions as: How skillfully do individuals and teams give recognition? How confident are managers in giving recognition? How much recognition training is there in your organization? What did we learn from this reward or recognition program? Tests, performance assessment, observation, and debriefings are best for determining skill, knowledge, and lessons learned.

- **LEVEL 3-Application.** This level relates to the actual use of rewards and recognition in the organization, how much is done, and how well rewards and recognition are being used. Level 3 questions might include: How frequently do employees recognize one another? How many employees receive written praise from managers, peers, or customers? One of the best ways to

NO-COST IDEA

Share the Financials

At Carolina Safety Associates in Gastonia, North Carolina, profits went up more than 30 percent in the past two years. They attribute this to sharing financial results with employees and giving them freedom to make changes that have a positive impact on the bottom line. Employees report increased job satisfaction and have formed several off-line problem-solving task forces on their own.

Terry O'Neal, manager of the Oak Ridge, Tennessee, Chick-Fil-A restaurant, opens the books to employees, helping them see how their performance affects the results and links performance to month-to-month bonuses.

CLARIFY THE CRITERIA

Q We don't want to have our program be a popularity contest. What can we do?

—**Gary Flaxman,**
City of Long Beach, CA

A Clarify the criteria and ask nominators to be very specific about the behavior being recognized. If the nominations are vague, return them to the nominator for more detail, or talk them through why the employee seems deserving.

answer level 3 questions is to use records of reward and recognition activity and observations of its quality.

- **LEVEL 4 - Results.** This level of measurement assesses the impact of rewards and recognition on business outcomes. Because of its special importance, we will discuss level 4 measurement in more detail.

FOCUS ON RESULTS

Level 4 (or business results measurement) is really the most important for measuring reward and recognition effectiveness. It doesn't matter how people feel about recognition, or how good they are at using it, if the recognition isn't getting desired results. Even when the intent of a program is simply to increase employee morale, indirect measures exist (or can be built) to examine the results of the program's effectiveness beyond morale.

Here are some examples of questions you can ask at level 4:

- How much are sales incentive programs helping to increase sales revenue?

- What is the impact of employee suggestion programs on improving the business?

- How much do attendance programs reduce absenteeism?

- Are customer service awards improving customer retention?

- Are team awards enhancing inter- and intradepartmental cooperation?

- Are safety recognition programs increasing safe behavior and reducing on-the-job injuries?

- Are quality award programs increasing product quality?

Usually results are defined as the bottom-line outcomes of the organization (such as profits, sales, and so on), but the tendency to reduce everything to financial terms is dangerous because it trivializes many nonfinancial organizational effectiveness measures. (Kaplan and Norton's "balanced scorecard," which is currently revolutionizing management thinking about organizational evaluation, is a response to this "bean-counting," quantifying mentality.)

In addition to the traditional bottom-line results, there are countlesss intermediate results called "organizational effectiveness" indicators. These hundreds, even thousands, of operational measures exist in every organization and include manufacturing efficiency, inventory levels, lost-time accidents, order entry accuracy, abandoned calls, defects produced, equipment utilization, cycle time, and so on. These indicators are also level 4 measures. Conveniently, organizational effectiveness indicators already exist and can be used without any additional investment.

The four levels of measurement can be used on an individual, team, or organizational basis. Below is a table indicating some examples of appropriate measurement questions for each level.

> "High achievers love to be measured . . . otherwise they can't prove to themselves that they are achieving."
>
> —**Robert N. Noyce,**
> cofounder, Intel Corporation

LEVEL	INDIVIDUAL	TEAM	ORGANIZATION
LEVEL 1: Reaction	What was the employee's reaction to the recognition I gave?	What was the team's reaction to the recognition?	What were employees' reactions to the organizational recognition program?
LEVEL 2: Learning	What are my recognition skills?	What are the team's recognition skills?	What did we learn from the organizational recognition program?
LEVEL 3: Application	How much recognition am I giving?	How much recognition is the team receiving?	How many employees are participating in the organiztional recognition program?
LEVEL 4: Results	What was the impact of the recognition on the performance of the employees?	What was the impact of the recognition on the performance of the team?	What was the impact of the recognition program on organizational performance?

BEGIN WITH THE END IN MIND

One of the added benefits of good measurement, especially at level 4, is that the more recognition activities and programs drive significant organizational performance and strategic results, the easier it is to justify the effort and funds to support them. We all want to have recognition programs that are rewarding for employees, easy to use, and readily applicable on the job—and that

See pages 258–59
for "Recognition Planning Checklists."

TREATING PEOPLE RIGHT AT STARBUCKS

Starbucks virtually invented the market for high-quality coffee in the United States. Ever since the Boston Tea Party, Americans have been big fans of coffee. Surprisingly, however, in 1989—well before Starbucks made a big splash domestically—there were only two hundred coffeehouses in the entire United States. Today, there are more than eight thousand—more than sixteen hundred of which are Starbucks. Most of this growth can be directly attributed to the craze for high-quality, dark-roasted coffee and espresso drinks that Starbucks triggered in its quest to be the most recognized and respected coffee seller in the world. And it's not over yet. Consumers have already been enjoying the further expansion of the Starbucks brand, including bagged coffee for sale in grocery stores (to accompany its best-selling premium coffee ice cream), pricey ceramic vases, and a line of jazz CDs, and soon there may be much, much more.

However, it's clearly not just the coffee; it's the *people*. Although CEO Howard Schultz is riding high now, it wasn't always this way. Schultz grew up in the projects in Brooklyn, New York, where his father was a blue-collar truck driver for a diaper delivery service. Because the job carried neither worker's compensation insurance nor health insurance, a broken leg suffered on the job caused tremendous hardship for seven-year-old Howard Schultz's family. So when he bought Starbucks, Schultz was determined that his company would be different—that it would share its success with all employees, not just a select few in management. As Schultz points out, "No matter what business you are in, if you don't treat your people well, you can't expect the product or the service to be delivered well."

In an industry that is notorious for low wages and little or no benefits, Starbucks stands out. Wages above the federally required minimums are just the beginning. Every Starbucks employee who works more than twenty hours a week is eligible for a generous benefits package of which Starbucks pays 75 percent of the cost. For most employees, this translates to an average of only $32 out of their own pockets each month.

And what is included in Starbucks' benefits package? Medical insurance, dental and vision care, mental health and chemical dependency coverage, paid vacation time, sick leave, a 401(k) retirement savings plan, short- and long-term disability, life insurance—even a free pound of coffee each week. And that's not all. Employees get a 30 percent discount on product purchases and, subject to a formula based on wages, company profits, and stock price, employees are offered options to purchase Starbucks stock at a reduced price.

OWNERSHIP IS KEY

It's the stock options that probably have the greatest impact on how employees treat their customers, and how they treat one another. Says Corey Rosen, director of the National Center for Employee Ownership in Oakland, California, "This is really a key benefit. Ownership is deeply rooted in this company. And what American companies have failed to realize is that there's tremendous value in getting everyone in the company to share a common purpose of self-esteem, self-respect, and appreciation."

The result is that annual turnover, which often runs in the range of 400 to 500 percent for businesses in the retail and service sector of the American economy, is running at approximately 50 percent.

How can the company afford to pay for such an extensive benefits plan, estimated to cost the com-

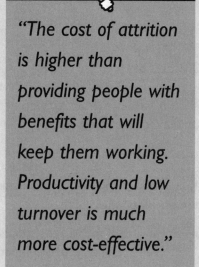

"The cost of attrition is higher than providing people with benefits that will keep them working. Productivity and low turnover is much more cost-effective."

pany more than $2,200 per year for each of the company's 25,000 workers? According to Schultz, "The cost of attrition is higher than providing people with benefits that will keep them working. Productivity and low turnover is much more cost-effective."

Employee training programs also play an important role in making employees more effective and in teaching them the skills they need to succeed on the job. New employees receive twenty-five hours of classroom training, including customer service, coffee-brewing methods, retail skills, and how to pour a perfect shot of espresso. Management trainees receive eight to twelve weeks of classroom training, including classes in recruiting, project management, and how to conduct performance appraisals.

Without a doubt, Starbucks employees are better trained than workers in almost any other retail food establishment. And they clearly like being part of the company. Says a Starbucks shift supervisor in Vancouver, British Columbia, "I think we're phenomenally important. People come for the coffee, but they keep coming back because they like the people behind the counter. I know my customers' names. I know their drinks. I know what they do on the weekends and holidays. I have a relationship with every customer who comes into my store. It's the personal service that makes people want to come back."

A worker in Manhattan adds, "I feel like this company actually cares about me."

NO-COST IDEA
36

Work Stoppage

At Kodak's Image Loops and Sundries Department in Rochester, New York, when operators reach their weekly goal for each type of loop, production is shut down so they can work on other projects. Employees have used the extra time to develop ideas for improving the operation and other team activities, which has resulted in quite a few improvements and great camaraderie.

See page 267
for "Measurement Strategy Worksheets."

improve organization performance in meaningful ways. To do this, you must reverse the evaluation strategy and begin with the end in mind. First, clearly understand your employees' needs and wants. Then define the results you desire to ensure that the program can achieve them. Starting with a clear idea of your audience and the goals and performance you want from them will strengthen the link of recognition to results now and in the long term.

The profound implications of these four levels escape most people. But remember: what you measure is what you are likely to get. The level where you focus most of your attention is where you are most likely to see results. Obviously, measuring at all four levels is most likely to achieve the most complete results, but you should measure other levels only if you feel it is necessary to obtain feedback from them.

THE THREE PHASES OF MEASUREMENT

In addition to the four *levels* of measurement, there are also three *phases* of measurement:

- **Preprogram measurement**, also referred to a "baseline" measurement, enables you to compare pre- and postrecognition reaction, learning, application, or results. If you don't measure *before*, you won't know if there was improvement *after*.

- **In-process measurement** occurs during the implementation of a reward or recognition activity or program. This phase is very important because this is the time when you can answer questions like: What is working well in the program? What is falling short of expectations? What can we do to make it better?

- **Postprogram measurement** comes after the recognition activity or program ends and is compared with the baseline measurement.

THE MEASUREMENT STRATEGY

You should now appreciate the importance of developing a comprehensive measurement approach. Turning once again to the department store chain customer loyalty example, let's look at the sixth element of the planning framework: measurement strategy.

MEASUREMENT

Method	Level	Phase(s)	Description
PROGRAM IMPLEMENTATION CHECKLIST	**LEVEL 3: Application**	In-process	Checklist was used to ensure that the program was implemented according to the program plan.
BUSINESS INDICATORS	**LEVEL 4: Results**	Preprogram, in-process, and postprogram	Tracking increased customer loyalty (as measured by repeat sales). This was done throughout the program implementation (in-process) and on completion of the program. Improvement was compared with preprogram (baseline) measurements.
SALES ASSOCIATE SCORECARD	**LEVEL 3: Application**	In-process	Measurement instrument was designed to track customer problem identification behavior on the part of sales associates and department managers; this instrument triggered recognition.
SALES ASSOCIATE INTERVIEWS	**LEVEL 1: Reaction**	In-process	Interviews during the program implementation monitored engagement in and satisfaction with the pprogram.
PROGRAM OBSERVATION	**LEVEL 3: Application**	In-process	Systematic observation of program implementation was conducted.
PROGRAM PARTICIPANT FOCUS GROUPS	**LEVEL 1: Reaction and LEVEL 2: Learning**	Postprogram	Group interviews were used to debrief participants after completion of the program; used to identify "best practices" and lessons learned.

Believe it or not, mastering the six essentials of planning an organizational recognition program is easier than it may seem. In fact, after a few experiences with successful programs in your organization, it may become second nature.

THE TAKE-AWAY

- Planning is the best way to transform intentions into reality. Remember the six P's of planning: Prior Planning Prevents Pitifully Poor Performance.

- There are six essential elements in good organizational recognition program planning: (1) action plan, (2) schedule, (3) resource requirements, (4) budget, (5) potential failure factors and preventive actions, and (6) measurement strategy.

- One of the best ways to mitigate potential failure factors in a new organizational recognition program is through the implementation of a pilot project before any organization-wide program is rolled out.

- Although measurement is the only way the progress of an organizational recognition program can be monitored, it is too often overlooked.

- There are four levels of measurement: reaction, learning, application, and results. Results are the most important, but the other levels can help you get there.

- Don't just measure bottom-line results; also track organizational effectiveness indicators.

- Using preprogram, in-process, and post-program measurements will help you get a complete picture of your recognition program—before, during, and after—and manage it for maximum impact.

CHAPTER II

Implementing Organizational Recognition

"One of the stepping stones of a world-class operation is to tap into the creative and intellectual power of each and every employee."

—**Harold A. Poling,** former chairman and CEO, Ford Motor Company

T he most important thing to remember about implementing organizational recognition is that you are about to introduce a significant change to your organization. As you know, people often resist change, even when the change is positive. Even under optimal conditions, a new program requires a high degree of focused energy for liftoff. Once airborne, however, it can build up enough momentum to keep flying for a very long time.

The magnitude of the change created by the introduction of a new organizational recognition program will depend on the organization's general climate for change. But even in organizations where recognition is already part of the culture, there's bound to be some *inertia* ("Thanks, but what we've already got is just fine") and *entropy* (the tendency of enthusiasm for new programs to diminish over time, as well as management's inclination to move on to the next "motivational program of the month" before the one that was recently implemented has had a chance to develop).

The key to avoiding both? Alignment, coordination, and communication.

ALIGNMENT

I f you've ever been to a chiropractor, you have a pretty good idea of what alignment is. Alignment means making sure that the desired behaviors/results that trigger recognition are "in line" throughout the organization, and are the right ones at each level to achieve the desired organizational goals, strategies, and results. Recognition programs don't exist in a vacuum; to be effective, they must be synchronized with the organization's vision, strategies, and goals.

Well-aligned organizational recognition has the potential to provide enormous benefits to the organization by positioning people emotionally around organizational goals and priorities.

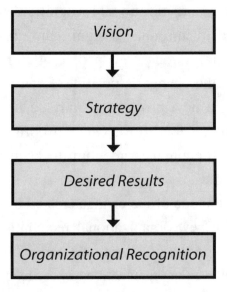

Recognition Alignment

> "For some reason, there never seems to be enough recognition. After a brutal day, walk up to employees and say, 'You were great. I'm so glad about what you did today.' You'll be surprised how far a simple gesture will go."
>
> —**Robert Preziosi,**
> president,
> Management Associates

Strong Capital Management, a mutual fund company in Meno-menee Falls, Wisconsin, developed a "recognition menu" that was fully aligned with its business priorities. When employees displayed these specific behaviors, they were eligible to receive rewards and recognition. The company's recognition menu included such behaviors as:

- Completing required tasks quickly

- Putting forth extra effort to satisfy customer requests

- Suggesting additional products and services to customers

- Implementing business improvement ideas

- Going above and beyond for the business unit

The importance of alignment cannot be overemphasized. So many potential behaviors and results can be recognized in any organization that it is absolutely vital that the *right* ones be recognized. When *everything* is recognized indiscriminately, recognition loses its focus and undermines its own potential.

COORDINATION

At an organizational level, it is best for recognition to be coordinated across the organization and not left up to isolated, arbitrary, individual efforts. Unfortunately, recognition is often viewed as a decentralized activity that cannot really be effectively tracked or managed.

When recognition is uncoordinated and scattered willy-nilly throughout an organization, there is inevitably going to be confusion, chaos, and waste. There can be no consistency in how recognition is delivered, no way to assess the program's results, and no way to ensure that the program supports the vision, strategies, and goals of the organization. As management consultants Garry Jacobs and Robert Macfarlane explain, "The real power of organization arises from its capacity for coordination and integration of people, activities, and systems." To have meaning, all the elements of any recognition program must be brought under control.

The larger and more decentralized the organization, the more vital it is to coordinate recognition. The business units, facilities, and employees of many organizations are scattered across the

WRECKOGNITION

One insurance company singles out low-performing sales-people at its quarterly awards ceremony and has them get up in front of the company's eight hundred other sales reps and explain why they didn't do a better job. This practice makes morale suffer drastically.

UP CLOSE AND PERSONAL

Q I read with interest your case study on Caterpillar. You say a centrally located program is doomed to failure. My experience is that decentralized programs fail due to employee dissatisfaction because others "have more fun," "have better treatment," "spent more money," etc. Please explain.

—**Colleen Fritsch,**
Training and Development,
Thompson, Manitoba, Canada

A **"Doomed to failure" might have been a bit strong, but I do believe that motivation is a very personal issue that best occurs between employees and their immediate managers as a function of the inter-actions, trust, support, and respect that you receive on a daily basis— more than from an occa-sional award or holiday party. "Recognition inequity" diminishes as you allow a greater quantity and variety of recognition activities. If employees like what they heard another depart-ment did or received, duplicate that success. Soon employees come to appreciate the success of others, knowing that when they achieve, they'll be recognized too.**

United States, or all around the globe. If any integrated benefits are going to be gained from recognition in such decentralized compa-nies, and if the wastefulness of repeatedly reinventing the wheel is going to be avoided, coordination is *essential*. Alignment and coor-dination of recognition can yield tremendous leverage for an organization because these two principles work to focus every employee in the organization on what is most important.

Alignment and coordination can produce significant synergy. The principle of synergy states that the whole is greater than the sum of its parts. As Peter and Susan Corning put it in their book *Winning with Synergy*, synergy "is to say that the whole produces combined or cooperative effects that are not otherwise attainable."[1] Organiza-tional recognition needs to be much more than a disjointed collection of individual instances of recognition. Bill O'Brien, former CEO of Hanover Insurance, talks about a "merit environment . . . where the conclusions, decisions, and rewards focus on the attainment of the organization's purpose and vision in a way that is consistent with its values."[2]

As you can see in the case study of the Arizona Department of Administration on pages 164–65, the existence of central coordi-nation does not remove the potential and need for local initiative. The purpose of this coordination is not to impose another level of bureaucratic control, but to create more organizational value and avoid unnecessary duplication of effort.

RECOGNITION VALUES

Nothing helps get organizations aligned around coordinated recognition like a compelling mission statement that can inspire passion in employees for the work they do and the cus-tomers they serve. Such a statement might be expressed in the fol-lowing way:

We want to use recognition to make our employees feel like cus-tomer service heroes. We want everybody in the organization to feel that recognition is their responsibility, but that our recogni-tion efforts are coordinated and aimed at achieving the organi-zation's goals. We want to use recognition to celebrate our major accomplishments, and we want to learn from our shortcomings.

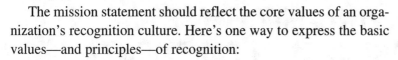

The mission statement should reflect the core values of an organization's recognition culture. Here's one way to express the basic values—and principles—of recognition:

- We will recognize behaviors and results that make significant contributions to achieving our goals.

- We will recognize collective accomplishments, not just individual accomplishments.

- Only behaviors and results that go beyond the routine should be recognized; otherwise, recognition will be devalued.

- We will celebrate major accomplishments.

- We will strive for fairness and objectivity in our recognition activities.

- We will use recognition as an opportunity to identify achievements of all types, share them, and learn from them.

- We will make recognition fun.

RECOGNITION GUIDELINES AND STANDARDS

Once the mission has been written, recognition guidelines and standards can be developed and implemented. Clear expectations are essential for effective performance. When well written, they never constrain creativity, but rather provide the boundaries within which creativity can take place. Boundaries and rules separate fun and creativity from chaos.

Guidelines and standards typically include the following kinds of items:

- The behaviors and results that should be recognized

- Guidelines about when to use individual, team, or organizational recognition

- Guidelines for when it is appropriate to give tangible recognition items

- Links between recognition and other related organizational systems (such as compensation and benefits)

- Role descriptions relative to organizational recognition, such as recognition coordinator (see below)

NO-COST IDEA

Three-Day Weekends

Employees at TRW in San Diego work nine hours each workday and have every other Friday off. Surveys of employees report that this "9/80" work schedule is more highly valued by many employees even than their health benefits, and plays a key role in helping keep employees.

INVOLVING EMPLOYEES AT THE ARIZONA DEPARTMENT OF ADMINISTRATION

The public sector is not typically known for its leadership in recognition. The Arizona Department of Administration (ADOA) is a notable exception to that generalization. The ADOA's organizational recognition program BRAVO! is dedicated to "celebrating outstanding performance." This comprehensive and multifaceted program comprises many component awards that recognize all aspects of employee performance: short-term and long-term, individual and team, and high performance and improvement.

If an organizational recognition program expands and becomes part of the fabric of the organization, advisory team members can be made into program coordinators in the various operating units.

As part of the BRAVO! program, a recognition coordinator is selected in each division to serve as the direct program contact with employees. If employees want to nominate another employee for an award, they do it through their local BRAVO! coordinator. If they have any questions about recognition, they ask the BRAVO! coordinator. Coordinators also help maintain the ADOA recognition center, which displays award winners' pictures, and write articles on awards and award winners in the ADOA newsletter. At the Arizona Department of Administration, recognition doesn't get overlooked, because the BRAVO! coordinators make sure that there are no weak links in the chain of recognition.

Given public sector financial constraints, organizations like ADOA have to substitute creativity for financial rewards. ADOA has done an excellent job of creating a comprehensive nonmonetary recognition program that recognizes the right things in the right ways. The BRAVO! program is designed to celebrate and reinforce the ADOA's core values: customer service, continuous improvement, teamwork, integrity, and quality. In addition to the awards (described below), all recognition recipients receive acknowledgment at an annual awards presentation, a picture in the ADOA recognition center, and an article in the ADOA newsletter.

The BRAVO! program's awards include:

- **"A Cause for Applause"**: Employees are encouraged to give on-the-spot recognition for employees who demonstrate core value behaviors. "Cause for Applause" certificates can be presented one-on-one, at a staff meeting, through interoffice mail, or through an employee's supervisor. Each month, ten "Cause for Applause" recipients are randomly selected to receive BRAVO! recognition items. The employee receiving the most "Cause for Applause" certificates at the end of the year receives eight hours of recognition leave, a designated parking space for a year, and a plaque.

- **Standing Ovation:** The ADOA director gives team-based customer service awards that represent the highest level of department-wide employee recognition. The Standing Ovation category includes two awards: the Director's Excellence Award for teams that receive a rating of 6.5 or higher on the ADOA Customer Satisfaction Survey, and the Director's Recognition Award for teams that experience an increase of one point or more on the ADOA Customer Satisfaction Survey. Awards include a plaque for the team and certificates for each individual.

- **A Round of Applause:** This award has four categories: Supervisor of the Year, Team of the Year, Career Excellence, and Public Service.

- The Supervisor of the Year award recognizes one department employee who has demon-

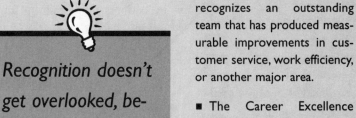

Recognition doesn't get overlooked, because the BRAVO! coordinators make sure that there are no weak links in the chain of recognition.

strated excellence in leadership, motivation, and staff support.

- The Team of the Year award recognizes an outstanding team that has produced measurable improvements in customer service, work efficiency, or another major area.

- The Career Excellence award is given to an employee who has made a particularly outstanding contribution to the department over the past year.

- The Public Service award recognizes employees who have demonstrated commitment to civic responsibility through volunteerism.

- Individual award recipients receive eight hours of recognition leave, a designated parking space for a year, and a plaque.

- Teams receive a team plaque and certificates for each team member. There are also A Round of Applause awards for the Employee of the Quarter and the Team of the Quarter.

- There are also Encore recognition awards for each five years of service, and Take a Bow seniority awards for employees who are retiring.

The BRAVO! coordinators are the glue that holds the program together. The Arizona Department of Administration's BRAVO! organizational recognition program itself deserves a big "bravo!" and "a round of applause."

- Requirements for a recognition program (such as the sponsorship and approvals needed, reporting requirements, and measurement expectations)

- Procedures for obtaining funding and other support for recognition

RECOGNITION COORDINATOR

Any organization serious about recognition should have a recognition coordinator. In most organizations, recognition coordinator is a part-time role, rather than a full-time job. And while the role can conceivably reside in any department, it might fit best into human resources. Recognition coordinator responsibilities typically include:

- Facilitating the development of the recognition vision, mission, values, guidelines, and standards—often with a cross-functional team made up of volunteers from across the organization

- Coordinating recognition-related communications

- Maintaining a recognition site on the organizational intranet

- Building a repository/database of recognition "best practices" and lessons learned

- Performing regular recognition inventories

- Maintaining a list of internal and external recognition resources

- Providing advice on how to maximize the positive impact of recognition initiatives

- Helping to find synergies among recognition programs and economies of scale

- Helping to identify sources of recognition information and recognition items

COMMUNICATION

Hand in hand with alignment and coordination, effective communication is needed to make organizational recognition work.

WINNING MANAGEMENT SUPPORT THROUGH COMMUNICATION

Management support is the foundation of any organizational change effort, and management support *always* begins with sponsorship. Of course, sponsorship at the top level—the president, CEO, or chairman of the board—makes it easier to win support at other levels of management. Influence usually flows better downhill. However, wherever sponsorship originates, sustaining a recognition program over time will require additional management support.

Managers often view organizational recognition programs as intrusive—at best a distraction, at worst something that must be resisted with considerable vigor. To gain the backing of management, you need to be able to show that recognition on an organizational level is different from recognition on an individual or group level, that it really can help achieve ambitious organizational goals. One way to accomplish this is through awareness meetings with senior executives. During these meetings, we recommend:

- **Emphasizing the benefits.** Show managers how the use of organizational recognition will benefit the organization *and* make them look good—that it really is a win-win proposition. In other words, stress both the business and interpersonal benefits.

- **Sharing successes.** Tell stories about "best practices," either from other companies in your industry or from elsewhere in your organization.

- **Minimizing the risks.** Be honest about the downside, but show executives that you have a strategy to protect against it.

"Recognition is something a manager should be doing all the time—it's a running dialogue with people."

—Ron Zemke,
senior editor,
Training magazine

LEADERSHIP COMMUNICATION

Once you've got management onboard, get them to lead by invoking some of these powerful recognition leadership examples.

- Toy Reed, former president of Eastman Chemical Company, rarely missed an opportunity to personally attend a company recognition meeting or celebration.

Call in Well

As a result of its commitment to a more balanced work life, employees at clothing outfitter Eddie Bauer can "call in well." The company's Redmond, Washington, store has even created Balance Day, an additional day off for all employees.

See page 269
for more
on "Recognition
Training Designs."

■ David Novak, CEO of KFC, spent a lot of his valuable leadership time reinforcing the importance of cleanliness, hospitality, and work ethic by making frequent visits to restaurants—pumping people up, motivating them, recognizing accomplishments large and small—even personally delivering the company's highest award, the Rubber Chicken!

■ Bill Marriott, Marriott International's CEO, personally leads the company's campaign to emphasize the importance of appreciation to a successful hospitality enterprise—rather than delegating it to a subordinate manager.

■ Jack Stack, chairman of Springfield Remanufacturing, in Springfield, Missouri, instituted "open-book management" as the way to get employees to take more responsibility for the company's bottom line. He personally leads what he calls "The Great Game of Business."

■ Roger Hale, president of the Tennant Company, in Minneapolis, Minnesota, personally acknowledges employee contributions and reinforces the importance of recognition in his "President's Column" in *Tennant Topics*, the employee newsletter. He's even coauthored a book on recognition!

The visible support of a top executive in your organization can accelerate the acceptance of a recognition program and help ensure its long-term survival. Many top executives enjoy being part of a program that will improve employee morale and productivity—especially when they have the opportunity to put their own stamp on it. Before you roll out your organizational recognition program, be sure you've got this base covered.

COMMUNICATING THE PROGRAM TO THE ORGANIZATION

Since good communication is essential at all levels of the organization, it is unfortunate how frequently organizational information is communicated only on a need-to-know basis. When employees are given the minimum information necessary to do their jobs, they often end up confused and resentful. When it comes

to organizational recognition, communication should be ubiquitous, consistent, and aligned with the company's mission and
goals.

Successful organizational recognition programs depend on
three phases of communication:

1 **Prelaunch communication:** Communication that
precedes launch of the program, including communication during the pilot of the program.

2 **Launch communication:** Communication that occurs
when the program is announced to the organization.

3 **Ongoing communication:** Communication that is
sustained throughout the program life cycle.

At each phase, decide the following:

- **The target of the communication:** *Who* should receive it?

- **The message:** *What* is it?

- **The source:** *Who* delivers it?

- **The schedule:** *When* does it arrive?

- **The method:** *How* does it get there?

Remember: different audiences require different approaches.
For instance, while direct communication is effective when speaking to management, communication to employees should often be
indirect. Research shows that communication to employees should
be channeled through their supervisors, rather than given to them
directly by senior management. Unfortunately, supervisors are the
most frequently ignored stakeholder group in any organizational
change initiative, ultimately leading to disappointment for those
who originally had such high hopes for the success of the program.
Any organizational recognition program that affects employees
and fails to target supervisors as a major communication link is
bound to fail.

INCENTIVIZING FINANCIAL SUCCESS

Q Can an incentive program work when pay
rates are below market
levels?

—**Carnario,**
online forum participant

A **Motivation does not
have to start with
money (not that money
isn't important). I've seen
cases in which managers
led with the "softer"
approach of inspiring performance and then were
able to be more finan-
cially successful and share
the wealth with those
who helped make success
possible. I've also seen
work environments in
which employees were
not that well paid, but
because they were well
respected and enjoyed
their work they were
happy.**

THE TAKE-AWAY

- Remember: people often resist change, even when it is for the better. Implementing a new organizational recognition program therefore requires focused energy to obtain alignment, coordination, and communication, and get successfully under way.

- Management support is critical to the long-term success of any organizational recognition program.

- There are three phases of communication for organizational recognition programs: (1) prelaunch communication, (2) launch communication, and (3) ongoing communication.

- Plan communications very carefully, with a clear understanding of each target audience.

CHAPTER 12

Managing Organizational Recognition

"There's a big difference between getting people to come to work and getting them to do their best work."

—Bob Nelson

Organizational recognition programs, like humans, need care and feeding. But instead of actively managing them, managers and employees too often move on to things that have a higher priority on their "to do" list, leaving the programs to die a slow death. The major continuing challenge of organizational recognition is figuring out how to *sustain* the initiative long enough for it to achieve its full impact.

THE ORGANIZATIONAL RECOGNITION LIFE CYCLE

Every organizational recognition program has a life cycle similar to the life cycle of a product: it is developed, launched, marketed, and eventually withdrawn from the market. Each phase of the life cycle needs to be managed, or else the impact will diminish sooner than expected or desired.

The Life Cycle of Organizational Recognition

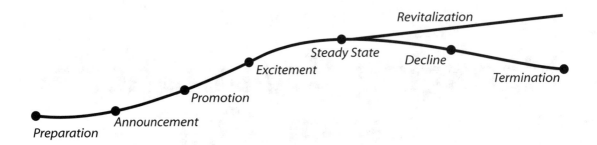

Organizational recognition programs begin with preparation, including an assessment of organizational readiness, design of the initiative, a possible pilot, and revision (based on the pilot). Once the organizational recognition initiative is ready for full-scale implementation, it is announced to the organization as a whole. Then it is promoted to build excitement. Over a period of time, when it is fully implemented, the initiative reaches a steady state. The steady state can continue for some time before decline due to entropy sets in. Finally, the initiative is terminated, once it has served the purpose for which it was intended. Alternatively, if you want to sustain the program longer, it can be revitalized.

FROM PROMOTION TO EXCITEMENT

Communication is crucially important during the promotion phase of the program's life cycle. This is where your communication plan will really pay off. Make sure you have identified all the major stakeholders, and that there are appropriate communications targeted to each stakeholder group.

While nothing creates excitement among employees like seeing the actual program in action and feeling the effects of giving and getting recognition, new programs can require relatively high effort and attention at the promotion stage. There will always be employees who ask themselves (and others), "Why are they doing this?" "What are the ulterior motives?" or "What do they expect of me?" The natural resistance to change needs to be counteracted dur-

> *"Continuous, supportive communication from managers, supervisors, and associates is too often underemphasized. It is a major, major motivator."*
>
> **—Jim Moultrop,**
> consultant,
> Management Perspectives Group

ing the early stages of any organizational program through communication—sharing successes from the pilot, having management give briefings, staging events that create anticipation, hanging signs and posters, and the like.

It is important to make a good first impression with your new organizational recognition program. That is one strong reason for piloting it. During the pilot program, the program will very likely achieve some successes, and these initial successes—when shared through e-mails, newsletters, or meetings—are valuable for spurring anticipation and excitement.

Nothing succeeds like success, so don't hesitate to communicate any successes widely and loudly.

STEADY STATE

Once the inertia that is a natural part of any startup phase has been overcome, there is typically a high degree of enthusiasm among employees. Novelty alone is sometimes enough to generate significant interest and excitement. However, this enthusiasm cannot be sustained for long, unless it's backed up by something more substantial—like real results.

It is then that the initial excitement of the recognition program gives way to a steady state—the plateau at which the program works well enough to be self-sustaining, at least for a while. At this point, a new enemy makes its entrance: complacency.

Most organizational recognition programs begin with great excitement and fanfare on the part of managers and employees alike. At the beginning, senior managers are typically involved, employees are made to feel special, and there is a lot of hoopla and celebration, but sooner or later entropy will lead to decline.

The unplanned, unexpected termination of a program can be hard on everyone—and especially demoralizing to the employees who placed their trust and energy in the program. However, the planned termination of an organizational recognition program—"time-bounding"—can in fact be a positive thing. The life cycle of recognition programs can become an accepted part of organizational life, and the regular replacement of old programs with new ones can be a vital part of an effective recognition culture.

NO-COST IDEA

39

Information, Please

At FedEx Corporation, based in Memphis, Tennessee, the most popular column in the company newsletter is about the company's competition.

At Subaru's Illinois plant, employees requested information about new models the company was planning to market, which helped them serve as ambassadors for the products.

TEAM SPIRIT AT GOOD SAMARITAN HOSPITAL

At Good Samaritan Hospital in Dayton, Ohio, organizational recognition is a major force toward creating a high-quality, customer-focused organization. The outstanding organizational recognition program is one of the reasons the hospital has been recognized for excellence both nationally and by the State of Ohio.

Good Samaritan Hospital uses a coordinating committee called the CREW (Celebrating and Recognizing Employees' Work) to foster employee involvement, consistency, and alignment. This committee has responsibility for planning and implementing a variety of formal and informal recognition programs to support Good Samaritan's core values (Reverence, Integrity, Compassion, and Excellence) and SPIRIT standards: Spirit, Professionalism, Information and communication, Responsibility, Initiative, and Teamwork.

SAMARITAN STARS SHOW SPIRIT

Six times a year, ten employees are recognized as "Samaritan Stars" for exemplifying each of the SPIRIT standards. Employees are invited to nominate peers for the award. The recipients are honored at a reception to which all employees are invited, and the hospital's president personally presents the awards. Another group, the Employee Cooperative Action Committee (ECAC) sponsors the employee-of-the-month program, which is presented by the hospital's president at a celebration brunch.

In addition to these programs, other recognition and fun activities are sometimes used. For example, at a time when employees' workload was particularly high, the CREW distributed $10 gasoline cards to say thank you. At the Blue Ribbons Bake-off, employees can demonstrate their baking skills and share the results with their follow employees. Workers are also treated to days at the ballpark and holiday celebrations.

CORE VALUES AND PERFORMANCE STANDARDS

Like all great organizational recognition programs, Good Samaritan Hospital's is totally aligned with the organization's core values and performance standards. Recognition is not merely an organizational benefit, but a dynamic, well-coordinated component of organizational strategy that unites senior management and employees.

Good Samaritan's CREW has made a real difference in the working lives of the hospital's employees, proving to them that someone really does notice their good work and appreciates what they do. And employees who feel appreciated are employees who will consistently do their very best job.

REVITALIZATION

Most organizations set up formal recognition programs, but never reevaluate their effectiveness and relevance to the organization's purpose and objectives. This is a vital step in keeping recognition efforts fresh. If you believe that a recognition program should be terminated, terminate it. Others may just need to be revitalized.

At Johnson & Johnson, employees were asked what items and activities they valued most. It turned out that more than half of the employees didn't consider the organization's traditional years-of-service awards meaningful recognition. What they wanted was recognition that involved their families, such as receiving a basket of goodies or movie passes for the whole family. The company made the necessary adjustments. Through this experience, Johnson & Johnson learned a very important lesson: One of the keys to recognition success is consistently surveying employees, not assuming that management knows best.

One of the best ways to revitalize an aging organizational recognition programs is through the use of *motivators*. Here are just a few of the possibilities:

- **Variety.** Sometimes simply adding a new celebratory activity can do wonders to revitalize recognition. We suggest that you brainstorm the ways that variety can be added, without necessarily changing any of the core aspects of the program: you might recognize all employees who recognize or nominate another employee for an award during a one-month period.

- **New recognition opportunities.** Establish new opportunities for recognition and celebration. Even within a well-defined area of recognition, you should be able to identify many new recognition opportunities. If you have individual safety awards, establish a new category for team safety awards.

- **New recognition levels.** Choose new triggers for recognition. To make sure employees do not perceive "recognition escalation" as a take-away, or as changing the rules in the middle of the game, keep lower levels of recognition intact.

- **Enhance the scorekeeping process.** Make use of this powerful measurement and feedback mechanism. Providing new score-

WRECKOGNITION

One of the authors was working in one corporation and stopped to read a plaque honoring annual top achievers, only to discover that the last entry was twelve years old!

REMEMBER: Keep recognition programs fresh and relevant—or retire them and start something new.

➤ See chapter 15
for more on revitalizing and sustaining your recognition programs.

MANAGING RECOGNITION AT IBM

No company has a more varied organizational recognition infrastructure than IBM Corporation. With approximately 350,000 employees scattered around the world, IBM takes rewards and recognition very seriously. Not satisfied with maintaining the status quo, IBM regularly reengineers their rewards and recognition program to respond to changing business needs. No recognition program we have studied is better aligned with the company's strategy and culture. IBM is striving to create a true climate of recognition throughout the company.

While recognizing outstanding performance is nothing new at IBM, the company has never had a unified, consistent program worldwide. IBM's new recognition program is designed to create a deeply entrenched culture of appreciation and recognition at all levels of IBM. The program was initially launched in Asia and later in the U.S.A., Latin America, and Canada.

NOT SINGING THE BLUES

The global recognition framework, called New Blue: Focused to Win, is an integrated system of targeted recognition programs that focuses on behaviors—speed, commitment, focus, passion for the business, teaming, and knowledge sharing—as well as results. These behaviors were not just selected by managerial intuition. Most of these "winning behaviors" are all aligned with IBM's strategic business priorities. Even the names of the

programs reinforce the critical behaviors and results being targeted.

This more streamlined recognition program came about as a result of the responses of 33,000 IBMers in seventy-eight countries to the Global Employee Survey. The new awards are meant to go beyond traditional means of compensation—things like salary and benefits—to make sure employees know how much they are valued by their managers, colleagues, and the company as a whole.

Now the emphasis is on behavior as well as results. Kay Reed, the human resources project manager behind New Blue, explained: "We want to reinforce and reward the behaviors that Lou Gerstner has identified as critical to the business worldwide."

New Blue features six different awards. Five of them enable managers to recognize individuals and teams; one award allows peers to recognize one another. It is a key element in the new initiative, according to Reed.

Here's a quick overview of the six awards, which have been enormously successful:

- "Thanks!" enables one employee to spontaneously recognize a peer for providing out-of-the-ordinary assistance with an item of up to $25 in value.

- "Bravo!" enables recognition (up to $2,500) for individual or team behavior, or for results beyond normal job and performance expectations.

- "Technical Recognition" (up to $25,000) enables three types of recognition: invention achievement, outstanding innovation, and outstanding technical achievement.

- "Knowledge Advantage" enables recognition (up to $2,500) for individuals who share knowledge, lessons learned, and key insights with others.

- "Execute Now!" enables recognition (up to $10,000) for truly outstanding contributions.

- "One Team!" enables recognition (up to $10,000 per team) for outstanding work done by a formal or informal team.

The global recognition framework focuses on speed, commitment, focus, passion for the business, teaming, and knowledge sharing— as well as results. Even the names of the programs reinforce the critical behaviors and results being targeted.

- "Win IBM!" includes awards and contests (up to $10,000) targeted at specific goals and measurements, and allows IBM management to selectively drive performance and recognize individuals or teams that have had a significant impact on the business.

In addition to these monetary awards, IBM has a wide range of nonmonetary forms of recognition:

- IBM Thanks! award cards enable employees to express appreciate to peers for going above and beyond in helping each other.

- Executives and managers are encouraged to send handwritten notes to employees in recognition of specific project accomplishments.

- Individual executives also develop recognition ideas that reflect their personalities, such as "Fun in the Sun Days" celebrations, bottles of Champagne, flowers, a day at the spa, or time off for a round of golf.

- One senior executive delivered on a promise that executives would personally wash the cars of employees who reached a sales goal!

Developing and maintaining a recognition program for more than 350,000 employees worldwide is no small undertaking, but IBM is doing it and putting its money behind its commitment.

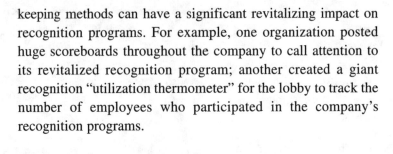

"The first responsibility of a leader is to define reality. The last is to say thank you. In between, the leader is a servant."

—Max de Pree,
CEO, Herman Miller

See page 268 ◄
for "Lessons Learned Worksheet."

keeping methods can have a significant revitalizing impact on recognition programs. For example, one organization posted huge scoreboards throughout the company to call attention to its revitalized recognition program; another created a giant recognition "utilization thermometer" for the lobby to track the number of employees who participated in the company's recognition programs.

TERMINATION

Sometimes the termination of a recognition program can't be avoided—it might even be desirable. Planned termination avoids the problem of an obsolete program's gradual decline, which can be extremely demotivating to employees, not to mention wasteful of scarce resources. When you do terminate a program, make sure it is done in a positive way. After all, terminating a recognition program that isn't working is the right thing to do.

Another positive action you can take is to encourage learning from the experience. If and when an organizational recognition program is terminated—for whatever reason—it is important to capture the lessons learned. Capturing and communicating lessons learned and "best practices" will enable everyone in the organization to learn from the experience and turn negatives into positives. We find it sad that so few organizations capture and share knowledge about recognition programs—especially when it is one of the best ways to continuously improve the effectiveness of your recognition efforts.

Another valuable postprogram activity is to document positive testimonials, including those from employees who initially were the most cynical about the program. Assign someone to make the rounds of employees who participated—you can even use a video camera to tape the testimonials so they can be used when rolling out new organizational recognition programs.

And to be sure you don't lose the benefit of hearing from people who were not happy with the program, solicit candid employee feedback by way of anonymous written surveys. Many employees are afraid to speak their minds unless they feel safe. Surveys are one of the best ways to know how people feel, and they serve as a record if you try a program again or modify it later.

OTHER MANAGEMENT TOOLS

Most of us are familiar with the old saying "The devil is in the details"—meaning that the causes of failure are often buried in the details of what might otherwise have been a great idea. As we have shown, there are usually many details in any organizational recognition program. We have already mentioned the importance of treating organizational recognition as a significant organizational change. We also believe that it is vital to *manage it* as you would any major initiative. In managing an organizational recognition program throughout its life cycle, it is important to use the basic tools of project management:

- **Action plan.** Monitoring the accomplishment of the action plan and the schedule become important control mechanisms for keeping things on track. You can turn your action plan and schedule into a detailed project plan using standard project management software (such as Microsoft Project) to help manage the program.

- **Exception reports.** Exception reports document deviations from plan, including the action plan (e.g., uncompleted tasks), the project plan (e.g., missed milestone dates), and the budget (e.g., budget overruns). Exception reports are often discussed at program review meetings.

- **Review meetings.** Review meetings should be held on a regular basis to discuss the progress of the program. The purpose of review meetings is to identify what is working well ("best practices") and what has not worked well (lessons learned). Review meetings are vital to program improvement and to the PDRI process (see pages 65–68).

- **Status reports.** Status reports are usually brief documents that summarize the program progress, accomplishments, major milestones, and problems encountered. This document is sometimes produced before and sometimes produced after the review meetings. Status reports should be provided to all interested stakeholders.

- **Audits.** It is a good idea to do a formal audit of the program every three or six months (or more often if the program is a brief

MAKING WOW CARDS WORK

Q How do programs like the WOW cards at the Swan and Dolphin Resort in Orlando work? How does anyone in HR or a newsletter editor know who received WOW cards to publicize it or put it in a personnel file? Also, how long should a program be kept, and how would we know when a program has run its course?

—**Catherine Strumbos,**
The Alpha Group,
Livonia, MI

A In many programs like this, written praise is submitted though a central recognition committee, which keeps a copy that might be published or posted. Sometimes memo pads are used that have a duplicate that goes to a person's manager or to HR. At the Dolphin Resort, "Captain WOW" (wearing a cape and motorcycle helmet!) hands out awards in person.

On your other question, most recognition programs should be evaluated every twelve to fifteen weeks. If people are still excited about the program and using it, it's still viable.

one). This program audit can be done internally or by an outside consultant.

Organizational recognition can be extremely enjoyable for participants, but it takes serious management work to yield extraordinary organizational benefits. We have provided you with all the tools you need to do recognition well—now it's time for you to make it happen in *your* organization.

THE TAKE-AWAY

- Every recognition program goes through a natural life cycle, from preparation and announcement, through promotion, excitement, and steady state, to revitalization or decline and termination.

- When a program grows old (and every program eventually does), it should either be revitalized or terminated.

PART IV
ISSUES AND CHALLENGES IN RECOGNITION

CHAPTER 13

Selling Recognition to Senior Management

"We realized that our largest asset was our workforce and that growth would come from asset appreciation."

—**Larry Colin,** president, Colin Service Systems

Sooner or later, you're going to have to sell senior management on the benefits of recognition. This time may come before you start your program or it may come when you need to continue or expand funding. For all programs, the support and credibility that comes from top management endorsement is essential. With active support from the top, recognition initiatives take on a new urgency, encouraging employee participation at every organizational level. Without it, recognition programs and activities tend to be considered optional, or are simply thought of as fads, and will consequently flounder or fail.

In this chapter we will cover the strategies and secrets that have worked best to sell senior management on what a powerful tool recognition can be.

See page 353
for article,
"Incentives for All
Generations."

Since the preferences and priorities of top management can vary widely, so too do the best approaches for selling them on recognition. Some managers may be older and more conservative, with "old-line" management values, and feel that employees shouldn't need to be recognized for the job they do because they are already being paid. Such managers might prefer old-fashioned perks and traditional forms of organizational recognition, and may be uncomfortable with the casual and creative style of contemporary recognition.

Other managers may have experienced some success with recognition and may be more open and comfortable with the idea of exploring new and different possibilities for recognizing employees. Typically, however, no matter who's the boss, you are bound to run into some resistance sooner or later. When you do, it will be helpful to know about the following strategies for influencing senior managers to recognize the importance of employee recognition and of the roles they can play in making it happen.

IDENTIFY YOUR ALLIES

Identify the senior managers who will be most receptive to recognition programs. Sell to the right leaders. Make alliances with key senior managers who you think might be the "innovators" or "early adopters" of recognition programs—those who enjoy championing new causes. Also, try to find senior managers who are championing programs or initiatives for which recognition might be a natural complement. For example, the senior vice president of human resources might already be interested in improving employee retention or promoting a "wellness program" with employees. Show him or her how recognition can be an integral component of those programs. In other cases, show the appropriate executives the linkages between recognition and other sought-after improvements. There is always going to be someone in the executive suite who can see the benefit of recognition as long as it is linked to performance or an objective near and dear to their hearts.

PROVIDE CHOICES

Everyone likes to have alternatives and options. Give key executives a choice for their level of involvement. Outline different roles they might play in the recognition program, and get

One busy executive, upon hearing for the umpteenth time that one of his employees did not feel appreciated, stormed out of his office and announced in a loud voice to the entire department, "From now on, I want everyone to assume they are doing a good job unless you hear otherwise from me."

WRECKOGNITION

their commitment to one or more of them. Here are some ways top managers can get involved with recognition:

- Host a recognition kickoff meeting.

- Present top individual or group recognition awards.

- Introduce recognition committee members at a company meeting.

- Point out recognition opportunities to other managers.

ASSESS WHAT MANAGERS ARE ABLE TO DO

You have to determine what top managers are able and willing to do, and help structure a specific plan that holds them accountable for their commitment. For example, one of the authors worked with the president of a company who confessed that—for whatever reasons—he was terribly uncomfortable directly praising employees. To tell such a person that he must personally praise employees would be counterproductive and unsuccessful. In this instance, more plausible alternatives were proposed. The executive ended up holding lunches with small groups of employees from different departments, and in the course of each meal he was able to get to know employees better—and employees had the chance to ask questions and get to know him better as well.

TALK TO THEM IN THEIR OWN TERMS

Probably the best way to influence top management is to demonstrate that an increase of recognition in your organization will have a bottom-line financial impact. This is especially true if you have lots of "old-line" top managers who feel that giving employees their paychecks should be reward enough to get the best effort from everyone. Make a case for recognition by pointing to the bottom-line impact that other companies have enjoyed when recognition programs helped drive desired performance objectives:

- An Amoco plant saved $18.8 million in two years through the use of various recognition gift programs and contests.

- The Travel Related Services division of American Express enjoyed a 500 percent increase in net income over eleven years,

SEEING IS BELIEVING

Q Help! We currently leave reward and recognition to the manager's discretion, but feel that this is ineffective. How can we convince the leadership team of the value and ROI (return on investment) to be gained from implementing a custom R&R (reward and recognition) program?

—**Maria Long,**
Electronic Data Systems,
Port Orange, FL

A You will be able to demonstrate the value best if you link the programs directly to desired performance in one's job, department, or organization. Start with the end in mind in terms of the impact on desired results, and when these results occur, the credibility of your recognition programs will be enhanced. For example, Sears Roebuck was recently able to link recognition to employee satisfaction, and further found that a 5 percent improvement in employee satisfaction led to a 3 percent improvement in customer satisfaction and a 1 percent improvement to the organization's bottom line.

DON'T WORRY, BE HAPPY (AND PRODUCTIVE) AT PERKINS COIE

On May 1, 1912, federal judge George Donworth and U.S. attorney Elmer Todd left public service to form their own law partnership, Donworth and Todd. What started with a handshake on a Seattle sidewalk has evolved through the years to become Perkins Coie, a law firm of 450 lawyers serving a veritable *Who's Who* of successful companies, from Boeing to Bristol-Myers Squibb.

While Perkins Coie has seen tremendous success over the years, the company's management is farsighted enough to know that there is always room for improvement. In fact, "Continuous Improvement" is the second of seven of the firm's formal guiding principles (another is "Rewarding Work Environment"). In 1996, Perkins Coie conducted a firm-wide employee survey to gauge job satisfaction. In the case of the firm's forty-person-strong finance department, the score was only "average"—lower than expected.

In response, Perkins Coie's director of finance and CFO Wayne Robinson created a "book club" with a focus on leadership. The group read books, discussed a selected chapter each month, and tried to apply the authors' concepts in a real-world setting. Included in this group of books was *1001 Ways to Reward Employees*. According to Carla Stroud, a project manager at Perkins Coie, reading the book started a chain of events that has not only improved employee morale within the finance department, but also improved employee productivity.

HAPPINESS IS WHERE YOU FIND IT

Says Stroud, "We decided that we didn't do enough to thank employees and that we needed to focus on that. During one of the first meetings we had regarding the issues, we came up with the idea of forming a Happiness Committee—I think the book called it a Morale Committee. Another supervisor from payroll and I just went around and asked people privately to participate. You see, it's a secret committee. At first we just gave people a basic outline of what we were doing and asked whether they'd like to join. And some really enthusiastic people jumped on board, but no one knew all five of the members. In fact, no one knows even now."

Employees never know what to expect from the Happiness Committee, or when to expect it. The group's first formal act was to fill little Easter eggs with candy and wrap each one in a Dilbert cartoon in which the artist Scott Adams made reference to a "happiness committee." Other creative Happiness Committee activities have included:

- An end-of-summer barbecue in the pouring rain on the outside forty-eighth-floor deck of the building (which just happened to be under construction at the time).

- On Earth Day, department employees received plants, bags of dirt, and fertilizer with a prize to whoever could grow a plant most successfully. (One unexpected benefit: employees are asking one another about their plants. Says one employee, "I don't know if I'd . ever have talked to some of these people before. These kinds of things really break down the barriers.")

- A sack lunch picnic trip on a ferry across Puget Sound. Employees were required to bring permission slips signed by a coworker allowing them to attend.

- A Veteran's Day celebration where the department's five veterans were honored by their thirty-five coworkers with a potluck lunch, complete with red, white, and blue balloons, and a sheet cake.

However, for a rewards program to be effective, it's not enough just to come up with a creative idea once in every blue moon. Rewards and recognition programs have to be sustained; employees have to know that the organization cares enough about their well-being to make them a priority.

"At the end of last year, people were a little burned out, and people began asking me, 'What are you guys going to do?' And I decided to hire a clown."

Stroud says, "It's interesting—it's like a garden. You've really got to tend it. And if you don't do something for a while—it's not that people feel entitled, but they notice. At the end of last year, people were a little burned out, and people began asking me, 'What are you guys going to do?' And I decided to hire a clown. It was only about $75 an hour, and well worth it. It's great to see forty adults making balloon animals. That was our kickoff for 1999."

And the Happiness Committee *has* been effective.

Not only did employee morale improve, but so did productivity. For example, accounts payable bookkeepers in the period from 1994 to 1998—during which workload increased some 36 percent and the staff decreased from ten full-time equivalents to nine—demonstrated a productivity increase of 52 percent.

All this fun—and the improved work environment—has not gone unnoticed by other employees in other departments. Says Stroud, "I see them slowly starting to do some things and forming their own ideas. They have a supervisor who is thinking of great ideas and trying to implement them herself. It has taken a while, but people in some other departments have noticed what we've done. Someone on the operations department staff said to me, 'You people seem so happy down there.'"

SELLING OWNERS

Q For over eight months I have been compiling information about the necessity of keeping employees informed and motivated. I have been able to convince my superiors that it's time to address employee concerns, but I still need to convince the company owners. I'm afraid my company will start to lose its best people because of low morale. How should I go about it?

—**Anonymous**

A **You want to meet owners and upper management on their terms, not yours. That is, show how recognition will positively influence whatever goals—including financial ones—are important to them. Show owners what the competition is doing. Have a pilot study in one department or division, and capture the impact of recognition programs on employee morale and productivity through pre- and post-tests of existing work measures.**

which is attributed in part to recognition programs such as the Great Performers poster campaign.

- Using their points-for-merchandise recognition program, American Airlines was able to purchase a new airplane with $50 million of savings derived from employee suggestions.

By pitching recognition as a means of enhancing productivity, performance, and profitability, you'll have a much better chance of convincing upper management that employee recognition is not just a feel-good, nice-guy activity.

HELP THEM LOOK GOOD

If you want upper management to be personally involved in supporting recognition in your organization, you need to find ways to make them look good. For example, if you want the CEO to write a letter to endorse a new recognition program or an upcoming recognition event, draft the letter yourself to make the task easier for him or her. If you are having your company's CEO present formal awards at a banquet, help him or her by researching some personal stories about each award winner, and go over the pronunciation of the winners' names with the CEO prior to the event. You might arrange for the CEO and award winners to meet after the ceremony to socialize, however briefly. Then close the loop by informing the CEO how much positive impact the meeting had on the award recipients.

SHARE STUDIES AND STATISTICS

Since many top managers are analytical by nature, they can be influenced by evidence from all the research studies and surveys you can marshal. Research and statistics give your proposal instant credibility by connecting recognition to goals and objectives that are important to the organization. Use any or all of the studies and research presented in Chapters 1 through 3 of this book.

SHARE INDUSTRY "BEST PRACTICES"

The information you share should also include industry "best practices," and especially what the organization's competition is doing to recognize and reward their employees. If you can show how other successful companies are innovating in how they manage and motivate their employees to produce bottom-line results, even the most hardened top managers are apt to listen more closely. "Best practices," and survey and research findings, can be found on the Internet, or obtained from human resource organizations such as the Society for Human Resource Management, the Department of Labor, the HR Institute at Eckerd College, or the Saratoga Institute.

MAKE A PERSONAL APPEAL

If the logical and data-based approaches described above fall short of selling senior management on the value of recognizing employees, you might try a personal appeal. At some point, managers must make a "leap of faith"; you need to reassure them that recognition is the right thing to do, and that the organization can become known as a place where people come first. After all, if people truly are the organization's most important resources—as many company mission statements and policies proclaim—then treating those people right should be a priority, not an afterthought, for the success of the organization. At the very least, you should be able to broker a plan to test your beliefs through a pilot program.

CREATE A PILOT PROGRAM

You can create your own success and build momentum for your recognition efforts by initiating a pilot program in your company and developing your own results data. This has the advantage of being more relevant, because it is done with your own employees, performance goals, culture, competitive pressures, and managers. You can also influence the success of a pilot program by carefully selecting positive, proactive participants and closely monitoring what is done to increase the chances of favorable results.

LEVERAGE AND COMMUNICATE SUCCESSES

Start a program that doesn't require a major investment of funds but instead uses creative, no-cost recognition, such as personal and written thanks, public praise, morale-building meetings, and information sessions. Collect anecdotal success stories and build a case for broader implementation by tracking and describing your successes in the organization's publications, in company-wide meetings, or on public bulletin boards. Better yet, schedule some "bragging sessions" for your own employees to share their successes, with senior management in attendance. You will be surprised how much you can do with so little to start, and in the process you will build momentum for additional recognition efforts—especially if you involve those employees you are trying to recognize.

GETTING SENIOR MANAGERS TO MODEL RECOGNITION

When top managers practice recognition, they set the behavioral tone for all managers in the organization, and symbolically say, "If I can make time to do this, no one else in the organization has an excuse not to." The publisher of *The Washington Post* writes notes by hand to reporters. The CEO of the Phoenix Textile Corporation hosts a monthly breakfast for representatives from each department of the company to acknowledge their efforts and see how the organization can better meet its employees' needs.

Here are some more examples of how top managers use open communications with employees as an important form of recognition:

- Scott Mitchell, president of Mackay Envelope in Minneapolis, Minnesota, holds a one-on-one, twenty-minute discussion with every employee every year to discuss ideas, improvements, or whatever is on the employee's mind. Mitchell devotes more than 170 hours to this task every year, an investment that he feels is time well spent.

- Home Depot stores across North America have a weekly satellite feed called "Breakfast with Bernie and Arthur," the company's president and chairman. Everyone gets to hear from the top of the organization what's new and important in moving ahead each week. This underscores, once again, the value of technology in making all employees feel involved and connected wherever they work.

"Good leaders make people feel that they're at the very heart of things, not at the periphery. Everyone feels that he or she makes a difference to the success of the organization. When that happens people feel centered and that gives their work meaning."

—**Warren G. Bennis,**
professor of management

- Mary Kay Ash, founder of Mary Kay, made a commitment to meet with every new employee within thirty days of hire. She once even turned down an invitation to the White House because it conflicted with a new employee orientation session she had committed to months before. Mary Kay's philosophy: "Make people who work for you feel important. If you honor and serve them, they'll honor and serve you."

- Herb Kelleher, CEO and cofounder of Southwest Airlines, based in Dallas, Texas, demonstrates his personal commitment and willingness to be personally involved by helping flight attendants serve beverages to customers when he flies on his airline.

- Andy Grove, chairman of Intel, conducts a half-dozen or so open forums every year at different Intel locations. Whenever Grove is in his cubicle (*all* employees at Intel work in cubicles), any employee is welcome to drop in and speak with him. "Management is about organized common sense," says Grove. "We communicate and communicate and communicate, at every level, in every form. Anyone can ask anybody any question."

RECOGNIZE TOP MANAGEMENT FOR RECOGNIZING OTHERS

Top managers are no different from other employees in their need to be recognized. If you provide positive consequences for top management's involvement in recognition activities, you will increase the chances of their greater future involvement.

- Allow them to announce recognition program successes to the organization when a milestone is achieved.

- Thank them in a letter from the employees and/or the recognition committee.

- Create a top manager's recognition award, nominated and voted on by employees.

To successfully design and implement increased recognition activities or a new recognition program takes not only conviction and persistence but also a strategic approach to winning over top

CEO SANTA

Marty Edelson has only one complaint about most people. "They don't understand business," the seventy-two-year-old says. "Specifically, they don't understand the people side of business." But *he* does.

The people side is the driving force that has made Boardroom, in Greenwich, Connecticut, a leader in newsletter publishing. Boardroom's cornerstone publication, *Bottom Line/Personal,* has a readership of more than 2 million, making it one of the most widely circulated newsletters ever published. Its ninety employees average more than $100 million in sales annually—about five times the productivity rate of most Fortune 500 companies.

Edelston expects a lot from his people—and gives a lot in return. For example, the I-Power program requires employees to submit two ideas a week to improve the company; in return, they share in the profits (often more than $1 million) that result from submitted ideas.

I-Power has a few specific rules. If an employee doesn't submit any ideas, he or she doesn't share in the profits. Edelston explains, "I noticed that this guy was submitting ideas and that guy was submitting ideas, but that guy wasn't. And all three were sharing the profits equally. Well, that's not fair."

He handles nonmonetary recognition in the same style. Edelston gets to know his employees personally. If he notices that someone is working late away from his or her family, he might delve into Marty's Closet—a closet filled with toys and puzzles—and give the person something to take home. He celebrates every associate's birthday and even helped some of his employees make down payments on new homes.

Edelston is also known for storing information about associates' likes and dislikes, which is useful when their work anniversaries approach. "I saw this great baseball book that's perfect for one of my guys," he says. "His anniversary's coming up, and it will make a great gift."

Boardroom employees have returned the loyalty. There was a span of several years, before the dot-com craze snatched up people from all over, that Boardroom's turnover rate held steady at virtually zero.

After a stroke, Edelston has semiretired. He wasn't sure the company was ready to fly on its own, until one day, in the hospital, he had a vision that he could relax—that his employees knew how to work together on their own. "I knew I'd built a company that nourishes its employees."

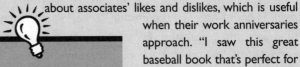

> *He might delve into Marty's Closet— a closet filled with toys and puzzles— and give the person something to take home.*

A MODERN-DAY GUARDIAN ANGEL

In this age when dot-coms have become dot-gones, and everybody's job is on the line, the associates of Maiden Mills can sit tight knowing that someone is looking out for their best interests—the legendary Aaron Feuerstein, seventy-five, CEO of the Lawrence, Massachusetts–based textile manufacturer.

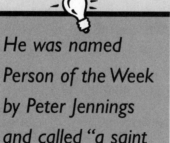

After a disastrous blaze destroyed three of his four factories in 1995, he stood by his more than three thousand employees, keeping them on the payroll while Maiden Mills was rebuilt. Feuerstein's actions made national news: he was named Person of the Week by Peter Jennings and called "a saint for the '90s" by Tom Brokaw.

It was perhaps one of the greatest examples of caring for your employees in the history of corporate America. But for Feuerstein, it was simply the right thing to do. "I really don't think that, as a human being, I deserve all this celebrity status."

At the time, many business leaders questioned Feuerstein's decision. They thought he should relocate the business or close it down. Many thought that keeping his employees on payroll was insane. Feuerstein disagreed. Time and time again, he explained that his employees are his company's greatest asset.

And he had more than his employees to think about. Feuerstein believed that he had a responsi-

bility not only to his workers, but also to the community. Feuerstein felt that letting his employees go would "deliver a death blow" to Lawrence, Massachusetts.

So he paid his employees three months' wages, gave them Christmas bonuses, and assured them that they would return to work. By summer, 85 percent of them were back in the factory, and for the four hundred people still at home, Feuerstein extended health benefits and assisted with job searches.

Feuerstein was no stranger to nonmonetary recognition. Long before the fire, he extended himself—and his success—to his employees; from handing out free soda pop and allowing extra breaks during the dog days of summer, to helping finance an employee's heart bypass operation.

Maiden Mills' employees and community members have responded in turn. Both employee and customer retention at Maiden Mills, according to one report, is above 95 percent. When it comes to recognition, that's amazing.

> *He was named Person of the Week by Peter Jennings and called "a saint for the '90s" by Tom Brokaw.*

management. Don't waste time complaining that your organization doesn't have satisfactory recognition programs or support; instead, propose a recognition program and sell senior managers on why it needs to happen now.

THE TAKE-AWAY

- Obtaining the support of top management is a critical step in the implementation of a successful recognition program, especially one that crosses organizational lines and requires financial resources to put into practice.

- Target key senior managers as allies for new recognition programs, especially innovators and early adopters—individuals who enjoy championing new organizational programs and initiatives.

- One of the best ways to influence top management is to demonstrate a bottom-line financial impact, or other performance results, that can be attained from your proposed recognition program.

- Be sure to recognize top managers who recognize others. This will further reinforce their behavior, increasing the likelihood that additional support for recognition programs and activities will be forthcoming.

CHAPTER 14

Troubleshooting Recognition Problems

"We are continually faced by great opportunities brilliantly disguised as unsolvable problems."

—**Lee Iacocca,** former CEO, Chrysler Corporation

Despite the best intentions, recognition can go wrong. And when recognition goes wrong, it can lead to far more problems for an organization than having no recognition program at all. The wrong people can be recognized, the wrong things can be recognized, the awards chosen can turn out to be meaningless or even insulting to those who receive them, or recognition programs can be ignored altogether. The result? Decreased morale, lowered performance, customer service problems, and a decline in profitability.

Here's a review of the most common recognition mistakes that are made at the individual, group, and organizational levels.

Decide for Yourself

At Xerox, one cus-tomer service center turned decisions about work schedules over to the employees. With employee work teams in charge of scheduling, the com-pany reported higher morale, better cus-tomer service, and a 30 percent reduction in absenteeism.

INDIVIDUAL RECOGNITION MISTAKES

In many ways, one-on-one thanks is the most important form recognition can take. Why? Because individual recognition is very personal, and thus meaningful to employees. Individual recognition can be given by anyone to anyone at any time; you don't need to fill out a form, submit a nomination to a committee, or get approval from top management.

Here are some of the most common recognition mistakes we see made with individuals:

Missed recognition opportunities. Probably the most common problem with individual recognition is ignoring or just not noticing the opportunities to use it. The reasons range from being too busy to take the time to acknowledge an employee who does a good job, to believing that employees don't need to be recognized, to feeling that employees need to receive positive feedback only once a year in their performance review or at the end of the year when bonuses are passed out to employees. One of the authors recently worked with a very successful manager who resented the fact that he received recognition only when it was given out publicly to every-one in his department. He reported that the public recognition seemed perfunctory and mechanical, and he never had the satisfac-tion of a simple individual thank-you from his boss for the results he had obtained. Missed opportunities can especially be a problem with good performers, who you feel must already know they are good since you've told them in the past.

Recognition that's not timely. Almost as bad as missing an opportunity to recognize others for doing a good job is doing so too late. The longer you wait to recognize someone, the smaller the impact. After a certain point, delayed acknowledgment only shows your employees just how out of touch you are with them and their accomplishments.

Insincere or mechanical recognition. One of the hallmarks of effective recognition is sincerity. Mechanical and superficial recog-nition can completely backfire. When you provide recognition mechanically, it seems manipulative: "Gary, here's some movie passes for helping out yesterday—can you work late again tonight?" For recognition to work, it needs to be honest and sincere, with no expectation of a favor in return. Likewise, an employee who received a glowing report back from her manager was upset when she learned that her manager had not actually read the report.

Public recognition for private people. Although, as a general rule, people value public praise, there is a percentage of the population that is made uncomfortable by public recognition. To force public recognition on someone who does not want it is demotivating and can even have negative ramifications. For example, one gentleman who was going to be given a perfect attendance award at an all-company awards banquet was so nervous about going up on stage—with the possibility of having to speak publicly—that he called in sick on the day of the banquet. One introverted Employee of the Month never used his designated parking spot close to the building, so a few of his buddies removed the sign and posted it in front of his car out in the middle of the employee parking lot.

Criticism should always be conducted in private in order to be more effective (as well as more respectful). The founder of one computer company had a tendency to berate employees in front of others if they were running behind schedule. The anticipated humiliation caused other employees to try to hide when they were running behind schedule or having trouble with a project—or rush to turn in less-than-perfect work.

Undercutting praise with criticism. It is very common for managers to immediately follow their thanks with a note of criticism. "You did a great job on that report, Betty, but I noticed quite a few typos." This approach undermines the positive impact of the recognition. Save constructive feedback for another time when the person can do something with it, and just focus on what they did right!

Giving recognition that is not rewarding. Managers often defeat their best intentions by doing something that ends up being non-motivating, or even insulting, to the recipient. A woman told us about a boss who took her to a baseball game as a reward. Her initial excitement was soon dashed when, after asking a question about the game, her boss replied, "What are you, stupid?" She spent the rest of the game staring in cold silence, and reported it as being "one of the worst days of my life."

THE EYES OF THE RECEIVER

Q We do a lot of things for people at Children's, but it doesn't seem to be enough. For example, we recently scored low on an employee survey question about whether they have been recognized by a manager within the past week. What can we do to improve these particular scores?

—**Anonymous,**
Children's Hospital,
Philadelphia, PA

A Just because you are doing things for all employees does not mean that you are making individual employees feel recognized. Many employees do not feel that organizational forms of thanks (such as a benefit or celebration) are anything special, precisely because everyone is getting those things. To make each employee feel recognized, you have to connect with each person and find out what items or activities make the person feel valued. Of course, some things are always important: sincere, timely praise for a job well done, for example, is almost universally important to everyone.

Code Pink: Recognition in Reverse

Scottsdale Memorial Hospital in Scottsdale, Arizona, was having a problem with doctors criticizing staff members in front of others, even patients. To alleviate the situation, they instituted a special code for use over the intercom. When someone started publicly reprimanding another, you'd hear "Code Pink, Station 7" over the intercom and personnel would rush to that location and stare at the perpetrator! The problem soon stopped.

TEAM RECOGNITION MISTAKES

One thing that makes recognizing teams especially difficult is that it can be hard to determine who on any given team is truly performing and who is slacking off. If you give a non-performer the same reward as a high performer, you risk totally invalidating the recognition in the eyes of the team members. And if you fail to reward the team stars, watch out!

Many of the same recognition mistakes that are made with individuals are made with teams, but some are more typically team-related. These include:

Treating everyone the same. Also called "jelly bean motivation," this strategy fails to differentiate between the deserving and those merely riding the productive team members' coattails. Guess who best knows who on the team is not performing? The members of the team. When you reward everyone on a team equally when some people clearly did not perform up to the standards of the rest of the team, you risk losing credibility in the eyes of the high performers—precisely those you can least afford to alienate. Worse yet is giving more work to the person who does good work, while allowing a nonperformer more time when they didn't meet a deadline.

Leaving someone out. Sometimes when a group is recognized, individuals are left out, either inadvertently or because team membership has changed over time. Sometimes only the manager gets credit for the entire group's work, which can be demotivating to the team. It's up to you to ensure that *everyone* who contributes to the success of a team effort—regardless of where they may be located in the organization—is recognized for their contributions.

Not letting the team help determine rewards. Often the team is not allowed any say in how they'd like to be thanked. As a result, the form of thanks can miss the mark completely. For example, a team leader in a chemical plant wanted to thank her project team for the work they had done, and purchased T-shirts for team members. Their response: "We saved the company all this money and all we get is this lousy T-shirt?!" The manager was smart enough to use the incident as a learning point and asked the team, "What would have been more motivating?" By involving the team in the selection of rewards, the recognition will likely be closer to the mark and more motivating as a result.

ORGANIZATIONAL RECOGNITION MISTAKES

Because of its scope and complexity, organizational recognition efforts are most likely to go awry. For this reason, many organizations avoid getting too creative with recognition programs, sticking instead with tried-and-true programs such as years-of-service and employee-of-the-month awards (which, unfortunately, are often not all that effective in motivating employees). Following are common problems that arise in organizational recognition.

The rush to recognition. The starting point of many organizational recognition problems is poor planning. Some action-oriented companies tend to take a ready-fire-aim approach to planning. But where a systematic plan is highly desirable for individual and team recognition, it is absolutely essential for organizational recognition. More than a few companies that have rushed to get an initiative rolled out have neglected one or more important components of an effective recognition program and have seen it blow up in their faces.

Rewards that aren't rewarding. We've seen many instances in which the awards given in a recognition or incentive program or contest created more problems than they fixed. Take, for example, a trip to Mexico. At first this seems like a great reward for desired performance, but for many employees it might only raise questions: "Can I bring my family if I win?" "If my children can't come, can I get someone to watch them while we're gone?" "Will I have to get new clothes, luggage, etc. for the trip?" Suddenly, a well-intentioned idea can backfire. Deciding what employees value without checking with them is a sure way to increase your risk of missing the motivational mark.

One size doesn't fit all. Another basic mistake people make is to provide—out of a false sense of fairness—the exact same recognition or reward to every employee. Few things are as unfair as the equal treatment of unequals. Younger employees, for example, often want to be passionately engaged in their work. Give them leeway and the chance to pursue their ideas and learn new skills. Challenge

> *"For any organizational problem first ask, 'What is the best solution?' Then ask, 'What can be done?'"*
>
> —**Peter F. Drucker,** management consultant

REVITALIZING RECOGNITION AT PIZZA HUT

What company uses 2.5 percent of all the milk produced in the United States each year (more than 3.2 billion pounds)? What company uses more than 700 million pounds of pepperoni each and every year (a quantity that, if the slices were laid side by side, would circle the earth twice and then stretch all the way to the moon)? What company did Russian president Boris Yeltsin and his comrades call during an attempted political coup several years ago to deliver food to the Russian Parliament building?

The answer is Pizza Hut, the world's largest pizza company. Pizza Hut was founded in Wichita, Kansas, in 1958, eventually purchased by PepsiCo, and in 1997 was spun off into a new company—Tricon Global Restaurants—along with its other PepsiCo fast-food stablemates, Kentucky Fried Chicken and Taco Bell. Today, Pizza Hut has more than 12,100 outlets around the world, with sales exceeding $5 billion a year, and controls 22 percent of the U.S. pizza market.

While the world is looking pretty rosy for Pizza Hut right now, this wasn't the case just a few years ago. After PepsiCo spun off the company into Tricon Global Restaurants, profits faltered and its chief competitors, including Domino's, Little Caesar's, and Papa John's, began to steal away market share. Employee turnover was at crisis levels, with about a third of restaurant managers quitting every year.

The solution? Tricon hired 6-foot-3-inch Mike Rawlings—a former football linebacker who studied art, communications, and philosophy at Boston College—as Pizza Hut's president and chief concept officer. "The company needed some serious mojo," Rawlings says. "There were very talented people here and great brand equity, but it needed an internal belief in itself, direction and spirit."

IT ALL STARTS WITH A PLAN

Rawlings developed a three-part plan to rejuvenate Pizza Hut's operations:

1. Improve the company's products.

2. Redesign the company's restaurants.

3. Energize the company's employees.

Rawlings quickly accomplished the first two goals by spending $50 million in 1997 to develop new toppings for the restaurants, selling off hundreds of restaurants to franchisees, and creating a plan to pump $500 million more into upgrading the company's remaining restaurants over the next five years.

Rawlings has devoted much of his time, however, to accomplishing the third goal—energizing the company's employees. "These people are competitive, bad to the bone," he says. "The way to get them to be even more competitive is to create a sense of winning and fun so they like to come to work each day."

THE KEY TO ENERGIZING

It didn't take Rawlings long to discover the key to energizing his employees: employee rewards and recognition.

Here are just some of the ways that Pizza Hut rewards and recognizes its employees:

- The Big Cheese award is perhaps Pizza Hut's most coveted award, and it is the highest level of corporate recognition. Rawlings has personally presented this award—a yellow foam rubber wedge of cheese that fits neatly on the recipient's head—to more than three hundred of the company's highest performing employees and franchisees. Each proud award recipient also receives a photo of the presentation.

- Star Tracks is an awards program that recognizes and rewards managers, area coaches, and market coaches for their ability to grow Pizza Hut, run great restaurants, develop great teams, and make plans. Rewards include team dinners and celebration trips for the recipient and a guest.

Edwards was totally surprised when Rawlings personally showed up at his restaurant to present him with a Big Cheese award.

So how does a mammoth company like Pizza Hut continue to energize employees, obtaining their best performance every day of the week? By putting people first, by supporting employee learning and initiative, and by creating a culture of recognition. Says Alywin Lewis, chief operating officer of Pizza Hut, "Our goal is to run great restaurants. And to that end, we need great people. We strive to create a nurturing environment and culture that provides our employees a place to contribute and succeed." When employees succeed, the company succeeds.

- Quarterly bonuses are awarded to general managers based on the size of the manager's restaurant and its performance on a variety of measures.

Do rewards and recognition make a difference at Pizza Hut? The answer is an unqualified yes! Just ask Harold Edwards, a twenty-five-year Pizza Hut veteran who manages an outlet in an inner-city Kansas City neighborhood. Edwards was totally surprised when Rawlings personally showed up at his restaurant to present him with a Big Cheese award, which Edwards now displays proudly at home on his fireplace mantel. "It shows that management cares. If they don't care, why should we? My customers call me Mr. Cheesehead now. Okay, I'll take that."

"It's just a piece of foam," says Joe Bosch, Pizza Hut's chief people officer, "but you see these twenty-year veterans get tears in their eyes when they get one. It's a powerful thing."

TRIVIAL PURSUITS

Q We're having problems with our employee-of-the-month program in that people nominate others for trivial things.

—**Susan Schmitz,**
Department of Transportation

A **I'm not a fan of such programs. I've rarely seen one that worked well and was truly meaningful to recipients. Speak with anyone who submits trivial nominations and help them be more specific, identifying and articulating their colleagues' behavior and performance.**

 See chapter 15
for more
on revitalizing
tired programs.

them with interesting work, or give them full responsibility to take control of a situation. For example, a young man in a recent session conducted by one of the authors said that he felt most motivated when his company gave him full contact with a key client, trusting him to do what needed to be done to meet that client's needs. Another person who manages younger employees tries to vary the routine at work to make things a little more exciting. When he wants to hold a group meeting, he finds he gets a better response by doing it outside on some picnic tables rather than in a conference room.

Loss of freshness and relevance. Yet another basic mistake managers and organizations make is to expect a recognition program or activity to remain effective forever. We see many formal recognition programs that were once very good, but along the way ran out of energy, got boring, or didn't engage everyone involved. This often happens with long-standing recognition programs such as years-of-service awards or employee-of-the-month programs. One employee told of feeling good about receiving his ten-year pin until a new employee came up to him and said: "How did you ever make it working here ten years?! I'm ready to quit today!" He found himself having to defend why he had been with the company so long. What had been an honor at one time had essentially turned into an "endurance award."

Maybe the program had lost touch with those it was meant to excite, so that the recognition was no longer a great honor, or had even become a joke in the organization. At another corporation, employees didn't view a years-of-service award as a form of recognition at all. Since everyone eventually got it, it didn't seem special. And since it was delivered very impersonally, the only emotions that were triggered were negative. "You misspelled my name!"

Even the best programs need to be reevaluated and renewed from time to time—usually sooner rather than later. As a general rule of thumb, the shelf life of a typical recognition program today is closer to sixteen *weeks* than sixteen years. Find out what's working and what's not—and adjust the program accordingly.

Confusing priorities and alignment. It is amazing how many organizations send confusing and conflicting messages in their recognition practices and systems. Without realizing it, what management chooses to recognize often sends a bewildering array of messages that confuse, rather than guide, employees. "Maximize production!" "Quality is job one!" "Give customers your complete attention!" "Reduce customer contact time!" "Increase long-term profits!" "Reduce costs immediately!" "Work faster!" "Work safer!" "Be innovative!" "Don't make mistakes!"

After a while, employees realize that if everything is a priority, nothing is a priority. Employees also sense that management is confused about what it really wants. When performance expectations are unclear, employees waste a tremendous amount of human energy trying to figure out what is *really* expected, and various individuals and groups that are supposed to work together end up working at cross purposes.

Subjective recognition. Too often we have seen recognition given based on subjective impressions, which are notoriously inaccurate. Subjective recognition is uneven at best, and wrong and unfair at its worst. Often when the authors are in their clients' companies, they look at the organization's newsletter and will typically find photos of employees with the president around an award or plaque. We'll stop an employee and ask what that reward is for. More times than not, the employee does not know. "Why do you suppose these people are in this photo then?" The reply: "They're management's favorites."

Some employees receive recognition based on a "halo effect"— that is, once they are perceived as top performers, they are *always* perceived as top performers, and can do no wrong. On the other hand, a "horns effect" (for lack of a better term) often exists around employees perceived to be inadequate. Under such circumstances, recognition becomes more of a demotivating influence than a motivating one.

To avoid these pitfalls, use carefully defined, objective criteria. Checklists can help identify behaviors and results that are worthy of recognition, and defeat the halo or horns effect. The tendency of supervisors to give some people more recognition than others can also be counteracted by using a recognition log, which helps keep track of who is receiving recognition and how often. This is a valuable feedback device for the supervisor or manager who wants to improve the quality (and quantity) of recognition giving.

Entitlement recognition. A common problem when recognition is done just to be nice is that it comes to be expected, leading to a cul-

OVERCOMING POOR MORALE

Q I'm a rewards and development manager for a prominent security industry. The rewards program is newly developed for the company, and my boss says the hype is not there. I feel as if I'm in a trap with no buy-in from top management, and low employee morale. Any advice?

—**Sharon Ragsdale,**
ADT,
Boca Raton, FL

A It takes time to change a culture. Start by bargaining for more time, then request your manager's support—no one can do it on his own! Then establish a motivational baseline and find out what employees would like to see more of. Once you can provide what employees want, morale will go up and management will see the value of your program.

ture of entitlement. Bring in doughnuts to celebrate performance, not just because it's a nice day; otherwise, by the third time you bring in doughnuts, employees will come to expect the recognition just for showing up. At one company, employees would complain that a recognition dinner was a buffet when last year it was a sit-down affair. When thousands of dollars was spent buying popcorn as a spontaneous thanks to all employees, people complained that the popcorn wasn't that fresh. Employees even complained that the tissue paper in the rest rooms wasn't as soft as it used to be!

Too often, recognition becomes "part of the landscape." Recognition should be special, not routine. When recognition is expected, it loses its value and authenticity. Entitlements (such as employee benefits) are fine. Just don't make recognition one of them.

Too much recognition is almost as bad as too little recognition. We advocate the generous use of recognition, but we have seen organizations that overdo it. In terms of results, recognition for everything has just about the same impact as recognition for nothing. Recognition should be viewed as a valuable organizational resource, and should be used as such. Remember, recognition is a strategic business resource, not simply a form of psychological compensation.

Recognition take-aways. When recognition programs end, which most eventually do, employees commonly feel deprived. The result can be a decline in morale and performance. To prevent this problem, we recommend "time-bounding" organizational recognition by setting clear start and end dates for the program. In this way, employees anticipate that recognition programs will come to an end, and they aren't disappointed when they do. Furthermore, when one recognition program is brought to a close, another one should be ready to immediately take its place.

Inappropriate recognition. Sometimes recognition is too small or too large. Telling someone in the hallway that they did a "nice job" at the completion of a two-year project can be inappropriate, as is (in a true example) giving a cruise to an employee of the month who was known by his colleagues to have fudged his numbers (and who was fired within the year).

It is very important to differentiate recognition from rewards. Recognition is positive reinforcement for something well done. A reward is something tangible that often accompanies recognition.

Rewards are often used as a proxy for recognition and too often are dumped at people's feet without sufficient recognition. The antidote? Focus on *high recognition value*—even if there is a significant reward associated with it.

Zero-sum recognition. Zero-sum games are those in which in order for somebody to win, somebody else must lose. This might make sense in competitive sports and games, but it doesn't make sense in the collaborative workplaces of today. There needn't be any losers. Picking one outstanding employee tends to send the wrong messages about teamwork—that it isn't important.

When establishing an organizational recognition program, *every* employee should be able to win. This doesn't mean that rewards shouldn't be earned. What it does mean is that competitive recognition can be extremely detrimental to what organizations want to accomplish today. In many recognition contests, there are very few winners and the rest are losers. A classic example is the top salesperson winning a trip to Hawaii, the number-two salesperson getting a bottle of Champagne, and the rest of the sales staff (and support staff) getting nothing. Likewise, in employee-of-the-month or employee-of-the-year programs, there is one winner, and everybody else loses. Why can't a lot of employees be "employees of the month"? Isn't that what organizations ought to be striving for?

Untimely recognition. Delay is the enemy of recognition. One of the challenges of organizational recognition is keeping it streamlined and nonbureaucratic so that people receive timely recognition. If every form of recognition needs management approval, many recognition opportunities will be missed. Avoid recognition decisions that have to go through level after level of approval, and always allow some forms of recognition—such as an on-the-spot award or a traveling trophy—that require *no* additional levels of approval.

RECOGNIZING THE WRONG THINGS

At any level of recognition, but especially at the organizational one, it's critical to identify exactly what you're rewarding. If your organization isn't getting the results it wants, or the behaviors needed to achieve them, perhaps you're just confused

"Silent gratitude isn't very much to anyone."

—**Gertrude Stein,**
writer

NO-COST IDEA

44

Special Assignments

AT&T has a program called "Resource Link," which lets employees from diverse backgrounds and with varied management, technical, or professional skills "sell" their abilities to different departments for short-term assignments. It has greatly increased retention and employee satisfaction.

about what you want. It's amazing how many times organizations do what management expert Steven Kerr calls "The folly of rewarding A, while hoping for B." In a classic article,[1] Kerr gives a wide range of examples of undesired outcomes that were, usually inadvertently, being reinforced.

Let's look at some examples of our own:

Many organizations recognize *any* sales revenue instead of real profits. It is amazing how many salespeople receive recognition—and significant cash rewards—for closing *unprofitable* deals. Recognizing sales revenue—period—can result in a big "top line" and a small—or nonexistent—"bottom line."

Many organizations recognize internal competition instead of real teamwork. If you are finding that there isn't enough teamwork in your organization, you probably don't have to look any further than your recognition system. In fact, most performance evaluation systems pit employee against employee, and department against department, in an internal competition for scarce rewards. When he was dismissed as CEO of Digital Equipment Corporation, founder Ken Olsen admitted that his major failing was not getting his engineering managers to team up with product and marketing managers, in part because of conflicting reward and recognition criteria.

Many organizations recognize inspection instead of real quality. For years, companies tried to *inspect out* defects, hoping that quality would improve. Factories that shipped no defects were recognized, even though they wasted millions of dollars on scrap and rework—quality was never built in. Some software firms even went so far as to give employees cash rewards for finding bugs in their products, creating an incentive for employees to plant these bugs in the first place, and then (they hoped) catch and fix them before the products were released to the public.

Many organizations recognize trainee attitudes or training time rather than the truly effective training. The desired outcomes of training should be skills and knowledge to be used on the job, and improved business results. However, rather than recognize these results, most organizations recognize the amount of training that employees receive, and the attitudes of trainees toward training events. Both of these factors have very little bearing on whether the skills being learned are valuable, and the extent to which they will be used on the job—much less the impact on organizational effectiveness. We have seen many training courses that receive rave reviews from trainees, but the skills are never used when the trainees get back on the job. This is often because the application of the new skills—which usually requires more effort than the use of existing skills—is never recognized (and therefore is never reinforced).

Many organizations recognize seniority rather than high performance. There is nothing wrong with celebrating service anniversaries, but not at the expense of performance. Some companies not only tolerate mediocre performance, but encourage it by giving mediocre, senior-ranking performers the same recognition they give outstanding performers. This sends a poor message to employees. Other companies recognize political astuteness and "gamesmanship," not real performance.

Many organizations recognize problem hiding rather than problem solving. What happens when an employee speaks up about a problem in your organization? In many companies, problem finders are viewed as troublemakers. No one can solve problems that are being hidden or ignored. Does your organization recognize whistle-blowers or punish them? Remember that problems are actually opportunities for improvement.

Many organizations recognize individual expertise instead of knowledge sharing. You might be surprised how many organizations that are investing heavily in knowledge management (KM) don't have the most critical KM enabler in place—a recognition system that recognizes knowledge sharing, and not knowledge hoarding. As long as individual expertise is recognized above corporate expertise, this will continue to be the case.

Many organizations reward management rather than leadership. According to Warren Bennis and Burt Nanus in *Leaders: The Strategies for Taking Charge,*[2] managers are people who do things right, and leaders are people who do the right things. Too many organizations say that they want visionary leaders, but tend to recognize only the managers who meet deadlines, manage

> *"A pessimist sees the difficulty in every opportunity; an optimist sees the opportunity in every difficulty."*
>
> **—Sir Winston Churchill,** statesman

NONMONETARY REWARDS

Q I agree with what you've said, that praise and recognition are very important, with money and perks a close second. I am working for a small company now, and did not get the money I thought I should have, but I've stayed on because I can work part-time flexible hours, travel only five miles to work, have paid vacation and holidays, a 401(k) plan, and the month of August off to be with my children. My boss is demanding, but always motivates and praises.

—**Leverne Moore,**
General Office Interiors,
Union, NJ

A I think your comments reinforce my belief that money is important, but certainly not the only motivator and, for most people, not even the top motivator at work.

budgets, and make sure that others follow procedures, leaving the real leaders unrecognized.

Many organizations recognize conformity rather than creativity. No organization can be successful without some degree of conformity. But no organization can be truly successful without a significant amount of creativity. Creative behavior manifests itself when employees go beyond the "normal" requirements of the job and take initiative. Unfortunately, in many organizations creativity is often punished rather than rewarded because it is messier and may not be fully understood at first, which often causes problems.

At one time or another most employees have tried to be creative only to encounter resistance, not recognition. This resistance comes with phrases like the following: "It won't work," "We've never done it that way before," or "That's just not feasible." Resistance also comes in the form of bureaucratic and cumbersome "suggestion" systems purporting to welcome ideas.

Many organizations recognize overperformance based on easy objectives instead of employees who aim high. How many performance reviews assess employees in terms of "not meeting," "meeting," or "exceeding" expectations? This often encourages employees to set low goals, so that they can be exceeded. When the bar is low, many employees may "win," but the organization loses.

Many organizations recognize not reporting accidents rather than safety. Recognizing "lack of accidents" often encourages employees simply *not to report* accidents or injuries. There are two ways to achieve excellent safety records: (1) maintain a safe workplace and recognize employees who engage in safe behavior, or (2) recognize employees for not reporting the accidents that will inevitably happen, especially in an unsafe workplace. Which approach do *you* think is better?

Many organizations recognize bloated budgets rather than cost containment. How many times have you seen managers "rewarded" for being under budget by getting their budgets cut the next year? In fact, that is the most frequent consequence of managerial frugality. Managers learn that the best way to defend against organizational cost-cutting is by having a bloated budget! In addition, across-the-board cost-cutting hurts those who have been running a tight ship much more than those who have bloated budgets and redundant staffs. This kind of cost-cutting actually reinforces budget padding, buffer stocks, and inventory cushions, just trying to protect against future shocks.

Many organizations recognize lack of complaints rather than excellent customer service. Truly outstanding hospitality organizations realize that it is virtually impossible to improve customer service *without* customer complaints. In fact, the best customer service organizations actually *solicit* complaints. There is another reason for wanting customers to report complaints: research has verified that effective recovery from a customer service problem is one of the key drivers of customer delight and building customer loyalty.

Recognition is a wonderful thing, but recognizing the wrong things can actually undermine your organization's competitiveness and threaten its very survival. The table below will help you identify the behavior it pays to recognize.

"Successful people are simply people who learn to solve their problems. . . . They are not people without problems."
—**Source unknown**

If you want . . .	Then recognize . . .	Not . . .
PROFITS	Profitable sales	Any sales revenue
TEAMWORK	Collaboration	Internal competition
QUALITY	Process improvement	Inspection
EFFECTIVE TRAINING	Skills used on the job	Training time
HIGH PERFORMANCE	Results achieved	Seniority
PROBLEM SOLVING	Problems found & solved	Problem hiding
KNOWLEDGE SHARING	Organizational expertise	Individual expertise
LEADERSHIP	Quality of leadership	Just management
CREATIVITY	Creative ideas	Conformity
AIMING HIGH	Meeting stretch goals	Overperformance
SAFETY	Safe behavior	Reported accidents
COST CONTAINMENT	Reduced spending	Keeping within budget
CUSTOMER SERVICE	Customer loyalty	Lack of complaints

EMPLOYEES CAN RUN RECOGNITION

Q In one business I've worked with, the employees came up with a list of things that motivated them (free dry cleaning, leasing a BMW, oil changes, weekends away, and so on). The owner took part in creating both team and individual rewards, but now has "no time" to implement anything that's been discussed.

—**Alayne White,**
Alayne White Success Group,
Bristol, RI

A If the owner is too busy to lead the efforts and doesn't have time to keep commitments he made, no one's behavior is going to change for the better. Consider having the employees run the recognition effort themselves, perhaps as a revolving responsibility for a week or month at a time. Sharing the work spreads it out and gives a great sense of ownership and commitment to people as their ideas are used. Ideally, those at the top of the organization would be involved, but if they are not, don't let it discourage you from acknowledging those who are doing good work.

BUILT-IN DEMOTIVATORS

In addition to common mistakes and "wrongful" recognition, there's one more trouble area that we need to consider: broad, but often subtle, demotivators that sabotage a recognition program. Some of the most common ones include:

Unclear expectations. Sometimes, due to poor design, planning, or communication, employees simply don't know what to expect from the recognition program. They don't know what their roles and responsibilities are, or what is supposed to happen during the program. The solution, of course, is to make sure that expectations are very clear and unambiguous.

Unnecessary rules. Recognition programs are sometimes so full of rules and guidelines that employees perceive the programs as being "just more bureaucracy." Keep recognition programs simple.

Lack of follow-up. Nothing is more demotivating than expecting a positive outcome and not getting it. Too many recognition programs make promises that cannot be kept—at least not in a timely fashion. The solution is to promise only what can be delivered, and to make sure that the recognition delivers on all promises.

Constant change. Change is particularly demotivating when employees perceive that the "rules of the game" keep changing. When you change recognition programs, make sure that you are making them better (such as by adding new recognition opportunities), and not simply changing the rules to the organization's advantage (such as making it more difficult for people to attain existing recognition levels). If you do need to "raise the bar" to address "recognition inflation," for example, it is important to consult with employees and explain why you are making the change.

Unfairness. If employees view recognition as unfair, your entire recognition program might be in serious jeopardy. Organizational recognition is particularly vulnerable to this concern, because the recognition criteria in one area of the organization could differ from the recognition criteria in another area. Don't think that employees don't compare—they do. The antidote: keep the perception of fairness in mind while you are designing the program, and keep track of any recognition disparities in different areas of the organization.

Hypocrisy. Nothing is more demotivating than managers who say one thing and do another. Many recognition initiatives have been sabotaged by inconsistencies between talking the talk and walking the walk. There is no quick fix for hypocrisy. The countermeasure is to make executives aware of this pitfall. Then monitor employee feedback that might indicate if hypocrisy is still a problem. If so, provide feedback to those who inadvertently might be sending the wrong messages.

Rewarding poor performance. If employees see that poor performers are being recognized, the program (and whoever put it into place) will lose credibility. Recognition should always be earned. Never recognize those who don't deserve recognition. Here are some tips for ensuring that you don't reward poor performance, from the book *Why Employees Don't Do What They Are Supposed to Do and What to Do About It,* by Ferdinand F. Fournies:

- Examine the consequences you deliver when an employee fails to perform or creates problems.

- Don't reward nonperformance with attention, lunch, coffee, or lengthy discussions about personal problems.

- Don't personally correct errors made by nonperformers. Make sure that the employee responsible for the mistake makes the correction.

- Give your attention to people who do things the way you want them done without creating havoc for you.

- Do not assign someone else to take over work from the nonperformer. Work with him until either his performance improves or you replace him.

- When an employee is difficult to control, apply the necessary controls and negative consequences. If performance improves, provide immediate verbal recognition and praise.

- If an employee repeatedly complains about work assignments that are both fair and unavoidable, ignore it. Respond to the person with verbal rewards only when they correctly perform the job.[3]

Management invisibility. Too often, senior managers are visible during the initial launch of the initiative, but then disappear. This makes employees believe that the program is not really important to

WRECKOGNITION

In one company, management asked employees to call an employee who was frequently late to wake him up in the morning.

Fellow employees felt invaded and resentful. Management should have dealt with the problem directly, and on company time.

See chapter 14 for a discussion on demotivators.

the organization, and is therefore not deserving of their efforts or attention. Keeping a recognition initiative healthy requires continual management visibility. Senior managers should have specific roles to play in a recognition program (such as presenting recognition to recipients), so that they will remain a visible part of it.

THE TAKE-AWAY

- Some of the most common mistakes made when recognizing individuals include missed recognition opportunities, recognition that's not timely, insincere or mechanical recognition, and public recognition for private people.

- Some of the most common mistakes made when recognizing teams include treating everyone the same, leaving someone out, and not letting the group determine their rewards.

- The majority of organizational recognition problems are the result of poor planning.

- Recognition often goes awry if an organization rewards one kind of behavior when it really wants an entirely different kind of behavior.

- Some of the most common recognition demotivators include: unclear expectations, lack of follow-up, constant change, hypocrisy, rewarding poor performance, and management invisibility.

CHAPTER 15

Sustaining and Reenergizing Recognition

"It's no good saying you can't afford to look after your staff. You can't afford not to."

—**Julian Richer,** founder, Richer Sounds

G etting married is not easy; after all, there's finding the right person, falling in love, deciding on the color of the bridesmaids' dresses, choosing the caterer. But the real trick is making a marriage work over time. So it is with recognition programs. As we have seen, there are many obstacles to getting a program up and running properly in the first place, but once the honeymoon's over even the most popular and successful program faces the daunting challenge of keeping the excitement going.

It is natural for a recognition program to become tired at some point after the initial excitement wears off and recognition diminishes in frequency or becomes routine. Once the spontaneity is gone, what remains often can be nothing more than the tedious administrative and bureau-

WRECKOGNITION

An office administrator whose boss initially supported new, more flexible, and fun recognition activities in the office quickly withdrew his support when his own boss didn't like the idea. This left the administrator hanging with a half-completed project, hours of wasted effort, and raised expectations on the part of employees. The worker left his job, feeling he'd lost face from the experience. Several others in his group followed him out the door.

cratic elements of award nominations and awards events (sometimes to the extent that they bore even the award winners themselves). Although no rewards and recognition program lasts forever, its life as a critical part of your company's culture and success will be enhanced if it is carefully sustained and occasionally reenergized. Sustaining a recognition program over time means raising and re-raising awareness of the importance of recognizing employees, constantly renewing the motivation to recognize, and periodically putting new skills and tools into place. Let's look at some strategies and techniques that will help you keep your recognition efforts fresh and effective.

SUSTAINING YOUR RECOGNITION PROGRAM

So you've got an effective recognition program in place. Employee morale is up. Customer service is up. Productivity is up. So are profits. Congratulations!

Now what?

The next step is to build upon this effort, linking recognition to other organizational elements. Build or rebuild momentum for recognition by amplifying and multiplying recognition practices throughout the organization until they become part of the organization's culture.

Link to strategic objectives. The best programs specifically tie recognition to the achievement of important objectives for the organization. Ideally, this is done in the upfront design of the recognition program, but it's never too late to make the link. Show progress toward that end by finding ways to measure the impact of recognition, demonstrating the actual, quantifiable differences recognition efforts are making on employee perceptions, satisfaction, and performance.

Renew sponsorship commitment. Few forms of support are more important to recognition than sponsorship. Any recognition program without an active upper-management sponsor is bound to run low on energy. If your program has been hanging on all this time without a sponsor, get one. If you need to reenergize the sponsor, do so. You might want to consider taking the sponsor to a conference on recognition, or on a benchmarking field trip to another organization that has a highly energized recognition program.

Conduct specific management follow-up. Get managers to recognize employees, and employees to recognize one another, on a continuing basis—and help them to do so by providing assistance, recognition tools, and a budget. Some organizations require all managers to develop a plan for implementing recognition on an individual and group basis, along with time frames to hold managers accountable. Plan elements can range from asking managers to have new hires (or all employees, for that matter) make a list of things they find rewarding, to hosting a group discussion about new ways to acknowledge work well done.

Some organizations assign specific employees—perhaps from the organization's recognition team—the job of following up with managers by reviewing progress on their recognition plans, reviewing recognition tools and programs that are available, and encouraging them to continue or expand their efforts. If a manager is stuck or having doubts about her recognition efforts, she might be teamed with another who has more experience and/or success with recognition.

Other organizations ask managers to conduct one-on-one meetings devoted to issues of importance to the employee with every worker who reports to them, at least once every two weeks. What initially might be an awkward meeting because it's so new often turns into a welcome opportunity for employees to seek advice, role-play a work problem, or discuss development plans and potential career paths.

Communicate. Every communication in the organization— whether it's a voice mail, an e-mail, a speech given at the end-of-the-year awards banquet, or a chance exchange in the hallway—is an opportunity to recognize employees. An exchange of praise and recognition in a company newsletter, an "applause" bulletin board on the company's intranet, or simply allotted time in meetings for acknowledgment of jobs well done are just a few possible forums for formalized recognition.

For example, a general manager from Xerox told one of the authors that whenever he gets his thirty managers together he

NO-COST IDEA

Start Out Right

At Business First in Louisville, Kentucky, the advertising department sends a broadcast voice mail daily with a motivational message, a joke, success story, or whatever helps the team enjoy what they do for a living.

NO-COST IDEA
46

Welcome New Hires

Nokia Mobile Phones in San Diego, California, assigns new hires a "buddy" and provides a mug and T-shirt to welcome each one on their first day on the job.

See page 269 ◄
for "Recognition Training Designs."

always saves time at the end of the meeting to go around the room and ask each manager to share something he or she has done to recognize a staff member since the last meeting. This simple technique renews the excitement of recognition while providing a practical source of new recognition ideas for managers to learn from one another. At other companies, meeting-holders ask, "Does anybody have any praisings?" at the end of department or company-wide meetings. Managers at the Swan and Dolphin Resort in Lake Buena Vista, Florida, meet monthly to brainstorm new and creative ways they can recognize their employees.

TIE RECOGNITION TO HUMAN RESOURCE SYSTEMS

For recognition efforts to last, they should be tied as much as possible to other human resource systems, including hiring and recruiting, orientation and training, and evaluation and promotion.

Hiring and recruiting. Because it is easier to hire the right attitude than it is to change long-established wrong ones, having good recognition skills needs to be one of the criteria for hiring new managers.

The Walt Disney Company, for example, aggressively recruits people-oriented individuals regardless of the position. Other hiring considerations pale in comparison to this fundamental value for the Disney organization. Likewise, Southwest Airlines' policy is to "hire for attitude, and train for skills."

Orientation and training. Management training in many organizations tends to focus more on business planning and operations at the expense of the "soft skills" related to managing others. In fact, few organizations have a new-manager orientation that emphasizes the importance of employee recognition.

By providing specific training on recognition, organizations can overcome the objection by low-use managers that they "don't know how to do it."

All employees at Disney are required to attend Traditions 101 and learn the values of the organization—including the importance of how people are treated—and what those values look like in practice. Managers and supervisors at AlliedSignal (now a part of Honeywell) are required to attend a four-hour recognition training session that includes real-job situations for discussion and role-playing. At CalPERS, the State of California retirement system, training in recognition skills is provided to all employees—not just managers—to encourage the use of recognition throughout the organization and at all levels.

Evaluation and promotion. If recognition is important to the organization, it makes sense that managers be evaluated for their use of it, and that people skills be a criterion for any promotion.

In their performance reviews, managers at Disney are evaluated in part on their ability to manage, develop, and encourage their employees. Managers who aren't considered competent people-developers receive additional training, and cannot advance in the organization until they demonstrate their commitment to the people side of their job. At AAA of southern California, one third of a manager's annual bonus is based on immediate employees' quantitative rankings of the manager's "soft skills," such as being available to listen to and help employees, being supportive, and having an interest in creating development opportunities.

REENERGIZE YOUR RECOGNITION PROGRAM

Even the best recognition programs can eventually become stale and lose their effectiveness. Perhaps the program incentives have lost their thrill, nominations have dwindled, or no one remembers the purpose of, or criteria for, the awards anymore. Perhaps the program just needs to be reassessed, reaffirmed, and renewed in some way. Sometimes, it can be as simple as tracking the names of those who nominate others for recognition awards over a period so that they too can be recognized. In other cases it may be time to replace the program with something else—ideally something you know your employees want.

Informal recognition efforts also might need to be revised and expanded. For example, one of the authors was working with an electronics firm based in Seattle, Washington, that had an excellent

REVIVING AN OLD RECOGNITION PROGRAM

Q I'm on a committee at work to give rewards. So far, they consist of "applause," "just a pat on the back," and "bravo" cards, given out quarterly for over-and-above performances, to either teams or individuals. The committee gives both a plaque and a monetary reward, along with company exposure and recognition. Any person can fill out the nominations, so it's not top-down. This program has been in place since 1994, and with all the company's restructuring, not many people are still participating. What do you suggest to perk up the program?

A Hold a focus group or find a way to collect information on why people have stopped using the program. Include the biggest cynics on the review team for feedback. Maybe the program just needs to be relaunched to remind people of its existence, and new incentives need to be established. Or, you may discover that it would be better to do something new and more exciting.

REHABILITATING REWARDS AT COMPREHENSIVE REHABILITATION CONSULTANTS

The managers at Comprehensive Rehabilitation Consultants, a health care consulting company with locations in Miami, Florida, and New York City, realized that interest was waning in their traditional employee-of-the-month program. They wanted to revitalize the program and drive change through employee initiative instead of through management.

To reinvigorate staff and eliminate the perception of a popularity contest, CRC developed the Star Employee program, which identified nine "star" qualities that embodied the company's philosophy. Every staff member was given a coffee mug listing the Nine Star Qualities and nomination forms.

Staff members nominate one another, and an employee committee reviews the nominations and awards "star" bucks of $20 or more. Employees may then purchase services or privileges on a dollar-for-dollar basis. Rewards include video rentals, car washes, time off, restaurant gift certificates, classes, massages, weekend getaways, gourmet coffee delivered to their desk, and any other item that the committee approves. Each year, a new group of employees volunteer to serve on the committee. Managers do not serve on the committee and are not eligible to receive bucks, but can nominate other staff. Bucks are awarded at monthly staff meetings, and nominations are read aloud so that both the nominator and nominated are acknowledged.

At year end, small trophies and star-shaped baskets of goodies are given to those who made the largest number of successful nominations, and the Star Employee of the Year is awarded to the person who received the most nominations.

The program has been in place for four years and has been a wonderful source of team-building, improving morale and giving everyone an opportunity to become involved in recognition.

Rewards include video rentals, car washes, time off, restaurant gift certificates, classes, massages, weekend getaways, gourmet coffee delivered to their desk.

decades-old informal recognition program that made use of pogs, the milk bottle cap–style tokens popular in the 1980s. Employees were given pogs as a simple and immediate form of thanks for work well done, and the pogs could be redeemed for company merchandise, logoed T-shirts, and similar items. Yet the program had flaws. While some managers handed out pogs like candy, others hardly dispensed them at all. Reintroducing the program, reminding managers of its purpose and intent, and counseling errant managers all helped to breathe many more years of life into what had once been a successful program.

In another example, recognition programs at the Commonwealth of Virginia's Department of Transportation in Richmond, Virginia, had become stale and ineffective. Human resources spearheaded a revitalization effort with the goal of increasing meaningful recognition within the agency.

A preprogram employee survey indicated that most employees felt that there was inadequate recognition. In addition, the survey found that various units throughout the agency administered existing recognition programs, but that these efforts often fell between the cracks.

To correct the situation, a "Recognition Guide," produced to increase awareness of existing recognition programs, was distributed, along with copies of the "365 Ways to Manage Better" perpetual calendar and *1001 Ways to Reward Employees,* to all managers and supervisors. They also created "Standing Ovation Recognition" pocket cards to remind managers of the behaviors and practices they needed to recognize their employees for.

A follow-up employee survey showed a significant increase in positive responses to the statement "Employees in my work group are recognized." Focus groups within the organization also revealed a significant increase in recognition.

MARKET YOUR SUCCESS

After your recognition program recommendations are made and the program has been revamped, it's time to reannounce it with all the gusto of a celebration. Hold special meetings to feature the revised program. Review the successes of the previous

---

NO-COST IDEA 47

Dog Days

Shawn Freeman, CEO of Focus2, based in Dallas, Texas, recommends bringing pets to work to reduce stress. Some people work as long as 90 hours a week at the Web-development company, so Freeman allows them to bring dogs into the office any time they want. Says Freeman, "They think of their pets as children, and if they go for long periods without seeing them they get sort of grumpy."

WRECKOGNITION

One organization told its managers they each had to recognize four employees every week, which, predictably, resulted in hundreds of superficial, insincere compliments that did little to motivate employees.

REMEMBER: *When recognition is performed mechanically, it comes across as insincere.*

program, focusing on the results achieved and the levels of participation. Explain program changes and improvements, emphasizing any that came from employees. Give as much emphasis to the program's renewal as you did to the initial rollout.

BankBoston bolstered its program's relaunch with new communication and marketing efforts. These included a nomination challenge, which gave people greater incentive to use the program (during the first thirty days, anyone who nominated another employee received a surprise gift), the addition of an overview of the recognition program to the new employee orientation program, and expanded efforts to ask employees for their opinions on the company's strategies and employee issues.

The program was marketed like a product. It was not mandated or required of anyone, but instead "sold" to employees and managers so that they would *want* to use it. BankBoston also sent monthly participation reports to managers showing who in their areas was using the recognition program. The company also designated a specialist to clarify any vague written nominations with the nominator so that no program nominations were declined.

Taking the time to reassess and revamp a recognition program is a minimal investment of effort that can offer great returns. The sooner you catch a deenergized or faltering program and make the necessary changes, the stronger your overall recognition culture will become. Over time, you can also make the overall recognition effort more robust by adding new elements, expanding successful programs, or focusing on increased participation, for example. After all, the best organizations continually look to be better.

BRING A PROGRAM TO A CLOSE

In some cases, it might take far more effort than it's worth to revitalize a recognition program. Then it's time to retire it—or at least put it aside until some later date when it can be reintroduced. How can you tell when a program is a candidate for closure? Sometimes it's painfully obvious that a program has degraded. For example, one company had a spontaneous recognition program that included the phrase "You're the best!" After the program had successfully been used for over a year, it became stale and was used only as an all-purpose sarcastic joke; for instance, if someone had a bad day, a coworker would say, "Remember, Joe, you're the best!"

Here are some general tip-offs that a program has run its course:

- The program was time-limited at the outset, and has reached the end of its planned duration.

- The program is generally ignored, no matter how much you publicize it and encourage its use.

- Employees do not value the rewards given, no matter what items you use.

- Changing market conditions force you to make major changes in your approach.

Timing is a crucial factor in recognition. Sometimes programs are initiated when business conditions are favorable, only to decline when business conditions worsen. If your program is suffering from poor timing, you might want to consider terminating or discontinuing it until conditions improve. Caution should be taken about changing a program too dramatically. If you want to radically change a recognition program, it might be more desirable to end the program and begin a new one.

Sometimes a program design was too ambitious to begin with. Realizing this too late, senior management might want to *downsize* the program. This is generally not a good idea, since employees might view such action as a take-away—one of the major demotivators of recognition we discussed earlier. That is why it is so important to heed the principles of organizational recognition design we've shared.

Be sensitive to these and other signs that it's time to bring your recognition program to a close. It's better to shut down a successful but declining program a bit earlier than necessary than it is to allow a marginal or counterproductive program to remain in place long after it should have been retired. There is nothing wrong with terminating a recognition program when it has run its course, especially if you have some new recognition ideas or activities that are likely to be more motivating to employees.

> *"Having a good time is the best motivator there is. When people feel good about a company, they produce more."*
>
> **—Dave Longaberger,**
> CEO,
> The Longaberger Company

THE TAKE-AWAY

- After the initial excitement of a recognition program wears off, it tends to diminish in use, and become progressively less effective.

- To sustain initial recognition efforts, it's important to link recognition to the organization's strategic objectives and values, renew sponsorship commitment, institute management follow-up, and tie the recognition program to the organization's ongoing communication vehicles.

- Recognition programs can be reenergized by reassessing them, reaffirming them, and sparking them in some new way.

- Don't be afraid to terminate a program when it has outlasted its usefulness and cannot be easily reenergized.

Epilogue

We hope you have enjoyed this fieldbook and find it of value now and for years to come. We are grateful that you have taken this journey with us toward more effective rewards and recognition.

Motivation is a moving target that requires frequent review of your recognition and rewards practices, activities, and programs as well as the needs and preferences of those people you are trying to motivate. Even the best-designed and -implemented recognition program will run its course and will need to be revitalized or terminated and replaced with new recognition programs and activities. This is natural and a part of the "recognition cycle" that we described earlier in the book.

We encourage you not to become complacent, but rather to continue to refine your skills, learn from the rewards and recognition you have given and the programs you have created, and continue to grow and have breakthroughs in how you recognize others. In so doing, you will have a positive effect on the people and circumstances around you and you will get better and better at achieving your goals. So, best of luck, and remember, "You get what you reward!"

PART V
RECOGNITION TOOLS

Recognition Assessment and Measurement Tools

I n this section, you will find various recognition assessment and measurement tools that were referenced earlier in the book. These tools can be used to measure different aspects of recognition and your organization's readiness for implementing recognition programs. The first two assessments—

■ Recognition Practices Inventory for Leaders

■ Recognition Practices Inventory for Employees

—can be used to determine current recognition behaviors of your leaders and employees. The other assessments—

■ Motivational Culture Assessment

■ Recognition Context Assessment

■ Organizational Culture Assessment

■ Recognition Skills Needs Assessment

—can help determine your organization's readiness for implementing recognition programs.

RECOGNITION PRACTICES INVENTORY FOR LEADERS

The "Recognition Practices Inventory for Leaders" can be used independently or together with the "Recognition Practices Inventory for Employees" that follows in this section.

Behavior/belief gaps. The "importance" ratings on the inventory can help you understand whether you are actually practicing the behaviors you feel are important in managing or supervising others. If your frequency ratings are not consistent with your importance ratings, you might want to try to align your recognition practices with your beliefs about managing and recognizing people.

Range of behaviors. This inventory can also provide you with a profile of how frequently you use a variety of forms of recognition. If you find that you are using only a few of the recognition practices listed, you might want to consider using other forms of recognition.

Pre- and postassessment. You can use this inventory to establish a baseline of beliefs and practices that can then be remeasured after an intervention such as recognition training, recognition program rollout, providing recognition tools, or all of these.

Comparison with other leaders. You can compare your scores with an aggregate of scores of all other leaders who completed this inventory or all other leaders within your organization. The scoring key allows for an initial comparison of your mean scores with those of other leaders who have taken this inventory.

Alignment with employee perceptions. After your employees take the "Recognition Practices Inventory for Employees," you will be able to easily see what recognition behaviors they deem most desirable. By comparing your own self-ratings with your employees' ratings, you will be able to identify gaps in both frequency and importance, and you will be better able to focus on increasing the behaviors that are most important to your employees.

RECOGNITION PRACTICES INVENTORY FOR LEADERS

This inventory measures the type, frequency, and importance of nonmonetary recognition that you provide to your employees in your current position.

RECOGNITION ITEM/ACTIVITY	IMPORTANCE: unimportant	not very important	somewhat important	very important	extremely important	FREQUENCY: never	seldom	occasionally	frequently	always
Employee is given a verbal praising.	1	2	3	4	5	1	2	3	4	5
Employee is given a praising on voice mail.	1	2	3	4	5	1	2	3	4	5
Employee is given a written thank-you note.	1	2	3	4	5	1	2	3	4	5
Employee is given a praising on e-mail.	1	2	3	4	5	1	2	3	4	5
Employee is given a public praising.	1	2	3	4	5	1	2	3	4	5
Employee is given a certificate of achievement.	1	2	3	4	5	1	2	3	4	5
Employee receives a gift, flowers, gift certificate.	1	2	3	4	5	1	2	3	4	5
Employee receives coupons: food, movie, car wash, etc.	1	2	3	4	5	1	2	3	4	5
Employee receives entertainment tickets.	1	2	3	4	5	1	2	3	4	5
Manager gives the employee dinner out for two.	1	2	3	4	5	1	2	3	4	5
Employee receives a small cash award.	1	2	3	4	5	1	2	3	4	5
Customer letters are posted on bulletin boards.	1	2	3	4	5	1	2	3	4	5
Employee receives a "pass-around" trophy.	1	2	3	4	5	1	2	3	4	5
Employee gets to use a preferred parking space.	1	2	3	4	5	1	2	3	4	5
Employee receives a special achievement award.	1	2	3	4	5	1	2	3	4	5
Manager buys the employee lunch or dinner.	1	2	3	4	5	1	2	3	4	5
Manager provides a celebration for successes.	1	2	3	4	5	1	2	3	4	5
Manager spends time with employee.	1	2	3	4	5	1	2	3	4	5
Manager gives employee time off from work.	1	2	3	4	5	1	2	3	4	5
Manager allows an employee flexible hours.	1	2	3	4	5	1	2	3	4	5
Employee is given a choice of assignment.	1	2	3	4	5	1	2	3	4	5
Employee is given special privileges or perks.	1	2	3	4	5	1	2	3	4	5
Employee is given increased job autonomy.	1	2	3	4	5	1	2	3	4	5
Employee is given increased authority in the job.	1	2	3	4	5	1	2	3	4	5
Employee is allowed to participate in a learning activity.	1	2	3	4	5	1	2	3	4	5

continued on next page ➤

Z1. In general, how important is it to you to recognize employees when they do good work? (circle one)

    1 *extremely important*   **2** *very important*   **3** *somewhat important*   **4** *not very important*   **5** *unimportant*

Z2. In general, how often do you recognize employees when they do good work? (circle one)

    1 *daily*   **2** *weekly*   **3** *monthly*   **4** *yearly*   **5** *seldom, if ever*

This inventory is available for electronic scoring, feedback, and comparisons with other leaders and organizations through Nelson Motivation at www.nelson-motivation.com, or call 1-800-575-5521.

SCORING FOR IMPORTANCE

Add up your responses under Importance for Items 1 to 25 and divide by 25 to calculate your average perceived importance of providing these various forms of recognition to your employees. The average response of previous leaders who have taken this assessment is 2.62, with an average response of 1.45 for Item Z1.

An average score of less than 2.62	indicates you feel providing employees recognition is **more** important than most leaders do.
An average score of more than 2.62	indicates you feel providing employees recognition is **less** important than most leaders do.
A score on item Z1 of less than 1.45	indicates you feel providing recognition to employees is **more** important than most leaders do.
A score on item Z1 of more than 1.45	indicates you feel providing recognition to employees is **less** important than most leaders do.

SCORING FOR FREQUENCY

Add up your responses under Frequency for items 1 to 25 and divide by 25 to calculate your average perceived frequency of providing these various forms of recognition to your employees. The average response of previous leaders who have taken this assessment is 3.33, with an average response of 2.10 for item Z2.

A average score of less than 3.33	indicates you provide **more** recognition than most leaders.
An average score of more than 3.33	indicates you provide **less** recognition than most leaders.
A score on Item Z2 of less than 2.10	indicates you provide **more** recognition than most leaders.
A score on Item Z2 of more than 2.10	indicates you provide **less** recognition than most leaders.

RECOGNITION PRACTICES INVENTORY FOR EMPLOYEES

This inventory measures the type, frequency, and importance of nonmonetary recognition that you receive from your immediate manager (supervisor, team leader, etc.) in your current position.

RECOGNITION ITEM/ ACTIVITY	IMPORTANCE unimportant / not very important / somewhat important / very important / extremely important					FREQUENCY never / seldom / occasionally / frequently / always				
Employee is given a verbal praising.	1	2	3	4	5	1	2	3	4	5
Employee is given a praising on voice mail.	1	2	3	4	5	1	2	3	4	5
Employee is given a written thank-you note.	1	2	3	4	5	1	2	3	4	5
Employee is given a praising on e-mail.	1	2	3	4	5	1	2	3	4	5
Employee is given a public praising.	1	2	3	4	5	1	2	3	4	5
Employee is given a certificate of achievement.	1	2	3	4	5	1	2	3	4	5
Employee receives a gift, flowers, gift certificate.	1	2	3	4	5	1	2	3	4	5
Employee receives coupons: food, movie, car wash, etc.	1	2	3	4	5	1	2	3	4	5
Employee receives entertainment tickets.	1	2	3	4	5	1	2	3	4	5
Manager gives the employee dinner out for two.	1	2	3	4	5	1	2	3	4	5
Employee receives a small cash award.	1	2	3	4	5	1	2	3	4	5
Customer letters are posted on bulletin boards.	1	2	3	4	5	1	2	3	4	5
Employee receives a "pass-around" trophy.	1	2	3	4	5	1	2	3	4	5
Employee gets to use a preferred parking space.	1	2	3	4	5	1	2	3	4	5
Employee receives a special achievement award.	1	2	3	4	5	1	2	3	4	5
Manager buys the employee lunch or dinner.	1	2	3	4	5	1	2	3	4	5
Manager provides a celebration for successes.	1	2	3	4	5	1	2	3	4	5
Manager spends time with employee.	1	2	3	4	5	1	2	3	4	5
Manager gives employee time off from work.	1	2	3	4	5	1	2	3	4	5
Manager allows an employee flexible hours.	1	2	3	4	5	1	2	3	4	5
Employee is given a choice of assignment.	1	2	3	4	5	1	2	3	4	5
Employee is given special privileges or perks.	1	2	3	4	5	1	2	3	4	5
Employee is given increased job autonomy.	1	2	3	4	5	1	2	3	4	5
Employee is given increased authority in the job.	1	2	3	4	5	1	2	3	4	5
Employee is allowed to participate in a learning activity.	1	2	3	4	5	1	2	3	4	5

continued on next page ➤

Z1. In general, how important is it to you to be recognized by your manager when you do good work? (circle one)

⊡ *extremely important* ⊡ *very important* ⊡ *somewhat important* ⊡ *not very important* ⊡ *unimportant*

Z2. In general, how often are you recognized by your manager when you do good work? (circle one)

⊡ *daily* ⊡ *weekly* ⊡ *monthly* ⊡ *yearly* ⊡ *seldom, if ever*

This inventory is available for scoring, feedback, and comparisons with other employees, leaders, and organizations through Nelson Motivation at www.nelson-motivation.com, or call 1-800-575-5521.

SCORING FOR IMPORTANCE

Add up your responses under Importance for items 1 to 25 and divide by 25 to calculate your average frequency of receiving these various forms of recognition from your manager. The average response for employees who have previously taken this assessment is 2.89, with an average response of 1.88 for Item Z1.

An average score of less than 2.89	indicates you feel recognition is **more** important than most employees do.
An average score of more than 2.89	indicates you feel recognition is **less** important than most employees do.
A score on item Z1 of less than 1.88	indicates you feel recognition is **more** important than most employees do.
A score on item Z1 of more than 1.88	indicates you feel recognition is **less** important than most employees do.

SCORING FOR FREQUENCY

Add up your responses under Frequency for items 1 to 25 and divide by 25 to calculate your average frequency of receiving these various forms of recognition from your manager. The average response of employees who have previously taken this assessment is 3.59, with an average response of 2.77 for item Z2.

An average score of less than 3.59	indicates you receive **more** recognition than most employees.
An average score of more than 3.59	indicates you receive **less** recognition than most employees.
A score on item Z2 of less than 2.77	indicates you receive **more** recognition than most employees.
A score on item Z2 of more than 2.77	indicates you receive **less** recognition than most employees.

MOTIVATIONAL CULTURE ASSESSMENT

Please respond to the statements below to the best of your ability based on your own personal experience in your work unit and/or the organization as a whole.

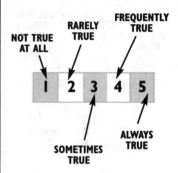

RATING

Use the numbers on the scale below to rate the following statements.

STATEMENT	RATING				
I look forward to going to work.	1	2	3	4	5
Employees are very productive.	1	2	3	4	5
There is a high level of energy.	1	2	3	4	5
Employees have positive and optimistic attitudes.	1	2	3	4	5
Employees seem to enjoy working here.	1	2	3	4	5
Absenteeism is low.	1	2	3	4	5
Tardiness is low.	1	2	3	4	5
Commitment to customer satisfaction is high.	1	2	3	4	5
Employees are encouraged to take initiative to satisfy both internal and external customers.	1	2	3	4	5
Employees' health and safety are important to management.	1	2	3	4	5
I am made to feel like an important part of this organization.	1	2	3	4	5
Management encourages employees to have fun at work.	1	2	3	4	5
Working in this organization is more than just a job to me.	1	2	3	4	5
Employees are careful and respectful in dealing with the organization's facilities and resources.	1	2	3	4	5
I am well informed about the organization's vision, mission, strategy, and goals.	1	2	3	4	5
I feel that management is interested in my opinions.	1	2	3	4	5
Senior managers are highly visible.	1	2	3	4	5
I have input into the organization's planning processes.	1	2	3	4	5
Employee suggestions are actively solicited.	1	2	3	4	5

The rating scale:

NOT TRUE AT ALL — 1
RARELY TRUE — 2
SOMETIMES TRUE — 3
FREQUENTLY TRUE — 4
ALWAYS TRUE — 5

continued on next page ➤

RATING

Use the numbers on the scale below to rate the following statements.

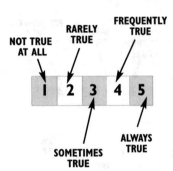

STATEMENT	RATING				
Management takes prompt action on employees' suggestions and provides employees with feedback on actions taken.	1	2	3	4	5
Employees are encouraged to be creative.	1	2	3	4	5
Employees are encouraged to suggest improvements in work methods.	1	2	3	4	5
Management strives to reduce or eliminate barriers to my success.	1	2	3	4	5
Employees are encouraged to learn from mistakes, and are not reprimanded for them.	1	2	3	4	5
Managers tend to view problems as opportunities for learning.	1	2	3	4	5
Management is committed to continuous improvement.	1	2	3	4	5
Employees are encouraged to use the full range of their skills.	1	2	3	4	5
Learning is a high priority in this organization.	1	2	3	4	5
Employees have input into the training they receive.	1	2	3	4	5
There is assistance provided after training to help employees use what they learned on the job.	1	2	3	4	5
I am involved in training decisions that affect my career.	1	2	3	4	5
A high priority is placed on doing quality work.	1	2	3	4	5
There is frequent two-way communication between employees and management.	1	2	3	4	5
Employees are kept well informed.	1	2	3	4	5
Information is not withheld from employees.	1	2	3	4	5
The meetings I attend are productive and well led.	1	2	3	4	5
Organizational communications are informative and helpful.	1	2	3	4	5
Managers are responsive to employees' needs and concerns.	1	2	3	4	5
Everybody works together as one team.	1	2	3	4	5
There are no conflicts between departments or work units.	1	2	3	4	5
Management values each and every employee.	1	2	3	4	5
Labor-management issues are promptly resolved.	1	2	3	4	5
Management is willing to take responsibility for its mistakes.	1	2	3	4	5

continued on next page ➤

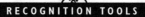

There is a high degree of trust between employees and management.	1	2	3	4	5
I believe that what management tells me is the truth.	1	2	3	4	5
There is excellent teamwork among employees.	1	2	3	4	5
I receive frequent and objective feedback on my work performance.	1	2	3	4	5
My performance is evaluated fairly.	1	2	3	4	5
I view performance appraisal as being a positive development experience.	1	2	3	4	5
Problems of poor employee performance are promptly addressed.	1	2	3	4	5
A lot of recognition is given to employees who deserve it.	1	2	3	4	5
Employees feel appreciated.	1	2	3	4	5
Rewards and recognition are given fairly.	1	2	3	4	5
I feel that I am fairly paid.	1	2	3	4	5
I am appreciated when I put in extra effort.	1	2	3	4	5
Outstanding performance is celebrated.	1	2	3	4	5
Both individual and team performance are appropriately rewarded.	1	2	3	4	5
Poor performers are not rewarded.	1	2	3	4	5
I don't hear others complaining about how they are treated in this organization.	1	2	3	4	5
If this organization were in financial trouble, employees would be willing to make a financial sacrifice to help out.	1	2	3	4	5
TOTAL SCORE					

SCORING

Add total score: _____ (divide by 300) = % Score: _____ %

90–100%	Extraordinary motivational culture
80–89%	High motivational culture
70–79%	Above-average motivational culture
60–69%	Average motivational culture
50–59%	Below-average motivational culture
Below 50%	**Deficient motivational culture**

RATING

Use the numbers on the scale below to rate the following statements.

NOT TRUE → **1**
SOMEWHAT TRUE → **2**
DEFINITELY TRUE → **3**

RECOGNITION CONTEXT ASSESSMENT

Organization/unit: _____

Date: _____

Please complete the following questions as accurately as you can.

STATEMENT	RATING		
There are one or more senior leaders who actively support and practice recognition.	1	2	3
A recognition vision has been communicated.	1	2	3
There is a person in this organization with responsibility for coordinating recognition activities.	1	2	3
Recognition is widely practiced by managers throughout the organization.	1	2	3
Peer-to-peer recognition is widely used.	1	2	3
Recognition-giving skills are high in this organization.	1	2	3
Recognition activities and events are common in this organization.	1	2	3
Nonmonetary recognition is widely used in this organization.	1	2	3
There is widespread understanding of the business benefits of recognition.	1	2	3
Organizational recognition programs have been successful in the past.	1	2	3
Organizational recognition programs have been sustained long enough to have a major impact on the workforce.	1	2	3
There is training available to improve recognition skills.	1	2	3
Recognition giving is measured.	1	2	3
Recognition giving is rewarded.	1	2	3
Managers have the resources available to facilitate recognition activities.	1	2	3
People are highly valued in this organization.	1	2	3
Management proactively addresses demotivators.	1	2	3
There is a high degree of consistency between what is said and what is done in this organization.	1	2	3

continued on next page ➤

There are few barriers to recognition in this organization.	1	2	3
This organization is receptive to change and improvement.	1	2	3
There is open communication in this organization.	1	2	3
People in this organization are encouraged to learn new skills.	1	2	3
People in this organization are encouraged to adopt new behaviors.	1	2	3
Risk taking is not typically punished in this organization.	1	2	3
TOTAL SCORE			

SCORING KEY

63–69	Ideal context for recognition
55–62	Receptive context for recognition
45–54	Questionable recognition readiness—care should be taken
Below 45	**Lacking in recognition readiness— significant improvement needed**

RATING

Use the numbers on the scale below to rate your organization on the following cultural characteristics.

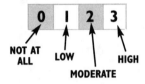

ORGANIZATIONAL CULTURE ASSESSMENT

Organization: _____

Date: _____

Multiply your **rating** by the **factor** to arrive at a score for each item. See the scoring key for interpretation.

CULTURAL CHARACTERISTIC	DESCRIPTIVE STATEMENT ABOUT ORGANIZATION	RATING				FACTOR	SCORE
Creative	There is a lot of creativity.	0	1	2	3	+1	
Collaborative	There is a lot of collaboration.	0	1	2	3	+1	
Communicative	There is a lot of communication.	0	1	2	3	+1	
Optimistic	Prevailing attitudes are optimistic.	0	1	2	3	+1	
Concern for quality	Quality is very important.	0	1	2	3	+1	
People-oriented	Management practices are people-oriented.	0	1	2	3	+2	
Clarity of strategy	Most employees understand the organization's priorities.	0	1	2	3	+1	
Traditional	Tradition is very important.	0	1	2	3	−1	
Customer focus	Customer satisfaction is of paramount importance.	0	1	2	3	+1	
Autocratic	Decision making is top-down.	0	1	2	3	−2	
Flexible	People are allowed to make changes.	0	1	2	3	+1	
Committed	Employees are highly committed.	0	1	2	3	+1	
Learning-oriented	Learning and development are important.	0	1	2	3	+2	
Risk taking	Calculated risk taking is encouraged.	0	1	2	3	+1	
Unionized	Employees are unionized.	0	1	2	3	−2	
TOTAL SCORE							

continued on next page ➤

SCORING KEY	
36–42	Ideal culture for recognition
30–35	Receptive culture for recognition
24–49	Questionable recognition readiness—care should be taken
Below 24	**Culture is hostile to recognition**

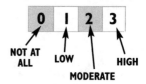

RATING
Use the numbers on the scale below to rate your organization on the following recognition skills.

0	1	2	3
NOT AT ALL	LOW	MODERATE	HIGH

RECOGNITION SKILLS NEEDS ASSESSMENT

Name: _____

Date: _____

RECOGNITION SKILL	RATING			
Explaining the importance of recognition	0	1	2	3
Differentiating between recognition and rewards	0	1	2	3
Explaining the dos and don'ts of successful recognition	0	1	2	3
Identifying the major pitfalls of recognition	0	1	2	3
Pinpointing behaviors and/or results to recognize	0	1	2	3
Assessing the recognition context	0	1	2	3
Developing a recognition action plan	0	1	2	3
Providing sincere praise to others	0	1	2	3
Giving spontaneous (informal) recognition	0	1	2	3
Providing formal recognition	0	1	2	3
Selecting appropriate recognition items to reinforce recognition	0	1	2	3
Learning from recognition experiences	0	1	2	3
Planning high-impact recognition events and celebration	0	1	2	3
Providing recognition to co-located teams	0	1	2	3
Providing recognition to virtual teams	0	1	2	3
Planning to maximize recognition value	0	1	2	3

continued on next page ➤

RECOGNITION SKILL	RATING			
Setting recognition goals	0	1	2	3
Measuring the impact of recognition	0	1	2	3
Designing organizational recognition programs	0	1	2	3
Planning organizational recognition	0	1	2	3
Implementing organizational recognition	0	1	2	3
Managing organizational recognition	0	1	2	3
Marketing recognition within your organization	0	1	2	3
Sustaining recognition	0	1	2	3
Revitalizing recognition	0	1	2	3
TOTAL SCORE				

SCORING KEY	
65–75	You are a recognition pro.
55–64	You have significant strength in recognition.
45–54	You have a good foundation of skills on which to build.
Below 45	**You should work on developing your recognition skills.**

Recognition Planning Checklists

I n this section, you will find checklists drawn from the content of each of the chapters in this book. These checklists can be used to guide your individual, team, and organizational recognition activities and programs as well as to quickly review important points covered in this fieldbook, identified by chapter.

You can use them before, during, or after a recognition effort—as a way of double-checking your priorities during the planning phase, for anticipating problems, or for evaluating the effectiveness of your effort.

CHAPTER 1 CHECKLIST
The Rewards and Recognition Revolution

❑ Many people feel that recognition is common sense, and falsely believe that their organizations already do a great deal to reward and recognize employees.

❑ Five important trends have led to the increased importance of recognition:

   ❑ Decline of traditional incentives

   ❑ Rise of nontraditional incentives

   ❑ Increased use of variable compensation

   ❑ Increased employee empowerment

   ❑ Increased change and uncertainty

❑ Recognition and performance should be closely linked.

❑ Effective recognition has a bottom-line impact.

❑ The use of employee incentives is changing dramatically:

   ❑ From one-size-fits-all to multiple programs and activities

❑ From centrally oriented to manager-oriented programs

❑ From formal and stuffy programs to programs that are informal, spontaneous, and fun

❑ From few choices to many options that constantly change

❑ From infrequent use to greater frequency and flexibility

❑ From cultures of entitlement to cultures of performance

❑ From selective use for top performers to use for everyone

❑ Recognition offers a low-cost strategy with a big-bang effect on morale, performance, recruiting, and retention.

❑ Some final (and reassuring) thoughts:

   ❑ Recognition works.

   ❑ Virtually everyone would benefit from increased recognition use.

   ❑ Learning to use recognition effectively is not difficult.

CHAPTER 2 CHECKLIST
The Salary Fallacy and the Seven Facets of Recognition

❏ Managers and employees differ significantly in what they perceive as the most rewarding aspects of employees' jobs. Ask most managers what his or her employees want from their jobs, and you'll probably get a list of items heavy on financial incentives such as increased pay, bonuses, promotions, and so forth. Ask most employees what they really want from their jobs, and you'll likely get very different answers.

❏ Although most people come to work because of money, they don't work just for money.

❏ The money employees are paid is compensation.

❏ Recognition is not compensation; it's what you offer employees above and beyond compensation to get the best effort from them.

❏ Motivators differ significantly from employee to employee.

❏ Money is a basic need, but it really isn't a motivator.

❏ The seven key aspects of recognition are:

1. Contingency

2. Frequency

3. Timing

4. Formality

5. Setting

6. Significance to provider

7. Value to recipient

❏ Recognition is most meaningful when it is performance-based, given promptly, given frequently, given informally, given in the appropriate setting, and valuable to both provider and recipient.

❏ The most effective incentives to employees are manager-initiated rather than organization-initiated, and are contingent on performance, not just on showing up to work.

CHAPTER 3 CHECKLIST
Why Managers Use and Don't Use Recognition

❑ Employees expect to be recognized when they do good work.

❑ As Bob Nelson found in his doctoral research, the major determinants of the frequency of recognition giving are:

   ❑ Sense of personal responsibility for giving recognition

   ❑ Skills and confidence in giving recognition

   ❑ Past reinforcement for recognition use

   ❑ Age of the recognition giver

   ❑ Role models

❑ Managers who use recognition frequently tend to see it as part of their job, and have developed skills and confidence in those skills, have received reinforcement for their previous recognition efforts, are under fifty, and have had a high-use-of-recognition role model.

❑ In addition, Bob found that:

   ❑ Time constraints are not a major factor in frequency of recognition use.

   ❑ Managers are concerned about not giving recognition fairly.

❑ Business pressures reduce the likelihood that recognition will be given.

❑ Budget and resource constraints do not significantly affect the recognition giving of high-use managers.

❑ A program for increasing recognition use must address the six major excuses for not giving it:

   1. "I'm not sure how best to recognize my employees."

   2. "I don't feel that providing recognition is an important part of my job."

   3. "I don't have the time to recognize my employees."

   4. "I'm afraid I might leave somebody out."

   5. "Employees don't value the recognition I have given in the past."

   6. "My organization does not facilitate or support recognition efforts."

❑ When converting managers who seldom use recognition into managers who often use recognition, small-step improvement works best.

CHAPTER 4 CHECKLIST
The Context for Recognition

❑ Differentiate *task* versus *context*.

❑ All recognition occurs in a context.

❑ The context has a major impact on recognition effectiveness.

❑ The major contextual factor is *culture*.

❑ Values create culture; culture determines practices.

❑ Remember that the "ground" (organizational context) determines how people perceive the "figure" (recognition).

❑ *Motivators* are major positive contextual factors (for example, action, fun, variety, input, stake-sharing, choice, and responsibility).

❑ *Demotivators* are major negative contextual factors (for example, unclear expectations, unnecessary rules, poorly designed work, unproductive meetings, constant change, dishonesty, and unfairness).

❑ Be careful about "noise" (extraneous things going on in the organization) that can detract from the "signal" (your recognition initiative).

❑ Rewards that are too powerful can obscure the recognition that should be communicated.

❑ Avoid the potential sabotage of recognition programs by understanding and adapting to the context.

❑ Create a conducive personal environment for recognition.

❑ Use context assessment tools.

CHAPTER 5 CHECKLIST
The Recognition Cycle

❑ Recognition is much more than a single skill; it is a collection of closely related knowledge, attitudes, *and* skills.

❑ The right knowledge and attitudes enable the right skills. These skills should then produce the right behavior, and the right behavior should produce the desired results.

❑ All learning involves risk—risk of failure, risk of feeling stupid, risk of wasting time.

❑ Anyone can become competent, but individuals do not necessarily become competent at the same rate. Some people learn more quickly than others. It is the speed of learning—not the capacity for learning—that distinguishes one person from another.

❑ It is all too easy to give up early in the learning process; the inevitable discomfort of conscious incompetence often leads to resignation.

❑ While everyone has the capacity to achieve a high level of competence, not everyone becomes an expert.

❑ Habits are both positive and negative forces in learning: People will continue *not* giving recognition, if that is their habit, or they will continue giving the same forms of recognition over and over again until there is some impetus to change.

❑ It's very easy to fall into a pattern. This can lead to recognition that appears mechanical—and *nobody* wants to be recognized mechanically.

❑ Fear of making mistakes, and looking bad, causes many people to shy away from learning new things.

❑ As people move up the learning ladder to higher and higher levels of competence in recognition, the learning path is not usually a straight one. Probably the best way to think about learning is in terms of a PDRI cycle. PDRI stands for: **Plan**, making a decision or intention to take some action or perform some activity; **Do**, performing the action or activity; **Review**, assessing how well the action or activity worked; and **Improve**, refining the action or activity to make it even better when it is next used.

❑ There's only one way to get better at anything—including giving recognition—and that is to practice it, using feedback to improve.

❑ When you have mastered your first PDRI cycle, you will want to innovate and to become even more effective. We refer to these jumps to another PDRI cycle as "breakthroughs."

❑ Breakthroughs are relative—a breakthrough for one person might be an incremental step for another.

❑ Good ways to stimulate breakthroughs are learning from others who demonstrate high skills, rehearsing, and joining or creating a support group.

❑ One of the reasons recognition still hasn't attained the usage that it should is that the recognizers don't get recognized themselves.

❑ Don't forget to reward yourself!

CHAPTER 6 CHECKLIST
Getting Started with Individual Recognition

Getting Started . . . JUST DO IT:

❑ Start in your immediate sphere of influence.

❑ Do *one* thing differently.

❑ Ask employees what motivates them.

❑ Focus on what you can do, not what you can't do.

❑ Don't expect to do recognition perfectly.

Before You Recognize . . . ASK YOURSELF:

❑ What do I want to recognize?

❑ Who do I want to recognize?

❑ When should the recognition be done?

❑ Where should the recognition be done?

❑ How should the recognition be done?

❑ What could go wrong (and how can I prevent it)?

❑ What kind of response can I expect?

During the Recognition . . . ASK YOURSELF:

❑ How am I doing?

❑ Am I getting the response I expected?

After the Recognition . . . ASK YOURSELF:

❑ How am I doing?

❑ Am I doing what I planned to do?

❑ Is the timing right?

❑ Am I getting the response I expected?

Remember ASAP³:

❑ As Soon   ❑ As Sincere

❑ As Specific   ❑ As Personal

❑ As Positive   ❑ As Proactive

Make Recognition Easy:

❑ Write notes.

❑ Be observant.

❑ Link the activity to your day planner.

❑ Harness the power of technology.

❑ Hold "one-on-one" meetings.

❑ Schedule time for recognition.

Use the Power of I's to Motivate:

❑ Interesting and important work

❑ Information/communication/feedback

❑ Involvement/ownership in decisions

❑ Independence/autonomy/flexibility

CHAPTER 7 CHECKLIST
Getting Started with Team Recognition

❑ Team recognition is really just a variation on individual recognition.

❑ The team recognition challenge: Recognize the team without slighting the individual.

❑ ASAP[3] applies to team recognition as well:

    ❑ As Soon   ❑ As Sincere

    ❑ As Specific   ❑ As Personal

    ❑ As Positive   ❑ As Proactive

❑ Try these ten ways to recognize teams:

  1. Have managers pop in at the first meeting of a special-project team and express their appreciation of the members' involvement.

  2. Open the floor for team members to praise anyone at the beginning or end of a meeting.

  3. Have team members thank individuals for their contribution.

  4. Create symbols of a team's work, such as logoed T-shirts or coffee cups.

  5. Hold a "praise barrage" for team members to acknowledge one person on the team.

  6. Use one member of the team to create an award for another member of the team.

  7. Rotate responsibility for group recognition.

  8. Host a refreshment hour, a potluck, or a special breakfast or lunch to celebrate interim or final results.

  9. Have a manager ask an upper manager to attend a "bragging session."

 10. Write thank-you letters to every team member at the end of a project.

  ❑ What do I want to recognize?

  ❑ Who do I want to recognize?

  ❑ When should the recognition for done?

  ❑ Where should the recognition be done?

  ❑ How should the recognition be done?

  ❑ What could go wrong (and how can I prevent it)?

  ❑ What kind of response can I expect?

❑ Some great team recognition principles:

  ❑ Focus on areas that will have the greatest impact.

  ❑ Involve your target employee group.

  ❑ Announce the recognition with fanfare.

  ❑ Publicly track progress.

  ❑ Have lots of winners.

  ❑ Allow flexibility of rewards.

  ❑ Renew the program as needed.

  ❑ Link informal and formal rewards.

  ❑ Find ways to perpetuate new behaviors.

  ❑ Recognize virtual teams.

  ❑ Use electronic technology to facilitate distance recognition.

  ❑ Take time for team-building activities.

  ❑ Don't let the virtual team members fall between the cracks.

CHAPTER 8 CHECKLIST
Getting Started with Organizational Recognition

❑ Organizational recognition is similar to and different from individual recognition.

❑ Organizational recognition requires a different perspective.

❑ Organizational recognition can have greater positive or negative impact.

Purposes of Organizational Recognition

❑ Performance improvement

❑ Modeling

❑ Showing appreciation

Starting Points for Organizational Recognition

❑ At the top

❑ In the middle

❑ At the bottom

What Works: The Five Essentials

❑ Aligned (vision, strategy, desired results, recognition program) plans

❑ Coordinated plans

❑ Well-designed plans

❑ Well-implemented plans

❑ Well-managed plans

The Skills of Organizational Recognition

❑ Organizational recognition requires the same skills as individual and team recognition *plus* systems thinking.

The Four Phases of Putting Organizational Recognition Programs into Practice

1. Design
2. Plan
3. Implement
4. Manage

Steps to Effectively Getting Started with Organizational Recognition

❑ Commit to doing it.

❑ Find an opportunity.

❑ Clarify the recognition goal and selection criteria.

❑ Ensure executive sponsorship.

❑ Maximize the recognition value.

❑ Consider the potential constraints.

❑ Develop the plan.

❑ Solicit feedback.

❑ Implement the program.

❑ Monitor the impact.

❑ Do it even better next time.

CHAPTER 9 CHECKLIST
Designing Successful Organizational Recognition

❏ The ultimate success of an organizational recognition program is very much dependent on the quality and clarity of the organizational programs themselves, and of the program design.

❏ The starting point of organizational recognition design is goal setting. A goal always reflects dissatisfaction with one or more aspects of the current state of the organization.

❏ The key to effective goal writing—creating goals that clearly communicate their intent—is specificity.

❏ The format of an effective goal is *action statement* (What will be achieved?), *target group* (Who will achieve it?), and *time frame* (When will it be achieved or for what period?).

❏ Once the organizational recognition goal is formulated, the organizational recognition program should be designed, guided by a set of design principles:

  ❏ Focus: Is there a clear focus to the recognition program?

  ❏ Clarity: Is the goal of the program clear?

  ❏ Readiness: Is the organization ready for the recognition program?

  ❏ Sponsorship: Is there executive sponsorship?

  ❏ Alignment: Is there alignment between the program and organizational priorities?

  ❏ Enhancement: Is the program built on the foundation of previous, successful recognition programs?

❏ Integration: Is the program integrated with other organizational initiatives?

❏ Systemization: Has the program been built into organizational systems?

❏ Responsibility: Is there clear responsibility for coordinating the program?

❏ Involvement: Are there opportunities for employee involvement?

❏ Accessibility: Is recognition accessible to a large number of employees?

❏ Visibility: Is the program visible?

❏ Knowledge sharing: Is there a provision for sharing knowledge about the program?

❏ Significance: Do employees feel that the program is significant?

❏ Presentation: How personal is the presentation of the recognition?

❏ Measurement: Are there adequate provisions for measuring the program, and for acting on feedback?

❏ Modifiability: Can the program be easily modified?

❏ Closure: Can the program be reversed if necessary?

❏ Sustainability: Has the program been built to be sustainable?

CHAPTER 10 CHECKLIST
Planning Successful Organizational Recognition

❑ Planning is an investment of time made in the present to improve performance in the future. Every hour spent in effective planning can save many hours (and much frustration) during execution.

❑ Albert Einstein: "Everything should be as simple as possible—but no simpler!"

❑ There are six elements of an organizational recognition plan: action plan, schedule, resource requirements, budget, potential failure factors and preventive actions, and measurement strategy.

❑ The best way to prepare an action plan is to identify the major categories of activities, and then identify the activities under each category.

❑ While an action plan provides a basic outline of what needs to be done, it doesn't usually explain *when* the activities need to be done. This is the purpose of the schedule. The schedule provides another perspective on the program—especially in terms of dependencies.

❑ The resource requirements can be identified from the action plan and the schedule. And almost all resources are time-critical. They must be designed, ordered, or otherwise acquired *before* they are needed. Slippage in meeting these individual resource acquisition dates can cause the entire program to be delayed.

❑ A budget is an estimate of the amount of money needed to fund the various elements of the program. Without one, you won't get funding approval, and people won't think proactively or economically.

❑ The way to avoid ambushes is by closely examining the many "contextual" factors in your organization that can undermine or sabotage the best intentions—and then plan how to avoid them, or deal with them if you can't. One of the best ways to mitigate potential failure factors—particularly with a high-risk initiative—is to implement a pilot project.

❑ Although measurement is the only way that progress can be monitored, it is too often overlooked. In addition, measurement provides crucial feedback about what to improve.

❑ Bottom line: With organizational recognition, as in so many other areas of life, "Those who fail to plan . . . plan to fail."

CHAPTER II CHECKLIST
Implementing Organizational Recognition

❑ View organizational recognition as organizational change.

❑ You will need to overcome inertia (resistance to change) and entropy (the tendency of enthusiasm for new programs to diminish over time).

❑ The keys to overcoming inertia and entropy are alignment, coordination, and communication.

❑ Make sure that your organizational recognition is aligned with your organization's vision, strategy, and values.

    ❑ Coordination of organizational recognition is essential to realizing its full benefits.

    ❑ Uncoordinated recognition will result in conflict, confusion, and duplication of resources.

❑ Alignment and coordination will increase synergy, and ensure that the impact of your organizational recognition is more than the sum of its individual parts.

❑ Nothing facilitates alignment and coordination of recognition like a recognition mission statement that clearly articulates your organization's values relative to recognition.

❑ Clarify expectations by providing recognition guidelines and standards.

❑ Any organization that is serious about organizational recognition should have a recognition coordinator.

❑ Communication is essential to the effective implementation of organizational recognition.

❑ Communicate the benefits of recognition.

❑ Share successes.

❑ Nothing communicates more powerfully than organizational managers who lead recognition.

❑ There are three phases of communication:

    1. Prelaunch

    2. Launch

    3. Ongoing

❑ Don't economize on communication.

CHAPTER 12 CHECKLIST
Managing Organizational Recognition

❑ Organizational recognition has a life cycle.

❑ It is important to manage the program throughout the life cycle.

   ❑ Stage 1: Preparation (prepare for the program).

   ❑ Stage 2: Announcement (announce the program).

   ❑ Stage 3: Promotion (promote the program).

   ❑ Stage 4: Excitement (build excitement for the program).

   ❑ Stage 5: Steady state (keep managing the program).

   ❑ Stage 6: Decline (don't let entropy take over).

   ❑ Stage 7: Revitalization (most recognition programs need to be revitalized).

   ❑ Alternative stage 7: Termination (sometimes it is best to terminate the program before it declines due to entropy).

❑ Being aware of the life cycle of organizational recognition can help you anticipate and make the most of each stage.

❑ The key to promoting organizational recognition is effective communication.

❑ The keys for managing the steady state of organizational recognition are:

   ❑ Ongoing communication

   ❑ Recognizing the recognizers

   ❑ Fine-tuning the program

❑ Ideas for revitalizing recognition:

   ❑ Add variety

   ❑ Establish new recognition opportunities

   ❑ Establish new recognition levels

   ❑ Enhance the scorekeeping process

❑ Ideas for positively terminating organizational recognition programs:

   ❑ Collect lessons learned: Those who don't learn from the past are destined to repeat it!

   ❑ Document positive testimonials: Don't dwell on the negatives!

❑ Don't forget to use valuable management tools for managing organizational recognition programs (for example, action plans, exception reports, and review meetings).

CHAPTER 13 CHECKLIST
Selling Recognition to Senior Management

❑ Consider the values of senior managers.

❑ Talk to them in their own terms.

❑ Enhance credibility.

❑ Share studies and statistics.

❑ Share industry "best practices."

❑ Make a personal appeal.

❑ Create a pilot program.

❑ Leverage and communicate successes.

❑ Nothing succeeds like success!

❑ Help senior management look good.

❑ Let senior managers choose their level of involvement.

❑ Recognize senior managers for recognizing others.

❑ Get senior managers to model recognition.

❑ Give employees access to the top.

❑ Small actions by senior managers yield big results.

❑ Help senior managers create a personal recognition plan.

CHAPTER 14 CHECKLIST
Troubleshooting Recognition Problems

❑ Despite the best intentions, recognition can go wrong.

❑ It is important to be aware of individual, team, and organizational recognition problems so that they can be avoided and/or fixed.

❑ Common individual recognition mistakes:

   ❑ Missed recognition opportunities

   ❑ Recognition that's not timely

   ❑ Insincere or mechanical recognition

   ❑ Misdirecting public recognition to individuals

   ❑ Undercutting praise with criticism

   ❑ Giving recognition that is not rewarding

❑ Common team recognition mistakes:

   ❑ Treating everyone the same

   ❑ Leaving someone out

   ❑ Not letting the group determine rewards

❑ Common organizational recognition mistakes:

   ❑ Rushing to recognition

   ❑ Rewards that aren't rewarding

   ❑ Making one size fit all

   ❑ Loss of freshness and relevance

   ❑ Confusing priorities and alignment

   ❑ Subjective recognition

   ❑ Entitlement recognition

   ❑ Recognition take-aways

   ❑ Inappropriate recognition

   ❑ Zero-sum recognition

   ❑ Untimely recognition

   ❑ Rewarding the wrong things

   ❑ Built-in demotivators

CHAPTER 15 CHECKLIST
Sustaining and Reenergizing Recognition

❑ There are many obstacles to getting a program up and running properly in the first place, but once the honeymoon's over, even the most popular and successful program faces the daunting challenge of keeping the excitement going.

❑ To sustain a recognition program over time, a number of things have to happen: new skills and tools have to be put in place, there has to be an ongoing focus on recognizing employees, and the motivation to recognize others in the organization has to be reenergized as needed along the way.

❑ To sustain your recognition programs, try the following:

  ❑ Link to strategic objectives.

  ❑ Gain renewed sponsorship commitment.

❑ Encourage specific management follow-up.

❑ Increase communication.

❑ Tie recognition to human resources systems.

❑ Reenergize recognition by:

  ❑ Increasing management involvement

  ❑ Providing new and improved recognition

  ❑ Holding recognition events

  ❑ Marketing your success

❑ Don't be afraid to terminate a program when it has outlasted its usefulness and cannot be easily reenergized.

❑ When the program is ready for termination, bring it to a close gracefully.

Recognition Planning Worksheets

In this section, you will find recognition planning worksheets that have been described in chapters 6, 7, 9, and 10 for use in planning individual, team, and organizational recognition programs and activities. These blank worksheets are designed to help you plan and implement effective recognition step by step, as described in earlier chapters. Make copies as needed so that you can use the worksheets in different contexts and for different recognition efforts.

See Chapter 6
to get started
with individual
recognition.

INDIVIDUAL RECOGNITION PLANNING WORKSHEET

WHAT do I want to recognize?

WHO do I want to recognize?

WHEN should the recognition be done?

WHERE should the recognition be done?

HOW should the recognition be done?

WHAT could go wrong?

WHAT response can be expected?

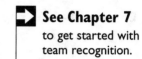

TEAM RECOGNITION
PLANNING WORKSHEET

➡ See Chapter 7
to get started with
team recognition.

WHAT (team performance) do I want to recognize?

WHO (what team) do I want to recognize?

WHEN should the recognition be done?

WHERE should the recognition be done?

HOW should the recognition be done?

WHAT could go wrong?

WHAT response can be expected?

See Chapters 8–12 ◀
to get started
with organizational
recognition.

ORGANIZATIONAL RECOGNITION PLANNING WORKSHEET

Current State

Desired State

Goal

ACTION PLANNING WORKSHEET

ACTION PLAN

Step No.	Major Activity	Responsibility

SCHEDULE WORKSHEET

SCHEDULE

Major Milestones	Critical Dates

REQUIRED RESOURCES WORKSHEET

HUMAN RESOURCES REQUIRED

Personnel	Program Role

REQUIRED RESOURCES WORKSHEET (continued)

OTHER RESOURCES REQUIRED

Resource	Purchase/Develop	Date Required

BUDGET WORKSHEET

PROGRAM BUDGET

Items	Estimated Cost	Actual Cost

POTENTIAL PROBLEMS WORKSHEET

POTENTIAL FAILURE FACTORS AND PREVENTIVE ACTIONS

Factor	Probability	Preventive Actions

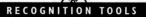
MEASUREMENT STRATEGY WORKSHEET

Method	Level	Phase(s)	Description

LESSONS LEARNED WORKSHEET

What Lessons Did I Learn from This Recognition Effort?

What Would I Do Differently Next Time?

Recognition Training Designs

Companies are realizing that if they expect managers, supervisors, and team leaders to take the job of recognizing their employees seriously, they need to provide training in recognition skills. Such training can greatly raise awareness, develop specific skills, and help overcome obstacles regarding the use of recognition, making it easier to develop a momentum that can greatly impact the organization's chances of creating a cultural change.

Training and follow-up programs can also be invaluable in creating "breakthrough" learning, as discussed in Chapter 5, "The Recognition Cycle."

Managers can learn from one another about what recognition strategies have worked well in the organization, and they should solicit feedback about new recognition activities they are considering.

A NOTE ON TEACHING RECOGNITION

Since people learn in different ways and at different rates, a variety of approaches should be used when teaching recognition in order to maximize the potential for learning. Here are a few techniques that you will find of value in teaching the topic of recognition and its related skills.

Activities and discussion. Getting individuals involved in the topic is an effective way to get them to think about the importance or recognition. You might want to start by asking participants to think of the last time they felt appreciated or the best recognition they ever gave to or received from another employee, and to describe that experience. The resulting discussion and sharing give the group a common baseline of experience upon which to build. Group discussions can also be held to share recognition techniques that have worked for attendees in their jobs or in previous positions or organizations, or to brainstorm low-cost recognition ideas.

Research and statistics. Using motivation studies or statistics from studies such as the ones provided in this book persuasively underscores the importance of recognition, especially for more analytical participants. Motivation studies are commonly reported in the business press, and quotations can be used to make a point and give credibility to your ideas.

Stories and case studies. Often even more persuasive than research is the power of a good story. The recent knowledge-management literature provides extensive evidence of the power of storytelling for both disseminating knowledge and sustaining an organization's values. A story can be based on the trainer's own experience or one the trainer heard from an employee, manager, or in previous training. If the story is humorous, it is even better for holding the group's attention and offering a change of pace to the content. A full-blown story can serve as a case study, which adds depth of understanding to the topic. For the greatest relevance, use case studies directly from your own organization so that trainees can readily relate to them. A video case study example can also go a long way toward showing what recognition looks like when it's an integral part of a company's culture.

Behavioral modeling. An ideal way to teach any skill, especially interpersonal skills, is to model behaviors related to that skill. When teaching recognition skills, it is important to demonstrate whenever possible what effective recognition looks like, by providing a quick, specific, and sincere informal personal praising to a participant in front of the class, or more formally by role-playing (live or on videotape) examples of good and poor recognition. Other ways of demonstrating recognition in a training setting follow.

- Use an in-class pass-around trophy such as a water gun to recognize certain behaviors (compliments of Peg Murray, trainer, Skillpath Seminars).

- Create an award out of a piece of crumpled paper and ask participants to make the award meaningful (compliments of Amelia Armitage, principal, Performance System Associates).

- Provide a certificate for participants to write something they would like to be recognized for and have a partner present the certificate to the person (compliments of Toni La Motta, author of *Recognition: The Quality Way*).

In general, although it is important to make managers, supervisors, team leaders, and, increasingly, all employees aware of the importance of recognition and to train them in the skills of providing recognition, it is even more critical to get them to personally experience the power of recognition. The classroom can be an effective environment in which to help them take the first step in practicing recognition skills and developing an action plan for using those skills once they return to the workplace.

Following are several training designs that the authors have used, which can be readily adapted for your own situation.

GENERAL RECOGNITION TRAINING OUTLINE

TOPICS	ACTIVITIES	SUGGESTIONS
Introduction	■ **Welcome** ■ **Objectives** ■ **Agenda** ■ **Participant introductions** ■ **Expectations**	*Make sure that participants are clear about expectations. As they introduce themselves, you might want to have each participant share what he or she personally expects to get out of the program.*
Definition of terms ■ Recognition ■ Incentives ■ Reinforcement ■ Reward ■ Etc.		
Value of recognition	**Discussion**	*Have participants share their personal experiences about how recognition has made them feel.*
Monetary versus nonmonetary recognition		*Interactive presentation*
Levels of Recognition Individual Team Organizational	**Interactive presentation**	*Ask participants to volunteer to share a recognition experience at each level.*
Recognition Quotient (RQ) ■ Age ■ Experience ■ Skills/confidence ■ Frequency of use ■ Organizational role ■ Available time ■ Fear of negative consequences ■ Others	**Interactive presentation**	*Ask participants to suggest other factors that might contribute to higher RQ (Recognition Quotient).*
Organizational Enablers ■ Manager ■ Organizational support ■ Recognition culture ■ Resources ■ Others	**Interactive presentation**	*Ask participants to suggest other organizational enabling factors.*

continued on next page ➤

Organizational Constraints	Discussion	Ask participants to identify any constraints that might discourage recognition. If any constraints are identified, point out that recognition is always possible.
Dimensions of Recognition • Contingency • Timing • Frequency • Formality • Recognition setting and context • Significance of the provider • Value to the recipient	Interactive presentation	
Recognition Cycle	Interactive presentation	Discuss the Plan-Do-Review-Implement (PDRI) cycle and its implications for developing incremental and breakthrough recognition improvement.
Getting Started with Individual Recognition	Interactive presentation	Emphasize the importance of "getting started" and not "being perfect." Point out simple planning questions.
Guidelines for Effective Recognition	Interactive presentation	Focus on "ASAP" model. Optional: role-playing.
Best Practices	Interactive presentation	Discuss the "ten best ways."
Getting Started with Team Recognition (optional)	Interactive presentation	Discuss both in-person and virtual team recognition best practices.
Getting Started with Organizational Recognition (optional)	Interactive presentation	Emphasize that organizational recognition requires more careful planning.
Making Time for Recognition	Discussion	Focus on what can be done (opportunities) rather than what can't be done (constraints).
Recognition Commitment	Action planning	Get participants to complete the "Recognition Action Plan."
Summary	Discussion	Brainstorm major learning points.
Evaluation	Survey completion	

SAMPLE FULL-DAY RECOGNITION WORKSHOP

	The following full-day training design combines elements of the two previous half-day designs and can also be delivered in separate half-day modules.
8:30–8:45	**Introduction and Overview**
8:35–8:45	**Opening activity:** The importance of energy
8:45–8:55	**Trends affecting the need for recognition**
8:55–9:10	**Activity and Sharing:** The last time you felt appreciated (Conclusion: the best recognition was simple, personal) (Provide *1001 Rewards* books to three participants who share)
9:10–9:20	**Benefits of recognition** **Bottom-line impact of recognition**
9:20–9:40	**Definitions:** ■ Recognition and reward ■ Formal/informal/day-to-day ■ Tangible/intangible ■ Extrinsic/intrinsic
9:40–10:00	**Video clip best practice:** Southwest Airlines
10:00–10:15	Break
10:15–10:20	**Questions about recognition and rewards**
10:20–10:50	**Small group discussion:** Why don't we use recognition
10:50–11:00	**Two Principles of Performance Management** #1 All Performance Starts with Clear Goals #2 You Get What You Reward Three types of consequences: Positive, Negative, None
11:00–11:45	**Activity:** Three types of feedback with debrief (demonstration of the value of different types of feedback)
11:45–12:00	**Video clip best practice:** Walt Disney Dolphin Hotel
12:00–1:15	Lunch
1:15–1:30	**Questions & discussion:** Developing a motivation baseline
1:30–2:00	**Research overview:** 3–4 studies with Graham capstone research study: Top Motivating Techniques Reported by Employees with techniques. Conclusions: (1) Money is not the top motivator and (2) The best motivators are manager-initiated and based on performance

continued on next page ➤

2:00–2:20	**Group Activity:** A nonmonetary recognition that has worked for you (group discussion and report; capture items for distribution to group)
2:20–2:30	Break
2:30–2:45	**Putting recognition into practice** **Guidelines for effective praisings**
2:45–2:55	**Activity:** Praising practice with partner
2:55–3:00	**Revisit goal list, divide into groups by topic interest**
3:00–3:30	**Group Activity:** Discussion and brainstorming of needs, report out
3:30–3:50	**Energizing Employees:** The Power of I's (with examples): ▪ Interesting and important work ▪ Information, communication, and feedback on performance ▪ Involvement in decisions and a sense of ownership ▪ Independence, autonomy, and flexibility ▪ Increased opportunity for learning, growth, and responsibility
3:50–4:00	**1001 Energize video:** Motivation: Igniting Exceptional Performance (show entire video, if time permits)
4:00–4:20	**Action planning and handout review with one thing you'll do differently** (Provide 1001 Energize books for those who share their plans)
4:20–4:30	**Summary and Close**

SAMPLE HALF-DAY RECOGNITION WORKSHOPS

Conducting a half-day follow-up workshop 2–3 weeks after the initial training helps build momentum and resolve obstacles.

SAMPLE A

8:30–8:45	**Introduction and Overview**
8:45–9:00	**Activity and Sharing:** The last time you felt appreciated
9:00–9:05	**Definition of Recognition**
9:05–9:25	**Types of Recognition:** formal/informal/day-to-day
9:25–9:35	**Activity:** The power of informal interaction
9:35–9:40	**Guidelines for Giving Effective Praise:** ASAP[3]
9:45–10:00	**Video clip best practice:** Walt Disney World
10:00–10:20	Break
10:20–10:35	**Discussion:** What keeps us from using recognition?
10:35–10:55	**Two Principles of Performance Management** 1. All Performance Starts with Clear Goals 2. You Get What You Reward
10:55–11:15	**Research Overview**
11:15–11:35	**Group Activity:** A recognition activity that has worked (group discussion, brainstorming and report out)
11:35–11:50	**Action Planning and Sharing**
11:50–12:00	**Summary and Close**

SAMPLE B

8:30–8:40	**Introduction and Goal-setting**
8:40–9:10	**Activity:** Group discussion and report—what worked and what did not?
9:10–9:30	**Review of the Principles of Effective Recognition and Rewards**
9:30–9:45	**Video Clip Best Practice:** Southwest Airlines
9:45–10:00	Break
10:20–11:00	**Further discussion and brainstorming**
11:00–11:25	**Action Planning and Sharing**
11:25–11:30	**Summary and Close**

PART VI
RECOGNITION RESOURCES

Bob and Dean's Recognition Honor Roll

Following are our top dozen picks for best overall recognition organizations, based on our experience in researching, writing, and working with hundreds of organizations on the topic of recognition and rewards. These organizations all enjoy strong recognition cultures, with active and diverse recognition practices, and a long-term commitment to their employees. Rather than use a rigorous set of criteria or quantitative ratings, we selected organizations based on our qualitative assessment of the organizations that best represented the principles and practices advocated throughout this fieldbook.

ARIZONA DEPARTMENT OF ADMINISTRATION

This state government agency has demonstrated, on many levels, that it is truly a recognition culture. The approach to recognition is strategic and tied to organizational values, yet tactical and decentralized in its implementation. The BRAVO! program is multifaceted, comprised of many components that focus on all aspects of employee performance.

What we like best about the ADOA's program is that it is both comprehensive and well balanced. It recognizes many types of performance and provides recognition in numerous ways. For example, there is a strong focus on recognizing teams (not just individuals), and team awards include recognition for the team as well as for individual members.

See pages 164–65 for more information about ADOA's BRAVO! program.

Given the limited resources of a state government agency, the ADOA has been very resourceful and creative in how they have made recognition relevant and meaningful, keeping it vibrant and fresh.

ChevronTexaco

See pages 114–15
for more information about ChevronTexaco's recognition programs

CHEVRON/TEXACO

ChevronTexaco's recognition program is based on a well-conceived set of principles, "The ChevronTexaco Way," which are consistent with the principles and practices of effective recognition we have described in this book.

ChevronTexaco's approach is also systemic. In addition to the corporate-wide Chairman's Award program, human resources staff members consult with each division to set up its own recognition programs. Recognition at ChevronTexaco is centrally coordinated but decentralized enough to provide a lot of recognition accessible to all employees in the company. Within its guiding principles, ChevronTexaco encourages diversity of recognition programs, depending on the subculture of the division or organizational unit.

ChevronTexaco's approach to recognition is a motivational "fill 'er up" for employees and an energizer for the entire organization.

See pages 100–01
for more information about Seattle Works!

CITY OF SEATTLE

A high-recognition culture in a city government almost seems like an oxymoron . . . but not for the City of Seattle. Dedicated, concerted effort on the part of a lot of people has contributed to an exemplary employee recognition program called Seattle Works!—part of a citywide commitment to excellent performance.

Seattle Works! is an outstanding model for organizational recognition, utilizing a wide range of recognition policies and practices throughout city government that make employees feel good about working: peer nominations, multiple approaches, decentralized programs with centralized coordination, a mix of formal and informal recognition, ongoing education on recognition giving, and an effort to ensure that recognition is spread around, so that all employees in all areas and in all job categories have the opportunity to earn recognition.

DISNEY CORPORATION

No Recognition Honor Roll would be complete without Disney Corporation. Few companies do organizational recognition better. The Disney model is powerful, dynamic, and flexible.

Disney doesn't look at recognition as an isolated program; it is an integral part of a larger strategy to direct, manage, and retain customer service–oriented "cast members" (employees). Disney is constantly looking for new ways to recognize people, both formally and informally.

As we have pointed out many times in this book, the best organizational recognition is aligned with the organization's culture and business strategy. Disney has one global recognition program that supports the company's performance excellence initiatives, including guest satisfaction, cast excellence, and operational/financial excellence—called Partners in Excellence. Like many great organizational recognition programs, Partners in Excellence has multiple tiers. They also have many other local programs, all aligned with core Disney values.

Another reason for liking Disney is that their approach to recognition was developed based on extensive benchmarking with other high-recognition companies. They are not satisfied being less than the best, and they are always striving to get better. This same approach applies to revitalizing recognition that might have lost its edge. Disney is not afraid to change in order to get better.

FEDEX CORPORATION

FedEx Corporation is one of the best-known and most respected companies in the United States, and perhaps in the world (*Fortune* magazine voted FedEx one of its 100 Best Companies to Work For in America as well as one of the Most Admired Companies in the world). We thought that it also belonged on our Recognition Honor Roll.

FedEx, like most of the companies we have profiled, has a varied array of recognition programs clearly aligned with desired business results. It also provides a large number of opportunities for employees at all levels to be appropriately recognized. In our opinion, FedEx is a company that "gets it"—one that realizes that

Walt Disney World Co.
© Disney

➤ **See pages 12–13**
for more information about Disney's recognition programs.

➤ **See pages 56–57**
for more information about FedEx Corporation's recognition programs.

recognition is not a matter of throwing plaques or a collection of entitlements at people. For example, when reassessing its Bravo Zulu awards, management focused on how well-written, personalized letters presented in front of a person's work group are often just as meaningful as cash or costly mementos.

FedEx's recognition includes awards selected by supervisors, by senior managers, and by customers, but all recognition reinforces the company's core values—quick, reliable delivery and a high level of customer service. FedEx even has a formal award for humanitarian contributions to the community.

FedEx also does a lot of informal recognition. The example that really got our attention was the manager who sings to the employees as they are sorting packages each morning.

The bottom line is, FedEx appreciates that recognition has value for its bottom line.

GOOD SAMARITAN HOSPITAL

A member of **Premier Health Partners**

Hospitals can be pretty depressing places to work. Not so at Good Samaritan Hospital in Dayton, Ohio, where organizational recognition is a major force toward creating a high-quality, customer-focused organization that is also fun to work in. Effective organizational recognition is one of the reasons the hospital has been honored for excellence both nationally and by the State of Ohio.

Like all great organizational recognition programs, Good Samaritan Hospital's program is well coordinated and dynamic, it includes both senior management and employee involvement, and it is aligned with the organization's core value and performance standards. However, employee involvement is the hallmark of the Good Samaritan program. By necessity, Good Samaritan has avoided a costly recognition infrastructure—in fact, compared to most organizations listed in our Honor Roll, it is done on a shoestring—but it has not sacrificed quality. We have been particularly impressed by Good Samaritan's CREW (Celebrating and Recognizing Employees' Work) team, which is the driving force behind the recognition program.

Recognition has a lot to do with why both smiles and high performance are more common at Good Samaritan than at most hospitals.

See page 174 ◀
for more information about Good Samaritan Hospital's recognition programs.

IBM CORPORATION

One of us might be biased, but we both ultimately agreed that IBM was a worthy member of our Recognition Honor Roll. Admittedly, IBM probably puts a greater emphasis on monetary recognition than other Honor Roll members do, but they also have a serious commitment to other forms of recognition.

No company is more focused on performance than IBM, and IBM's recognition programs reflect this focus. Likewise, no recognition program we have studied is better aligned with the company's strategy and culture, and IBM is actively creating a true *climate of recognition* throughout the company.

"New Blue: Focus to Win" is an integrated system of targeted recognition programs. This program recognizes a wide range of behaviors and results. The programs range from low-cost peer-to-peer recognitions to payments of up to $25,000 for significant impact on the business—and virtually every level in between.

IBM also uses a great deal of nonmonetary recognition: e-mail thank-you cards, tokens of appreciation, executive visits, celebrations, contests, and so on. Another meritorious aspect of recognition at IBM is the company's commitment to management development—and its education on recognition in all management development programs.

Developing and maintaining a recognition program for more than 350,000 employees worldwide is no small undertaking, but IBM is doing it, and putting its money behind its commitment.

➜ See pages 176–77 for more information about IBM's recognition programs.

LANDS' END

We selected Lands' End, the direct merchant based in Dodgeville, Wisconsin, as an example of an organization that is extraordinary by being ordinary. That is, the company believes that recognition should be a routine, everyday activity, and not something that happens only sporadically on special occasions. That's why you might not see as much formal recognition here as in some other organizations, and why a company like Lands' End might not get as much attention as some other companies that are known for flashier recognition programs. However, we believe that the company's day-to-day informal recognition practices are among the best in the country.

See pages 34–35 ←
for more
information about
recognition
programs at
Lands' End.

Call centers are notoriously stressful and unforgiving workplaces. That is why we are so impressed with Lands' End. It is open twenty-four hours a day, seven days a week, 364 days a year, and it can be an extremely stressful and hectic place, especially during the holidays. Yet the atmosphere at Lands' End is different from that of any other call center we have studied. A lot of this difference has to do with a genuine commitment to recognizing employees' contributions on an ongoing basis.

The company is constantly trying to find better ways to serve customers and its employees. Even if founder Gary Comer hadn't built the 80,000-square-foot activity center for employees, they would know that management cares for them and appreciates their efforts—and that is just an ordinary fact of life around Land's End.

See pages 186–87 ←
for more information
about Perkins Coie's
recognition programs.

PERKINS COIE

Named for the first time in 2003 as one of the 100 Best Companies to Work For in America, the law firm Perkins Coie is an excellent example of a company systematically building a culture of recognition over a three-year period, combining all the elements we've discussed in this book. From a fun and simple Happiness Committee, comprised of five anonymous members, any one of whom can initiate a new morale-building activity, to flex time and paid sabbaticals available to everyone, to a systematic method for measuring recognition efforts through periodic surveying of employees, Perkins Coie serves as a model for how recognition can take root and spread in any organization.

SOUTHWEST AIRLINES

Although we don't always like getting to the airport early enough to get a low number for early boarding on a Southwest flight, we were unanimous in our admiration of the company's approach to recognition.

The major distinguishing feature of the corporate culture at Southwest Airlines is the emphasis on fun and playfulness, a spirit and sense of camaraderie that is unequaled in American business and is evident as soon as you arrive at the ticket counter or board an airplane. It is not surprising that, even in tough economic times,

Southwest is one of the only airlines that is still making a profit. Southwest has proven that recognizing people really pays off.

We are impressed by companies, like Southwest Airlines, that realize that employees are the company's first customers. If employees are not feeling good about themselves, they can hardly make customers feel good about interacting with them.

No corporate leader has done more personally to create a culture of recognition than Herb Kelleher. Our favorite story about Kelleher is when employee Ed Stewart turned down a better-paying offer to stay with Southwest. The CEO walked into his office and kissed him.

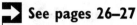

See pages 26–27 for more information about Southwest Airlines' recognition programs.

STARBUCKS

Few companies have sought to do as much for its front-line and part-time employees as Starbucks. From part-time benefits to extensive learning, training, and growth opportunities, Starbucks sets the stage for a new type of employer-employee contract in which employees are treated as partners. Starbucks' employees like working for the company, and their service to customers reflects that fact. Founder Howard Schultz knows from personal experience what it's like to work and not have a safety net, and in his view, the cost of training programs, stock options, and comprehensive medical coverage is more than offset by the value to the company of employee loyalty and the sense of cohesion that is passed on to the customer. Starbucks is all about quality, not only in its product but in its attitude toward people.

See pages 154–55 for more information about Starbucks' recognition programs.

U.S. OFFICE OF PERSONNEL MANAGEMENT

It may not seem as if an agency of the federal government could serve as a role model for other organizations, including those in private industry. But the Office of Personnel Management is not a typical government agency. Charged with advising federal agencies that employ some 2 million people (representing the most diverse employer in the world) about recognition programs while adhering to constant public scrutiny and legislative constraints, the OPM has become a skilled adviser about the power of recognition and how agencies can creatively tap its principles.

See pages 72–73
for more
information about
the federal
government's
recognition programs

"The challenge that the Office of Personnel Management faces," says Doris Hausser, director of performance management for the OPM, "is to encourage people to be innovative and creative, yet keep them from doing something that the law does not allow them to do." The OPM does this by providing clear principles of recognition, while allowing and encouraging agencies to design their own programs. In addition, they encourage agencies to exchange ideas and successes and bring in outsiders to train agencies and learn from the "best practices" of other organizations.

In just one of hundreds of programs by one of its agencies, the Unsung Heroes Award was given as part of the fiftieth-anniversary celebration of the Smithsonian Institution honoring fifty outstanding peer-nominated employees who had distinguished themselves through an ongoing commitment to excellence.

Recognition Best Practices

In this section, we showcase a variety of recognition Best Practices—specific recognition programs created to achieve specific performance results. These examples come from organizations of all sizes in a wide variety of industries and were written to make it easy for you to understand what was done and to use that information to create templates for similar programs within your own organization. Several blank recognition planning forms are provided at the end of the section for the purpose of creating your own recognition programs.

Featured on the upcoming pages you'll find:

PERFORMANCE TARGET(S)	FEATURED ORGANIZATION
"Above and beyond" behavior	Honeywell
Cost savings and suggestions	Boardroom
Employee and customer appreciation	IKEA Furniture Stores
Employee retention	Frito Lay
Exceptional performance	American Express
Hiring and recruitment	Land's End
Initiative	ComputerWorld
Service, teamwork, and innovation	CalPERS
Learning and development	Brodeur Worldwide
Morale improvement	Perkins Coie
Outstanding customer service	The Ken Blanchard Cos.
Patient satisfaction	Good Samaritan Hospital
Peer recognition	Johnson & Johnson
Positive behaviors	Strong Capital Management
Quality improvement	Tennant Company
Safety	Martin Marietta Materials
Sales, service, and teamwork	JC Penney
Suggestions and achievements	Sony Pictures Entertainment
Teamwork, performance, and pride	Hilton Hotels
Values	Caterpillar
Years of service and tenure	Datatel

"ABOVE AND BEYOND" BEHAVIOR RECOGNITION BEST PRACTICE

Target Performance	"Above and beyond" performance
Program Name	Winning Edge
Organization/Location	Honeywell, Honeywell Technology Center, Minneapolis, Minnesota
Industry	Technology
Need	Honeywell wanted to encourage more employees to strive for superior performance.
Recognition Provided	$100 in cash and a publicly presented certificate
Recognition Criteria	Any "above and beyond" behavior of an employee
Program Time Frame	The program had run its course in about a year and was discontinued after it was felt that a majority of worthy employees had received the award.
Program Administration	Administered by human resources with the aid of a selection committee.
Selection Process	A selection committee reviewed written nominations by management and peers with final approval by upper management.
Presentation/Celebration	Awards were presented at a brief ceremony, and all award winners were publicized in the company newsletter.
Results	The program was considered a success in getting employees to pay extra attention to helping others, recognizing those who were committed to excellence, and increasing the general morale and excitement of the work environment. Although there were some program costs, the benefits of the program were felt to be far more beneficial.

COST SAVINGS AND SUGGESTIONS RECOGNITION BEST PRACTICE

Target Performance	Cost savings and suggestions
Program Name	I-Power
Organization/Location	Boardroom Greenwich, Connecticut
Industry	Publishing
Need	To increase employee involvement in the business and improve the quality of meetings; this was to be done by recognizing the number and quality of suggestions for improvement. The ideas actually came as a result of a suggestion from management guru Peter Drucker to Martin Edelston, Boardroom CEO, to improve meetings by having participants suggest two things to make them better.
Recognition Provided	■ Nominal monetary recognition ($2 or $5 per suggestion), along with feedback on the suggestion ■ $100 each month for the best "A" ideas ■ $50 each month for the best "B" ideas ■ Various nonmonetary rewards ■ Quarterly profit sharing, based on overall business improvement
Recognition Criteria	Every idea gets some recognition, but the best ideas are categorized with an "A" (should be implemented) and good ideas with a "B" (more study needed).
Program Time Frame	Open-ended
Program Administration	Administered by an I-Power director; each department has an I-Power coordinator; there is also a data manager to handle the paperwork. The program can be fairly labor intensive because of the commitment to respond to every suggestion in a timely manner.
Selection Process	Martin Edelston, CEO, used to personally review each idea; however, due to the high volume, they are now reviewed and the best are selected by department managers.
Presentation/ Celebration	All employees receive feedback and some token of appreciation. The developers of top-rated ideas get their awards. A list of all ideas and award winners is circulated throughout the organization.
Results	Boardroom credits this program with a fivefold increase in their revenues plus cost savings of millions of dollars. Employee morale and retention in the company has also improved dramatically as a direct result of the program. The program has been so successful that Martin Edelston wrote a book about it and has marketed training programs to share its concepts.

EMPLOYEE AND CUSTOMER APPRECIATION RECOGNITION BEST PRACTICE

Target Performance	Employee and customer appreciation
Program Name	Big Thank-You Sale
Organization/Location	IKEA Furniture Stores Sweden (with stores in 30 countries)
Industry	Retail
Need	To show appreciation to employees for sales results through a public marketing program
Recognition Provided	Employees receive shares of the entire day's receipts.
Recognition Criteria	All full-time employees receive an equal share of the day's revenues, regardless of their position; part-time employees receive a prorated share. This reinforces the company's egalitarian philosophy toward employees.
Program Time Frame	One day each year
Program Administration	Administered by company management
Selection Process	All employees participate in the recognition; there is no differential recognition.
Presentation/Celebration	The entire day is a big celebration for employees and customers. There are free chocolates, free massages, reduced prices, and extended hours. Every two hours, customers waiting in line at the checkout win their purchases free.
Results	Increases employee morale and energizes sales long after the event.

EMPLOYEE RETENTION RECOGNITION BEST PRACTICE

Target Performance	Employee retention
Program Name	N/A
Organization/Location	Frito-Lay (a division of PepsiCo) Plano, Texas
Industry	Food products
Need	Reducing employee turnover. Turnover in a manufacturing plant in West Valley City, Utah, had reached an annual rate of 30 percent.
Recognition Provided	The program provided a more stable and predictable work schedule that allowed employees to better plan family activities. In addition, involvement in designing and selecting alternative work schedules was very motivating.
Recognition Criteria	All employees were eligible for the new work schedule.
Program Time Frame	Open-ended
Program Administration	The program was developed in conjunction with a local consulting company. Interviews with employees were conducted. Alternative work schedules were designed, and employees were able to make the final decision about the ultimate work schedule chosen.
Selection Process	Volunteer employee groups developed alternative proposals to address high turnover. Selection of new policies was determined by a company-wide vote of all employees.
Presentation/Celebration	The ultimate work schedule decision was announced. All employees knew that they had had input and had contributed to the selection of the new work schedule. Employees felt very positive about the process and the outcome.
Results	Attrition declined immediately from 30 percent to 5 percent and leveled off at 20 percent. Savings to the company were $120,000 during the first year; there were also unforeseen improvements in safety.

EXCEPTIONAL PERFORMANCE RECOGNITION BEST PRACTICE

Target Performance	Exceptional performance
Program Name	The Great Performers Program
Organization/Location	American Express, Travel Related Services New York, New York
Industry	Travel
Need	To promote pride and exceptional employee performance
Recognition Provided	Life-sized posters showing famous people and referencing their greatest achievements were displayed throughout the facilities for many weeks. Then the company began to picture American Express employees on posters, with a statement of a major accomplishment by each employee. Afterward, the employee could take the poster home.
Recognition Criteria	The program was established to recognize and reward "truly exceptional performance."
Program Time Frame	This program ran for several years.
Program Administration	Unknown
Selection Process	Nominations were made by fellow employees, supervisors, and customers. There was no limit on how many people could win, and in a recent year thirty-eight employees captured the award. Award winners were eligible to become Grand Award winners, chosen by the worldwide governing committee.
Presentation/Celebration	Prizes for Grand Award winners included an all-expense-paid trip for two to New York, $4,000 in American Express traveler's checks, a platinum "GP" logo pin, and a framed certificate.
Results	The Great Performer's program is just one of the factors that helped to increase TRS's net income 500 percent in eleven years, or about an 18 percent annual compounded rate. The company's return on equity since the program began has been 28 percent.

HIRING AND RECRUITMENT
RECOGNITION BEST PRACTICE

Target Performance	Hiring and recruitment
Program Name	Recruitment Incentive Program
Organization/Location	Land's End Dodgeville, Wisconsin
Industry	Retail (mail order and Internet)
Need	High growth; ongoing need for reliable new employees (especially in seasonal jobs and difficult-to-fill jobs) in a small community
Recognition Provided	■ $35 for every seasonal applicant who is referred and hired ■ $1 for each new hire is set aside for a drawing at the end of each holiday season for which all those who referred employees are eligible ■ $500 for a referral for a hired full-time professional or hourly employee ■ $1,000 for referred new employees for the computer department ■ Drawing for Green Bay Packers tickets for which all previous successful referral award winners are eligible
Recognition Criteria	Referred applicant is hired.
Program Time Frame	Different time frame for each subprogram; depends on need for new employees
Program Administration	Administered by the human resources department
Selection Process	When referred employees are hired, the employee who referred them is given the award and entered for whatever lottery drawing is occurring at that time.
Presentation/Celebration	Awards are presented by a human resources representative.
Results	The program has generated many more qualified and local new employee applications at a much lower cost.

INITIATIVE RECOGNITION PROGRAM BEST PRACTICE

Target Performance	Initiative
Program Name	Enterprise Awards
Organization/Location	Computerworld Magazine Framington, Massachusetts
Industry	Publishing
Need	For employees to take more initiative and be more innovative
Recognition Provided	$200 cash awards
Recognition Criteria	Demonstrating "enterprising behavior." Examples: ■ Going beyond the call of duty on urgent projects ■ Helping needy people ■Writing particularly clever headlines
Program Time Frame	Open-ended
Program Administration	Administered by management
Selection Process	Candidates are nominated by other employees and selected by management.
Presentation/Celebration	Awards, along with prolific praise, are given "very publicly" by managers. Even though the award is relatively small, the recognition is large.
Results	The company reported an increase in "enterprising behavior" and improved morale for a nominal cost.

SERVICE, TEAMWORK, AND INNOVATION RECOGNITION BEST PRACTICE

Target Performance	Service, teamwork, and innovation
Program Name	The Rock
Organization/Location	CalPERS (California Public Employees' Retirement System) Sacramento, California
Industry	State government
Need	The organization wanted to strategically revamp and improve its approach to providing employee recognition.
Recognition Provided	Day-to-day recognition consists of thank-you note pads incorporating the words "You're a rock," along with a photo of a real rock. "The Rock" pass-around award is periodically passed to another outstanding individual or team.
Recognition Criteria	"The Rock" pass-around award is awarded by one employee to another according to the following five criteria: ■ Taking responsibility or initiative to help achieve a common goal or purpose ■ Proactively or consistently going above and beyond to accommodate internal customer needs ■ Helping others in the organization achieve results through effective decision making or problem solving ■ Consistently exemplifying core values in dealing with internal customers ■ Contributing to strengthening relationships and achieving optimum results through teamwork, encouragement, and positive reinforcement
Program Time Frame	Open-ended
Program Administration	In addition to several program coordinators, a cross-functional team helps to coordinate recognition activities, assisted by external recognition consultants. Training in effective recognition skills is also provided to all employees: managers, supervisors, and professional staff.
Selection Process	Any employee can give any other employee a Rock note at any time for almost any reason he or she decides merits it, e.g., support, service, or innovation.
Presentation/Celebration	The current holder of the "Rock" schedules an informal celebration to present the award to the next recipient(s), who is posted on the CalPERS Insider Recognition Page on the organization's intranet. Recipients of the "Rock" also receive a personalized certificate to serve as a permanent memento of the award after it is passed on to the next recipient.
Results	The program has received widespread enthusiasm and has greatly helped to increase the amount of informal recognition that has been conducted.

LEARNING AND DEVELOPMENT RECOGNITION BEST PRACTICE

Target Performance	Learning and professional development
Program Name	Professional Development Program
Organization/Location	Brodeur Worldwide Boston, Massachusetts
Industry	Public relations consulting
Need	The program was instituted to promote learning and professional development among employees and to "create a culture of learning." Employee development is one of the key values and strategic drivers of the company.
Recognition Provided	This multifaceted program includes such professional development opportunities as: ■ In-house training sessions develop skills in areas such as people management, media relations, client service, presentations, and writing ■ Creativity workshops, led by an outside consultant; the company even hired a full-time "creatologist" to evangelize creativity throughout the organization ■ BookSmart Program provides best-selling business books to employees given at the time of the job offer letter, each annual performance review, and each promotion ■ Professional education allowance of $300 can be used to join professional associations, professional journal subscriptions, and so on
Recognition Criteria	Available to all employees at the company's expense.
Program Time Frame	Open-ended
Program Administration	Unknown
Selection Process	All employees qualify.
Presentation/Celebration	Learning is celebrated throughout the organization and is recognized by managers as being vital to the company's success.
Results	The program won a SABRE Certificate of Excellence for best practices in public relations, and it has contributed to the company's selection as PR Agency of the Year in 2000 by *PR Week*, and the number-one ranking in high-technology PR by *Inside PR* for many years.

MORALE IMPROVEMENT RECOGNITION BEST PRACTICE

Target Performance	Morale improvement
Program Name	Happiness Committee
Organization/Location	Perkins Coie Seattle, Washington
Industry	Legal services
Need	There was a sense that employees were not feeling adequately appreciated and morale was not as high as the partners wanted.
Recognition Provided	A variety of "happiness events"
Recognition Criteria	Periodic determination by the Happiness Committee that morale-boosting and recognition are needed
Program Time Frame	Open-ended; events are not programmed; surprise is an important feature of the program.
Program Administration	Administered by the Happiness Committee, composed of five volunteer employees who are anonymous to the organization.
Selection Process	"Happiness events" are open to all employees.
Presentation/Celebration	Each event is different, and the Happiness Committee is constantly thinking of new ways to recognize and surprise Perkins Coie's employees. Past "happiness events" have included: ■ Company picnics on the roof ■ Barter with neighboring limo service for rides ■ Easter egg hunts ■ Earth Day planting celebration ■ Ferry trip on Puget Sound ■ Happiness Committee members serving "happy meals"
Results	There have been dramatic improvements in morale since the inception of the program. For example, employee morale scores almost doubled in the finance department alone.

OUTSTANDING CUSTOMER SERVICE RECOGNITION BEST PRACTICE

Target Performance	Outstanding customer service
Program Name	The Eagle Award
Organization/Location	The Ken Blanchard Companies Escondido, California
Industry	Management training and consulting
Need	To recognize employees for "legendary service" to customers—one of the organization's strategic objectives
Recognition Provided	A spontaneous celebration and photo of the honoree for the Eagle Wall of Fame with a brief description of the service provided, a pass-around trophy of an eagle and credit toward an Eagle Plaque (for multiple occurrences), and consideration for Eagle of the Year, determined by a company-wide vote of all the year's recipients
Recognition Criteria	Outstanding customer service, noticed by any employee. Examples include staying late to ship materials, helping a customer locate a lost order or resolve a billing problem, rearranging trainer schedules for emergencies, and so forth.
Program Time Frame	The program ran for several years with modifications.
Program Administration	The Eagle Committee, a small group of volunteer employees whose membership was periodically rotated, administered the program.
Selection Process	Any employee could nominate another employee who had demonstrated exemplary service to customers. The employees' names were submitted with a brief description of the activity that was considered exceptional. A volunteer committee reviewed the nominations, primarily to screen out items that were expected to be part of someone's job. The program was later modified to include "internal" customer service: exceptional service provided by one employee to another within the company.
Presentation/Celebration	Members of the Eagle Committee surprised the winners with a visit and took a picture of the person holding "an eagle award"—one of several eagle trophies that rotated around the company. The photo was displayed on a lobby bulletin board along with a brief description of the activity being recognized. The winner got to keep the eagle trophy on his or her desk until it was needed for a new recipient—typically a week or so. Eagle Plaques were presented at company meetings, and an annual dinner was conducted with awardees and their spouses.
Results	This program successfully drove customer service from being the seventh or eighth customer-cited attribute in working with the organization to one of the top attributes.

PATIENT SATISFACTION RECOGNITION BEST PRACTICE

Target Performance	Patient satisfaction
Program Name	Good Samaritans of the Month Program
Organization/Location	Good Samaritan Hospital Dayton, Ohio
Industry	Health care service
Need	To increase patient satisfaction survey results
Recognition Provided	Certificate and recognition ceremony
Recognition Criteria	Outstanding patient care and service
Program Time Frame	Monthly
Program Administration	Most of the hospital's recognition programs are administrated by a Celebrating and Recognizing Employees' Work (CREW) committee, composed of twelve staff drawn from throughout the hospital.
Selection Process	The employee must be specifically named on a patient satisfaction survey as having rendered particularly meritorious care.
Presentation/Celebration	Recognition is presented at a monthly ceremony sponsored by the hospital's customer service department.
Results	The program has increased excitement about providing outstanding patient care and has been nationally ranked in the top 1 percent for patient satisfaction.

PEER RECOGNITION BEST PRACTICE

Target Performance	Peer recognition
Program Name	Applauz
Organization/Location	Johnson & Johnson Medical Products Division, Peterborough, Ontario, Canada
Industry	Health care
Need	To fix perceived lack of peer-to-peer recognition—all recognition was "management's responsibility."
Recognition Provided	An assortment of expressions of recognition, including: ■ Applauz Post-It Notes ■ Photo greeting cards with envelopes ■ Little Favors (such as packs of Lifesavers, chocolates, or nuts available in the mail room) ■ When someone nominates another employee for an award they are entered into a drawing for a monthly $25 gift certificate.
Recognition Criteria	Depends on the award. In the Applauz Kits, which all employees receive, there are cards with descriptions of each type of recognition and recommendations for selection criteria.
Program Time Frame	Open-ended
Program Administration	Self-administered using the Applauz Recognition Kit. A program coordinator maintains the program and makes sure that the Recognition Cupboard in the mail room has sufficient Little Favors. This program is a part of a larger organizational recognition program.
Selection Process	Peer selection is based on recommended criteria.
Presentation/Celebration	Peers present recognition (Post-Its, cards, Little Favors, and so on) to peers.
Results	Increased morale, teamwork, and peer-to-peer interaction

POSITIVE BEHAVIORS RECOGNITION BEST PRACTICE

Target Performance	Positive behaviors
Program Name	Strong Recognition Program
Organization/Location	Strong Capital Management Menomonee Falls, Wisconsin
Industry	Banking and finance
Need	To encourage behaviors that Strong Capital's management considers instrumental for the company's success
Recognition Provided	Gift certificates, company logo items, and other items. Managers also receive a Recognition Toolkit (including a copy of Bob Nelson's *1001 Ways to Reward Employees*, thank-you cards, and other items to facilitate creative recognition).
Recognition Criteria	Managers and supervisors provide recognition based on observing "Behaviors to Look For" listed on "Strong Capital's Recognition Menu."
Program Time Frame	Open-ended
Program Administration	The company's associate services department administers the program. Managers can request recognition items, which are delivered to the managers within twenty-four hours. A team of associates (the Recognition Rapid Action Team) helped review and fine-tune the program, which was originally developed by associate services.
Selection Process	Selection is based on managers' and supervisors' observations of behaviors suggested on the Positive Behavior Menu. Each Behavior Menu item has a certain value. Examples of positive behaviors include: ■ Smiling at a customer ■ Fast turnaround in completing work ■ Extra effort to satisfy a customer's request ■ Helping a coworker ■ Implementing a business-improvement idea When the employee has reached a certain value, they get to choose an item for that value from another menu, the Recognition Menu.
Presentation/Celebration	Managers and supervisors present recognition items personally to employees as soon after the behaviors are observed as possible.
Results	The program has increased targeted behaviors, improved performance, improved morale, and made work more fun. The managers report that they enjoy the program as well.

QUALITY IMPROVEMENT RECOGNITION BEST PRACTICE

Target Performance	Quality improvement
Program Name	Koala T. Bear Award
Organization/Location	Tennant Company Minneapolis, Minnesota
Industry	Manufacturing
Need	To recognize individuals who were contributing to quality improvement throughout the year but might not qualify for the annual rewards program
Recognition Provided	A small stuffed koala bear wearing a Tennant Quality T-shirt, and a certificate
Recognition Criteria	■ Extra effort to meet or exceed customer needs ■ Going above and beyond job standards ■ Exhibiting a commitment to quality
Program Time Frame	An employee can receive only one Koala T. Bear Award in any twelve-month period.
Program Administration	A committee composed of eight Tennant employees from different ranks and departments administers the program.
Selection Process	■ Employees are nominated for the Koala T. Bear Award by their peers or managers ■ The committee sends a thank-you note to all nominators ■ The committee contacts those who work with the nominee to verify their qualifications for the award ■ Qualified nominees who have already received an award within the past twelve months receive a sticker to add to their certificate
Presentation/Celebration	A committee member dressed in a Koala T. Bear costume reads a proclamation, reinforcing the commitment of the individual to Tennant's quality values, and personally delivers the award. Over the years, a Koala T. Bear pin and Koala T. Bear cookies have been added to the award. Further program enhancements are anticipated in order to continue to revitalize the program.
Results	Tennant continues to be an industry leader in product quality. The Koala T. Bear Award program has recognized individual contributions to quality improvement at Tennant for twenty years at a very low cost. The program continues to have an extraordinary level of participation.

SAFETY RECOGNITION BEST PRACTICE

Target Performance	Safety
Program Name	Safety Activity Recognition Program
Organization/Location	Martin Marietta Materials Raleigh, North Carolina
Industry	Natural resources
Need	To reduce accidents
Recognition Provided	Publicity (newsletter articles, bulletin boards); points to be redeemed for prizes or cash
Recognition Criteria	Individual and team participation in safety activities
Program Time Frame	Three years old; revised after one and a half years to include behavior-based safety
Program Administration	Corporate safety director and the human resources manager of each division
Selection Process	Points systems for participation in safety activities. Different activities have different points (for example, attending a safety meeting—1 point; presenting at a safety meeting—10 points). Selection is criterion-referenced (not competitive). Teams receive recognition when they have attained a certain number of points.
Presentation/Celebration	Recognition is presented by human resources in divisions. Recipients receive publicity, and there are team celebrations. There is a celebration for teams that get maximum points. Meal and a cake commemorate the achievement.
Results	Tremendous increase in safety, lower accident rates, and increased participation in safety program activities

SALES, SERVICE, AND TEAMWORK RECOGNITION BEST PRACTICE

Target Performance	Sales, service, and teamwork
Program Name	Senior Merchandising Assistants (SMA) Contest
Organization/Location	JC Penney Dallas, Texas
Industry	Retail
Need	To increase sales, service, and teamwork among senior merchandising assistants (SMAs) in each store
Recognition Provided	Cash award and a plaque
Recognition Criteria	■ Greatest customer service profile (CSP) score improvement ■ Highest overall CSP score in the district
Program Time Frame	Annual
Program Administration	Administered by corporate headquarters
Selection Process	Award is given to the SMA team in each district that gets the highest total score in the company's annual customer service profile (CSP) and the one that shows the greatest year-to-year improvement.
Presentation/Celebration	The district manager presents the award with great pomp and ceremony.
Results	The program has significantly increased the sales, customer service, and team-work among senior merchandising assistants in each store.

SUGGESTIONS AND ACHIEVEMENTS RECOGNITION BEST PRACTICE

Target Performance	Suggestions and achievements
Program Name	ScreenLighter Program
Organization/Location	Sony Pictures Entertainment Los Angeles, California
Industry	Entertainment
Need	To give employees recognition and rewards for outstanding contributions
Recognition Provided	Cash awards between $100 and $250,000
Recognition Criteria	Three distinct award programs, each with its own criteria: ■ ScreenLighter Suggestion Awards for employee ideas that save the company money or generate new revenues ■ ScreenLighter Achievement Awards for employees (or teams) who have made exceptional contributions ■ ScreenLighter SpotLight Awards: on-the-spot awards given for extraordinary effort or accomplishment
Program Time Frame	The program has run for several years.
Program Administration	A full-time program manager coordinates the program with the help of the employee-run ScreenLighter Committee.
Selection Process	■ ScreenLighter Suggestion Award nominations are submitted by employees or teams in four areas: revenue generation/cost savings, customer service, improved work environment, and personal effort. ■ ScreenLighter Achievement Award nominations are made by managers and reviewed by the ScreenLighter Committee. ■ ScreenLighter SpotLight Award nominations are made by managers or coworkers with the approval of the employee's manager.
Presentation/Celebration	■ ScreenLighter Suggestion Award: $100 plus a percent of the savings over several years up to $250,000 ■ ScreenLighter Achievement Award: $500 to $1,500 for individuals; $1,000 to $3,000 for teams, a special plaque and a certificate presented in a brief ceremony ■ ScreenLighter SpotLight Award: $100, and mention on Screenland (intranet) and in *Sweeps* (newsletter)
Results	In the first two years, a multitude of Achievement and Spotlight Awards have been granted, and the suggestions alone have generated over $2.3 million in savings and $97,000 in cash awards for employees.

TEAMWORK, PERFORMANCE AND PRIDE RECOGNITION BEST PRACTICE

Target Performance	Teamwork, performance, and pride
Program Name	The Hilton Pride Program
Organization/Location	Hilton Hotels (260 hotels throughout the world) Beverly Hills, California
Industry	Hospitality
Need	Designed to build teamwork, enhance shareholder value, and empower employees to take greater pride in their jobs by recognizing exceptional employee and team performance.
Recognition Provided	Company stock, public recognition
Recognition Criteria	Employees and teams are measured against seven different performance criteria: ■ Revenue maximization ■ Boosting room sales ■ Controlling expenses ■ Customer satisfaction ■ Results of mystery shopper visits ■ Team-member surveys ■ Guest comment cards
Program Time Frame	Initially planned to be a two-year program, the program has been modified and the end date extended.
Program Administration	Unknown
Selection Process	Employees and teams are rated against each of the performance criteria and placed in "zones" of red (the lowest), yellow, or green (the highest).
Presentation/Celebration	If a hotel scores 100 percent (green zone) for all seven performance criteria, Hilton has promised to divide $1 million of company stock equally among all employees of the winning hotel.
Results	Although none of Hilton's hotels has yet won the $1 million in company stock (several are close), employees are performing better as a result of the program and they are stretching to achieve the company's goals. The program has also offered a tremendous spirit of fun, competitiveness, and focus on customer service and has spawned the Innovation Awards program, which encourages employees and employee teams to submit ideas on how to improve their hotels.

VALUES RECOGNITION BEST PRACTICE

Target Performance	Company core values
Program Name	Barrier Buster Award
Organization/Location	Caterpillar (Track-Type Tractor Division) Peoria, Illinois
Industry	Manufacturing
Need	The program was instituted because the Track-Type Tractor Division ranked at the bottom of the all-employees survey results.
Recognition Provided	The program has two levels: ■ Level 1: Low-cost or no-cost recognition with a value of $5 or less (thank-you notes, lunchroom passes, coffee mugs, pens, and so on). ■ Level 2: The "Barrier Buster Award," a small plaque
Recognition Criteria	Based on observed behaviors consistent with company values: teamwork, commitment, trust, mutual respect, empowerment, sense of urgency, risk taking, continuous improvement, and customer satisfaction. Level 1 recognition is given when values-consistent behavior is observed; level 2 recognition is given to employees who exhibit "exceptional display of the Division's value."
Program Time Frame	Monthly
Program Administration	The division's recognition coordinators administer the program.
Selection Process	The Barrier Buster Award is based on employee nominations; the final decision is made by the division's recognition coordinators.
Presentation/Celebration	In addition to the presentation of the plaque, Barrier Buster Award winners are written up in the local newspaper and highlighted in the monthly company video.
Results	There has been a dramatic improvement in the all-employees survey results. Before the program, the Track-Type Tractor Division was 30 to 40 points below the rest of the company; now it leads all other U.S.-based divisions in all categories.

YEARS OF SERVICE AND TENURE RECOGNITION BEST PRACTICE

Target Performance	Years of service and tenure
Program Name	Tenure Recognition Program
Organization/Location	Datatel Fairfax, Virginia
Industry	Information management
Need	To recognize employees for longevity with the company
Recognition Provided	■ A pin and $500 at ten and fifteen years ■ Every ten years, an additional $1,000 and an extra week's vacation ■ At twenty years, $5,000, an extra week's vacation, and a chauffeured limousine ride to work
Recognition Criteria	Years of service
Program Time Frame	Open-ended
Program Administration	Administered by human resources
Selection Process	Human resources tracks tenure.
Presentation/Celebration	The most innovative aspect of this program is that the employee with the twenty-year anniversary is picked up by a limousine chauffeured by the president of the company dressed up in a tuxedo! When the employee arrives at the office, he or she is treated to a company-sponsored breakfast celebration with coworkers.
Results	The company has an extraordinary record of employee longevity. The program also sends the message to other employees that loyal employees are greatly appreciated.

YOUR RECOGNITION PROGRAM DESIGN

Target Performance	
Program Name	
Organization/Location	
Industry	
Need	
Recognition Provided	
Recognition Criteria	
Program Time Frame	
Program Administration	
Selection Process	
Presentation/Celebration	
Desired Results	

YOUR RECOGNITION PROGRAM DESIGN

Target Performance	
Program Name	
Organization/Location	
Industry	
Need	
Recognition Provided	
Recognition Criteria	
Program Time Frame	
Program Administration	
Selection Process	
Presentation/Celebration	
Desired Results	

More No-Cost, Low-Cost, and Informal Recognition Ideas

Following is a continuation of the 101 no-cost recognition ideas that have appeared in the margins earlier in the book, plus a dozen low-cost recognition ideas, and finally, 327 informal recognition ideas.

Organize "Good Job" Tours

48 Get the highest-ranking person you can to tour and visit your department, suggests Jeffrey J. Fox, author of How to Become CEO. "Before the tour, write out a single 3″ × 5″ index card on every person. Write a one- or two-line report of some achievement or contribution that the person made. Use the cards as 'cue cards' for the top guy, so that he can personally and specifically thank and compliment each person."

Real Meal Deal

49 Once a month, Integrated Marketing Services in Princeton, New Jersey, invites employees to a "Bagels and B.S." meeting, at which management discusses year-to-date performance and plans for the future, then fields questions from the group, reports manager Jim Mullins. "Employees are also invited to complain to management about whatever might be on their minds," says Mullins. "The meetings have opened up the lines of communication and are very popular."

The Human Touch

50 Don Eggleston, director of organizational development at SSM Healthcare in St. Louis, Missouri, says, "I mark my calendar and then send flowers or cards to employees on the anniversary of important events in their lives. For example, I've sent cards on the anniversary of a parent's death or for a child's graduation or birthday. There are subtle ways to let employees know I'm interested without prying into their lives. After all, we're working with human beings, and we can all be more effective and sensitive if we understand one another better."

Thanks a Bunch

51 Reports Terry Horn, human resources director at Household Automotive Finance in San Diego, California, "I recently wanted to thank all the employees in my department for their great work in meeting financial goals. The group is all women, except for one man, who is very health conscious and eats a banana at break daily. I gave each of the women a bunch of flowers and the guy a bunch of bananas. They all really appreciated the gesture. It was fun!"

Conference Room Play Time

52 First International Bank and Trust in Harvey, North Dakota, opens up their conference room to employees' school-age children every afternoon; they can pull open the bank of cupboards to turn on the big-screen TV, dig out a box of crackers, and settle in with homework while Mom or Dad finishes up the workday. Dennis Walsh, bank president, says, "People here feel wanted and special. I see that in the amount of work they get done." He reports that it's been at least four or five years since anyone has left the company.

Who's Got the Rubber Ducky?

53 The president of a teacher's union in Vancouver, Canada, explains that when he worked in the construction industry, what started as a joke became a coveted honor each workday. One morning, a foreman placed a yellow rubber ducky on the desk of the person who had done a great job the previous day. The tradition continued and soon everyone looked forward to seeing who would receive the day's honor.

Disco Madness

54 As an incentive to staff at the Newark, California, branch of Pro Staff Personnel Services, Josh Parker, northern California regional manager, promised to disco dance on his desktop if they met specific quarterly goals. Polyester pants, gold chain, and all, Parker hustled his way into Pro Staff's manager hall of fame. Since Parker's disco debut, the employees at the Newark office anxiously await his next challenge.

Simple Silly Stretches

55 Suzy Armstrong of State Farm Insurance in Tulsa, Oklahoma, reports, "We watch a video of cute songs and silly stretches to release stress. I lead the fifteen members of the team of underwriters in aerobics exercises in the common area. We do a lot of close computer work so it's great to relieve the tension." Pam Wiseman, training coordinator for Designer Checks in Anniston, Alabama, says, "For eight minutes every afternoon, I have department heads lead their employees in stretching exercises at their desks. It's a little silly, but it's fun and it gives everyone a break. I think we're more productive because of it, and we feel better too."

Record-Breaking Haircut

56 At a pizza party to celebrate a record sales month, Michael Phillips, director of sales for Seattle-based Korry Electronics, told his sales force that if they ever beat their new record he'd shave his head. Reports Phillips, "Everybody got involved in trying to break the record, even the customers. To celebrate the "unbelievable" month, Phillips brought in his own personal "Hair Terminator," who shaved Phillips's scalp in front of approximately 565 employees at a rooftop party celebrating Korry's sixtieth year in business. The first snips were taken by reps who had contributed the most sales. Key customers and sales reps from around the world were present.

Employees Get the Savings

57 In an effort to reduce both turnover and expenses, the Daniels Company, a trucking firm in Springfield, Missouri, challenged its drivers to cut their costs of fuel by improving mileage—then let them keep the difference. Since then, turnover has been cut by 25 percent and trucks are logging fewer miles, thus cutting overall costs.

Let the Best Decide

58 A McDonald's restaurant franchise in St. Louis, Missouri, gives first choice of work schedules to those employees who have the best attendance/tardiness records. This practice promotes better attendance and—because many employees are students—gives them the chance to better coordinate their work and class schedules.

Recognizing Good Ideas

59 The Office of Human Resources and Administration at the U.S. Department of Energy in Washington, D.C., once sponsored an "Ideas Day" for all employees to examine ways to improve the way they worked. They collected 2,134 ideas, 68 percent of which were implemented.

Rewarding Daredevils

60 Ziff Davis of La Jolla, California, has "daredevil awards" that are used to "catch people in the act" of doing something above and beyond the call of duty that is innovative or helpful to others or the company. Award recipients are regularly announced to the entire company via e-mail.

Surprise Shifts

61 Crate and Barrel store managers in Houston, Texas, started a program for their associates involving a "surprise hour off." Once a week, each store manager would pick a sales associate and take his or her shift on the floor for an hour, saying, "You've been working hard, and I appreciate it—take an hour off and come back refreshed and ready to sell some more."

Appreciation Day

62 A division of Hewlett Packard in San Diego, California, named a day of appreciation for an exceptional employee. Any employee in the division was able to reserve a time slot to visit the employee on her day, present her with a flower, and thank her for something she had done for the individual in their working relationship.

Maydays

63 At Workman Publishing in New York, the subject of how great it was to have time off came up, and someone suggested that they offer three-day weekends during the summer. This was the birth of "Maydays," in which every employee is allowed to take off either a Monday or a Friday each month from May to September, with the approval of their supervisor. It has become a popular benefit, and they've been doing it every year since.

Share the Work

64 At Claire's Boutique in Wooddale, Illinois, district managers reward store managers for highest sales volume by working in their stores on a Saturday so the manager can take the day off. The regional managers present simple traveling trophies to district managers, which move from one district to another within the region.

Get out of Your Office

65 When employees of AAA of southern California were asked what the company could better do to support them, the overwhelming response was, "Have managers get out of their offices more often."

A Special Invitation

66 A Motorola manager on the Iridium satellite phone project in Schaumburg, Illinois, rewarded star performers for a job well done with special attention. For example, she would invite a broad spectrum of engineers, MBAs, salespeople, and customer service staff to brainstorm for an hour at lunch about their most intriguing business problems and solutions. People loved being singled out, and business problems got solved as well.

Hoops Break

67 As a break for busy assembly or warehouse workers who are meeting quota or ahead of schedule, some firms call for a surprise fifteen-minute basketball break, although Ping-Pong™ or pool would work as well. At Microsoft, it's not uncommon for employees to take a break to throw a Frisbee.

Special Service

68 To recognize those who take extra effort to cover for vacationing coworkers, the Donaghey Student Center at the University of Arkansas in Little Rock gives a special award for "going above and beyond the call of duty" to see that the office continued to operate smoothly in the absence of vacationing employees.

Share the Spotlight

69 The San Diego Unified School District in California allows any student with at least a 4.0 grade point average to be listed as a valedictorian, which has resulted in as many as thirty-two valedictorians at one of the district's high schools. Students interviewed claimed that they had worked harder knowing they might be one of those recognized, although there was no chance of being the "top" person.

Eye-Opener

70 The Hydraulic Specialty Company in Fridley, Minnesota, makes many improvements as a result of sharing sales and revenue results with employees. The company says everyone pulls together without any pressure from management now that they can see how improvements pay off for the bottom line.

Lessons from the Minor Leagues

71 Baltimore Orioles manager Ray Miller didn't have much personalized attention from his coaches as a minor league pitcher back in the '60s and '70s. "The way I was treated hurt me," he recalls. Miller learned from this experience that paying attention to players is important, whether they are performing well or not. To be sure that he communicates with all players, Miller keeps a "Talk-to List" on a yellow legal pad. "Just talking really matters," Miller says. "Take Cal Ripken. If he is playing great and for some reason you don't talk for four or five days, he looks at you and says, 'What's wrong?'" Miller has learned an important lesson. Feedback and recognition go a long way.

Scavenger Hunts

72 Dick Eaton, owner of the Urban Outing Club for Business in New York City, knows how to structure fun. Eaton hosts scavenger hunts in the city for corporate clients, designed to promote teamwork and build morale. Mercer Management Consulting, headquartered in New York City, also uses a scavenger hunt to orient team members who travel to new cities. They are asked to visit client offices, large hotels, and the convention center when they arrive, bringing back "proof" of their visits to each location.

Remember Their Names

73 Southwest Airlines president Herb Kelleher has an uncanny knack for remembering employee names. Flight attendant Sandy Poole happened to meet Kelleher one day and spoke with him for a few minutes. Says Poole, "Six months later, I was walking down the hall of the headquarters and he said, 'Hi, Sandy Poole. How's the new job?' And that is just so flabbergasting. And you do feel important; it really makes a difference."

Distribute Responsibilities

74 When the supervisor of the membership-development department of the Girl Scouts of Santa Clara County, California, left the organization, chief executive Nancy Fox declined to fill the vacancy, instead handing over responsibility of all department duties to its staff. Now membership-development department employees have the power to set their own work schedules and determine how they will do their jobs. Says Fox, "Individuals on the team tell me they feel more responsible and connected to what they do."

Time Off with Pay

75 Pro Staff Personnel, a chain of temporary help agencies, recently held a drawing for paid time off. All employees who were in good standing were eligible. The winner received two weeks off, and two others received one week off as part of the company's campaign to recruit and retain employees. Jeff Dobbs, president of Pro Staff, explains: "Our research shows that time off is of great value to employees."

Listen and Learn

76 Sue Copening says she learned an important lesson about listening the hard way several years ago when she was promoted to store manager for a retail chain. She was not taking time to really pay attention to her staff. When two employees quit within a few weeks, one had the courage to tell her that she was creating an unfriendly work environment. Sue realized that she needed to make time to listen to employee concerns and help them to cope on the job. She now reports, "A manager's job is 95 percent being sensitive to employees and keeping them happy. It's easier to change your own behavior than to expect other people to adjust to you."

Birthday Calls

77 Manny Fernandez, CEO of Gartner Group, the Stamford, Connecticut, technology consulting and research firm, finds time to call every one of his employees on his or her birthday. Says Fernandez, "It used to be a lot easier when we were small. Now I sometimes make twelve calls a day, but it's a great way to keep in touch with what's going on in the company, and employees seem to enjoy it." Marty Edelston, chairman and CEO of Board-

room in Greenwich, Connecticut, personally sings "Happy Birthday" to each of his eighty-five employees on their special day.

Take Time for Fun

78 Rebecca Rogers at University Hospitals in Augusta, Georgia, has a fun activity she calls "communal captions." She posts photos from newspapers and magazines over the copy machine and invites staff members to write funny captions for them, helping make time spent making copies more interesting.

Walk the Dog Day

79 Xerox Corporation in Palo Alto, California, had fifty dogs this year for Take Your Dog to Work Day, June 23, up from thirty last year. Systems Engineer Greg Newell says there wasn't a single complaint from the five hundred employees.

On-Site Visits

80 Ray Kroc, founder of the McDonald's restaurant chain, used to visit endless stores. He'd send his grandchildren into each McDonald's to see how they treated children.

Casual Day Is Here to Stay

81 Customer sales representatives at Emerald Publications in San Diego, California, are allowed to wear casual clothing every Friday. Says one employee, "It's often my best sales day, because I don't have to worry about sitting properly and whether my skirt is riding up or not. I wish we had even more latitude on other days." American Airlines now allows employees at company headquarters in Ft. Worth, Texas, to dress in "business casual" attire every day. The policy applies to about twenty thousand management employees. Jayne Allison, vice president for human relations, says, "We have heard from our employees that they believe they are more productive in casual dress."

Change of Pace

82 Japanese appliance manufacturer Hitachi is doing away with formal titles, somber suits, and morning calisthenics in their Tokyo headquarters. Their goal is "to promote individuality." Company spokeswoman Emi Takase says employees are being urged to wear polo shirts and slacks, hoping that more casual clothing will bring out people's personalities and stimulate their creativity, which in turn will lead to new ideas for how to improve the company. Workers are also no longer required to address their supervisors by formal titles, but may use personal names. Takase says, "We want to give employees freedom to make their own judgments."

Allow Choice of Work Assignment

83 Reference International Software in San Francisco, California, allows one day a week for customer service reps to work on any project they choose. Results have been better systems and salable products—and really great employee morale.

Air Memos

84 Pacific Power and Electric in Portland, Oregon, uses Frisbees to deliver memos on Frisbee Memo Day.

Joy Breaks

85 Matt Weinstein of PlayFair in Berkeley, California, suggests giving joy breaks, during which employees can do something fun, such as look at cartoons or listen to tapes. He feels that often the best thing to do when under pressure is to take a break, get away from the task, and recharge your batteries. Weinstein recommends that people play a childhood game such as marbles or pitching pennies that puts all team members on the floor together having a fun break. They then can go back, refreshed, to the job at hand.

Take a Nap

86 Lowney and Associates, a Palo Alto, California, consulting firm, has a nap room at its headquarters to help employees take a break in peace and quiet. Magic Pencil Studios, a creative services company based in Orlando, Florida, has a "time-out" room that is complete with children's furniture and toys that any employee is free to use—sometimes with their children, whom they're allowed to bring to work.

Working for Health Care

87 George MacLeod, a restaurant owner in Bucksport, Maine, allows his employees to run the restaurant by themselves one Sunday every month, and then to split the profits among themselves to help pay for their health insurance. Participating employees have made enough money to cover the entire cost of their insurance premiums.

More Flexibility, Less Turnover

88 At Deloitte and Touche's West Palm Beach, Florida, office, Ann Blanchard has the freedom to move between part-time and full-time schedules as she raises her young children. "I have a lot of opportunity," Blanchard says. Her boss, Susan Peterson, sees such flexibility as the only way to go: "You can't afford to reestablish your professional staff every few years."

Roll up Your Sleeves

89 Jeff Bezos, CEO of Amazon.com, spends about twelve hours at work six days a week, and often stocks shelves along with workers in order to hear their problems firsthand.

Double Duty

90 J. P. Morgan Chase, a New York investment bank, recently opened a lactation room for nursing mothers on its Wall Street trading floor so they would be able to return to work sooner after maternity leave.

Pitching in Is Practical

91 A former manager at UA Consulting and Training Services, now in Tucson, Arizona, often spontaneously took over phone duties for the busy receptionist. It served a double purpose of staying in touch with life on the front lines and hearing customer concerns firsthand.

Let Them Decide

92 Management at AT&T Universal Card Services in Jacksonsille, Florida, allows employees to use their own judgment about whether to waive late fees or raise credit limits when talking to customers on the phone. This has not only made customers happier, but has improved efficiency and given employees a greater sense of control over their jobs and a sense of autonomy.

Travel Companions

93 At Parrett Trucking in Scottsboro, Alabama, Mike Parrett allows drivers to take their pets on the road. But he did have to limit the policy to cats and dogs only in the break room after one of his drivers came inside with a boa constrictor around his neck, causing some alarm for office workers.

Split the Difference

94 At Pfeiffer and Company, a publisher now part of John Wiley and Sons, employees were financially rewarded for prolonging their business trips by an extra day or so. For example, a plane ticket with a return on Friday night might be $150 cheaper than one with a Sunday return, so they would give the employee $75 of that savings. "It turned out to be a great way for employees to bond with clients, vendors, or coworkers in the other city when there simply had been no time during the normal work week for social activities," reports Marion Mettler, former CEO of the company.

Discounts on Your Products

95 One night a year, employees of Sears are allowed to bring in immediate family members for a shopping spree using the employee's discount.

Pick and Choose

96 Hi-Tech Hose, makers of flexible hoses and ducting products in Newburyport, Massachusetts, lumps all vacation time, holidays, and sick days into a single account. Employees can take time off whenever they need it, for whatever personal reasons.

Share in the Savings

97 In San Diego, California, seventy-one county employees who came up with ideas that saved money or improved efficiency the previous year were honored at a year-end ceremony. The workers' ideas generated nearly $400,000 in savings, and cash awards to employees ranged from $25 to nearly $5,000.

The Exalted Order of the Extended Neck

98 Richard Zimmerman, chairman and CEO of Hershey Foods in Hershey, Pennsylvania, created a special award called "The Exalted Order of the Extended Neck" for people who find ways to go "outside the box." Says Zimmerman, "I wanted to reward people who were willing to buck the system, practice a little entrepreneurship, who were willing to stand the heat for an idea they really believe in."

Share Ownership to Drive Motivation

99 Science Applications International Corporation (SAIC) in San Diego, California, was founded on the principle of the importance of employee ownership. Founder J. Robert Beyster knew that owning even a small stake in a business that is growing exponentially can be a powerful incentive. SAIC has gone further than most companies, however, relinquishing 98 percent of the company to employees. Says Beyster, "It just seemed like the right thing to do" to keep employees motivated and morale high.

Park It Here

100 WRQ, a software company based in Seattle, Washington, offers dock space for kayaking commuters, as well as a nap room with futons, on-site massages, and a flexible work hours policy (which 94 percent of employees use).

Take a Sabbatical

101 Employees at the Container Store, based in Dallas, Texas, get sabbaticals after ten years of service to the company—just one of the reasons they have ranked as the number-one best company to work for in America for several years in a row.

A DOZEN LOW-COST RECOGNITION IDEAS

A Cool Notion

1 "When it becomes extremely hot during the summer months, I carry an ice chest full of freezer pops around and give them out to employees who are working in areas that are not air-conditioned," reports Cynthia M. Wood, team manager at International Paper in Eastover, South Carolina. "You should see their faces light up!"

An Eggcellent Idea

2 Linda Fuller, supervisor of business development at Jevic in Delanco, New Jersey, reports, "Last year at Eastertime, I purchased plastic eggs and filled them with candy, a bit of pocket change (mostly pennies), and coupons to take off an hour early, come in an hour late, or have lunch with me (my treat). To be able to participate, my folks had to meet their weekly quota and then pick an egg out of a beautifully decorated basket. It made that Monday morning a little more exciting and set the tone for the whole week!"

BBQs Galore

3 As a sales manager for Westinghouse in Los Angeles, California, Robert Partain threw a barbecue lunch for his sales staff the first time they made their group sales goal. He promised to do it again if the group again made its goal. Seventeen months later, he had done sixteen team barbecues, missing only the month of the Northridge earthquake.

Warming up a Cold Day

4 Kathleen Capristo, chief motivational strategist at Awards.com in Lynd- hurst, New Jersey, reports, "One really cold winter day last year when wet snow was coming down and freezing on the streets, we hired local high school students to scrape the ice off the windshields of the employees' cars, and then handed each employee a bottle of Heet as they left for the day. Everyone felt special, and that we were looking out for them."

Worth Their While to Show Up

5 Mary Jo Stuesser-Yafchak, president of Accudata in Cape Coral, Florida, found a way to encourage her employees to attend monthly after-hours training sessions. She has a monthly drawing for $50 and enters the names of everyone who has attended in a drawing for $1,000 worth of travel credit at year-end.

Reverse Motivation

6 SCA Hygiene Products, based in Philadelphia, Pennsylvania, honors cor- porate managers with a trip to the company's manufacturing plant in

Bowling Green, Kentucky, to spend a day with line workers, reports George Mapson, director of North American HR. A three-member Country Management Team makes the selection and keeps the process bureaucracy-free. Selected plant workers are also honored when they are especially productive, or when they offer an innovative, money-saving idea, by being allowed to visit any of the company's sales offices in the United States or Canada.

Grab a Handful

7 One manager of cable installers holds a lottery for installers who had a customer send in a positive letter about him or her. One of the eligible winners is selected to grab as many quarters as possible out of a fish bowl. It's very exciting for the winners (the average grab is about $30 in quarters) and keeps all employees focused on exceptional customer service.

Cut the Deck

8 Kym Illman, managing director of Messages on Hold in Perth, Australia, shares, "Our client contact is over the phone, so we need our people to wow those clients to overcome the distance factor. I read the compliments I receive in a team meeting and ask the person to pick from a deck of playing cards. For cards 2 through 9, they receive the dollar value. For a 10 or picture card, they receive $10, and $20 for an ace. It's fun and helps to spur all the reps to wow the clients."

Holiday Wrap-Up

9 Corey Wedel, employment services manager for Central Missouri State University, shares how last year their staff of seven offered to wrap holiday presents for other employees of the university, even providing gift wrap. "We picked up the gifts at people's desks and brought back their wrapped packages," he continues. "People loved it! They enjoyed the hassle-free service and the results, especially one person who has eight children."

$1,000,000 Flowers

10 Rhonda Lowe, publisher of the *Los Banos Enterprise* newspaper, found a way to thank loyal advertisers by creating Thanks a Million bouquets. Using a computer program that makes currency, she designed some $1,000,000 bills and printed them out on her color printer. Lowe then wrapped them around the top of twenty-five-cent suckers to look like petals on a flower. She bought some inexpensive potted plants and inserted the "flowers" into the potted plant, and added a bow and a sign that said "Thanks a Million for Being Our Customer." Sales representatives signed his or her name and personally delivered the award to their top accounts. It gave them the chance to create a buzz—and clients prominently displayed the awards.

Include the Family

11 "One thing we do that is especially a big hit with the employees' families is to send flowers or a cookie-gram to the place of business or to the home of all spouses on their birthdays and anniversaries," says Michael L. Finn, chairman and CRO (Chief Remover of Obstacles) at Fortress Safe and Lock in Cincinnati, Ohio. Every child (up to age sixteen) is also sent a birthday card with $20 in movie tickets. "Including the families has meant a lot to everyone," Finn concludes.

Floppy Chicken Awards

12 Employees who go the extra mile at KFC Corporation headquartered in Louisville, Kentucky, are presented with a Floppy Chicken Award, a handwritten note of thanks, and a $100 gift certificate, reports Diane Zile, manager of employee recognition. Former president and CEO David Novak started the program one day when he flew to an awardee's city and personally presented a rubber chicken he pulled out of a crumpled brown paper sack. A photo of the presentation is taken and placed on permanent display in the Walk of Leaders, a prominent area of corporate headquarters.

327 INFORMAL RECOGNITION IDEAS*

1. Magazine subscription
2. Letter with copy to manager
3. Special chair/throne
4. Family day at office
5. Sabbatical (paid)
6. Informal dress
7. Senior management–hosted party
8. "Time-at-the-top" day
9. Prime parking spot
10. Plaque
11. Cash to spend at company store
12. Special project clearance
13. Professional membership fee
14. Savings bond
15. Limo ride to work
16. Breakfast
17. "You measure up" ruler
18. T-shirt
19. Points add up to award
20. Valet parking
21. Fishing trip
22. TV appearance
23. Porsche for a month
24. Violinist at your desk
25. Hot-air balloon ride
26. Special holiday dance/party
27. High school band serenade
28. Special name tag
29. Gift catalog
30. Weekly acknowledgment
31. Project kickoff party
32. Extravagant trip
33. YMCA family night
34. One year off
35. Use of company condo/cabin
36. Gift certificate
37. Coffee cups
38. Bumper sticker
39. Dinner gift certificate
40. Attendance award
41. Continuing education opportunity
42. Company-sponsored sports teams
43. Key chain
44. Golf outing
45. Compensation for benefit plan
46. Mileage for a week
47. Cafeteria theme—dress and food
48. Supervisor for a day
49. Interdepartmental tours
50. Star on forehead
51. Flowers
52. Free movie tickets
53. Corner office for a day
54. Work-from-home option for a week
55. "Expert" status
56. Host party for friends
57. Day off with pay
58. Pen
59. Trip
60. Recent best-seller book
61. Balloon bouquet
62. Cross-training opportunities
63. Cash on the spot
64. Visit from company president
65. Free training seminar
66. Photo on bulletin board
67. Visit to customer site
68. Popcorn party
69. Services at barber/beauty shop
70. Shares of stock
71. Statue in front yard of employee's home
72. Skywriting message
73. Cleaning service at home
74. Shopping spree
75. Work area enhancement
76. Health club membership
77. Cultural event tickets
78. Social event tickets
79. Sporting event tickets
80. Anniversary gifts
81. Spouse/family recognition
82. Company car
83. Well days
84. Chocolates
85. Jacket
86. Calculator
87. Service award
88. Recognition in newsletter
89. Free coffee
90. Ski trips
91. Letter from company president
92. "Honorary" degree
93. Handshake
94. Stuffed animal
95. Standing ovation
96. Pat on the back
97. Miniature product model
98. Trade show attendance
99. Smile
100. Day at camp
101. Pool party
102. Personalized stationery and pen
103. Valentines
104. Group/family picture

*Adapted from a list compiled by the Tennant Company, Minneapolis, Minnesota

105. Videos
106. Poems
107. Birthday card
108. "Zero defects" bonus pay
109. Welcome letter to new employees
110. Boat trip/dinner
111. Ring
112. Pin
113. Free vacation day
114. Use of company equipment
115. Overnight at a hotel
116. Golf balls w/logo or ad
117. Favorite snack
118. Free postage for holiday cards
119. Weekend at the coast
120. Present to upper management
121. Event tickets for the family
122. Trophy
123. Certificate of accomplishment
124. Buck knife
125. Captain Quality shield
126. Stickers
127. Coupons for office services— clean desk, take meeting minutes, pick up doughnuts for lunch
128. Raffle tickets
129. Celebrity visit
130. Safety shoes
131. Dessert tickets for café
132. Suspenders
133. Hall of fame induction
134. Charm bracelet
135. Dry cleaning
136. Mobile phone for a month
137. On-the-spot tokens, redeemable for cash
138. Ice cream sundaes

139. Grocery store gift certificate
140. Watch
141. Banners
142. Rubber stamps
143. Public announcement
144. Lunch "on me"
145. Barbeque
146. Babysitting for a week
147. TV set
148. Free soda for a day
149. Athletic equipment
150. Movie night
151. Software
152. Hardware
153. Manager answers own phone for an afternoon
154. Cassettes
155. Buttons
156. Photo finishing discounts
157. President's face on a placard
158. Upward performance appraisal
159. Breakfast meeting off-site
160. Name on electronic billboard (like at Baskin-Robbins)
161. Holiday cards
162. Interdepartmental recognition
163. Comp time
164. After-work get-together
165. Manager attends an event with the recipient
166. Gag gift (when appropriate)
167. Gas for car
168. Summer Olympics party
169. Display individual's safety record
170. Singing telegram
171. Train trip
172. Potluck dinner
173. Jewelry give-away

174. Lakeside party
175. Day with a client
176. Day at the races
177. Allow spouse to accompany on business trip
178. Letter opener
179. Offer free checking account
180. Lottery tickets
181. Retreat
182. New office furniture
183. Fishing pole/lures
184. Snow brushed off car for a week
185. Trip to art exhibit
186. Umbrella
187. Company blazer
188. Sweeper team to neighborhood
189. Landscaping
190. Pay for credit card use for a month
191. Golf lessons
192. Coupon for personal services—house cleaning, yard work, shopping
193. Weekend with an expert
194. Chef-prepared meal at home
195. Lawn care for a summer
196. Travel upgrade to first class
197. Attend a conference of choice
198. Socks
199. Brag board
200. Screen saver banner
201. Make-your-own-taco party
202. Thermometers for recognition temperature
203. Pass-along note
204. One week of service/cleanup
205. Accomplishment collage
206. Internal customer party
207. Car

208. Party for employee's children
209. Car insurance paid
210. Belt buckle
211. Big office
212. Six-month car lease
213. Headband
214. Fish fry
215. Oil change
216. Coasters
217. Car seat
218. Off an hour early
219. Blanket
220. Doorknocker
221. Soda/beer can holder
222. Necktie
223. Travel bag/tote
224. Theme party
225. Wooden nickels for points
226. Susan B. Anthony dollars
227. Group roast
228. Sandwich board statement
229. Wok cooking party
230. Bowling party
231. Personalized golf balls
232. Employee notices in local papers
233. Turkey
234. Golf clubs
235. Secretary
236. Employee picture on cup
237. Fire extinguisher
238. Parcel payment on anything
239. Massages
240. Frisbee
241. PA announcement
242. Start an hour later
243. Trip to vendor
244. Headphones
245. Plant
246. Gift for hobby
247. Sunglasses
248. Choice of assignment

249. Spouse's day
250. Give-a-hand gloves
251. Snowbrush
252. Video of group accomplishment
253. Sit in on top management meeting
254. Car allowance
255. Outward Bound trip
256. "Lettuce entertain you" visit from fun committee
257. Free physical
258. A pet
259. Safety glasses
260. Temporary help for a day
261. Car wash
262. Dust Buster
263. Desk supplies
264. Extended lunch hours
265. Las Vegas night
266. Company honor roll
267. Flashlight
268. Cruise
269. Calendar
270. Barrette
271. CDs or tapes
272. Sweatshirt
273. Speaker for group
274. Job sharing
275. Framed memento
276. Paperweight
277. Qu-owl-ity owl
278. Gift to charity
279. Barometer—weather or not
280. Society meeting
281. Movie videotape
282. Cooler
283. Billboard public display
284. Portfolio
285. First aid kit
286. Artwork
287. Dance lessons

288. Afternoon at the mall
289. Congeniality award
290. Portfolio
291. Pony rides
292. Valor awards
293. Authorship
294. Candy
295. Personalized merchandise
296. Represent manager at meeting
297. Bungee jump
298. Comedy club tickets
299. Airline tickets
300. Michael Jordan basketballs
301. Thermos
302. Fanny pack
303. Scholarship
304. Appliances
305. Tools
306. Atlas
307. Visit to company headquarters
308. Medal
309. Magnet
310. Collectibles
311. Job exchange
312. Makeover
313. Bus pass
314. Birthday off
315. Entertainment books
316. Blue ribbon
317. Sports bottle
318. Lunch bag
319. Roadside emergency kit
320. Umbrella
321. Travel mug
322. Disney tickets
323. Potluck lunch
324. Concert tickets
325. Car detailing
326. Earthquake kit
327. Letter to family

Top Ten Most Frequently Asked Questions

Throughout the margins of this book we've scattered questions about rewards and recognition that we have received over the years. Here we present the ten most frequently asked questions, followed by additional questions (and answers) we have received over the years about recognition and rewards.

FAQ **If you recognize one person, aren't you *not* recognizing everyone else?**

A Whenever someone in your organization is upset about someone else being recognized (and not him- or herself), this could be a red flag that there is not enough recognition being given. When recognition is scarce, people have a tendency to be envious when others receive it. Leaving employees out does not tend to be a problem in organizations that have developed a strong recognition culture, that have a variety of formal and informal programs and tools, and where managers place an emphasis on daily recognition practices and behaviors. As a start toward encouraging such an "abundance" mentality, avoid recognition activities and programs that have a single "winner" or quota of recipients. Instead, create opportunities for everyone to be a potential winner, such as having an honor roll for those employees who have all practiced a key value or set of behaviors of the organization within a given time period, instead of an employee-of-the-month award, which honors a single person at the expense of everyone else. Also, because the best forms of recognition tend to have little if any cost associated with them (e.g., verbal and written praise, public praise, symbolic gestures by managers, pass-around awards, and so on), there is absolutely no reason not to do more of these activities in a timely, sincere, and personal way.

FAQ **What can we do about managers who know they should recognize their employees but feel too time-constrained to do so?**

A Making recognition happen is iterative, so try to build on and expand from your successes—no matter how modest they might be. Discuss with the

managers the increasing problem of attracting and retaining employees, the hidden costs, the loss of productivity and competitiveness. Show them the demographics and what your competition is doing. Relate the issue to the bottom line. You can't force managers to recognize their employees, but you can make a persuasive case for why they should want to do so. Also remember that "no time" can be merely an excuse. In fact, Bob Nelson's doctoral research found that managers who used recognition frequently actually valued recognition in part because it can be well done with very little time.

FAQ **If you praise employees, won't it be more difficult to discipline them, if that becomes necessary?**

A If you are specific about what you are praising the person for, this should not be a problem. Broad, all-inclusive praise such as "You're one of my best employees" or "You're doing a great job" should be avoided, since it does not specify a particular accomplishment. This kind of praise is often misleading to the employee because it seems to indicate little, if any, need for improvement. It can also lead to the problem you mentioned about discipline. Instead, you can leverage specific things the individual is good at as evidence that he or she can improve in other areas of the job; for example: "Gary, I know you can make these new changes we've discussed, because I've seen how well you handle assignments that you put your mind to." As the person makes improvements, be sure to notice and acknowledge those improvements. This will be one of the best ways to ensure that the improved performance continues. When you discipline someone, you have to make sure that the person feels you are on his or her side. If someone is on a performance improvement plan, it is essential that you notice when the person has made improvement of any type, in order to start to build the positive momentum toward enhanced performance. Typically, doing so will make the employee's progress easier and show that you are committed to their success.

FAQ **My company does a lot to recognize employees, but employees report that they don't receive much recognition. What's going on?**

A Many organizations confuse employee activities with employee recognition. For example, employee social activities may help morale and promote social interaction among employees, but tend not to make any individual employee feel special. In fact, when you do things for all employees, you promote a culture of entitlement rather than of performance. The best recognition singles out individuals or groups for extraordinary performance and is contingent on those things that make the biggest difference to the group's mutual success.

FAQ How can we get top management to support recognition activities?

A There are many aspects to this question, which is addressed more fully in chapter 13. Different people are persuaded differently. The best advice is to think of other times when your top management has been persuaded to support a change (purchase equipment, approve a policy exception, hire a person). What served to convince him or her (data, cost/benefit, urgency of the problem, competitor doing it, personal appeal)? Now mimic what worked in those cases.

FAQ Our recognition programs are feeling stale. How can we reenergize them?

A Any recognition program or activity can get old and lose energy, especially over a number of years. Do a focus group or find a way to collect information about why people do not use the existing program. Include the biggest cynics on the review team to gain their feedback. It may be that the program just needs to be relaunched to remind people of its existence and new incentives need to be established. Or, you may discover that the program has run its course and it would be better to terminate it in favor of something new and exciting.

FAQ We hold some recognition events that a lot of employees—even ones receiving the awards—do not attend. How can we get employees to come to these events?

A If you throw a party and no one comes, was it really a party? It is very likely that the events you describe don't do much for those who are invited to attend. You need to host recognition events that create a buzz with employees, where fun things happen. Build anticipation: announce that upper management will be serving the refreshments, list door prizes that will be given for attendance, or stage some skits. Another possible reason for poor attendance may be the choice of time and venue. For example, one hospital held all recognition events during off hours so that employees had to stay an extra hour or two after what was usually already a long shift or even forced overtime. Was there any wonder that employees weren't excited? Employees who feel overworked and stressed prefer to be thanked and allowed to go home to their families. The last thing they want to do is spend more of their limited free time at work.

FAQ Can too much recognition lead to constantly escalating forms of recognition or unfulfilled expectations on the part of employees?

A Employee motivation today is a moving target. You've got to be in constant contact with your employees to determine what they most value and then find ways to systematically act on those desired forms of recognition and rewards as they perform well. You need to vary your forms of recognition, adding new ones and experimenting, but you can also stop doing other things that have run their course and are no longer very motivating to employees. If you keep doing the same things year after year, you'll likely end up with a very boring workplace. Variety is the spice of life, and as you try new programs—especially ones your employees are interested in—your rewards will be higher morale, productivity, performance, and retention. Certainly that should provide some motivation for you to stay the course! By the way, the one form of recognition that never seems to get old is effective praise. If you are timely, sincere, and specific in thanking employees when they have done good work, this form of recognition will never become stale.

FAQ **What's the best way to get employees really involved and invested in the decision-making process—that is, motivated to perform for the good of all?**

A Without a doubt, the best decision making involves those people who are expected to implement the decisions being made. Too often, employees are asked to take ownership in decisions and activities that they will never have the opportunity to implement. Ask their opinions, involve them in discussion, and also give them the authority to handle the situation as best they can. This is highly motivating for most people, and of course reaching goals they've set helps keep people going. As you give people responsibility, they are bound to act more responsibly.

FAQ **What is the best way to make recognition become part of an organization's culture?**

A Create a motivation goal and move in the desired direction one step at a time. Start small and build on your success. Ask, "Who wants to help?" and run with those individuals who see the need and are positive about the change. Build momentum to a critical mass, and every manager in your organization will one day know the value of recognition and act on it as a matter of course in his or her daily interactions with employees.

Creating a recognition culture is a messy, nonlinear process that involves taking time to assess what employees believe could most make a difference and then taking that feedback seriously in making change happen in the organization. Start with those employees who have the most energy for improving the level of recognition and build on your successes, learning along the way. Training is an important part of raising awareness about the need to recognize employees systematically in meaningful ways, helping managers develop the skills they need to recognize others well, and instilling in all managers the understanding that they need to make recognition a priority in their jobs. The ability to manage and motivate staff should be an integral part of how managers are evaluated in their jobs; otherwise, the activity is not likely to be taken seriously.

ADDITIONAL QUESTIONS AND ANSWERS TO JUMP-START RECOGNITION

DOS AND DOUGHNUTS

Q I work for a chemical manufacturing company with roughly 50 percent of the workforce unionized. We conduct monthly safety meetings, paying eight hours overtime and providing doughnuts and lunch to those who are not on shift to come in. This is the way it has been for as long as I can remember—for twenty-plus years. Many have questioned the value of these meetings and want more proactive participation in the continuous improvement of safety. Our safety performance is pretty good.

Do you have any thoughts on how we can use incentives more effectively to get more value out of these meetings?

—**Anonymous,** St. Louis, MO

A Any time you feel you are just "going through the motions," you probably are. I'd get some volunteers to discuss how the program can be improved and freshened and start to incorporate those ideas. For example, having people share safety success stories, or only having doughnuts if there have been no accidents since the last safety meeting. Doing this makes doughnuts part of the celebration and gets it away from being an entitlement or "something for nothing."

Getting away from paid overtime is a more daunting challenge. The obvious choice is to conduct the safety meeting on each shift instead of in a single all-hands meeting. My guess is that there would be no loss of value and communication by doing this (except by those who were not getting overtime to attend a meeting). There's a good possibility that smaller work group meetings might even be more motivational—especially if you get upper management to visit the work groups on each shift.

RETAIN AND GAIN

Q How can the motivation formula be used to retain graduates in civil service or the public sector?

—**Khalid Al-Mallam,**
Liverpool, England

A Recognition should be used to make employees feel they are doing important work that is valued by the organization. Most public service employees are drawn to public service in part as a calling; that is, it's work for the greater good of society. When people are systematically acknowledged for their contributions and achievements, it tends to affect how they feel about their jobs, how successful they are in those jobs, and how long they stay in those jobs. If you base the recognition on performance, you will get not only the performance you desire, but also people who will want to stick around.

LEVERAGING RECOGNITION

Q Have you run across a situation in which management will not give recognition to an employee who just received an outstanding letter from a customer because they feel that the employee's overall performance is poor? This is a paradox! What do you do?

—Claire Lauzon Vallone

A Clearly, the company does not want to send mixed messages, since recognition creates role models in any organization. For me, the conflict is diminished if recognition is made specific. If an employee receives a positive letter from a customer and you want him to continue with exceptional customer service, it would be a mistake to not thank the individual. Later, you can leverage the recognition by showing how the employee can improve in other areas of his or her job.

TOO MUCH RECOGNITION

Q How do you counteract a salary system that forces managers to rank employees, but only recognizes a few as exceptional, with corresponding higher raises?

—online forum participant

A Companies often force a quota system on their managers when they've given up trusting their managers' ability to be objective. No manager wants to give a poor review and risk an employee not receiving a raise he or she expected. Unfortunately, this means that managers are also willing to—and do—give employees good and even excellent performance reviews when the employee's performance may be average or even below average. (Worse still, they may promote a poor performer in the hopes that the person will be moved to someone else's area!) I worked with one large insurance company recently that had 85 percent of their employees rated as being "excellent"—the highest rating. Whereas it may be true that many employees were exceptional, why was the company experiencing a 12 percent loss of market share? There was obvious disconnect between goals and rewards. One predictable response is to force the evaluations to be spread evenly over a bell curve.

If you are forced to use such a ranking system, you should explain the intent of the system to your employees (not blame upper management or human resources), do your best to evaluate each employee fairly and objectively, and then work with those employees who were not ranked as "excellent" to show them how they could be in the future. Of course, such a situation increases the need for and importance of nonmonetary recognition to make all employees feel appreciated when they do good work.

RECOGNIZE IMPROVEMENT

Q How do you motivate a poor-performing employee once you have given a very substandard review to the person?

—online forum participant

A When you discipline someone, you have to make sure that the person feels that you are on his or her side. If someone is on a performance improvement plan, it is essential that you notice when the person has made improvement of any type to build the positive momentum toward enhanced performance and a better future review. Typically, doing so will make the employee's progress easier and show that you are in it together.

PERFECT ATTENDANCE

Q I'm drafting a proposal for a perfect attendance award for our market and being met with resistance from our director's staff, as they believe one's check is the reward for perfect attendance. I managed to overcome their resistance and gain approval for $10,000 yearly, in addition to quarterly cash incentives. I want to have a pool, and everyone with perfect attendance would have a chance to win the $10,000.

—**Laura Eberly,** BellSouth Mobility, Lexington, KY

A It's naive to think that a paycheck is the only thing needed to motivate employees to come to work every day. People today have too many choices and discretionary energy to be expected to do their best without being acknowledged for that effort. As far as giving everyone a chance to win such a large prize, it's far better to do many smaller things than one tremendous one that only one person can win, and that will make everyone else jealous. Spread out the money as much as possible and do not rely on monetary incentives alone to encourage the desired behavior.

THE MILLION-DOLLAR DECISION

Q The last two employers I have worked for have severely limited themselves by not valuing employees. An organization would never spend thousands of dollars on a piece of machinery and then not maintain it, but that's what they do with their employees! I hope people will take your advice and invest in the people who literally "spend" their lives working for them.

—**Diane L. Schmitt,** Pittsburgh, PA

A At IBM, they refer to hiring as "the million-dollar decision," because they calculate that's the average of what will be spent on each employee who joins the organization. "Employees are our most important asset" is a statement found in most every company's annual report, but your people will never believe it if you don't show them on a daily basis.

WORK FOR FREE

Q I'm writing a story about why elected officials are often motivated to work for free. Is it odd that someone would do this?

—**from a reporter for the** *Star-Ledger,* Newark, NJ

A It's not odd at all. There are a lot of reasons why someone might work for free, ranging from the altruistic (helping others, creating a better community, possessing a sense of civic duty) to the selfish (seeking fame or developing a network of contacts that can lead to financial gain). Hundreds of thousands of people work for free every day as volunteers for causes they believe in, for something to do, to spend time with others, or to feel they are making a difference with their lives. Money isn't everything, and most people want to get more out of life than simply greater wealth.

MEANING, NOT MONEY

Q My employees don't seem to be motivated by cash bonuses. What can I do about this?

—**Anonymous**

A Giving cash bonuses and the like is one of the least effective means of motivating employees. While money may induce short-term improvements in morale, it does not create motivation for the long term. In the long run, the following items are much more important than money.

1. Giving employees autonomy to do their jobs without having to constantly check in with higher-ups.

2. Giving employees flexibility in how they solve problems and issues, rather than tying them up in corporate rules and red tape.
3. Providing employees with sufficient resources to do their jobs efficiently and effectively.
4. Creating a fun and stimulating work environment.

LENGTH OF SERVICE

Q **We develop business intelligence software and currently have over seventeen hundred employees worldwide and are growing fast. Our problem is that we have acquired so many other businesses, we don't know how to handle awards for length of service. This is quite an emotional issue among people who have been with Cognos and feel slighted when someone acquired from another company is recognized first.**

—**Rohan Persaud,** Cognos, Ottawa, Ontario, Canada

A Ask those who are directly affected for their thoughts. You could pull together a focus group of employees from each part of the organization to brainstorm alternatives and make a recommendation. I'd give credit to years of service, but try not to make this program the cornerstone of your overall recognition effort. I might suggest making the award less coveted at an organizational level, while allowing individuals at the local level to acknowledge and celebrate the achievement with the people being honored in a form of their choice. Also, make sure that the bulk of recognition is focused on performance and not on longevity. Years-of-service awards are important, but it is even more important to recognize performance. If years of service is the primary or only way employees in your company are recognized, you are actually recognizing past endurance over current performance and contribution—a big mistake if you want everyone to strive for exceptional performance now.

MEANINGFUL MOTIVATION

Q **Some people think that any rewards we give would be meaningless.**

—**Margaret Frederick,** Florida Department of Education, Tallahassee, FL

A Don't believe it! No reward is ever meaningless, especially if it's timely, specific, sincere, and directly linked to desired performance.

INCENTIVE VENDORS

Q **We are setting up an incentive program for our sales reps that would include rewards of frequent flyer miles or free travel. I've been looking everywhere for information on this type of program.**

—**Adam Ziegelman,** Patagonia, Ventura, CA

A You might want to use an incentive vendor instead of finding someone on your own. Incentive providers are located in most markets and many operate on a national basis; see the appendices of *1001 Ways to Reward Employees* for a broad spectrum of incentive providers.

TURKEY ALTERNATIVES

Q I recently read the article Bob wrote in *Potentials* about holiday turkeys. I couldn't agree more. I think giving turkeys every year is tasteless. My company gives turkeys or gift certificates for meat from a local grocery store. This year I'd like to suggest something more personal and meaningful. We have eighty employees. Could you offer some suggestions?

—**Deborah Green,** NuTec Design, York, PA

A I'd recommend an activity or event; for example, having management serve a turkey lunch at which the past year's successes are discussed. I know of a company that handed out gift certificates and had employees go and spend them on the spot, then come back and share what they brought, and why, with everyone. It was a fun, team-building experience.

SICK ABOUT NEVER BEING SICK

Q It burns me up that where I work there is no recognition whatsoever for perfect attendance, not even a thank-you. It takes the energy right out of a person when a company doesn't recognize perfect attendance in today's workplace. When you write a book called *1001 Ways to Discourage Employees,* put that near the top of the list.

—**C.S.,** West Henrietta, NY

A In today's work environments, with the rise of flexible working hours and more part-time employees and contracted workers, the notion of honoring perfect attendance might be a bit outdated. Still, it's not that difficult to do: creating an honor roll, giving out perfect attendance certificates, or hosting a lunch with upper management for perfect attendees are just a few ideas.

MAKING EXCEPTIONS FOR THE EXCEPTIONAL

Q In our non-sales cost center last year, we began to have managers audit reps' calls. We attached rewards to "exceptional" calls (having found that only exceptional service improves customer retention). We have been struggling with the definition of an exceptional call. At the same time, managers feel pressured to rate calls as exceptional,

because if they don't, their reps won't earn an award. We are thinking about telling the staff that we have budgeted "X" dollars to
reward exceptional calls. Once we have defined what "exceptional"
means, we will begin to reward each exceptional call. Do you think
this will work?

—**Caroline Strumbly,** Progressive Insurance, Mayfield Village, OH

A I would modify your approach. Don't use money as an award for
exceptional sales call, but rather use other forms of desirable recognition. The problem with using money is that it becomes perceived as
compensation, and—as you have found—no manager wants to keep
employees from earning the most they possibly can. Your managers may
be more focused on the short-term goal of keeping people happy as
opposed to the longer-term goal of systematically reinforcing the most
important behaviors leading to individual, group, and organizational
performance.

The problem that will also arise is that once an employee earns this
form of financial incentive a few times, he or she will come to expect it,
so that it becomes a demotivator on those occasions when the money's
not forthcoming. Remember that good recognition—especially a formal,
publicized program—needs to have very clear criteria, or else the recognition can seem like favoritism. Take time to set the criteria for "exceptional" calls soliciting the affected employees' input, if possible.

DEADLINE REMEDY

Q I work for an ad agency with about eighty-five employees. Our
issue is reporting time. About 30 percent of the staff doesn't record
their time in a timely fashion, so we can't pull up current cost-to-date
reports. It slows down our billing cycle, and even a few days' delay
costs us big money. Of course, reports are not as accurate because
people try to catch up all at once and cannot remember what they did
on any particular day. Even worse, the executives are among the
worst offenders. How can I turn this situation around?

—**Bill Truesdell,** Biggs-Gilmore Communications, Kalamazoo, MI

A Appeal to your executives to "walk their talk." Once they are modeling this administrative task, find ways to notice employees for turning in
accurate and timely reports. At the same time, go to a few of the worst
offenders and ask them what they need to get their information in on time.
Try whatever they suggest, which will increase their commitment. Then
set weekly (or even daily) deadlines that everyone must meet. Use the
simplest possible reporting form, whether online or on paper. Assign
someone to follow up with everyone and then post names (like an honor
roll) of people who met the deadlines. Hold some type of celebration the

first time everyone's information is in on time. The point is to make a big deal out of even the little behaviors you want to see repeated.

WHAT'S IN A NAME TAG?

Q We have over twelve thousand employees in thirty-five states. I'm writing a proposal to replace our current name badges, which are tied to years of service. Do you have any ideas on using them for various types of recognition? Also, what are some other ways we could recognize years of service?

—**Millie Lozano,** La Petite Academy, Overland Park, KS

A Much status can be built into a name tag. At Disney, they use silver "Shining Star" tags to indicate that someone has been nominated for the distinction by a coworker. Name tags can also be holders for other types of awards and distinctions, such as stars or pins. Many hotels list employees' home towns, which is a good conversation starter with guests.

First check with your employees to see whether the tenure distinction is important to them or not, and what other ways they can think of to recognize years of service besides receiving a different name tag. Often I find that it's important *how* you do recognition more than *what* you do. Personally, I think it's important for most employees to be recognized on their anniversary date by their manager. Anything more formal, such as a letter, should be hand-delivered by the manager. The use of such things as pens or logo jewelry are less popular today; the trend now is to provide a greater degree of choice in the gift selection that an employee is offered.

PRESENT AND ACCOUNTED FOR

Q I have heard that Toyota and others have full-fledged attendance reward programs. Is that type of program effective? Has attendance increased? My feeling is that you do not want to have too much of a reward, because then sick people may come to work and infect others. Also, those with sick children at home feel demotivated when they are forced to miss work and can't possibly win an award. I don't want to set up a program and then find out that it doesn't work!

—**Caroline Strumbly,** Progressive Insurance, Mayfield Village, OH

A There are some amazingly rich attendance reward programs, as attendance is critical in many companies. For example, Isuzu and Toyota both offer a lottery for those employees who have perfect attendance—they give away six new cars each year. Lottery tickets (one per year) are given to employees with perfect attendance. I have heard that the losers feel quite a bit of disappointment. However, 65 percent of Toyota employees in the United States have perfect attendance, many for as long as ten years in a row, so it seems to be working.

SUCH PROBLEMS!

Q What can we do to provide incentives to employees who are now millionaires due to stock options? How can we keep them motivated to stay?

—**K. Morrison,** online forum participant

A We all should have such problems! I'd say the only thing you can do is to get them involved in helping their stock gain value. Ask them what they'd like to do to have a positive impact in the organization and then work hard to give them that opportunity.

PRODUCING RESULTS

Q I'd like some ideas on incentives or recognition programs that work in a manufacturing/production environment.

—**D. Pyle,** online forum participant

A Every work environment has nuances, but I find that the majority of effective recognition activities crosses industry lines. At Honeywell Industrial Fibers in Moncure, North Carolina, they post "Coach's Award" certificates for doing a good job. Once a month, they draw from those employees for a day off with pay. The same plant allows any employee to give praise to another at their morning plant-wide meeting, which they have found to be very motivating.

THE UNCOLA

Q What advice do you have for an organization that is moving its ten-thousand-plus employees from an annual COLA (cost of living adjustment) and standard 5 percent merit increase to a system that rewards employees with a 0, 3, 5, or 7 percent pay increase depending on performance?

—**Tom Mauter,** Fairfax County, VA

A Involve people in the process. Don't take on too much at once, and don't expect to make the change perfectly. Stop and see what's going right and what's going wrong along the way. Recognize and celebrate your successes and milestones in making the change.

TIERS OF RECOGNITION

Q Our recognition program, in place for about eighteen months, has three tiers: an informal program with verbal and written thanks from managers or peers; a performance-based departmental/team program initiated by management with lunch, gift certificates, or token rewards; and a formal program with nominations submitted to a committee quarterly, and an evening event to recognize winners, who receive debit cards and a traveling trophy. I want to know about tax implications, but I also have two other questions:

1. The number of nonexempt employees nominated and selected for the formal program is much lower than we would expect because managers tend to see production workers as doing their jobs, whereas exempt workers have control of whole projects and can more easily go beyond expectations. What can we do to involve those in nonexempt roles?

2. Another problem is that sometimes the nominations themselves are written in ways that just don't sell the candidate. What can we do to be sure others know what is being rewarded?

—**Michelle Hildreth,** GuideOne Insurance, West Des Moines, IA

A What are the indicators of exceptional work in your production areas? Attendance, consistency, continuous improvement, suggestions, peer helpfulness? Find ways to quantify and recognize those achievements. Perhaps seek both exempt and nonexempt nominations for the company-wide awards. Have someone from the committee review all the nomination letters first, and if one is vague or unclear, interview the nominator to determine why the nominee is exceptional. Another idea is to provide specific guidelines, or even an outline on the nomination forms, including some examples and a list of adjectives or sample phrases.

IT'S ACADEMIC

Q Do you have any suggestions for energizing staff within the cultural constraints of a school environment? Perhaps other educators have also been looking for similar ideas.

—**Richard A. Simon,** The Wheatley School, Old Westbury, NY

A I do hear from a lot of educators and school administrators. I'm convinced that often the most powerful motivators are things that cost little or nothing, and work in most environments. Consider involving people in decisions that affect them; setting goals together; allowing increased autonomy and flexibility; implementing systematic manager-based and peer-based recognition; and supporting people when they make mistakes and encouraging them to learn from those mistakes. Some specific rewards in an educational environment might be public praise, special assignments, reading letters from parents at staff meetings, a pass-around award, spotlighting teachers and staff in a community newspaper, access to you or the board, lunches or breakfasts, a suggestion box that you personally handle, an opportunity to attend a conference of their choosing, and so on.

SHIFTING RESPONSIBILITY

Q **What can be done about major morale problems created by a management mandate that some workers rotate shifts?**

—Anonymous

A Any time management "mandates" something, it's going to be unpopular. The proactive approach would be to ask employees to come up with recommendations and then select the best option. The creativity of employees might surprise everyone involved. If there's no way for workers to have input at this point, at least try to keep employees from feeling like second-class citizens for working on a different shift. Provide plenty of communication, celebrations, and recognition so that they feel that their contribution is valued. Even if top management does not visibly support shift workers, their immediate supervisors can do so.

QUICK BUT QUESTIONABLE FIXES

Q **Our administration wants to spark interest in our employee-of-the-month program by increasing the dollar value of the award from $50 to $1,000, in spite of the fact that research shows that "timely, specific, sincere praise from supervisors/coworkers" is the number-one desire of our employees. I'm afraid that by giving one larger award rather than multiple smaller ones we'll just make things worse and people will feel even less appreciated. I want to build a system for instant recognition instead.**

—Anonymous civil servant

A I agree with you. My guess is that the administration doesn't believe the results of the research. It sounds like your bosses want a quick fix and think the extra money will spark interest in the program. While interest will likely be sparked, resentment will likely follow, as a substantial reward leaves a single person feeling great and everyone else feeling undervalued. You could do a lot more with that money that would have a greater impact on a larger percentage of your staff. With the increased budget, you could set criteria and recognize whoever meets those criteria every month. Winners could have lunch with the CEO to discuss concerns and receive his or her personal thanks. That could stir a lot of interest in your program. Why don't you pull together a focus group in your organization, representing all functions, to discuss options and prioritize preferences? I believe your focus is better spent on no-cost recognition that all your managers should be doing on a daily basis, rather than on a single, larger financial reward.

AVOIDING "AVERAGE"

Q My fifty-year-old educational service company is trying to introduce a "performance culture." One possible strategy would be a five-point rating system, and our senior officers believe that most people should receive a three most of the time. They think that a four or five should only go to people who can "walk on water." So when we do the midyear reviews, we are going to be giving threes to a lot of professionals who don't like being "average" and have been rated higher in the past when in fact they are not doing things any differently. How can we avoid morale problems and motivate people to keep up their good work?

—**Anonymous**

A It's hard to motivate people to strive to be average. It's not difficult to predict what will happen. Because so few people will be ranked as exceptional, you'll have many top performers who are demoralized and either leave or start putting in more "average" performances. A much more motivating environment is one in which everyone is encouraged to do his or her best.

Here are some alternatives: (1) base evaluations on performance objectives, not standard, so that everyone has the potential to be excellent if the objectives are met; (2) start a profit-sharing plan that reimburses everyone at the same level if the organization is successful; (3) move toward a more variable pay plan in which employees are paid increases based on success criteria; and (4) scrap the annual reviews. Review compensation when warranted by a change in a position's responsibilities or in its market worth. In general, there's a lot to be said for separating performance evaluations from salary adjustments.

QUANTIFYING SUCCESS

Q We have a quarterly bonus system that I want to integrate into the new performance appraisal system. However, most targets can only be measured once a year, whereas the bonus calculation is done quarterly based on sales. Do you have any ideas how to solve this problem? How can performance recognition be linked to the idea of flexible payment?

—**Linda Hovius,** online forum participant

A If bonuses are calculated quarterly based on sales, that's a form of measurement right there. What milestones or supporting activities lead to successful sales? Have your employees come up with a list of relevant performance achievements, prioritize that list, and have the top ones serve as general standards. You can also quantify intangible measures, such as helpfulness, teamwork, and the like, and track those items quarterly.

As far as linking recognition to flexible payment, some companies do this with programs in which individual objectives and responsibilities each have a targeted range of financial incentives. Or you could divide incentives according to success at meeting individual, group, and company objectives, and over time increase the percentages of base pay.

GOING FOR THE GOLD

Q We have wide variety of employees, from engineers to truck drivers, clerks to supervisors. In addition to base pay, salaried employees are given bonuses based on position and profit level. Our committee agreed on an incentive plan, but we don't know whether to apply the discretionary portion to the regular bonus for salaried personnel, and how to decide how much. We review each employee against preset goals at the beginning of each year and set new goals, but if we preset a bonus amount, where's the incentive? And how can managers review one another for determining bonus amounts?

—**Alan Postel,** Commercial Metals, Dallas, TX

A Keep your cash bonus plan simple and relevant to the desired performance. Have objective criteria that are announced in advance and that all employees have an equal chance to achieve. Increase the frequency of the bonuses so that people can see better how their efforts influence the amount of money they receive. You could also consider devoting a portion to reward team achievements, as well as individual ones. Many companies are starting to rely on evaluations from a cross section of people. AAA, for example, has employees rate managers; W.L. Gore has associates rank other associates they work with. Employees tend to work together better when they know they can affect each other's compensation. Of course, don't overlook the value of nonmonetary recognition as you make changes.

EXPECTATIONS FOR REWARDS

Q I need your help! I work for a company as a manager of a department store, and every year we give rewards to employees, up to 100 percent of their salaries. This year we won't be able to give out any rewards because sales were down. I'm afraid people will be unmotivated for this coming year.

—**Sandra Alexandre Costa,** Sao Paulo, Brazil

A What an unpleasant situation! If the money was previously given as a generous, unilateral gift from the owners, it could easily have set the tone that employees are "entitled" to such largesse. If the money was previously given based on the organization's performance, you have a better chance of justifying the missing financial bonus, and focusing on the future opportunity for employees to receive the incentive next year.

I'd have a talk with everyone about what you all learned this last year and how the situation could be turned around in the future. Separate morale issues, such as celebrating over the holidays, from the expected financial bonus/incentive. At a holiday potluck luncheon, you could give each person a nominal cash amount and let them go shopping for an hour to buy something for themselves. It becomes a type of team building if they go together in small groups. Have them return and share what they purchased and why. It may not be in the same category as 100 percent salary bonuses, but it can still serve as a fun, team-building experience.

PART VII
SELECTED ARTICLES

You Want ToMAYtoes, I Want ToMAHtoes

Bob Nelson, Gail Good, and Tom Hill

Recognizing employees' good work is one of the more exasperating tasks that managers face. It's not that rewarding workers is a discomfiting thing to do, like performance appraisals. But in trying to demonstrate their appreciation for a job well done, managers confront a damned-if-you-do, damned if-you-don't dilemma.

Some employees adore the plaques and pins and other trinkets that are the staples of the typical rewards-and-recognition program. To those workers, plaques are tangible evidence, suitable for showing friends and relatives, that they are valued at work. But others look on them as cheap gewgaws which merely demonstrate that management is too parsimonious to thank employees meaningfully.

As if the situation weren't already complicated enough by employees' radically different notions of what constitutes proper recognition, it's further muddled by the preconceptions of the very people giving the recognition. Most managers probably don't realize they're part of the problem. Unthinkingly, they tend to recognize most frequently the behaviors they themselves value. For instance, a risk-averse manager who prides herself on punctuality

might give out perfect-attendance pins with all the pomp of a coronation, but ignore risk-taking by employees (especially if the risks failed).

Sure, the whole situation could be cleared up substantially if managers would just ask individuals what sort of recognition they might like should the occasion arise. But that would be time-consuming, and you might end up with quite an astounding wish list.

There is another way. It involves having managers make an educated guess about what kinds of recognition people might appreciate, based on their personality. What we call temperament is a tool for understanding personality type.

We are born with our temperament; it's the core of our personality. Four distinct temperaments have been observed and described for many centuries. In this century, the most well-known system for describing personality is the Myers-Briggs typing system, which contains sixteen personality types. Working with that system, psychologist David Keirsey grouped the sixteen types into four after determining that there were four types within the sixteen that had more in common with each

other than the remaining twelve. He called those categories Guardians, Rationalists, Artisans, and Idealists. In this article, we are using nicknames two of us devised, which we believe describe the four temperaments more uniformly (see the chart on page 348).

We call the four types of personalities Preservers, Strategists, Mavericks, and Energizers. For each category, it's useful to know not only what the personality is like and what kinds of recognition each group craves, but also how managers of each persuasion behave.

PRESERVERS

Preservers prefer the concrete over the abstract, order over flexibility, and past experiences over future possibilities. They like making clear-cut decisions rather than mulling multiple options. Preservers' daily activities are driven by responsibility, obligation, and duty—what they "should" do. They endlessly try to ensure that stability prevails.

As the traditionalist, trustee, and guardian of the company, the Preserver is willing to follow established business protocol, often without question. Other people may consider it blind allegiance to authority, but Preservers view it as their duty to carry out the organization's policies, procedures, and plans.

Preservers also tend to focus on present issues and are guided by past experience to solve problems. They may not see the big picture or new alternatives because they focus on the here and now. They avoid taking risks.

Preservers as managers. In the Preservers' quest to maintain the status quo, resentment might surface because some workers may see them as trying to act like an all-knowing parent. For their part, Preservers often view others as not pulling their weight because others do not spend the time Preservers do in maintaining the status quo. Until they understand each temperament's unique skills, Preservers will be unable to judge others fairly.

There is almost an inevitable tension between Preservers, who esteem the status quo, and certain other personalities who are constantly agitating for change. Consequently, Preservers must keep reminding themselves that people with very different personalities can make valuable contributions. Others might not prize the same qualities Preservers hold dear, but that doesn't mean they're insubordinate.

It's also important to note that a Preserver's decisive nature, while certainly a great strength, becomes a hindrance when it halts discussion or discourages input from others. Preserver managers should involve others in exploring an issue thoroughly instead of making a quick decision. They must get everyone's opinion of alternatives and be flexible when circumstances change.

There are other ways Preserver managers can become better leaders and enhance the productivity of their teams.

■ Preservers should try to lighten up. Work can be productive and fun, and the workplace ought to be an enjoyable place to be. Rather than viewing lighthearted moments as slacking off, Preservers must consider that other temperaments may need to have fun to be productive.

■ Attention to the bottom line is an important focus for Preservers. They must remember, however, that the other temperaments tend to value the bottom line differently. It's simply not as high on their priority lists.

■ Preservers need to learn that the workplace is not black and white. To improve their leadership skills, Preservers need to adopt a more flexible participatory management style, and consciously reward other kinds of strengths. If they can figure out how to nurture the personality assets of others, Preservers can be the instruments for developing a well-balanced organization.

Type and Temperament

Myers-Briggs Personality Type		Temperament Code	David Keirsey Nickname	Good & Hill Nickname
■ ESTJ ■ ESFJ ■ ISTJ ■ ISFJ		■ SJ	■ Guardian	Preservers
■ ENTJ ■ INTP ■ ENTP ■ INTJ		■ NT	■ Rationalist	Strategists
■ ESTP ■ ESFP ■ ISTP ■ ESFP		■ SP	■ Artisan	Mavericks
■ ENFP ■ INFJ ■ ENFJ ■ INFP		■ NF	■ Idealist	Energizers

Rewarding Preserver employees. Employees with the Preserver temperament value dependability, responsibility, and stability. They want to be recognized for follow-through, adherence to rules and policies, and dedication and loyalty. They respond best to managers who praise them daily for their industriousness and all the tasks they accomplish. There are a number of ways managers can reward these achievements:

■ On a regular basis, write a letter of praise to recognize specific contributions and achievements. Then send a copy to your boss or higher managers in the personnel department.

■ Recognize company tenure and loyalty in a big way. For example, engrave on a plaque the names of employees who have reached ten, fifteen, twenty, or more years in service.

■ Take time during a quarterly company meeting to acknowledge individual achievements, such as cost-saving measures, productivity increases, or thoroughness.

■ Use tangible awards such as a company coffee mug, plaque, T-shirt, or jacket to mark a project completion or to congratulate workers for a job well done.

■ Create a dependability award—most error-free reports, for example.

STRATEGISTS

Strategists are visionaries and architects of change. They are imaginative and analytical, exploring all possibilities inherent in any situation. They like to build systems for the future. While planning for the future is a good thing, it can be a problem if a Strategist ignores today's details while searching for tomorrow's perfection.

Strategists believe very strongly that an organization's daily activities need to be consistent with its mission. They are the first to question the relevance of people's activities and will create sweeping changes if they believe those tasks are not helping the company reach its goals. Strategists typically detest rules for the sake of rules and will challenge or change anything they believe impedes progress.

Strategists relish ideas. They love the work of solving complex theoretical problems that require innovation and creativity. Because Strategists believe that intelligence and competence are inseparable, they often find it difficult to respect people they perceive as unintelligent or who fail to work up to their potential. In contrast, they admire verbally articulate, skilled communicators who are able to analyze problems logically.

Strategists also tend to be visionary, with an ability to figure out what the organization needs to be more effective in the future. They work tirelessly on change that improves the system. Strategists tinker and revise until they get things just right. With their eyes fixed on the future, it's easy for Strategists to forget that others do not see change in this way. In fact, they may feel as though they've just been flattened by a steamroller.

Strategists as managers. All managers are most effective when they surround themselves with people who have different strengths. This approach appeals particularly to Strategists, who continually strive for perfection in themselves and in others. Care must be taken, however, to give credit where it is due and truly respect the skills of others. Here are other ways a Strategist can become a better leader:

■ Strategists' need for perfection often makes them intolerant of anything less. Strategist managers cannot expect others to share this same workaholic philosophy. They must realize that their work style is different and that other personalities do not place the same emphasis on the value of work.

■ For Strategists, delegating work is crucial. They flourish during a design phase, but as a project gives way to day-to-day implementation, they often become bored. To complete the project effectively and efficiently, a Strategist manager should surround himself with individuals who have different temperaments so that others will carry through the implementation and be glad to have the Strategist out of their hair.

■ Strategists dislike situations where there is no opportunity for creativity or self-determination, or when people are focusing exclusively on human issues. They have little patience for meetings devoted to the development of policies and procedures. Again, if Strategists can delegate the task of attending these types of committee meetings to others, everyone will be happier.

■ Lifelong education is a lifetime love of Strategists. Yet they cannot assume that additional training will be seen as a reward by other workers, who may view it as a chore or a comment on the quality of their current work.

Rewarding Strategist employees. Strategist employees respond best to a work environment that allows them to assume enough authority and responsibility to get results, while imposing minimal oversight, structure, and constraint.

Because Strategists value autonomy and work better when given this freedom, consider rewarding and recognizing them by:

■ Giving them freedom to set their own schedule and work plan.

■ Letting them telecommute or work at home on projects if feasible.

■ Allowing them to choose their next work assignments.

Because Strategists love to learn, rewards that enhance their education and personal growth will delight them. Ideas to consider include:

■ Paying membership dues for a professional organization or buying the person a subscription to a magazine, journal, or newsletter of her choice.

■ Paying for additional training or college classes of the person's choice and/or allowing the Strategist to attend classes during usual work hours.

■ Asking the Strategist to assist you with a project that offers a real challenge or to serve on a task force with the president of the company. In many large companies, employees rarely get the chance to see the president, let alone have the opportunity to work with him or her.

MAVERICKS

Mavericks prefer action over reflection, quick response over planning, the concrete over the abstract, and today over the past or the future. They are the ultimate negotiators and troubleshooters. Give them a problem to fix—especially a concrete, hands-on task—and they will swoon. Mavericks are the ones to call to respond to crises.

The most pragmatic of the four temperaments, Mavericks possess a keener sense of current reality than the others. In the workplace, they use their quick sense of the obvious to scan the environment and determine the best way to outmaneuver an adversary.

Mavericks will strive to perfect a particular skill, but once perfection is achieved they may never be interested in doing that again. They are ready to move on to new challenges, perfecting new skills along the way.

Mavericks have a unique picture of reality. Anything is negotiable, and the higher the stakes, the better. Because they value freedom more than possessions or relationships, they are likely to be easily frustrated by people who avoid risks. While they may not believe it is their job to change the views of others, they do want those who confine them to get out of their way and let them do what they need to do.

Mavericks as managers. Mavericks tend to dislike bosses. It makes little sense to place them in traditional management positions that demand directing, structuring, implementing, and monitoring— the kinds of things Mavericks don't do well. They like to live life fully and dislike being limited by traditions, policies, and procedures. Mavericks also detest being confined to an office, doing paperwork, and attending meetings. Mavericks will be effective managers only when they are in positions that provide ample opportunity to troubleshoot, negotiate, or take action. Otherwise, they will quickly become disenchanted and quit. Not surprisingly, Mavericks are often entrepreneurs.

As managers, Mavericks tend to operate in a fraternal style and prefer an informal atmosphere with built-in flexibility whenever possible. While this is reflective of their generally easygoing nature, Mavericks can be very demanding taskmasters when they are passionately involved in a project. They tend to disregard time, family, and other obligations when in the middle of something—and expect others to do the same.

Mavericks usually are good at delegating; however, they must take caution not to delegate too much. In delegating tasks, mavericks may fail to provide the structure and information others need

Rewarding the Four Types

	What They Value	What They Need Recognition For	Their Preferred Form of Recognition
Preservers	▪ Dependability ▪ Responsibility ▪ Stability	▪ Follow-through ▪ Adherence to rules and policies ▪ Dedication and loyalty	▪ Tangible thanks for steady work
Strategists	▪ Intelligence and innovation ▪ Competence ▪ Tireless effort	▪ Ideas ▪ Knowledge ▪ Competence	▪ Freedom to learn or explore a challenge
Mavericks	▪ Superior skills ▪ Grace under pressure ▪ Risk-taking action	▪ Responsiveness ▪ Cleverness ▪ Ingenuity	▪ Unusual reward for successful and risky action
Energizers	▪ Commitment and passion ▪ Independent thinking ▪ Sincerity and kindness	▪ Ideas ▪ Uniqueness and personal contributions ▪ Championing change	▪ Social recognition

to complete the project. If employees fail to perform tasks as a Maverick sees fit, he will do it himself—making it difficult for people to learn from their mistakes. To Mavericks, this makes sense; they're getting the job done as expediently as possible.

Among the things Mavericks can do to be more effective as managers:

▪ Adopt a "hands-off" policy. Mavericks often believe success is a perfected skill or superior product. If they are not doing the job themselves, they feel unproductive. Their natural instinct is to take action and to do the task, making it difficult to develop employees. Mavericks must learn to let go of tasks they enjoy and grant others the same independence they value.

▪ Mavericks need to remember that while they thrive on change,

others may regard Mavericks' need to upset the status quo as bullheaded and stubborn. Certainly, Mavericks believe that the freedom to act, respond, and work in their own way is an inalienable right, but they need to temper their independent streak if it interferes with gaining cooperation and support from others.

Rewarding Maverick employees. Mavericks respond best to managers who recognize them for their ability to excel in specific ways. Because of their pragmatic nature, Mavericks may prefer rewards involving practical activities or time off.

▪ Give Mavericks a chance to negotiate what they want for their reward.

▪ Challenge Mavericks to achieve a goal that seems difficult to reach.

▪ Provide on-the-spot cash awards in recognition of specific performance.

▪ Give assignments with specific quality expectations and deadlines. If the Maverick gets the work done before deadline, give her the remainder of the time as free time.

▪ Grant two-hour lunches or a three-day weekend.

ENERGIZERS

Energizers prefer the big picture over details, fairness over consistency, ideas over policies, and the future over present and past experience. As people pleasers, their first and last concern is always centered on people and relationships. They constantly strive for superior customer service, harmony in the work group, and self-actualization for themselves and others. They deal with people with great enthusiasm and passion. They like to champion people, causes, and anything new.

Energizers would rather focus on ideas than on tasks. They have trouble fitting into large, impersonal, bureaucratic organizations where the traditional ways of doing business are the norm. Energizers' idealism and enthusiasm for change may be appreciated more in creative work environments that encourage personal freedom.

Energizers as managers. Energizers seek positions where they have the chance to influence others. They are naturals at getting people involved and committed to the goals of the team. They tend to give praise generously (and seek approval in return), but may need to learn to give and receive constructive feedback without seeing it as personal criticism. They must realize that other personalities may not need as much approval as they do and they must get better at making objective decisions and giving reprimands.

Energizers also must doff their rose-colored glasses and become more realistic. Energizers cannot simply visualize a better workplace; they must learn to recognize problems, collect practical information, and use concrete data to resolve problems.

Energizers pride themselves on being congenial, and they often avoid disagreement. However, friction plays a valuable role in forming an effective team. Once Energizers accept the role of conflict, they can

become skilled mediators or counselors in problem-solving because they are already comfortable dealing with feelings.

The managerial strengths of Energizers can become liabilities if carried to extremes. They are often unable to separate business and personal relationships. They can create anarchy in their pursuit of democratic decision-making, and they often fail to finish tasks or projects that they find routine or boring. For these reasons, it is critical for Energizer managers to surround themselves with—and value—people who have strengths that they do not. Their natural penchant for cooperation, involvement, and people development, coupled with the skills of each of the other temperaments, can help form an ideal work team.

Rewarding Energizer employees. Energizers respond best to managers who value them personally for their contributions and provide constructive criticism with sensitivity and tact. Energizers like being rewarded with training that is people-oriented as well as useful, and they prefer to choose what and where it will be. Other ideas to consider include:

■ Using interpersonal (a personal note of thanks) and social forms (public praise) of recognition as much as possible.

■ Giving Energizers personalized gifts that recognize their contributions.

■ Rewarding superior interpersonal skills, particularly those demon-

strated in customer service or teamwork. Award a silver pin or similar prize for positive customer comments. Designate a prime parking space for the customer service Employee of the Month.

■ Have top managers meet periodically with selected employees to congratulate them on their hard work and to recognize specific achievements.

■ Send Energizers to special seminars, workships, or meetings outside the company on topics they are interested in.

With a little thought, it's not that hard to recognize employees in ways that are meaningful to them. To encourage employees to excel, a manager must remember that not all employees are alike—and especially, that they're not all like the manager himself. Individuals are motivated intrinsically by a variety of factors, all of which are affected by temperament. Leaders must discover how best to motivate each employee and must then provide the recognition and rewards that fit each worker's personality.

Originally published in
Training Magazine

Incentives for All Generations

Bob Nelson

Incentives have long played an important workplace role motivating, rewarding, and energizing employees and providing employers with powerful tools to retain valuable employees. However, the "one size fits all" incentive plans of the past no longer encompass the diverse needs and desires of today's multigenerational workplace.

Today, the Silent Generation, Baby Boomers, Generation Xers, and the now-emerging Generation Y are working side by side. This means that companies need to create incentive programs that motivate a workforce that, at times, spans some fifty-plus years. This is a challenging task, and companies that meet the challenge will gain a distinct competitive edge in retaining and attracting the talent they need to be successful.

Flexible work arrangements and other work/life initiatives aimed at enhancing employees' quality of life continue to have universal appeal. But the definition of "quality of life" varies by generation. Realizing that each of these generations has different values and ideas of what is important, progressive companies are committing to delivering rewards and incentives that are aimed at meeting the diverse needs of *all* employees.

So, just who are today's workers and what motivates them to give their best performance? Stretching over many generations, they include:

THE SILENT GENERATION: BORN BETWEEN 1920 AND 1945

Today there are nearly 16 million Americans age fifty-five and over (about 21 percent of the workforce) who are either working, or seeking work. They like the idea of reentering the job market, dipping a foot back into the labor pool, or even remaining there for the long haul. In a 1988 study of mature workers by the American Association of Retired Persons (AARP), 40 to 50 percent of those polled said they would work past retirement age if they were offered flexible schedules, part-time and temporary employment. But these are not the only incentives that are effective with mature workers.

Employees who fall into this group have generally had predictable career paths, working hard for one or two companies, moving up the ladder of success. They are characterized by dedication to their employer and as a group are considered nonrisk-takers and conformers.

Formal recognition is highly valued. In a recent survey, 76 percent of American workers ranked recognition at a company meeting as a meaningful incentive—and this is particularly true for the Silent Generation. These workers greatly value formal awards, publicly presented. For example, at Ceramics Process Systems Corporation, a technical ceramics manufacturer in Milford, Massachusetts, the Extra Mile Award is given each December to several people who have gone above and beyond the call of duty. The winner's name is announced at a company meeting and then engraved on a plaque that hangs in the company's lobby. The chosen employee also receives either cash or equity in the company.

Other ways to publicly recognize and motivate this group follow:

■ Take a photo of the person being congratulated by the company president. Frame the photo. Place photographs of top performers in the lobby.

■ Write a story about the employee's achievement and place it in the company newsletter.

■ Engrave on a plaque the names of employees who have reached ten, fifteen, twenty, or more years of service. Acknowledge and personalize such anniversaries as well as other individual achievements during a company meeting each quarter.

Team-based recognition incentives. Workers of the Silent Generation are the early pioneers of "the team" and are primarily credited with developing the "team-building" concepts used in business today. As a result, they greatly value programs that recognize the contributions and successes of teams. At First Chicago, the Service Products Group Performance Award helps develop teamwork by recognizing high-performing groups of employees each month. The award includes a group outing—dinner, theater—as well as a plaque for the group. All monthly winning team members attend the annual SPG Performance Banquet, at which additional awards are given out to team members.

Company stock and retirement planning. As Silent Generation workers consider their retirement, they also value recognition programs that offer stock awards, 401(k) contributions, and even retirement planning. At Mary Kay Cosmetics, employees receive increasing stock contributions in celebration of service anniversaries.

Ewing Kaufmann, chairman and founder of Marion Laboratories in Kansas City, Missouri, uses stock awards to reward employees for the best money-saving suggestions. One year he handed out $7,000, $12,000, and $15,000 worth of company stock to three employees for their ideas.

Another year resulted in an average of $1,000 worth of stock apiece for the employees whose 237 suggestions were accepted.

BABY BOOMERS: BORN BETWEEN 1946 AND 1963

Baby Boomers, otherwise referred to as the "Me" generation, make up the largest population of today's workers—76 million strong, accounting for 52 percent of the workforce. And that number is growing. According to the Bureau of Labor Statistics, within the next ten years, one out of every three workers will be older than fifty-five. Today, this large group makes up most of middle and upper management in most organizations.

This generation came of age at a time of economic boom in the United States. It is a generation that likes to win, to be in charge, and to have an impact. Having grown up in postwar prosperity, boomers were the focus of society and, as a result, they now focus on themselves. "It's the first generation that hasn't had to live with the notion that what you're trained to do, you do for the rest of you life," says Marc J. Wallace, founding partner of Center for Workforce Effectiveness in Northbrook, Illinois.

Boomers are set squarely in middle age. They are a gold mine of knowledge and very valuable to companies. To retain these workers, employers must work hard to provide incentives that are of value to this group.

New experiences and adventures. Among the most valued

forms of incentives and rewards for boomers are those that recognize their interest in new experiences and adventures. For example, at Valvoline Oil Company, six buyers from distributorships around the country were awarded a trip to Road Atlanta, a racing school. There they learned professional racing techniques and spent a day on the two-and-a-half-mile Grand Prix track.

Self-indulgent items and activities. Boomers appreciate self-indulgent treats. At Nordstrom, the Seattle-based department store chain, employees who have exceeded goals by a considerable margin receive the Pacesetter Award. As a Pacesetter, an employee enjoys a lavish evening of dinner, dancing, and entertainment to share with a guest. For the following year, the Pacesetter enjoys a 33 percent discount on all Nordstrom merchandise, 13 percent greater than the standard employee discount.

Flexibility and work-home balance. According to the AARP, one of the most significant factors that stands in the way of employment is that older workers are forced to choose between full-time work and retirement. But today, more boomers plan on staying in the workforce beyond the traditional retirement age of sixty-five than ever before. As a result, employers who recognize boomers' desire for flexibility and longing for a comfortable work-home balance will be rewarded.

Patagonia, an outdoor-clothing maker in Ventura, California, supports its employees by providing them with the flexibility needed to achieve a work-home balance. The company encourages its employees to take time away from the office for outside activities. In a speech to employees, founder Yvon Chouinard said, "You are allowed to take time off, whether it's two hours or two weeks, as long as your work gets done and you don't keep others from doing their work." For boomers, this valuable time might be spent with children and family, attending a conference of choice, or working on a hobby.

GENERATION X: BORN BETWEEN 1964 AND 1981

Much has been written about the disenfranchised new generation of workers. Whatever the label—"Generation X," "TwentySomethings," and "The 13th Generation" (that is, the 13th generation since the founding of the United States)—this group of employees can be quite challenging to manage.

They've been told that they will not have a better standard of living than their parents—that, in fact, many of them will still be living at home until their late twenties. They've been told they are the least skilled workers to enter the workplace in decades, with MTV attention spans that last fifteen minutes, tops. They've been told they will not have careers but, rather, will be lucky to have steady work—or even full-time, hourly work for that matter. They've been told they are unambitious slackers, and it's just as well, since their managers aren't going anywhere anytime soon anyway.

Granted, some of these generalizations have a foundation in truth. The nature of work is drastically changing in the United States with the extensive degree of downsizing and merging. Full-time jobs are being eliminated at record speeds, and companies are increasingly turning to contracted, part-time workers when they do seek to rehire. Their preparation for the jobs that do exist is scant. According to demographers Neil Howe and Bill Strauss, coauthors of *13th Gen,*

Just as they [Generation X] started graduating from college, the Nation at Risk report marked the end of the reform era that had spanned their entire school careers. As the cutting edge of educational philosophy suddenly swung back the other way, the college classes of the middle '80s became the target of a searing academic whiplash. Ever since elementary school, they had constantly been told that there weren't any standards, that they were doing well, and that they had to listen to their feelings. Now after all those years, they heard that there had indeed been standards, that they had failed to meet them, and that no one much cared how they felt about that failure.

Still, there appears to be more reason to rejoice than fret about this new breed of workers, provided managers take into account certain learnings. Following are several such insights for managing this new generation of workers.

Provide the larger context for work. When they're not worried about getting a job, workers in this generation would like to have a job that gives their life meaning. Says one twenty-six-year-old account executive for a communications firm, "We're more interested in contributing to society—whether it's via working for a company or a nonprofit, or volunteering our time—than any past demographic of workers." Often this meaning can be best provided by their manager, who can explain the mission and purpose of the company and how the employee's job fits into the overall goals of the organization. If this context is not provided, Generation Xers will revert to looking at work merely as a means of survival, a means to an ends, as only a way to make money. If not engaged on the job, they'll seek excitement when the workday is over—and be eager to get out the door each day to that part of their life.

Gear work to action, not talk. This generation has a low tolerance for talking about work and would rather "just do it." They prefer action over talk, results over process, and accountability over excuses. They pride themselves on their speed and their multitasking abilities. They hate meetings, philosophizing, and political maneuvering in the office. They are attracted to work that directly rewards initiative, such as sales or incentive work.

Focus on results, not rules. They know how to get the job done. This generation takes special pride in what they picked up on their own and in their ability to succeed in life despite less-than-desirable circumstances. They prosper when they can apply themselves to new tasks and problems never before experienced, rather than when systematically following predetermined work procedures. Make it clear what results you are after and then leave them alone to do the job as they see fit. This requires a trusting, respectful, supportive, and open manager.

Take time and listen; don't lecture. They may not want to be micromanaged, but they have a strong craving for their manager's approval. This need for approval comes in part from having possibly the lowest collective self-esteem of any living generation. Take time to listen to them. As Roy Moody, president of Roy Moody & Associates says, "The greatest motivational act one person can do for another is to listen." Yet many managers can't imagine that a young employee might have an idea or thought that has not already occurred to them. That's disappointing, because in many ways this generation is more attuned to the times. They are more "here and now" and market savvy than the future-oriented mindset of many of their managers. Claire Raines, coauthor of *Twenty-Somethings: Managing and Motivating Today's New Work Force*, says, "A big, big motivator for [this generation] is

time spent with their boss. They feel they didn't have enough time with their parents while they were growing up, and they transfer that need to the workplace. They're really motivated by spending time with their superiors, whether it's having a cup of coffee or being invited to lunch or a meeting."

Recognize and appreciate whenever possible. Although all employees have a need to be appreciated, for this group the need is particularly acute. "Unlike yuppies, younger people are not driven from within. They need reinforcement. They prefer short-term tasks with observable results," says Penny Erikson, forty, of the Young & Rubicam ad agency. Says Cathy Sigismonti, a twenty-eight-year-old marketing analyst, "Tell me that I did a good job. Let me know." Adds John Doyle, a thirty-one-year-old programmer, "We want recognition because when we were growing up the family unit wasn't very strong. It can be financial or something else. At a company event, it could be just pointing someone out and saying their name." Andy Moore, a twenty-six-year-old circulation and marketing manager for a national magazine, puts it this way: "When management shows, through actions rather than words, that you're a valuable employee, that your input is valued no matter what level you work at, it's very motivating." Make sure you recognize and reward the results you get in a timely, specific way.

Encourage skill development, not loyalty. This generation constantly wants to learn new skills, both to keep the job exciting and challenging as well as to increase their marketability. In the words of Liesel Walsh, a consultant with Big Picture Marketing in Charleston, Massachusetts, and a twenty-something herself, "Manage me by teaching me things." Adds Raines, "Young workers today see themselves as marketable commodities, as an item for sale. So if managers can help them to see how an assignment we give them today makes them more marketable, how it builds their resume, that really motivates them." Says Robert Lukefahr, one of the founders of Third Millennium, a political group that represents Generation X, "Training is one of the best motivators. The opportunity to increase their portfolio of skills through training, either formal or informal, ranks high on their list of motivators." Being highly individualistic, their loyalty is to themselves and their profession, not to a company that cannot guarantee them a career anyway.

Promote new responsibilities, not promotions. Job promotions are harder to come by during times of downsizing, so new responsibilities or job rotations are the next best thing to providing the change of pace that keeps this generation engaged. Says Margaret Regan, a principal with New York–based Towers Perrin who consults with companies about this generation of workers, "To these workers, promotions don't necessarily mean movement up the corporate ladder. Often the movement can be lateral, to a new position that will offer new challenges and build new skills. When Xers get bored with a job, they'll want to move on to the next, either within your company or outside it. They like job swapping; they think it's great fun."

Make work fun, not routine. This generation wants to have fun—at work, if at all possible—otherwise they'll focus on that activity when they're not on the job. This is part of a balanced life they decided was missing from their parents' lives as well as that of their workaholic managers. So loosen up and try some new activities to help keep things exciting. Says Raines, "Fostering a spirit of fun in the workplace by giving employees an occasional afternoon off for sporting activities or arranging humorous office events and competitions will improve the morale of [Generation X] and increase their productivity." Better yet, elicit the help of one or more of your youngest employees to come up with activities that can make work fun. This can range from each person taking turns bringing innovative refreshments to staff meetings (scones and tea, milk and cookies, ice cream, etc.) to planning team outings to celebrate project milestones.

All in all, the challenge of managing Generation X is to challenge them—to engage them with new tasks, problems, and skills—and recognize and reward them for re-

sults. Michael Gose of Pepperdine University conducted a study comparing Generation X with their parents' generation of Baby Boomers. Of forty-three measures of aptitude and achievement, the Generation X respondents scored higher in "skills in negotiation," "defenses to prevent extreme dependency on parents or authorities," "skill interacting with adults on an equitable basis," and "information about where to go for business, consumer, or personal wants and needs." He concluded that the students of this generation are "more aware of what's going on, how institutions work, how to manage social relations, how to cope with adults, and how to get things done in the community." In short, they are survivors, used to confronting problems and unfavorable circumstances on their own, sorting out the best solution and acting upon it.

Every day, managers have an opportunity to encourage and foster employee initiative and excitement with this type of employee—or to hinder and erode it. For example, I worked with one company that had a national chain of automotive parts stores. One store manager mentioned a young hire who came to him one day and very excitedly asked that the manager follow him to the back storeroom. When they got there the young man announced, "Look at this," gesturing to an inventory of freshly stacked oil cans. A manager in this situation has two choices. He can say something like, "What do you expect, a medal?" and shame the employee for taking pride in such a boring,

rote task—in the process possibly demotivating him forever—or he can say something like, "I've never seen oil cans so neatly stacked in all my life. You sure must take pride in your work. I could really use someone with that type of work ethic; in fact, tomorrow I'd like to start showing you how to take inventory." Wisely, the store manager chose the latter course.

Every company I know wants to have employees who are flexible and action-oriented, independent and self-directed, technically competent, and comfortable with the constantly changing nature of work today. In 1989 the U.S. Department of Labor commissioned a task force to determine the skills that American businesses desire in high school graduates. Among the most important were: "work in changing settings with people of different cultures," "learn new skills," "identify and suggest new ways to get the job done," and "work without supervision." If you look closely, that task force is available now.

Originally published in
HR Professional

Motivating and Rewarding a Global Workforce

Bob Nelson

As U.S. companies continue to expand their operations at breakneck speed, one of the most significant challenges organizations face in the process of going global is learning how to motivate, recognize, and reward people of all cultures. The key to success lies in understanding the cultural attitudes and business practices of other countries. Companies that foster cultural sensitivity and help workers from varying backgrounds feel comfortable can increase employee productivity and job satisfaction.

In general, other countries don't rely as much as we do on formal gestures of recognition. In Germany, for example, business is taken especially seriously and workers are conservative and very private. Rather than energize workers, public ceremony and recognition tend to embarrass the German worker. Other cultures look at the American focus on praise and recognition as a weakness. "Why are Americans so insecure about themselves?" an Asian businessman might ask. "Why do they have to be reassured about everyday activities they were hired to do?"

Let's look at some areas of potential crosscultural conflict in terms of recognizing employees.

TIME

In the U.S., time is a major driving force, a precious resource not to be wasted. Americans are always in a hurry. Many foreign visitors complain that Americans are more concerned with getting things done on time than with developing meaningful relationships. As a result, Americans are much more abrupt in their business dealings. They conduct meetings, review agendas, and make snap decisions with an eye on the clock. Most of Northern Europe is also time-sensitive.

In contrast, much of Latin America, Africa, and the Middle East take a more casual view of time. In these countries, greater emphasis is placed on developing relationships. In Mexico, it may take several breakfast or lunch meetings before people feel comfortable together and are ready to begin conducting business.

U.S. companies operating in countries where "time" is not a controlling factor and relationships are greatly valued will need to consider these differences when determining how to reward and recognize employees. Company policies that reward employees for meeting timeliness standards might be modified to place more emphasis on the desired results, and less on how quickly they were obtained.

COMMUNICATION

Americans typically prefer open and direct communication. In Sweden, a direct approach is also valued as a sign of efficiency, but unlike in the U.S., heated debates and confrontations are very unusual. The Swedish business culture strongly favors compromise. In Germany, Sweden, and Switzerland, the role of humor in business relationships is much more limited than in the U.S. In Asia, company leaders are expected to be much more politic and sensitive to the feelings and needs of subordinates in their communication.

Then there's eye contact. In France, direct eye contact is a frequent and intense part of communication, as it is in Latin America—much more so than in the U.S. In other cultures, such as Japan, direct eye contact is considered challenging, aggressive, and a sign of disrespect. Japanese employees usually prefer quiet recognition. Open praise at a staff meeting or singling out individuals for praise in public generally will not be effective.

Finnish and German employees tend to prefer written communication to face-to-face interaction. For these workers, a letter recognizing employee accomplishments would be most effective.

In Mexico and Latin American countries, communication is open and personal, with a strong emphasis on developing relationships. Recognition of employees' successes in building relationships will be well received.

FAMILY/WORK ORIENTATION

While U.S. businesses have taken steps toward creating a "family-friendly" work environment, the prevailing belief around the world is that Americans live to work and a significant part of most Americans' identity is determined by "what they do for a living." The individual's family life is taken into greater consideration in foreign workplaces than is generally the case in the U.S.

In Latin America, the Middle East, and Africa, there is a clearer division between work and family. In Mexico, the family is of vital importance, and issues affecting the family take priority over work. In many Asian and European cultures, the family is viewed as an essential institution, and business treats it with the highest regard. In Singapore, the strength of a worker's family is seen as a real factor in the company's success. In these cultures, economic and social progress are viewed as inextricably linked.

In some Asian countries, though, this leads to a blurring of the line between work and private life. Japanese companies often expect employees to work late or on weekends, and entertain business guests at home.

In cultures such as these, it makes sense to send a letter to the family acknowledging the employee's accomplishment. Allow time off, or at least a flexible work schedule, so employees can attend to family matters. Send birthday cards, get-well cards, and flowers to family members when appropriate. Hold "open houses" at work and invite family members to company celebrations. Grant time off to volunteer in a child's classroom or to attend school field trips or sporting events.

COMPETITION VERSUS COOPERATION

Americans adore competition. We love contests and the public sharing of work progress. Americans conduct business at rapid speed with intense focus on results, and are often compelled to make decisions quickly without soliciting input from other employees, clients, or vendors. Although many U.S. companies are striving to be more participatory, many still tend to invest top executives with extraordinary power and authority.

But many cultures outside the U.S. promote cooperation and teamwork over competition. In Sweden and Japan, a good manager is seen as a coach who leads through cooperation and consensus, not through his power and position. In Asia and the Middle East, teaching is considered the most important job a person can perform. The manager's role is seen as a teacher and facilitator—someone who helps those around him learn. For instance, in Asian corporations, particularly Japan, the manager is always present when a subordinate is being trained. This indicates that the manager believes that the learning is important. In these cultures, it is important for an employee to be seen as a whole person—with needs far beyond professional and technical ones. This is also true for Africa.

Japan has a collectivist culture in which workers do not want to be conspicuous. Individual pay for performance is considered potentially disruptive to pleasant working relationships. Instead, year-end bonuses are given based on loyalty, years of service, and one's family situation. Team awards have been effective—some include salary increases and an allowance system as incentives for outstanding performance.

Many European and Asian companies seek employee input on nearly every business issue. In Sweden, employees have a voice in management decisions, particularly those that relate to compensation, safety, and capital expenditures. Training begins when employees start new jobs. It is also important to incorporate new employees into the corporate culture. Management is based on the premise that the individual is willing and able to do a good job. A Swedish manager is generally thought of as a coach—motivating staff, leading employees through principles of cooperation and agreement—and is a good listener. Getting emotional when discussing a problem is considered inappropriate. All employees have the freedom to make decisions and solve unexpected problems without asking permission from superiors. Sweden has a high rate of employed women and a high ratio of family-oriented men who seek a better integration of work and family. Thus, there is a broad acceptance of home-based telework.

So in order to be successful overseas, U.S. companies may need to deemphasize individual contributions and do a better job of recognizing teamwork and cooperation. Recognizing employees who make group decisions, offer team suggestions, and manage themselves may work wonders. In Japan, where employees like to be valued as team players, compliments in the workplace need to be subtler and more indirect. A manager wishing to compliment a subordinate could ask an employee's opinion or he could invite him to a meeting to which he would not normally be invited.

U.S corporations must not make the mistake of assuming that American views and business practices are universal. "In the United States we've made a mistake thinking that because we're U.S.-based, what's good for us is good for everybody around the world," says Carol Kaplan, manager of global compensation and benefits at Applied Materials, Inc. "What happens then is that we export programs that aren't culturally sound and then end up creating animosities toward corporate headquarters."

With so much real economic growth over the next decade expected to take place outside the U.S., it's essential that American companies learn how to inspire, recognize, and reward a multicultural workforce.

Originally published in
Global Workforce

How to Design a High-Motivation Compensation System

Dean Spitzer

If you want an organization full of top performers who constantly delight customers with innovative, high-quality products and flexible, caring service, then you will probably want to redesign your organization's compensation system. Many organizations have discovered that traditional compensation systems are often black holes into which millions, even billions, of dollars are being spent with an extremely disappointing return on investment. Not only are most compensation systems not particularly rewarding, but for most employees they are actually demotivating! This article will show you how to make financial compensation a much more powerful and cost-effective part of your organization's motivational arsenal.

PROBLEMS WITH TRADITIONAL COMPENSATION

The most important question to ask when evaluating a compensation system is: Do the rewards induce the kind of performance the organization wants? Unfortunately, in most organizations, the answer is no. I have identified six major problems with traditional compensation that account for this situation.

1. The "entitlement" mentality.

Most employees have grown accustomed to viewing pay as something they are entitled to receive regardless of performance. Regular pay increases are also taken for granted as being virtually automatic. Consequently, financial compensation usually does little more than get employees to show up for work. It rarely gets them to work longer, harder, or smarter.

2. Lack of performance-based rewards.

The most important aspect of any compensation system is the relationship that exists between performance and rewards. Unfortunately, most employees receive few, if any, performance-based rewards, not even for exceptional performance. In a nationwide survey, it was found that only 13 percent of employees think they would personally benefit from increased production in their organization (Nelson, 1994). Employees have learned they are more likely to be rewarded for seniority, conformity, and personality traits than for superior performance.

3. The wrong performance is rewarded.

Many organizations have found that compensation often has exactly the opposite effect of the intended one. This is because organizations frequently reward the wrong things . . . and get them! As Kerr (1989) explains, "Managers who complain that their workers are not motivated might do well to consider the possibility that they have installed reward systems that are paying off for behaviors other than those they are seeking." The compensation systems in most American companies tend to reward short-term, rather than long-term, performance. Prevailing rewards tend to foster playing it safe, not making waves, and getting along with others rather than initiative, risk-taking, and creativity. And, even when most organizations today are trying to encourage teamwork, employees are rewarded only for individual performance. As Kanter (1987) puts it, "We talk about teamwork at training sessions . . . and then we destroy it in the compensation system."

4. Inadequate rewards for outstanding performance.

Merit pay, as typically used, has little or no

motivating value and is extremely costly to companies. Because they are built into employees' base pay, merit increases are essentially "annuities" that are awarded in perpetuity based on one year's performance. They also have little motivating value because of the small differential between the increases given to "satisfactory" employees and those who are "outstanding" performers. In one study, it was found that the increases were 4.7 percent and 7.7 percent, respectively (Schuster and Zingheim, 1992). In other words, outstanding performers received only a 3 percent reward for their outstanding efforts! When this amount is added to existing base pay, and adjusted for increased deductions, the difference is minuscule.

5. Poor performance is rewarded. Some companies not only tolerate poor performance, but reward it by providing across-the-board compensation increases. One employee described his company's approach to compensation in this way: "In our company, if you do a really outstanding job, you get very well rewarded. And if you do a mediocre job, you also get very well rewarded!" When good performers see that poor performers are receiving the same treatment (and the same compensation), they eventually question the wisdom of their own performance commitments ("Why should I bother working so hard?").

6. Perceived unfairness. One of the major irritants in almost every compensation system is the perception of unfairness. Very few employees feel they are being paid fairly. This is because people tend to be more sensitive to what they are not receiving than to what they are. It has been found that, regardless of how much they earn, employees want, on average, 25 percent more (Brim, 1992). In addition, 83 percent of all hourly employees and 53 percent of management employees feel "underrewarded" (Huseman and Hatfield, 1989).

These problems have combined to undermine the effectiveness of most existing compensation systems. However, the prognosis is not as bleak as it might at first appear. The salvation of compensation systems lies with performance-based approaches.

TOWARD PERFORMANCE-BASED COMPENSATION

It is surprising that, despite all the evidence affirming the efficacy of performance-based pay and the years of success in using it as a sales motivator, most companies still don't offer performance-based incentives to their rank-and-file employees (Peters, 1989). In fact, research has shown that using performance-based pay alone can improve employee performance by as much as 40 percent (Lawler, 1990). Listed below are some of the major forms of performance-based compensation.

Piecework. One of the oldest and most misunderstood forms is piecework. According to this approach, employees receive wages based on their individual productivity. This form of compensation has proven very effective for increasing short-term productivity. When misused, it has a number of negative side effects (Deming, 1986). However, if production is all you want, piecework is a good way to get it.

Performance bonuses. Another approach is using performance bonuses. This approach allows organizations to reward meritorious performance over a particular period of time, without having to keep paying for it for the rest of an employee's career (as is the case for merit increases). Companies that once gave annual wage or salary increases of 4 percent or 5 percent are now finding that they can give much more generous financial rewards because the lump sum bonuses aren't being added to base pay. Because these rewards permit greater differentiation among levels of performance, they tend to be much more powerful and effective motivators. When well implemented, performance bonuses are the most cost-effective way to financially reward individual achievement.

Gain-sharing. Gain-sharing is a method for sharing specific organizational improvements (gains) with the employees who contributed to them. Under this plan, employees' efforts toward increased productivity, improved quality, or reduced costs can be appropriately rewarded. The organization splits the increased profits or reduced costs with them according to some predetermined formula.

Gain-sharing can sometimes be used as a more motivating substitute for a portion of base pay, if employees agree to its use. In one particularly interesting case, a grocery chain won a 25 percent wage concession from employees in certain stores in exchange for participation in a gain-sharing program. According to the agreement, if employees could keep labor costs to 9.5 percent of sales, they would receive a cash payment equal to 1.5 percent of sales, 1 percent if labor costs were 10 percent, and .5 percent if labor costs were 11 percent. Stores that participated in this program experienced a 24 percent increase in sales, while labor costs fell from above the industry average to well below it (Ulrich and Lake, 1990). In another gain-sharing program, this time in a small manufacturing company, management shared 50 percent of the $40,000 it saved from implementing 300 employee ideas. The following year, the company received more than 3,000 suggestions!

Profit-sharing. Profit-sharing awards a percentage of the company's profits to employees, usually in proportion to their salary or wages. It is generally less motivationally effective than gain-sharing because the payments are not clearly linked with any specific employee contribution to the result. The effectiveness of profit-sharing as a motivator is significantly compromised by the delay of payment, usually several months after the end of the fiscal year. As a result, employees tend to view profit-sharing more as an entitlement than a performance-based reward.

ESOPs. Employee stock ownership plans (ESOPs) allocate company stock to employees according to a predetermined formula. ESOPs are supposed to increase employees' sense of ownership in the company, and provide them with a sense of having a real stake in the company's success. However, like profit-sharing, the reward value of ESOPs is often difficult for most employees to appreciate since they are rarely tied to any specific employee contributions. Since the purpose is to get employees to feel more like owners, the most successful ESOPs treat employees like owners, share business information openly, and solicit their input into key management decision-making.

Pay-for-knowledge. Pay-for-knowledge is the practice of pegging base wages or salary to increased job knowledge and skills. Competency levels are established and then correlated with pay rates. Employees work toward those rates by acquiring new skills. Pay-for-knowledge is intended to encourage employees to take more initiative in increasing their knowledge and skills levels, presumably resulting in a more skilled and flexible workforce. Unfortunately, pay-for-knowledge has sometimes rewarded the accumulation of training credentials and the acquisition of unnecessary skills.

As you can see, there are a great many innovative compensation options. When all the combinations and variations of these are considered, there is a virtually infinite number of ways to compensate employees. No longer must organizations be locked into a traditional compensation system limited to base wages or salary with cost-of-living adjustments and annuity-like merit increases. Organizations interested in really motivating their workers can draw on a wide variety of compensation approaches to create an optimal compensation system, tailored to the specific needs of the organization. It is likely that more paychecks in the future will took a lot different from those most employees currently receive, including less base pay and more incentive pay.

GUIDELINES FOR DESIGNING A HIGH-MOTIVATION COMPENSATION SYSTEM

The goal of any compensation system redesign should be to increase the motivational impact of financial rewards. High-motivation compensation systems should be both performance-based and cost-effective. Here are some design guidelines to consider to maximize the motivational impact of your organization's compensation system.

Plan carefully. Determine precisely what you want the compensation system to accomplish. Review past successes and failures. Determine which aspects of your current compensation system satisfy you and which don't. Investigate compensation systems in other organizations, especially those using nontraditional compensation arrangements.

Start small. Don't overcommit resources to a compensation plan your organization can't afford. Your organization certainly doesn't want to be put into a position of having to take away rewards that were recently added. Therefore, it is advisable to pilot test any new compensation arrangements before making them permanent.

Provide an equitable base compensation package. A performance-based compensation plan should be built on a foundation of equitable base compensation. Employees should receive a decent wage or salary based on their job responsibilities. The most important factor in determining base compensation should be the demands of the job. They should be based on a thorough job analysis. All organizations should also conduct regular competitive analyses to ensure that base compensation is comparable to that of other employers in the same industry and within the same geographical region. However, remember that base compensation is viewed by most employees as an entitlement rather than a motivator, so don't expect it to do much more than get employees to show up for work.

Emphasize performance-based compensation. The key to a high-motivation compensation system is to maximize the proportion of compensation that is truly performance-based. In the future, smart organizations will be paying less for years spent on the job and more for desired performance—

not only for production, but also for improvements in quality, cost-savings, and increased safety.

Reward the right behaviors and results. The importance of rewarding the right behaviors and results cannot be too strongly emphasized. Organizations should put their money where the payoff is. Determine the results and behaviors your organization wants to encourage. Then make sure the compensation system rewards them.

Make sure the link between performance and rewards is highly visible. No compensation system will be effective unless employees can clearly see the relationship between their own specific actions and the rewards they receive. (As we saw earlier, this is why profit-sharing is not as successful as gain-sharing.) Make sure employees understand the performance-based rewards being offered. By making both rewards and performance contingencies as visible as possible, your organization will be sending a powerful message to employees that performance is important and that it *will* be rewarded.

Never reward poor performers. Poor performers should never be recipients of performance-based rewards. If you do reward them, your organization will be sending entirely the wrong message, and it may negate many positive aspects of the compensation system.

Compensate promptly. Promptness is another important effective

compensation system feature. As we saw with profit-sharing, the value of rewards is discounted by delay. Performance-based rewards should be paid as soon as possible after the performance they are rewarding. In one interesting study, employees were offered $100 immediately or $500 after a year. You would probably not be surprised that most employees chose the $100. This is why the most successful gain-sharing programs pay employees monthly, rather than quarterly or annually (Lawler, 1990).

Use a variety of compensation options. It is virtually impossible for one compensation arrangement to adequately reward everything desirable. Therefore, any high-motivation compensation system should allocate total compensation through a variety of compensation methods.

Ensure cost-effectiveness. Nothing is more important to compensation in today's organizations than cost-effectiveness. When your organization spends money on ineffective rewards, high-motivation compensation shouldn't cost more; it should actually cost less!

Keep it simple. Too many compensation plans are so complex it takes a Ph.D. to understand them. The best compensation plan is simple enough to be understood by everyone. The comprehensibility of any compensation plan is one of the most crucial determinants of its success. This will become an increasingly important issue as employees' total pay comes from a variety of different plans.

Involve employees. Many excellent compensation ideas come from employees. Alas, organizations are reluctant to ask for their help. Since employees know a lot about what motivates them and what doesn't, soliciting their input into compensation planning may help to avoid pitfalls in compensation design. In addition, such involvement will increase their commitment to making the system work.

Be flexible. In a dynamic business environment, organizations must learn—sometimes through trial and error—which compensation arrangements work and which don't. They must be willing to admit their mistakes.

Ensure fairness. Nothing will sabotage a compensation system like the perception of unfairness. More than anything else, employees want to be treated fairly. They want the recognition and rewards they feel they deserve and have earned. They also want to make sure that others don't receive more of the pie than they deserve. The Japanese have long realized how important the perception of fairness is for motivating compensation. In fact, in Japan, reward criteria are always as explicit and objective as possible; if pay cuts are ever necessary, management takes them first (Abbeggler & Stalk, 1985). The research findings are clear: In planning motivating compensation, it is actually more important to be fair than to be generous!

It's time for performance-oriented organizations to stop wasting money on ineffective compensation arrangements and to invest their resources in a compensation system that will get the results they really want. According to Michael LeBoeuf (1985), "Establishing the proper link between performance and rewards is the greatest key to improving organizations." I hope you will agree that a high-motivation compensation system is an excellent thing to strive for.

Originally published in
Performance & Instruction

References

J. C. Abbeggler and G. Kaisha Stalk, *The Japanese Corporation* (Basic Books, 1985).

G. Brim, *Ambition* (Basic Books, 1992).

W. E. Deming, *Out of the Crisis* (MIT Press, 1986).

R. C. Huseman and J. D. Hatfield, *Managing the Equity Factor* (Houghton Mifflin, 1989).

R. M. Kanter, "The Attack on Pay," *Harvard Business Review* (March–April 1987), p. 66.

S. Kerr, "On the Folly of Rewarding A, while Hoping for B," *The Management of Organizations,* eds. M. L. Tushman, C. O'Reilly, and D. Nadler (Ballinger, 1989), p. 174.

E. E. Lawler, *Strategic Pay* (Jossey-Bass, 1990).

M. LeBoeuf, *The Greatest Management Principle in the World* (Berkley, 1985), p. 25.

B. Nelson, *1001 Ways to Reward Employees* (Workman, 1994).

T. Peters, "Letter to the Editor," *Inc. Magazine, Managing People* (Prentice Hall Press, 1989).

J. R. Schuster and P. K. Zingheim, *The New Pay* (Lexington, 1992).

D. R. Spitzer, *SuperMotivation: A Blueprint for Energizing Your Organization from Top to Bottom* (AMACOM Books, 1995).

D. Ulrich and D. Lake, *Organizational Capability* (Wiley, 1990).

Beware Tax Implications of Recognition Rewards

Bob Nelson

As a big believer in the importance of recognition, I get discouraged when companies shy away from the use of recognition awards because of a fear of the potential tax implications. Much of this fear is unwarranted and can be put to rest with knowledge of the facts and a strategy to build an effective program within the tax code. Following are relevant guidelines from the tax code regarding employee awards and how you can make the most of this information.

TAXABLE AWARDS

Most prizes, awards, and gift certificates are taxable as part of the recipient's gross income. If nonmonetary, the award's fair market value is included in an employee's gross income. This also applies to contest awards, including radio and television giveaway prizes and door prizes. If the winner of an employee contest is allowed to buy a television set at a nominal price, the amount to be included in gross income is the difference between the fair market value of the set and the price paid. Travel awards to individuals are taxed at the cost of the award.

NONTAXABLE AWARDS

Companies are allowed up to $25 per year to spend on employees tax free. This is known as "di minimis fringe" and, depending upon how the program is structured, can climb to $50 per employee. (Note that if you use $25 awards, you may still need to track recipients if employees are eligible for repeat awards.)

Achievement awards of tangible personal property given to your employees in recognition of *length of service* or *safety achievement* are excluded from employee income, as are achievement awards that are transferred to charity at the recipient's request. Special deduction limits apply to such achievement awards provided they are given as part of a presentation under circumstances indicating that they are not a form of disguised compensation. For example, awards will not qualify if given at the time of annual salary adjustments, or as a substitute for a prior program of cash bonuses, or if awards discriminate on behalf of highly compensated employees.

The amount of your deduction depends on whether the achievement award is considered a "qual-

ified plan" award. To be a qualified plan award, the award for length of service or safety achievement must be given under an established written plan or program that does not discriminate in favor of highly compensated employees.

You may deduct up to $1,600 for all qualified plan awards (safety and length of service) given to the same employee during the taxable year. The *average* cost of all awards under the plan for the year (to all employees) must not exceed $400. In determining this $400 average cost, awards of nominal value are not to be taken into account. The $1,600 limit applies if the same employee receives some qualified plan awards and some nonqualified awards in the same year. If the award is not a qualified plan award, the annual deduction ceiling for each employee is $400.

The employer's deductible amount for an employee achievement award is tax free to the employee. For example, if you give a qualified plan award costing $1,800 to an employee, you may deduct only $1,600. The employee is not taxed on the award up to $1,600; the $200 balance is taxable.

LENGTH OF SERVICE AWARDS

Every employee can get a $400 service award every five years of service (this can be combined with cash awards for each five-year period). A length of service award is not subject to the above rules if it is given during the employee's first five years. Furthermore, only one length of service award every five years is considered an employee achievement award. However, the value of an employee achievement award is deductible if the cost to the employer does not exceed the amount allowable as a deduction to the employer.

For example, an employee receives a crystal bowl from his employer as a length of service award. The bowl cost the employer $25 less than the deduction limit, but its fair market value was $25 more than the deduction limit. The employer made no other awards to the employee in that year and did not make any such awards to him in the previous four years. Employee can exclude the entire fair market value of the bowl since its cost is fully deductible by the employer.

SAFETY ACHIEVEMENT AWARDS

Ten percent of your employees can get up to a $400 gift annually related to safety.

Safety awards granted to managers, administrators, clerical employees, or professional employees are not considered employee achievement awards. If, during the year, more than 10 percent of other employees (not counting managers, administrators, or chemical or professional employees) previously received safety awards, none of the later awards is subject to the employee achievement award rules.

Currently, 50 percent of the cost of group travel awards are deductible as a business expense. In addition, a $200 to $300 allotment of work clothes is allowed each year, which can be factored into certain aspects of an overall recognition program.

WORKING WITHIN THE TAX GUIDELINES

How can you get the most from your recognition program while still working within the tax guidelines? The best advice is to plan for the tax consequences of your recognition program as you design the program. This can be done using a savvy and knowledgeable tax attorney or an appropriate incentive, but be prepared for the fact that the tax code is not always favorable to what we know from research and experience to be the most effective recognition practices.

If using monetary awards or gift certificates, another way to deal with the tax consequences is to add any awards directly to employees' paychecks, with the necessary taxes withheld. Some companies add the employee's income taxes to the award so there is not a "take-away" effect; for example, for an employee to receive a $250 performance bonus, the company may actually pay the employee $330 so the net amount the employee receives after taxes is $250 (if the employee's tax rate is 32%).

Perhaps the best strategy, however, is to design your program to first make the best use of nonmonetary awards in which no cash or personal property is exchanged. This might include raising awareness on the part of your managers of the importance of using no-cost verbal and written praisings. As Mark Twain once said, "I can live for two weeks on a good compliment." The same is likely true for your employees.

Information for this article was taken from the Research Institute of America Inc., *J. K. Lasser's Income Tax Guide*, and several incentive industry consultants. For specific applications of the tax code to your recognition program, consult your tax attorney or a qualified incentive company.

Originally published in
Bob Nelson's Rewarding Employees
newsletter

The Care of the Undownsized

Bob Nelson

We could begin by asking whether layoffs are really needed to get organizations back on the right track.

Maybe not. According to one study by Watson Wyatt Worldwide, a pension and profit-sharing company located in Washington, D.C., only 46 percent of the companies surveyed met their expense-reduction goals after downsizing, less than 33 percent met profit objectives, and only 21 percent enhanced shareholders' return on investment. In another study, the American Management Association found that fewer than half of the firms downsized since 1988 had increased their profits after layoffs, and only one third reported an increase in productivity. Worse, the study revealed that downsizing seems to beget more downsizing. Two thirds of firms that cut jobs do it again the next year.

Kim Cameron, a University of Michigan professor and downsizing expert, sees layoffs as a quick fix that usually doesn't work. Cameron studied thirty auto-industry companies that had been through layoffs. "Only five or six had a marked increase in productivity," he says. "In all other cases, performance went down."

But the big issue about downsizing, however, may not be that it exists but that so many companies don't plan properly for it. They just reduce head count, neglecting to figure out how they're going to move forward in their new "leaner and meaner" environments. The most important element of downsizing is ignored: the survivors. As downsizing analyst David Noer points out, "Survivors are left to fend for themselves, to somehow manage on their own."

FROM GUILT TO GROWTH

Downsizing is a traumatic experience—for those who remain as well as for those terminated. Joel Brockner, professor of management at Columbia University and an expert in survivor guilt, says, "When people react negatively to change such as downsizing it shows up in reduced productivity and low morale. The real cause is that people's self-esteem is threatened."

Ironically, survivors are perhaps the most critical factor in determining the future success of a downsized company. They are expected to assume additional workloads, work more efficiently, and adapt quickly to the new work environment in order to attain company goals. Managers must anticipate survivors' reactions to downsizing and help them grow in spite of the situation. Management must find ways to help survivors cope with concerns that they might lose their jobs, with guilt about the termination of coworkers, and with resentment and burnout because of pressure to work harder.

Though the steps below aren't a panacea, they can help management channel its energies and efforts in the right direction.

Lead by vision and values, not commands. In a downsized company, it's increasingly difficult for

---

THE MISCONCEPTIONS OF DOWNSIZING

Here are some common myths about downsizing:
- Downsizing occurs quickly and centers around a definitive event.
- Survivors are glad to still have jobs.
- Time heals all wounds.
- The weak people are the ones who leave.
- Survivors that seem to be OK really are.
- People take what management tells them at face value.

Source: Drake Beam Morin, New York

management to tell employees exactly what they should be doing to be most effective in their jobs. That's because their jobs—and their work environment—are changing so fast. In fact, in many cases, employees are in the best position to know how to solve problems or serve their customers because they are closest to the situations.

It is more important for management to help employees focus on a larger vision of what is needed, emphasizing the strategies and values that will help make the vision attainable. For example, instead of telling people what to do (and risk being wrong), management should encourage workers to take the initiative when appropriate. Managers should meet regularly with employees to map goals and to seek ideas on how they can work together to meet the goals.

Managers and employees should agree on goals, both big and small. In addition, management should identify the kinds of rewards and recognition that motivate employees to try to attain goals. Having the end in sight and empowering employees to be creative and to develop their own skills and abilities can tap into a tremendous reserve of energy, ideas, and initiative.

Communicate more, not less. During times of change and downsizing, communication assumes even greater importance. Surviving workers need to talk to managers and coworkers about their guilt, anger, and concerns. They also need information about what's going on in the company. Immediately after

a downsizing, management should hold a company-wide meeting to explain the reasons for layoffs, to outline the changes and their impact on survivors, to spell out the company's future, and to discuss what's needed from those employees who remain.

Management must communicate to employees what is expected of them in order to keep the company profitable and avoid more layoffs. Management should update employees regularly about the possibility of future layoffs. Never let employees read it first in the newspapers. Rumors must be addressed so that survivors understand what lies ahead.

Management must realize that it's impossible to "overcommunicate" with employees during turbulent times. That's when the quality and quantity of communications should be greater than usual. One reason is that more distortion occurs in a rapidly changing environment. The lines of communication that worked well in the past may be inadequate now. Past communication channels may be overloaded, too formal, or too slow to provide employees with information when they need it most.

To enhance communication, management may choose to experiment with new ways of talking with employees, including:

- Informal sessions between management and small groups

- Message boards in the rest rooms or lunchroom

- Department visits by top managers

- Electronic displays of announcements and updates

- Chat sessions on the organization's intranet

- Hotlines for employees' questions and concerns

Some of these suggestions will work; some won't. By experimenting, an organization can discover what meets employees' needs best. In return for the efforts, survivors will respect and continue to serve the organization well. *Involve people early on.* Managing is what you do *with* people, not to them. To get the most from employees and obtain their commitment, start with them: who they are, what they want, and what they need. Then, build on that foundation by putting the best interests of employees first. Let them take part in decisions that affect their workloads and work environment. That can make them feel important and reassure them that they are truly making a contribution.

One way to involve employees in decision making is to let them assist with a downsizing. Noer recommends that employees be involved in preliminary discussions so they can help shape the criteria on who will go and who will stay: "If you can involve people in the process and give them options such as job-sharing or part-time work—you'll be better off." Then, layoff survivors are less likely to experience feelings of guilt and depression.

Another way to involve survivors in decision making is to have them help management determine how they all can work together in the leaner organization. After downsizing, peoples' roles and responsibilities will be new, and they may seem overwhelming. Involving employees in crucial decisions will help secure their commitment. They will have a better understanding of what is expected of them, and they will see how their support and hard work fit into the overall picture.

Involving employees in decisions also builds trust—vital to sparking their motivation and enthusiasm to do their best. By working through issues as a team, management is telling survivors, "We're in this together." The way employees are treated during stressful times of change says a lot about how they're regarded by management. Are they pawns in a game? Or are they individuals to be treated with respect? Involving employees in decisions will demonstrate that even when times are rough, management has their best interests—and those of the company—in mind.

Recognize and reward performance. Many companies fail to recognize and reward the performance of survivors—thinking, perhaps, that they will be criticized for spending tight dollars foolishly. Nothing could be further from the truth.

After downsizing, management should recognize and reward

performance that makes a difference. Employees feel ambiguous and unclear in times of flux, they are likely to be skeptical about their future with the company. So that vital employees don't jump ship, they need to feel that their hard work and devotion are appreciated. Rewards and recognition go a long way to keeping

THE REALITIES OF DOWNSIZING

Here are some truisms about downsizing:
▶ When survivors are more involved in changes in the workplace, their reactions become less negative.
▶ The intensity of survivors' emotional reactions is proportionate to the speed of change.
▶ The longer an employee has been in a position, the greater his or her resistance to change.
▶ Though rewards and incentives may not lessen survivors' feelings of loss, they can motivate people and help them react positively to change.

Source: Drake Beam Morin, New York

employees motivated, satisfied, and committed.

Management should recognize employees for both their progress toward and achievement of desired performance goals. It should show appreciation for small accomplishments as well as big ones. The recognition must be ongoing to reinforce employees' need to feel that they're doing a good job.

Moreover, the best forms of recognition typically have little or no cost. Here are some suggestions for managers.

■ Thank each employee personally for his or her hard work.

■ Conduct morning chat sessions

to update employees on the status of projects and to highlight desired performance by team members.

■ Hold weekly team lunches so employees can share with co-workers and managers their ideas on how things are going.

■ Write about employees' accomplishments in the company newsletter. Circulate company-wide bulletins of outstanding results.

■ Institute and encourage an open-door policy—from lower-level workers to people at the top. Encourage employees to talk about their concerns and their ideas for new approaches.

Above all else, management must treat employees with trust and respect. Because survivors are likely to feel that their career paths are unclear, management must reassure them that it cares about them and their future with the company.

Originally published in Training & Development

Punished by Rewards: A Rebuttal

Bob Nelson

I*n his book* Punished by Rewards, *Alfie Kohn, the most vocal critic of rewards, explains how much he is opposed to rewards, and why. Essentially, he views rewards as bribes that send the message "Do this . . . and I will give you this." Kohn is most concerned about the controlling nature of incentive systems. He believes that such incentives encourage employees to engage in short-term performance that is not rewarded, and discourages risk-taking. Kohn further argues that rewards undermine authentic relationships and lead to disappointment when people feel underrewarded. He also believes that rewards replace intrinsic motivation with external incentives. His book is primarily concerned with preannounced monetary rewards, and says little or nothing about nonmonetary (or symbolic) forms of recognition. Following is Bob Nelson's response to Alfie Kohn's arguments as originally published by the Small Business Forum.*

—Dean Spitzer

There's a recent school of thought in management and incentive circles that argues that rewards are punishing. Led by author and lecturer Alfie Kohn, this message has reached a significant audience and as such should be more closely examined for its merits. Following are Kohn's major contentions and my attempt to sort out fact and fiction.

ISSUE: INTRINSIC MOTIVATION

Fact: Intrinsic motivation produces the best results from employees. I agree with Kohn that the best motivation is intrinsic. Unfortunately, in reality most jobs are not intrinsically very motivating. Managers must work with employees to mesh individual needs and interests, such as career aspirations and individual learning goals, with the organization's needs for performance and results.

Fiction: Extrinsic motivators (such as rewards) destroy an individual's intrinsic motivation and enjoyment of work itself. This assertion by Kohn is not true if a manager approaches the job of managing as a partnership with employees, looking to exchange work on organization goals for help in meeting the employees' individual and career goals in a positive work contract. In such a case, mutually agreed upon goals are more likely to be intrinsically motivating for the employee. Likewise, rewards need to be individualized to the desires of individual employees. Managers need to ask employees what would be rewarding to them if they obtained their goals. Involving employees in both setting goals and determining desirable rewards, intrinsic motivation can be preserved.

ISSUE: CONTROL AND MANIPULATION

Fact: Incentives effectively control behavior and produce short-term compliance. Over one hundred years of research has substantiated the finding that all behavior is controlled by its consequences. And positive consequences are more effective at motivating behavior and goal accomplishment than negative consequences. This is true from both a research perspective and a practitioner's perspective, and is simply common sense!

Fiction: Controlling behavior is bad; it makes people feel manipulated, and only gets people to obey resentfully for the short term. Control for control's sake is bad, but following through on aspects of a positive work contract; that is, providing rewards for agreed upon results, is good management. If you create a motivating environment that helps employees reach their goals as partners, they will be motivated.

Kohn seems to feel that *any* use of rewards is manipulative, but this is just not the case. If you share your strategy of managing with employees and develop mutually supportive goals, rewards will be rewarding, not manipulative. Rewards are only manipulative if managers don't tell employees first what they are doing and then use rewards to trick employees into doing certain behaviors they wouldn't otherwise want to do. This is poor management, not a poor use of rewards.

Over time, if properly managed, employees will come to take responsibility for their behavior without simply focusing on what's in it for them. This comes with developing individuals so that they take responsibility and pride in their abilities and their work.

ISSUE: COMPETITION AND RELATIONSHIPS

Fact: Competition can impede productivity. You don't want excessive internal competition among team members; you are trying to build into a team. This can happen if your reward program is ill conceived. If the high sales producer gets the only trip to Hawaii, you'll end up promoting cutthroat competition. If the high sales producer gets a weekend at a local resort and the entire sales team gets a party if the company makes its sales goals, you're more likely to encourage working together. It is

possible to have multiple-level incentive programs that work simultaneously with both individuals and groups.

Fiction: Rewards always create competition among workers and ultimately destroy relationships. This is not true if the team or relationships are geared to achieving joint goals in mutually supportive ways. In such cases, rewards are but one of many ways a manager can encourage and motivate employees to do their best. Far from creating an imbalance of power between a manager and employee or among employees on a team, praise, recognition, and rewards are a means to enhance trusting and mutually supportive relationships—to let others know you value and appreciate their efforts.

ISSUE: RISK TAKING AND CREATIVITY

Fact: You get what you reward. If it is important to get people to take risks, to be creative, or to work together to solve problems, you need to clearly focus employee attention on those goals. For example, if it is important to obtain suggestions from employees regarding ways to save costs, an effective reward program would focus on cost-saving ideas and in the process it will release creative energy of employees in trying to obtain that goal.

**Fiction: Rewards are ineffective— and even counterproductive—for getting people to take risks, think

creatively, or to work together to solve problems.** Kohn feels that people do exactly what it takes to get a reward and no more. All of his concerns are true only if inadequate goal setting is done, not because rewards don't work. If you have fuzzy goals, you'll get fuzzy results. If you reward behaviors you don't want, you'll get undesirable behaviors. If the goal clearly focuses on a desired behavior—be it risk taking, creativity, or problem solving—rewarding that behavior will produce more of the behavior.

ISSUE: INCENTIVE PROGRAMS

Fact: Incentives and other reward systems can be ineffective, failing to do the job they were intended to do. Again, this shortcoming of incentive programs is often due to poorly conceived or administered incentive programs or poor management practices, not to defective motivation theory.

Fiction: Financial incentives are the most important form of incentive. Kohn mainly addresses financial incentives, but there is abundant evidence that the most motivational forms of rewards and recognition tend to be nonfinancial [as cited in Chapter 1 of this book]. Note that all cited studies were done of working adults in workplace environments, not of school children or college students in contrived experiments— the type of research Kohn prefers to cite.

Fact: Most incentive programs don't effectively use coaching. The most effective incentive programs are individualized to those who are participating in them. A manager somehow answers the question "What's the best way I can reward this specific employee if he or she does what we both agree needs to be done?" To do this requires better individual coaching on the part of managers through: (1) individual performance planning in which goals, expectations, and rewards are set; (2) day-to-day coaching to help employees achieve their goals; and (3) performance evaluation and personal feedback.

Kohn has a three-word solution to all he feels is wrong with the theory and practice of rewards and incentives: choice, collaborate, and content. He recommends allowing workers *choice* in making decisions about what they do, letting them *collaborate* together in teams, and making sure the *content* of employees' jobs is worth doing. I hate to tell you, Alfie, but good managers already do these things—and not as a replacement for effective rewards!

In summary, Kohn's complaints about the use of rewards and incentive programs are more fiction that fact. Shortcomings he cites are due less to motivation theory being simplistic and outdated and more to his lack of understanding about the principles and practice of good management. Don't scrap your incentive programs yet!

Originally published in
Small Business Forum

Notes

Introduction: Motivation—The Fire Within

1. John Naisbitt, *Megatrends: Ten New Directions Transforming Our Lives* (Warner Books, 1986).
2. The Gallup Organization, as reported in *Training* (August 2000): 64, and *Workforce* (May 2000): 33.

Chapter 1: The Recognition and Rewards Revolution

1. C. E. Schneier, "Capitalizing on Performance Management Recognition and Reward Systems," *Compensation and Benefits Review* (March–April 1989): 23.
2. "Pre–September 11: Organizations More Than Ever at Risk of Losing Key Talent," *Canada at Work 2002.*
3. Peter F. Drucker, *Management: Tasks, Responsibilities, Practices* (Harper & Row, 1974), 239.
4. Cecil F. Hill, "Generating Ideas That Lower Costs and Boost Productivity," *National Productivity Review* 8, no. 2 (1989): 161.
5. K. Moore, "Downsizing Alters Recruiting," *Washington Post*, June 6, 1998.
6. Rosabeth Moss Kanter, "Kanter on Management— Holiday Gifts: Celebrating Employee Achievements," *Management Review* (1986): 198.
7. Lawrence G. Lindahl, "What Makes a Good Job?" *Personnel* (1949): 263–66.
8. Kenneth A. Kovach, "Employee Motivation: Addressing a Crucial Factor in Your Organization's Performance," *Employment Relations Today* 22, no. 2 (1995).
9. From a survey by the Minnesota Department of Natural Resources, Nancy Branton, project manager.

10. D. C. Boyle, "Ideas for Action: The 100 Club" *Harvard Business Review* (1987): 27.
11. Beverly Kaye and Sharon Jordan-Evans, *Love 'Em or Lose 'Em: Getting Good People to Stay* (Berrett-Koehler, 1999).
12. Robert Half International, press release for survey conducted by the company, August 1994.
13. J. A. Maciariello and C. J. Kirby, *Management Control Systems: Using Adaptive Systems to Attain Control* (Prentice-Hall, 1994), 7.
14. Henry Mintzberg, *The Structuring of Organizations* (Prentice-Hall, 1979), 270–71.
15. Maciariello and Kirby, op. cit., 15.
16. Schneier, op. cit.
17. Robert B. Nelson, "Factors That Enhance or Inhibit the Use of Non-Monetary Recognition by U.S. Managers," Ph.D. diss., Claremont Graduate University, 2001.

Chapter 2: The Salary Fallacy and the Seven Facets of Recognition

1. Lindahl, op. cit.
2. Gerald H. Graham and J. Unruh, "The Motivational Impact of Non-Financial Employee Appreciation Practices on Medical Technologists", *Health Care Supervisor* 8, no. 3 (1990): 9–17.
3. Families and Work Institute, "National Study of the Changing Workforce," survey reported in *New York Times*, September 19, 1993, F21.
4. Frederick Herzberg, "One More Time: How Do You Motivate Employees?" *Harvard Business Review* (September–October 1987).

Chapter 4: The Context for Recognition

1. Peter R. Scholtes, *The Leader's Handbook* (McGraw-Hill, 1998).
2. Ralph Stayer, "How I Learned to Let My Workers Lead," *Harvard Business Review* (November–December 1990).
3. Quoted in Jack Welsh and J. Jack Byrne, *Straight from the Gut* (Warner Books, 2001).
4. Available at: http://www.southerncompany.com/careerinfo/culture.asp.
5. Available at: http://www.susq.com/company/company_culture.html.
6. *U-inspire Employee Motivation Report* (January 2002): 9.
7. Ibid., 21.
8. Ibid., 19.

Chapter 5: The Recognition Cycle

1. Philip Crosby, *Quality Is Free* (New American Library, 1979).
2. PDRI is a refinement of the Shewhart Cycle, which has become a central concept in the total quality management movement. W. Edwards Deming publicized the Shewhart Cycle in his landmark book *Out of the Crisis* (Cambridge Institute of Technology Press, 1986). The Shewhart Cycle used slightly different terms: Plan, Do, Study, Act. Others have used the acronym PDCA (Plan, Do, Check, Act). We like Plan and Do, but feel that Study and Act are misleading for the application of recognition.
3. Jack Canfield and Mark Victor Hansen, eds., *Chicken Soup for the Soul: 101 Stories to Open the Heart and Kindle the Spirit* (Health Communications, 1993).
4. Napoleon Hill, *Think and Grow Rich* (Fawcett Books, 1990).
5. Canfield and Hansen, op. cit.

Chapter 7: Getting Started with Team Recognition

1. "Pitney Bowes Study Finds U.S. Workers Less Overwhelmed Despite Increased E-Mail Volumes," ebiz Chronicle.com, August 21, 2000.

Chapter 9: Designing Successful Organizational Recognition

1. Garry Jacobs and Robert Macfarlane, *The Vital Corporation* (Prentice-Hall, 1990), p. 143.
2. Dean Spitzer, *SuperMotivation: A Blueprint for Energizing Your Organization from Top to Bottom* (AMACOM), p. 14.

Chapter 10: Planning Successful Organizational Recognition

1. Richard Sloma, *No-Nonsense Planning* (The Free Press, 1984), p. 3.
2. Bob Nelson and Peter Economy, *Managing for Dummies* (IDG Books, 1996), p. 274.

Chapter 11: Implementing Organizational Recognition

1. Peter and Susan Corning, *Winning with Synergy* (Harper & Row, 1986), p. 10.
2. Bill O'Brien, in P. M. Senge, *The Fifth Discipline* (Doubleday, 1990) p. 214.

Chapter 14: Troubleshooting Recognition Problems

1. Steven Kerr, "The Folly of Rewarding A, while Hoping for B," *Academy of Management Journal* 19, no. 4 (1975).
2. Warren Bennis and Bert Nanus, *Leaders: The Strategies for Taking Charge* (HarperCollins, 1985).
3. Ferdinand F. Fournies, *Why Employees Don't Do What They Are Supposed to Do and What to Do About It* (Liberty Hall Press, 1988).

Index of Companies

About the Authors

BOB NELSON, PH.D.

Dr. Bob Nelson is one of the leading authorities on energizing and motivating employees and inspiring them to new peaks of performance. He is a frequent presenter at management meetings, conferences, and associations and has worked with a wide variety of clients, including most of the Fortune 500 companies. He is the author of twenty books on management, including *1001 Ways to Reward Employees,* which has been on *Business Week*'s bestseller list for over seven years, and has sold more than 1.5 million copies worldwide; *1001 Ways to Energize Employees; 1001 Ways to Take Initiative at Work; Managing for Dummies;* and *Please Don't Just Do What I Tell You! Do What Needs to Be Done.*

Dr. Nelson is president of Nelson Motivation Inc., in San Diego, California (www.nelson-motivation.com), and served as an executive for ten years with the Ken Blanchard Companies. Before that, he worked in human resources for several corporations in the banking and computer industries. He has been featured extensively in the media, including television—CNN, MSNBC, and PBS; radio—National Public Radio, USA Radio Network, Business News Network; and print—*The New York Times, The Wall Street Journal, The Washington Post, USA Today, The Chicago Tribune,* and *Fortune,* among others. He is the publisher of the *Rewarding Employees* newsletter and writes columns for *American City Business Journals, Corporate Meetings and Incentives, SAM's Club Source, Bank Marketing,* and *Strategies for Nurse Managers,* among others.

He holds an MBA from the University of California at Berkeley and received his Ph.D. in management from the Peter F. Drucker Graduate School of Management at Claremont Graduate University in Los Angeles. His dissertation was titled *Factors That Encourage or Inhibit the Use of Non-Monetary Recognition by U.S. Managers.*

DEAN R. SPITZER, PH.D.

Dr. Spitzer is one of the world's foremost authorities on organizational motivation. He is the author of six books and 130 articles and chapters on organizational performance improvement. His book *SuperMotivation: A Blueprint for Energizing Your Organization from Top to Bottom* is widely recognized as the pioneering work in this area. *SuperMotivation* received the Outstanding Communication Award from the International Society for Performance Improvement (ISPI), it was honored as one of the thirty best business books of the year when it was published, and it has been translated into numerous languages.

Currently a senior consultant with IBM Global Services, Dr. Spitzer has over twenty-five years' experience in helping individuals and organizations achieve superior performance. He has directed over 150 successful performance improvement projects for a wide variety of organizations in the United States and abroad. Dr. Spitzer has served as a human resources manager and internal consultant for several Fortune 100 companies, including Digital Equipment Corporation, Kimberly Clark, James River Corporation, and with the U.S. Department of Veteran's Affairs. He has taught at five universities, including a two-year visiting professorship in Australia, and has lectured in many countries. He is also a past vice president of the International Society for Performance Improvement (ISPI).

Dr. Spitzer earned his Ph.D. from the University of Southern California and his M.A. from Northwestern University. He also has pursued graduate studies at the London School of Economics.

*Bob Nelson and Dean Spitzer welcome
your questions, comments, and anecdotes about
rewards and recognition.*

Bob Nelson, Ph.D.
President, Nelson Motivation, Inc.
12245 World Trade Drive, Suite C
San Diego, CA 92128
Telephone: 858-673-0690
fax: 858-673-9031
www.nelson-motivation.com

———

Dean R. Spitzer, Ph.D.
Senior Consultant
IBM Business Consulting Services
IBM Global Services
Telephone: 863-425-9641
e-mail: spitzer@us.ibm.com

OTHER BESTSELLERS
BY BOB NELSON

1001 WAYS TO REWARD EMPLOYEES • *Foreword by Ken Blanchard* • The *Business Week* national bestseller, with over 1 million copies in print. This chock-full guide to motivating the people who work for you by recognizing and rewarding them offers more than a thousand innovative (and often no-cost) ideas to help you think beyond the expected raise and promotion.
ISBN 1-56305-339-X, $10.95 paperback.

1001 WAYS TO ENERGIZE EMPLOYEES • *Foreword by Ken Blanchard* • Take the brakes off your business as Bob Nelson reveals what real companies across America are doing to get the very best out of their employees—and why it's the key to their success. "A motherlode of practical ideas and practices."—Dr. Steven R. Covey, author of *The Seven Habits of Highly Effective People.*
ISBN 0-7611-0160-8, $10.95 paperback.

1001 WAYS TO TAKE INITIATIVE AT WORK • The first management guide for employees, this book weaves together case studies, quotes, research highlights, and the author's own "Tool Box" of techniques and exercises to show every reader how to develop self-leadership, set goals, and learn firsthand that the "biggest mistake you can make in life is to think you work for somebody else."
ISBN 0-7611-1405-X, $10.95 paperback.

AND ALSO BY DEAN SPITZER

SUPERMOTIVATION: A Blueprint for Energizing Your Organization from Top to Bottom • *SuperMotivation* shows how to "motivationally transform" an entire organization. This book provides a completely new approach to an age-old dilemma, explaining how to identify "motivators" that exist in a company, find ways to increase them, uncover "demotivators"—and reduce or eliminate them—and weave the principles of high motivation into six core organizational—systems. New York: AMACOM, 1995. ISBN: 0814402860. $23.95.

LINK TRAINING TO YOUR BOTTOM LINE • *With Malcolm Conway* • This book discusses the critical concepts for effective training evaluation and presents an immediately applicable model for linking training to the bottom-line business value of an organization. The model aligns training with the business results and bridges the gaps between learning, on-the-job behavior, individual performance, and organizational performance. Info-line. American Society for Training & Development, January 2002. ISBN: 156286310X. $14.00.

DEVELOPING A SAFETY CULTURE: Successfully Involving the Entire Organization • *With Terry L. Mathis* • This innovative book can help you reduce workplace accidents through the use of the latest safety improvement methodology—Performance-Based Safety. It works by focusing your employees' mindset more toward safety and helps make awareness and accident prevention seem automatic. Learn training and performance improvement techniques needed to develop proper safety habits, make the most of accident data, gain management support, and motivate employees. Neenah, WI: J. J. Keller & Associates, 1996. ISBN: 187779872X. $20.00.

IMPROVING INDIVIDUAL PERFORMANCE • This book provides a overview of what it takes to change human behavior and improvement performance and presents a compendium of innovative techniques for doing so. This book is full of methods that you can use to enhance the impact of your training programs and improve the performance of employees in your organization. Englewood, N.J.: Educational Technology Publications, 1986. ISBN: 0877781974. $34.95.